CHRISTIAN THEOLOGY

Christian Theology

AN INTRODUCTION TO ITS TRADITIONS AND TASKS

Edited by
PETER C. HODGSON
and
ROBERT H. KING

Newly Updated Edition

FORTRESS PRESS Minneapolis

CHRISTIAN THEOLOGY
An Introduction to Its Traditions and Tasks

Cover design: Pollock Design Group

Library of Congress Cataloging-in-Publication Data
Christian theology : an introduction to its traditions and tasks / edited by Peter C.
  Hodgson and Robert H. King.—Newly rev. ed.
      p.   cm.
   Includes bibliographical references and index.
   ISBN 0-8006-2867-5
   1. Theology, Doctrinal—Introductions.   2. Theology, Doctrinal—Study and
teaching.   I. Hodgson, Peter Crafts, 1934–   .   II. King, Robert Harlen, 1935–
BT65.C47   1994
230—dc20   94-4764
                                                                            CIP

The paper used in this publication meets the minimum requirements of American National Standards for Information Sciences—Permanence of Paper for Printed Library Materials, ANSI Z329.48-1984.   ∞™

Manufactured in the U.S.A.   AF 1-2867

                              10   11   12   13   14   15

CONTENTS

4. Revelation (George Stroup)

Ambiguity of "revelation." Objective and subjective dimensions, revelation as illumination (Origen, Augustine, Aquinas) and as encounter (Luther, Calvin). Challenges (Locke, deists, Hume, and Kant), and responses (Schleiermacher, Hegel, and liberals), God's self-disclosure (Barth), human experience (existentialism) and history (H. R. Niebuhr). Narrative theology and future issues.

5. Creation and Providence (Julian N. Hartt)

Decline of traditional teaching. Biblical images of creator and provider, the classic consensus (Origen to Calvin), and its persistent tensions. Challenge to teleology, defenses (Descartes and Leibniz), pantheism (Spinoza) and skepticism (Hume), historical consciousness (Hegel), liberalism (Kant and moral teleology), revivals (Barth, Bultmann). Origins, creativity, openness, freedom, goodness and evil.

6. Human Being (David H. Kelsey)

Classic themes: human nature as created (body and soul, social being, teleology, temporality), human nature as fallen. The modern "turn to the subject," moral autonomy and fulfillment, historicity of the subject. New strategies: the subject's consciousness, the moral subject, authentic freedom, self-making, self-choosing, God as subject (Barth). Problems of explanation, of abstraction, and of dependency; need for sense of createdness, and persons as agents.

7. Sin and Evil (Robert R. Williams)

The Adam story (O.T. and Paul), Augustine on original righteousness, sin and guilt, interpretations (Aquinas and Reformers). Problems of sin and responsibility, historical criticism, the fall. Centrality of redemption, reinterpretations of the fall. Phenomenology of sin, Augustinian and Irenaean theodicy (Hick).

8. Christ and Salvation (Walter Lowe)

The relation of doctrines of salvation and Christ. Biblical foundations and early centuries (Nicaea, Chalcedon); Anselm, Abelard, and Luther. Reason as critical, self-critical, and self-aware; modern reformulation (Schleiermacher, historical Jesus and apocalyptic, Barth and Bultmann), beyond existentialism (process theology, later Barth, Rahner, Pannenberg, liberation theology). The worshiping community, mystery, Trinity.

PREFACE

This book, which first appeared in 1982, is the product of a collaborative process begun seven years earlier at a meeting hosted by the theological faculty of Vanderbilt Divinity School. Those attending this meeting included theologians from several major theological centers in the United States. In spite of obvious denominational and methodological differences, we shared a desire that theology should become a more effective practice and a hope that collaboration could contribute to that outcome. We would help each other in various ways; we would address the needs of theological education; and we would be concerned with specific theological issues, themes and problems affecting the church as a whole. We decided to call ourselves the Workgroup on Constructive Theology.

We soon recognized that the teaching of theology both in seminary and college could benefit from a text that would provide an understanding of the transformations undergone by the tradition, but we found the work of collaboration required to produce this text more difficult than anticipated. By meeting together for periods of several days at the Institute of Ecumenical and Cultural Research in Collegeville, Minnesota, we were eventually able to achieve consensus on the development of Christian theology and the manner in which it could best be presented. All of the members of the group, some fifteen to twenty altogether, shared in the discussion and critique of the early chapter drafts that were extensively revised before achieving their final form. The result is a book written by individuals with different points of view yet a shared vision of the "traditions and tasks" of Christian theology.

The purpose of this work is twofold: (1) to introduce the student of theology to the Christian tradition by setting forth in brief compass its primary shape and substance, and (2) to pose the issues for systematic theology in the present day by showing how that tradition has been challenged and transformed under the pressures of modern thought. Our intent is not to write a history of theology, though it will be evident that we attach great importance to the historical development of Christian thought. Neither are we attempting to set forth a full-blown systematic theology, though there is considerable consensus among the contributors to this volume about what the outstanding issues are. Certainly the book is not designed simply as a review of past accomplishments. In an important sense it is meant to set the agenda for future theological discussion.

The way in which the book is laid out may initially strike the reader an anachronistic, for we have adopted a very traditional format: the *loci* of doctrine. This format was quite common in the period of Protestant scholasticism and rested on assumptions that are now largely discredited, primarily the view of Christian truth as consisting of a deposit of discrete doctrines that have simply to be expounded by the theologian in order to become intelligible. (A notable instance of this approach would be Heinrich Heppe's *Reformed Dogmatics*, which Karl Barth credits with having set him on the path to his own constructive theology.) Clearly, though, this is not our viewpoint. We have adopted the format as a useful way of making contact with the tradition, but within that structure we have attempted to show how fundamental a transformation the tradition has undergone. Were any one of us to set out to write an actual systematic theology this would not be the format we would employ.

And even the format itself has been modified to accommodate changes in the theological agenda. Some traditional topics have been dropped (for instance, divine election), others combined (creation and providence, Christ and salvation), and still others added (notably the Christian life and the religions). Even those that have been retained from the tradition are treated in an untraditional way—less as discrete items of belief and more as distinctive perspectives upon the whole of Christian understanding. It would not be inconceivable, in fact, to construct an entire systematic theology from any one of these "perspectives," but we have not attempted to do so because of limitations of space and our conception of the present task as primarily introductory.

Most of the chapters of this book, as should be evident, have a common structure. We begin by placing the topic for discussion within the context of contemporary theological reflection. Then we look back at how the doctrine (or combination of doctrines) received its "classic formulation." The authors at this point have had to be highly selective, ignoring the many variations and transmutations which the doctrine has undergone at the hands of creative thinkers in various periods of the church's history. The objective has been to identify those thinkers who have contributed most decisively to the shaping of a particular doctrine and to abstract from their work something approximating a theological consensus.

We then go on to consider "challenges and contributions of modern consciousness" in an effort to show how the doctrine or topic has been reconceived in modern times. The chapters tend to view the eighteenth-century Enlightenment as a critical watershed in the history of theology, demanding new paradigms or models of theological reflection in light of the impact on the tradition of critical methods, new scholarly disciplines, the increasing pluralization and secularization of Western culture, and so forth. This "paradigm shift," as we are calling it, is in fact the central motif of the book as a whole. Each chapter approaches it from a somewhat different vantage point, yet the cumulative effect is to document the massive and far-reaching transformation of theology which took place at that time.

We conclude with a brief look at new and persistent issues relating to the doctrine and suggest possible directions for a constructive response. Several chapters take the view that the cognitive, sociopolitical, and cultural challenges of our own time constitute a second watershed comparable in significance to the first and setting the agenda for future theological work. But only a beginning is made at defining issues and setting forth proposals, which are addressed more fully in a sequel to this book.

The introductory essay, "The Task of Theology," is on the order of a prolegomenon to the work as a whole; it gives a historical overview of Christian theology, identifying the main contributors to the formation of the Christian tradition and raising in a preliminary way issues that will be discussed more fully and in greater depth in subsequent chapters. The chapter entitled "Theological Method" sets the work of theology in the context of a new paradigm, which requires that theology as such be understood as "interpretation"—an interpretation worked out in terms of mutually critical correlations between the Christian tradition and the contemporary situation. This chapter does not address classic formulations of theological method but rather develops a model for current discussion. The following chapter, "Scripture and Tradition," is transitional to the main body of the work. It belongs to theological prolegomenon insofar as it is concerned with the sources that serve as the criteria of theological claims, but it belongs among the topics of theology to the extent that these sources themselves become an object of theological reflection and belief.

The main body of the work consists of chapters on specific topics: God, revelation, creation and providence, human being, sin and evil, Christ and salvation, church, sacraments, Spirit and Christian life, kingdom of God and life everlasting, and the religions. They are written so that they can be read separately or together, in the order in which they appear or in some other order, with accompanying readings from primary sources or independently. There are certain common themes that run through the chapters, yet no attempt was made to ensure that every theme would be treated in every chapter. On the contrary, we recognize that certain issues, themes, or theologians have played a more prominent role in the development of some doctrines than others. Thus, if it seems that a particular issue or individual has not been adequately covered in one chapter, the reader may look for more ample coverage in another. In some respects the book is like a mosaic in which each piece contributes to the overall pattern; in other respects it is like a room of mirrors in which each glass reflects the whole from a different angle. The Epilogue draws together some of the most prominent themes from the preceding discussion and offers some general reflections on the present state of theology.

Footnotes have been held to a minimum, with some variation from chapter to chapter, but we have provided suggested further readings at the conclusion of each chapter. Following the Introduction, the reader will find a more extensive set of bibliographic "Aids for the Study of Theology," including a list of major works in constructive theology, both classical and modern, and a selection of source books, histories, dictionaries, encyclopedias, and creeds and confessions. In the suggested readings at the end of each chapter, publication facts are not repeated if they are given in the "Aids"; and in the footnotes these facts are not repeated if they are given in either the chapter bibliographies or the "Aids." Abbreviations used throughout the book are listed at the beginning of the "Aids" section. Both the chapter bibliographies and "Aids for the Study of Theology" have been updated for this revised edition.

With the publication of the second edition of *Christian Theology*, we produced a companion volume of readings from classical and contemporary sources entitled *Readings in Christian Theology*. This anthology includes selections from most of the seminal thinkers of the Christian tradition organized around the major themes of the textbook. Now there is a third volume, a sequel to this work, which explores more fully the social and political issues confronting the contemporary theologian. Entitled *Reconstructing Christian Theology*, it is edited by Rebecca S. Chopp and Mark Lewis Taylor. It includes essays by some of the contributors to this volume but many others as well.

The Workgroup on Constructive Theology, which produced these three volumes, has undergone considerable transformation since its inception. Whereas it was once composed almost exclusively of white, male theologians from mainstream liberal denominations, it is now evenly divided between men and women with significant minority representation and a much younger membership. *Reconstructing Christian Theology* reflects this transformation insofar as it approaches theology not from within the framework of traditional doctrine but from the perspective of the pressing issues of our day—sexism, classism, ecology, addiction, and war among others. These issues are brought into juxtaposition with the primary beliefs of the church—God, creation, sin, Christ, and salvation—with the result that both our understanding of the issues and our interpretation of doctrine are contextualized and transformed. Our intent, however, remains the same—to assist and encourage students to take up for themselves the task of constructive theology.

THE EDITORS

INTRODUCTION: THE TASK OF THEOLOGY

WHERE WE ARE

Some would say that theology is in a state of disarray. There are no commanding figures on the order of Karl Barth, Paul Tillich, or the Niebuhrs, and no major system of thought elicits widespread support in the way that liberalism, neoorthodoxy, and existentialism did a generation ago. What theological writing there is tends to be fragmentary, occasional, and somewhat idiosyncratic, but that is not true in every case. Some recent work, most notably the theologies of liberation, gives evidence of systematic intent, if not of full systematic development, and may in time become the nucleus of a new theological consensus. At the present, however, there is no general agreement even as to what theology is, much less how to get on with the task of systematics.

There are some advantages to the present situation. For one thing, there is greater ecumenicity than at any time previously. A person beginning the study of theology now is free as never before to draw upon the resources of many different traditions—Catholic as well as Protestant, Calvinist as well as Lutheran. Even the Eastern Orthodox tradition has become accessible to theologians from the West, as it was not in earlier times. In fact, if there is any one characteristic that sets the present situation off from all previous ones, it is the manifest pluralism of religious traditions. Christianity is conceived far more broadly today than at any time in its history, and traditions outside Christianity are taken more seriously than they once were. It is not inconceivable even that a Christian theologian should learn from a Buddhist, Hindu, or Islamic thinker.

Another positive feature of the present time is the increased recognition that theology, for all its reliance upon tradition, is a *constructive* undertaking. What has previously been set down cannot

1

simply be taken for granted. The tradition we have received has evolved over time, and we ourselves contribute to its further development by the way in which we appropriate and apply it. We had therefore best take responsibility for what we say and for the way in which we say it. That is especially true if what we seek is a "systematic theology," for whatever else that term may mean, it surely connotes a deliberate ordering of ideas, the self-conscious articulation of a theological position.

Still there is no real consensus about either the substance or the task of Christian theology. The tendency is rather toward a kind of laissez-faire eclecticism, with theologians pursuing various thematic interests but no one undertaking a genuinely inclusive, unified approach to the exposition of Christian doctrine. Even a serious and sustained critique of traditional theological positions is difficult to mount, because it is not at all clear from what stance or on what grounds such a critique would be carried out. We are, for the most part, uncertain even as to what the options are.

So perhaps the best approach would be to review how we have arrived at where we are: to examine what have been the paradigms for systematic articulation of Christian faith in the past and the ways in which these paradigms have been challenged, transformed, and replaced in the modern period.[1] We are, in other words, proposing to tell the story of Christian theology, with a view to better understanding the present exigency. This approach ought not to be expected to resolve the outstanding issues, but it should put us in a better position to appreciate what those issues are and to take the measure of the task before us.

CHRISTIAN THEOLOGY IN ITS CLASSIC FORMULATIONS

The Beginnings of Systematization

We will look in vain for anything in the first century of the church remotely like a fully articulated theological system. The literature of

1. The term "paradigm" derives from Thomas Kuhn's work on the history of science, *The Structure of Scientific Revolutions*, 2d ed. (Chicago: University of Chicago Press, 1970). It refers to exemplary formulations of scientific theory, such as Copernicus's explanation of planetary motion and Newton's theory of mechanics. Embedded in these standard examples of scientific understanding are the presuppositions—both metaphysical and methodological—that will guide future research. The work of Augustine, Aquinas, Luther, and Calvin can be said to have been in this sense paradigmatic for Christian theology.

2

this period primarily takes the form of letters and occasional treatises answering the critics of Christianity. It does not include any major work of a comprehensive or systematic sort. Still there is to be found within these "confessional" and "apologetic" writings the beginnings of systematic reflection upon the central content of the Christian faith.

In the attempt of the second-century apologist Justin Martyr to commend the faith to Greeks, for instance, the concept of *logos* is brought into play. Borrowed from Greek philosophy, the term had a meaning sufficiently broad that it could connote either "word" or "reason." In the service of theology it formed a bridge between the transcendent God and the created universe. Whether as the word by which God called the world into being, or the rational structure of that world, it gave access to the mind of God. Following the suggestion of the prologue to the Gospel of John, it was also a concept through which one could interpret the person of Christ. It was sufficiently generalizable to bring together the seemingly disparate acts of creation and redemption, yet sufficiently personal and particular to be the determinative factor in the life of a single individual. The *logos* concept was a truly integrative, systematizing principle in early Christian literature, even if it was not yet firmly lodged within a major theological system.

Another type of theological literature, which began to appear about this time, was that directed against "heresy." The intent of this literature was to mark out and define what was truly Christian and what was not. In the process certain features of later systematization began to emerge. The most notable instance of this type of writing was Irenaeus' *Against Heresies* (182–188). In the first part of that work he describes and criticizes Gnostic systems of belief which had in the minds of many come to be confused with Christian belief. He appeals to scripture and tradition as the basis for "true" belief, citing an unbroken line of successors within the churches as the principal guarantee of authenticity. In the second part he expounds at length upon the central teachings of the church within a framework drawn from this same scriptural tradition: the history of salvation.

That framework is important, for it enables him to hold together creation and redemption. It also locates the redemptive experience of the individual within the larger context of human experience. Ac-

3

cording to this scheme, God created human beings for blessedness and immortality. When they sinned, God did not abandon this original intention but pursued it actively through successive interventions in history until it culminated in the appearance of Christ. In one of his most striking phrases, Irenaeus speaks of Christ "recapitulating," summing up or perfecting in his own person, the previous history of humanity and thus bringing it to a new level of being. Extending this principle to the cosmos as a whole, he envisions the entire creation radically transformed, perfected by God.

It is an extraordinary theological vision, but probably not yet a system. That achievement awaited the next generation and the work of the great scholar-theologian Origen. His *On First Principles* (212–215) is a truly monumental work of systematic reflection. Not only does it cover a broad range of topics, it also organizes them into a coherent scheme starting with certain fundamental concepts—God, Christ, the Holy Spirit, rational natures—and proceeding to a highly elaborate, and some would say speculative, account of creation, redemption, and final consummation. Though firmly committed to scriptural authority as the basis of Christian belief, Origen was not at all reluctant to speculate about matters on which there was no authoritative teaching or to draw upon a philosophical tradition remote from the biblical literature for the elaboration of its essential truths. Thus he adopted without question the Platonic principle of ascribing to God nothing unworthy of divinity, and he relied implicitly throughout his work on the Neoplatonic view of creation as a process of emanation from God.[2] According to Origen's grand cosmic scheme, souls preexist in God, fall away, and ultimately return to God. So complete is this cycle of emanation and return that even the demons are eventually restored to union with God.

One unacquainted with the history of theology might suppose that a major systematic work of this sort would close off further discussion, since it would answer all the important questions. In fact, it had the opposite effect. Origen's comprehensive treatment of Christian doctrine, particularly his views on the relationship of God the Father to God the Son, contained ambiguities which, when clarified, opened up further issues for debate and thus prepared the way for the great

2. For a helpful introductory discussion of Neoplatonism, see J. N. D. Kelly, *Early Christian Doctrines*, pp. 14–22.

ecumenical councils of the fourth and fifth centuries. It is as though first an attempt had to be made to provide a unified, coherent account of Christian belief before the difficulties, the apparent inconsistencies, and mistaken understandings could be identified and dealt with. Besides, there were features of Origen's thought that were subsequently perceived to be unorthodox, if not heretical—notably his speculations regarding reincarnation and the restoration of all things—so that it was unlikely, even with the resolution of certain ambiguities, that his systematic rendering of Christian belief could have become common ground for future discussion.

The Augustinian Synthesis

The premier systematic theologian of the early period of church history, and perhaps all time, was Augustine (354–430). More than any of his predecessors, he succeeded in weaving together the various strands of Christian doctrine developed up to that point into a comprehensive and unified synthesis which could serve as the basis for future theological development.

He wrote on a variety of topics, including a major work on the Trinity, yet it is generally agreed that his principal contribution to Christian thought came in the area of theological anthropology, the analysis and interpretation of human existence in relationship to God. In his early anti-Manichean writings he makes a strong argument for free will over against the predominantly deterministic philosophy of that day. In his controversy with Pelagius, he sets forth for the first time a fully developed doctrine of original sin, maintaining that the prevenient grace of God is the necessary condition of any truly good act. In over a dozen different treatises, he expounded upon the dynamics of sin and grace, freedom and destiny. For this body of work alone he would have to be recognized as a major systematic thinker. Yet he went further. He actually constructed out of the totality of his reflections a systematic work of major proportions. Written near the end of his lifetime, The City of God (413–426) is undoubtedly the most important work of systematic theology prior to the Middle Ages.

On the face of it, The City of God is a work of apologetics, for at the outset the book addresses charges brought against the church by its pagan critics, namely, that it was traitorous and had brought on the collapse of the Roman Empire. In answering his critics, however,

Augustine does more than just meet their objections. He constructs for the first time a fully developed Christian interpretation of history and, within the framework of that history, takes up the principal Christian doctrines (creation, sin, atonement, predestination, grace, the church, the life everlasting). It is not wholly fortuitous that he should have chosen this particular framework for the elaboration of Christian belief, for that same historical scheme is deeply embedded in the biblical writings—both Old Testament narrative and New Testament proclamation. Augustine, who began with a basically Platonic interpretation of Christianity, came increasingly to regard the biblical-historical perspective as fundamental to a Christian understanding of reality.

As the chief organizing principle for this Christian interpretation of history, Augustine fixed upon the metaphor of the city, using it to distinguish two mutually exclusive forms of life. Either one's life is oriented toward love of self to the exclusion of all else (in which case one belongs to the earthly city), or it is oriented to love of God as the supreme good (placing one in the city of God). History as a whole is ambiguous, involving as it does the intermingling of these two forms of life; yet running as a thread through history (for those with the faith to comprehend it) is the divine purpose wherein those whom God has predestined are brought to fullness of life while the rest are given over to judgment. Thus, for all its ambiguity, history has meaning, and for those whose orientation is toward God it has *redemptive* meaning.

The logic of Christian faith, as the mature Augustine came to conceive it, is most fully exhibited through the unfolding of this history. Yet in making salvation history the framework for a systematic presentation of Christian teaching, he did more than simply confirm a previous pattern of interpretation. He established a *paradigm* which would serve as the structure for most theological reflection in the West, at least until the Enlightenment. That paradigm includes, among other features, (1) a narrative structure that interprets the history of a particular people within the context of world history as a sequential story whose development and outcome is determined by God; (2) the theme of divine sovereignty with its implicit teleology and supporting motifs of governance, intervention, and causality; (3) the periodization of history and fixing of the time of revelation in the past; and (4) the task of theology conceived as the working out of a systematic body of doctrine corresponding to the major moments or motifs in this sacred history.

For the greater part of the Middle Ages the "Augustinian synthesis," as it has been called, was normative.[3] It provided the context within which theological discussion was carried on. If there was disagreement—as there was regarding predestination and the Eucharist—it was expressed in Augustinian terms with each side citing Augustine as the authority for its position. The eleventh-century theologian Anselm would be an example of one who wrote with brilliance and originality, yet clearly from within this tradition. His basic methodological principle, "faith seeking understanding," is explicitly Augustinian, while his major work on the atonement, *Why God Became Man* (1098), is an extension of this method of reasoning to a subject which Augustine himself had not considered in any great depth. Gradually, however, new currents of thought began to infuse the theological world. Western theologians were for the first time confronted with the ideas of Aristotle. In addition they had to deal with Islamic religion through the writings of some of its most brilliant interpreters. With the formation of universities there was a context in which a more critical spirit could flourish. The time was ripe for a new synthesis.

The *Summa* and the *Institutes*

The great medieval synthesist was Thomas Aquinas (1225–74). In a far more ambitious way than anyone before him, he undertook to give a systematic account of the totality of Christian teaching. There were already available compilations of the teachings of the fathers organized under major doctrinal headings, such as Trinity, creation, incarnation, and sacraments. But he sought to go beyond mere compilation and to present in a unified and rational way the sum of all knowledge pertaining to God. His *Summa Theologica* (1267–72) was the first real attempt to present theology as a "science," that is, to investigate rationally what faith professes on the basis of authority. In terms of sheer elegance of conception and economy of execution it is probably unsurpassed.

3. Jaroslav Pelikan, *The Christian Tradition: A History of the Development of Doctrine*, 3:50.

In his approach to theological issues, Aquinas was confident—as few others have been—of the capacity of reason to arrive at the truth. The existence of God, he thought, is not self-evident, yet it can be demonstrated by rational inference. Likewise, certain things can be known about the nature of God—omnipotence, omniscience, and eternity, for instance—solely on the basis of reason. Other matters, such as the creation of the world or the trinitarian nature of God, are known only on the basis of revelation. Yet even then there is no contradiction to reason. Revelation simply takes reason to a level higher than it could otherwise attain, for there is, according to Aquinas, a genuine hierarchy of knowledge corresponding to the hierarchy of being. As humans exceed lesser beings in their capacity to know, so by divine grace they are enabled to attain an even higher level of knowledge than their natures would otherwise allow. Revealed knowledge of God is the culmination, the perfection, of all knowledge.

Much of the substance of what Aquinas says in the main body of his work is Augustinian. In structuring the material and giving it systematic shape, however, he broke significantly with the Augustinian model. His conceptual framework, for instance, is more cosmological than historical, and his reasoning is much more deductive. He divides his work into three main parts, incorporating the Neoplatonic pattern of emanation and return encountered earlier in Origen. Part I has to do with the creation of all things by God, Part II with the return of the rational creature to God through its own acts, and Part III with the person and work of Christ as the means by which this return is accomplished. Within each of these divisions, he considers a wide range of topics, including traditional ones (creation, providence, sin, and grace) and others not so traditional (the unity of body and soul and the principles of human action). Every topic is broken down into discrete questions or units of investigation, which are then subjected to rigorous analysis and argumentation deploying with great subtlety the categories of Aristotle. The result of this endeavor is a masterful synthesis of philosophy and theology and a systematization of Christian teaching surpassing anything that had preceded it.

The sixteenth-century Reformation is sometimes seen as a repudiation of the systematic accomplishments of the Middle Ages—and to a certain extent it was. Luther in particular was critical of the excessive rationalism of scholastic theology. He sought to restore the personal immediacy of the biblical message and the assurance of salvation that comes from trust in the word of God. He was a prolific writer, but primarily in the mode of sermons, treatises, and biblical commentaries. He developed certain themes, notably that of "justification by faith," with great consistency and power, yet he did not undertake to write a major systematic work on the order of Augustine or Aquinas. That task was left to his contemporary John Calvin. Indeed, Calvin's *Institutes of the Christian Religion* (1536, 1559) is in many respects the Protestant summa. More than any other single work it provides a systematic framework for reformed theology. We may ask, though, whether it represents a real departure from previous tradition or simply a renewal and reaffirmation of elements within that tradition.

The structure of the *Institutes* follows the Apostles' Creed, with the first part devoted to God as creator and sovereign, the second to Christ as mediator and redeemer, the third to the Holy Spirit as justifying and sanctifying principle in the life of believers, and the fourth to the church and its relation to civil society. On the face of it, this would seem to be a way of organizing things quite different from any previous work of such magnitude. Yet at a more basic level it constitutes a return to the Augustinian model, for in following the Apostles' Creed, Calvin is actually adhering to the pattern of salvation history employed by Augustine. The movement from creation to redemption by way of the intervening agency of Christ is after all the normative pattern of that history. What he does that Augustine does not do is abstract the pattern from the history and subject it to analysis in terms of the fourfold division of the creed. Even the doctrine of predestination, for which Calvin is so well known, does not constitute a departure from this tradition. If anything it confirms it, for it is precisely from the perspective of divine election that human history takes on the character of salvation history.

It is certainly not insignificant that Calvin chose to organize his theology around the articles of the creed or that one of Luther's most successful ventures in the direction of systematics should have been his shorter catechism, for the Reformers were characteristically confessional in their approach to theology. Their primary interest was not in system-building but in witnessing to their faith. To this end they made far less use of philosophical argument than their predecessors and relied to a much greater extent upon scripture—and on creeds, as the key to the interpretation of scripture. In fact, if there is any distinctive contribution that Protestantism has made to the formation of a common theological tradition, it is in the prominence given to scripture in the formation of theological concepts and the resolution of theological issues. Ironically, by establishing scripture as the ultimate authority over tradition, Protestants made a contribution to that very tradition.

In the two centuries following the Reformation, there took place a general consolidation of theological positions and hardening of the lines between Protestants and Catholics. During this period no new ground was broken with respect to systematics, and some ground may even have been lost as the two groups reinstated many of the conventions of scholastic theology. It was a time in which orthodoxies of one sort or another were in the ascendancy. The critical spirit—whether evangelical or rational—was largely lacking. Not until the eighteenth century did it reappear to challenge the tradition as it had never been challenged before.

CHALLENGES AND CONTRIBUTIONS OF MODERN CONSCIOUSNESS

The Enlightenment

There are periods of history in which there occur intellectual changes of such magnitude that we are disposed to think of them as "revolutionary." The late eighteenth and early nineteenth centuries together constitute such a period in the history of Western religious thought. Set in motion were powerful intellectual forces that challenged many basic assumptions of the dominant religious tradition and called forth a major reorientation. In his study of scientific revolutions Thomas Kuhn speaks of such transitions as "paradigm shifts."[4] If we may think of the dominant tradition in Christian theology from Augustine to the Reformation as paradigmatic, then this was surely a time when a major paradigm shift took place, for not only did Chris-

---

4. Kuhn, *Structure of Scientific Revolutions*, p. 150. Compare Ian Barbour, *Myths, Models, and Paradigms: A Comparative Study of Science and Religion* (New York: Harper & Row, 1974), pp. 104–5.

tian theology come to be organized in a new way, but the very concept of theology underwent a significant change.

What precipitated the change was in the first instance the emergence and widespread acceptance of the scientific world view. Modern science did not, of course, have its beginning in the eighteenth century. The crucial discoveries of Galileo, Copernicus, Johannes Kepler, and Isaac Newton were earlier, but they laid the foundation for a different way of looking at things. This new outlook characteristically made no appeal to purpose—human or divine. It was expected that anything that happened would be in conformity with general law, and that if an event diverged from that expectation it must not be fully understood. This made it particularly difficult to credit any account of miracle. Since miracle was thought of as an event contravening natural law and brought about by the direct agency of God, it had no place in such a scheme of things. But beyond that it was difficult even to speak of God as active in history. The very notion of salvation history is incongruous with a world view which makes no provision for divine purpose.

Accompanying and reinforcing the scientific world view in the minds of many were the extraordinary accomplishments of science itself. The combination of mathematical precision and the experimental method had proven to be a powerful tool for the acquisition of new knowledge. Success in one area of inquiry quite naturally inspired confidence in other areas as well, so that a skeptical attitude developed toward any claim that could not be supported "scientifically." Superstition of all sorts was to be rooted out, while any appeal to authority, either institutional or doctrinal, was suspect. The best defense of Christianity was to show its essential reasonableness and social utility. Some Enlightenment thinkers went so far as to collapse the distinction between religion and morality, in effect reducing theology to ethics. That way there could be no conflict between science and religion, but also no distinctive claims on behalf of religion.

At the same time that science was reaching out to encompass new areas of knowledge, modern philosophy took a more reflexive turn. Beginning with René Descartes (1596–1650), philosophers directed their attention increasingly away from the known world and back upon the knowing subject. Descartes in particular tried to show that the self, while not open to empirical observation, could be known intuitively with absolute certainty. David Hume, writing a century later, did not share this sense of certainty regarding the self, but contributed nonetheless to a growing interest in the subjective conditions of knowledge. Immanuel Kant's *Critique of Pure Reason* (1781), with its transcendental deduction of categories, carried this approach even further. After Kant it would be difficult to make any kind of knowledge claim without taking into account the knowing subject. While not perceived as the immediate threat that science represented, this development too constituted a challenge to the theological tradition, since it brought into question the objectivity of many of its claims.

Finally, there was at this time the beginning of a new "historical consciousness." It was different from the salvation history espoused by Augustine and others in that it appealed not to a particular pattern in history but to a particular method of historical study—a critical method that sought to separate genuine history from mythological accretions. Moreover, there was for the first time some recognition of the historical conditionedness of human thought. The biblical writings began to be seen as reflecting the particular outlook, assumptions, and attitudes of the people that produced them. Johann Gottfried Herder, who probably more than any other pioneered this movement, actually celebrated historical particularity. His *Spirit of Hebrew Poetry* (1782) gives more attention to the "genius" of the Hebrew people than to "divine revelation." Clearly this approach to history had the potential to challenge the authority of scripture as nothing before it had, and with that challenge went a threat to the whole theological enterprise.

Schleiermacher and Hegel

Against such a background the theological writings of Friedrich Schleiermacher (1768–1834) are of particular significance, for if any individual can be said to have set theology on a new course in response to the challenges of the modern age, it was Schleiermacher.[5] He not only revived interest in religion as an intellectually respectable topic, but through his systematic rendering of Christian doctrine he laid the groundwork for much of the work that was to follow. It

---

5. Claude Welch, *Protestant Thought in the Nineteenth Century,* 1:2.

all began with an essay entitled *Speeches on Religion to the Cultured among Its Despisers* (1799), in which he argued that religion is neither a form of knowing, such that it might be in conflict with science, nor a form of doing, such that it might be reducible to morality. Rather, it is a matter of feeling or, as he came later to say, "immediate self-consciousness." As the latter definition makes clear, Schleiermacher's way of meeting the challenge of science was to embrace the turn to the subject already begun in philosophy and fully consistent with his own pietistic background. Theology, as he conceived it, consists of reflection upon the deliverances of religious self-consciousness. That reflection takes place within a historical context; nevertheless, it is the religious subject that is central.

In his major work, *The Christian Faith* (1821, 1830), Schleiermacher undertakes to reconstruct the whole of Christian theology from this perspective. He elaborates upon the notion of immediate self-consciousness by explaining that it includes a relationship both to God and to the world. God-consciousness derives from what he calls the feeling of "absolute dependence," or relationship to the ultimate *whence* of things. World-consciousness is distinguished from God-consciousness by the reciprocal nature of the relationship, the feeling of relative freedom and dependence that one has over against the world. Christianity, he argues, is to be distinguished from other religions in part by its clear articulation of God-consciousness and its emphasis upon the ethical implications of faith (what he calls its monotheistic and teleological character), but primarily by the fact that in it "everything is related to the redemption accomplished by Jesus of Nazareth."[6]

With these preliminary definitions in place, Schleiermacher turns to the task of systematically presenting the teachings of Christian faith. The way he goes about it is quite original. In keeping with his definition of Christianity, he organizes the material into three main divisions relative to the experience of redemption. First, he "brackets" the specifically Christian antitheses of sin and grace and considers the God-consciousness presupposed by consciousness of redemption. (In terms of traditional doctrine this section has mainly to do with creation.) He then takes up the consciousness of sin and its implications.

6. Friedrich Schleiermacher, *The Christian Faith*, p. 52.

In the third and final section he considers doctrines specifically related to the consciousness of grace (including the person and work of Christ, justification, sanctification, and the doctrine of the church). Within each division he further divides the subject matter according to the three main elements of religious self-consciousness: self, world, and God. Thus, in each division separate consideration is given to the human condition, the attributes of God, and the state of the world as illumined by a particular aspect of religious experience. It is a complex and elegant structure.

But just how much of a departure is it from tradition? If one considers the topics included and the general order in which they are taken up, it might appear to preserve intact the traditional structure of salvation history. Certainly most of the traditional topics are there, and they are expounded in a way congruent with that history—proceeding from creation to sin to redemption. Yet if one considers the primacy given to self-consciousness as the foundation of the system or to consciousness of redemption as its chief organizing principle, then clearly there has been a break with tradition. No longer can it be assumed that salvation history provides the objective ground for systematic theology. Nor must it be supposed that every doctrine previously included in the compendium of theology will necessarily find a place within a contemporary formulation of faith. In fact, even those that are included may be expected to take on new meaning in view of the radically different perspective taken toward them. In retrospect, what we seem to have here is the beginning of a new theological paradigm by one who stands within the tradition of Augustine and the Reformation, but who realizes that that tradition must be transformed if it is to be responsive to the challenges of the modern age.[7]

Along with Schleiermacher, the other major influence on the course of theology in the nineteenth century was G. W. F. Hegel (1770–1831). Though Hegel did not write a systematic theology and was not strictly speaking a theologian, he did develop a philosophical system within which theological issues could be approached in a fresh and creative way. He did not appreciate Schleiermacher's reduction of religion to feeling, but sought instead to bring out its es-

7. B. A. Gerrish, *Tradition and the Modern World: Reformed Theology in the Nineteenth Century* (Chicago: University of Chicago Press, 1978), p. 15.

sential rationality. To this extent he was very close to the Enlightenment. But Hegel also had a high regard for history, and probably more than any other thinker of the time he succeeded in incorporating the newly emergent historical consciousness into his theology. Perhaps even more important, however, Hegel addressed the issue of religious language in a way that was genuinely novel and that was to have a profound impact upon later theological developments.

Hegel is best known for his system, a speculative construct by which he sought to comprehend in its unity the whole of knowledge. The key to this system was the dialectic, a process of thought whereby each assertion generates a contrary assertion, and out of this tension there arises an encompassing and transforming synthesis. Though his thought was highly abstract and speculative, Hegel had great appreciation for the concrete and the particular. Thus he valued, as Enlightenment thinkers generally did not, the historical religions in all their concreteness and particularity. But he was not satisfied to leave it at that. He sought to comprehend these religions in terms of the system, to demonstrate their rational necessity and show how reason led necessarily beyond them. In his lectures on the philosophy of religion (1821-31) he provides an account of the development of religions wherein each successive stage is rendered intelligible in terms of the whole. Christianity is represented as the culmination of this process, the "absolute religion," in which the unity of the divine and the human is fully realized.

There was, as we have noted, a growing awareness of and appreciation for history. The Hegelian dialectic contributed to this awareness by providing a means for comprehending history as a dynamic process—one in which there was struggle, conflict, and risk, but also movement toward a higher end. What is more, the study of history as Hegel conceived it offered the promise of universal truth, truth of reason and not simply of fact. Small wonder then that his philosophy gave a strong impetus to the study of Christian origins and the history of Christian thought. Yet there was from the outset some doubt as to just how necessary historical occurrence was to the truth of Christianity. Perhaps history merely provided the occasion for the coming to consciousness of an idea, with events serving an incidental function.

In at least one instance, Hegel made it clear that he thought there was no actual historical occurrence back of an idea which had been assumed to be historically based. According to his interpretation, the "fall" does not refer to an actual event in history, but to a universal condition of history: alienation. To be *historical*, in the sense that history is something different from natural occurrence, requires freedom, self-differentiation, and (inevitably) alienation from God. One cannot remain in the state of innocence, naively doing what God wills, and at the same time be a responsible moral agent, deciding between good and evil. The doctrine of original sin therefore expresses a genuine truth having to do with the historical condition of humankind, but not a truth grounded in a specific historical occurrence.

Hegel could make this claim because of a fundamental distinction he had previously drawn between two types of language: the language of religion and that of philosophy. Both are concerned with truth at the highest level, but the form in which that truth is grasped differs significantly. The religious mind, according to Hegel, is restricted to thinking in terms of imagery or representation (*Vorstellung*), whereas the philosophical mind has access to the underlying concept (*Begriff*). Religious images are naturally more concrete and particular than the concepts of the philosopher, and they may have some reference to historical occurrence, but their truth does not depend upon their historical reference. Rather it derives from an implicit rationality which can be fully exhibited only in conceptual terms. It is the task of speculative philosophy to give religious truth this conceptual form.

Hegel's philosophy in its most fully developed state represents the attempt to appropriate the revealed truth of Christianity and put it into speculative form. The essence of Christianity he finds in such classic doctrines as the incarnation and Trinity. In these doctrines is disclosed the truly dialectical nature of God. As Father, God is one and absolute; as Son, self-differentiated; as Spirit, fully yet dynamically self-integrated. This same inner dynamic extends even to God's relationship with history. Our alienation from God is overcome by God's identification with us; through incarnation comes reconciliation. But the incarnation, unlike the fall, is an actual event in history. How important is it to show that the events associated with the incarnation—the ministry, death, and resurrection of Jesus—really happened? Is the truth of Christianity in any sense subject to historical verification? This is an issue that neither Hegel nor Schleiermacher fully confronted, but left to their successors.

The one who took up that challenge most explicitly was David Friedrich Strauss. His *Life of Jesus* (1835–36) poses the problem of history for theology with utmost clarity and force. It does so by questioning the historicity of much of the New Testament witness to Jesus and proposing instead a "mythical" interpretation. For some of the critics of Christianity this meant the death knell of religion. For the systematic theologian it meant that the history-of-salvation framework, anchored as it was to certain past events, could no longer be taken for granted. It would have to be defended if it was to survive at all. The key to Strauss's critical method was his concept of myth derived from Hegel's distinction between *Vorstellung* and *Begriff*. Myth, as he used the term, does not carry the connotation of false or invalid; rather, it signifies the poetic mode in which ideas characteristically come to expression within a religious community. Myth may have some historical basis, but that is not crucial. The meaning conveyed by the myth can be fully transposed into conceptual terms and has validity independently of any historical occurrence.

Thus the turn to history, seen by many at first as a way to reestablish contact with the source of Christian truth, came in time to be viewed as a threat to the viability of that truth. Perhaps there was after all no historical basis for the traditional claims of Christianity. But then Hegel had argued that these claims are ultimately grounded in reason. By way of the system, he had sought to show that Christian teaching contains in representational form truths that are universal and necessary. So history may not be required other than as an occasion for the emergence to consciousness of ideas that have their own independent grounding. The finality of Christianity is demonstrated by its position within the system. That, of course, was the other side of Hegel's ambiguous relationship to history—but it too came under attack, this time by the Danish philosopher Søren Kierkegaard (1813–55).

As the forerunner of modern existentialism, Kierkegaard vigorously opposed any attempt to contain Christianity within a system. He argued that religious truth was primarily subjective and could only be realized as an inward state. Moreover, this inward state could only be

17

attained through passionate choice, the so-called leap of faith. No rational argument, no metaphysical system, no dialectic of history could ever establish the truth of Christianity or relieve the would-be Christian of the burden of choice. The judgment that God is fully present and revealed in Christ is self-involving; it entails personal commitment. The task of theology is not to justify that commitment but to clarify it and thus to prepare the way for faith.

Kierkegaard, along with Schleiermacher, contributed to the subjective turn in theology. He did not, however, undertake a systematic reconstruction of Christian theology from this perspective. He was satisfied to leave the classical formulations largely in place and to concentrate on the communication and appropriation of Christian truth. A half-century later, however, the writings of Kierkegaard would be rediscovered and the implications of his ideas carried much further than he himself had envisioned. Then the attempt would be made to subject the whole of Christian teaching to an "existential" interpretation.

Liberal Theology and the Return to Earlier Models

The past hundred years have produced many creative efforts in systematic theology. The challenges to tradition brought on by Enlightenment and post-Enlightenment thought have been largely assimilated and some substantial efforts at theological reconstruction carried out. It would not be possible in this brief space to review all of them, yet we may at least examine some of the most representative with a view to determining the impact of these various new forces upon the shape of systematic theology.

Full and explicit recognition of the new situation in theology began about a century ago with a movement known generally as theological liberalism. The most influential spokesman for this movement was Albrecht Ritschl (1822–89). It is significant that he began his work as a historian and only subsequently took up the task of systematic theology, for liberal theology was (and still is) heavily committed to the historical method. When he did turn his attention to systematics, it was with a considerable degree of methodological self-consciousness. Theology, as he conceived it, is essentially an "ellipse with two foci"—one religious and the other ethical.[8] At the religious pole, he located the experience of forgiveness, justification, and reconciliation with God; at the ethical pole, the moral ideal symbolized by the kingdom of God. The point at which the two interests converged for him was the historical Jesus—conceived of as the revelation of God's will. In this way Ritschl and his fellow liberals maintained contact with the tradition while at the same time radically restructuring it. The principal effect of their restructuring was to give a strong practical impetus to theology, to emphasize the ethical implications of Christianity without losing sight of its distinctly religious character.

Though not without its detractors, liberal theology was clearly in the ascendancy as Europe entered World War I. With that war, however, came a massive disillusionment with the whole liberal ethos, and in particular its religious idealism. Liberal theology was naturally affected by that mood shift, but also by the publication of two works directly challenging its major theological premises. One of those works was Albert Schweitzer's *Quest of the Historical Jesus* (1906). By reviewing the century-long effort of German scholarship to establish an authentic historical record of the life and teachings of Jesus, Schweitzer succeeded in casting doubt on the liberal claim to an objective, historical understanding of Christ. Though he himself did not share the radical skepticism of Strauss, he left many wondering if that skepticism might not be justified. The other major challenge to the liberal consensus was Karl Barth's *Epistle to the Romans* (1918). Drawing to a considerable extent upon the thought of Kierkegaard, Barth denied that either history or religious experience could serve as bases for faith. Nothing short of God's ineffable grace could suffice to establish faith.

This critical assault on liberalism had a devastating effect upon an entire generation of theologians, though it did not result in the complete demise of liberal theology. What it did initially was revive interest in certain classic patterns of thought. Reformation theology in particular came in for reconsideration, with Barth once again leading the way. His *Church Dogmatics* (1936–69) was and probably still is the most impressive single effort to reestablish the Refor-

8. Albrecht Ritschl, *The Christian Doctrine of Justification and Reconciliation*, 3:11.

mation model in the face of eighteenth- and nineteenth-century criticism. In developing his constructive position, Barth set himself firmly against what he considered to be the subjectivist tendency in modern theology. What he found most appealing in Reformation thought was its emphasis on the sovereignty of God and the primacy of God's word. But that in turn meant the centrality of Christ for all theological reflection. Barth's attempt to carry out a consistently christological interpretation of Christian doctrine is undoubtedly his most distinctive contribution to constructive theology. Just how successful he was remains a matter of dispute.

In the course of writing more than a dozen volumes of the *Dogmatics*, Barth has sounded many traditional themes, yet invariably in a distinctive way. His treatment of the Calvinist theme of election is typical. In speaking of the "eternal decree," he makes no distinction between God's hidden will and revealed will. God's intention is wholly and irrevocably for humanity. Judgment is present, but it is included within acceptance, and the two moments are fully contained within the one event of reconciliation. For Barth, Jesus Christ *is* the event of reconciliation. And what becomes of the history of salvation? It would appear that it is totally taken up into the self-identity of Jesus Christ. He is the full and sufficient embodiment of this history. But then is it any longer "history"? Except for the persistence of the narrative mode in much of Barth's theology, the break with history—and therefore with the paradigm of salvation history—would seem to be virtually complete. Barth in his constructive phase turns out to have been no less a radical thinker than in his critical phase.

At the same time that a revival of interest in Reformation theology was occurring among Protestants, a comparable development was taking place among Roman Catholics with respect to the theology of Thomas Aquinas. The forces of change that had so profoundly shaken Protestantism a century earlier were just beginning to be felt on a large scale within Catholicism, and Aquinas's system of thought was seen as a possible bulwark against those forces. Much of the Thomistic literature is, as one would expect, very traditional, yet there were some fairly significant modifications in response to the challenges of the modern period. Thus, instead of "proofs" for the existence of God, we hear of intimations of the unconditioned. Deductive argument has for the most part given way to analogical description, and first principles have been replaced by rational postulates. Even the philosophical turn to the subject has had an effect, as witness Joseph Maréchal's reinterpretation of Aquinas along lines congenial with Kant's critical epistemology. Clearly a shift of major proportions has occurred all across the theological continuum.

One who has fully accepted this shift and attempted to integrate it into a systematic framework consistent with Catholic tradition is Karl Rahner. His *Foundations of Christian Faith* (1976) is a masterful piece of constructive theology exemplifying the systematic intent evident throughout his work. Perhaps the most distinctive feature of this work is the use he makes of what has been called the "transcendental method." Briefly, this method is an attempt to uncover at the preconceptual level a universal experience of divine presence or grace. It is important, Rahner thinks, to begin at this level if the specifically Christian experience of grace mediated by Christ is to be integrated with the whole of experience. But this also provides a way of relating Christianity positively to other religions, for there too one may expect to find an unreflexive, unthematic awareness of God. This is not to discount the importance of reflection or to minimize the significance of the uniquely Christian experience of grace—what he calls "categorical revelation"—but to put both within a larger context and to show that faith is actually constitutive of human subjectivity. For Rahner, as for Schleiermacher, the turn to the subject is decisive and irrevocable.

Radical Alternatives to Traditional Formulations

So considerable has been the effect of the nineteenth-century paradigm shift upon subsequent theology—even theology which has sought to be traditional—that some theologians have concluded that it is futile even to try to revive old models. What is needed is a radical reconstruction of the philosophical foundations of theology. Paul Tillich's *Systematic Theology* (1951–63) is a pioneering work in this respect, for he clearly sets out his philosophical presuppositions and consciously builds upon them. He characterizes his approach as the "method of correlation." What he attempts to correlate are existential questions generated by the ontological situation of people and religious symbols born of encounter with the "new being" who is Christ.

The starting point for Tillich's "existential ontology" is the self in relationship to the world. The self is primary, since it is primarily through the self that being discloses itself. Yet the self is never without a world, and the structural elements of being that come to light through the self are also found within the world. These elements are fundamentally polar: individuation and participation, dynamics and form, freedom and destiny. Moreover, they are in tension with one another at all levels of existence, so that one way of conceiving the human predicament is in terms of disruption and disintegration of the essential balance between these elements. Salvation then consists in their reintegration and reunification through union with that which underlies them, the ground of all being, God.

The most controversial feature of Tillich's system, for liberal as well as conservative critics, is his concept of God. Tillich has consistently opposed the traditional theistic understanding with its strongly personal characterization and its tendency to treat God as one being among others. In a way not unlike the mystics, Tillich regards God as outside all categories of understanding. But if there is one literal statement that can be made, it is that God is being-itself. All else that we might say is symbolic, expressive of our relationship to the ultimate but not really descriptive of the ultimate itself. It is important for Tillich to say this, in part because of the post-Enlightenment recognition of the symbolic nature of all religious assertions—and here there is obvious indebtedness to Hegel—but also because his ontology requires it, for if God is to unite the polarities of existence and secure being against the threat of nonbeing, then God must transcend the conditions of existence, including the requirements of literal speech.

Alongside this much discussed challenge to traditional ways of speaking about God has gone another and, in some ways, more radical proposal based upon quite different philosophical premises. Charles Hartshorne is the chief spokesperson for a viewpoint which has come to be known as process theology. Drawing primarily though not exclusively upon the philosophy of Alfred North Whitehead (1861–1947), he argues that God must be thought of more dynamically and in a way more consistent with a social conception of reality.

22

Rather than suppose that God is "above it all" and totally unaffected by what is going on in the world, we should presume that God is the most affected being in the universe, the one who experiences everything. Such a one might still be thought of as absolute, though not in the traditional sense of being totally self-sufficient but as needing no particular thing in order to be who it is. Hartshorne calls his viewpoint "panentheism" to distinguish it from "theism," which puts God wholly outside the world, and from "pantheism," which identifies God with the world. A number of American theologians (Schubert Ogden, John Cobb, Lewis Ford) have adopted this perspective and are using it to carry out a thoroughgoing reexamination of traditional doctrine.

A quite different sort of challenge to traditional theological formulation has come from philosophical reflection on the nature and function of religious language. Broadly speaking, two strands may be distinguished, the analytic and the phenomenological. The analytic strand traces its roots to the pioneering work of Ludwig Wittgenstein. While some have concluded, on the basis of Wittgenstein's investigations, that religious language has no real meaning, others have developed his insights into an analysis of the uniquely self-involving character of religious discourse. The phenomenological strand has been shaped primarily by the writings of Martin Heidegger, especially in his postwar years. Heidegger advanced a radical critique, not only of the objectifying metaphysics of pre-Kantian philosophy, but also of the turn to the subject inaugurated by the Enlightenment. Both philosophies, he argued, had "forgotten" the primordial occurrence of being in the coming-to-speech of an unconcealing, freeing word—a word that cannot be objectified but only experienced in our being "appropriated" by it.

These new philosophies of language have had a varied impact on theology. In the fifties and sixties, the movement known as the "new hermeneutic," associated with Gerhard Ebeling, Ernst Fuchs, and others, sought to work out a theory of "word-event" along lines suggested by Heidegger. More recently Paul Ricoeur, combining both the analytic and the phenomenological approaches, has engaged in an innovative series of reflections on religious language, attending to the way in which symbols, metaphors, and narrative texts evoke new, "poetic" possibilities of meaning that transcend the realm of ostensive

23

reference. Two American theologians, Gordon Kaufman and David Tracy, have responded to this complex of issues by attempting to reconstruct the reality-referent of the tradition through a fresh understanding of theological "imagination." Their work carries considerable promise of systematic development, though in ways quite different from any of the traditional formulations of Christian belief.[9]

Finally, there are the theologies of liberation. They are distinctive not only for their central theme but also for their social location. They derive primarily not from the reflection of academics but from the experience of oppressed peoples in their struggle with political and economic systems. The theme of liberation articulates both the hope and the goal of this struggle. Liberation for them is the symbol of salvation par excellence. But is it too political? According to Gustavo Gutiérrez, the most systematic thinker within the movement, the concept of liberation has three distinct levels of meaning: political, historical, and theological.[10] Each is important, and all three are integrally related. Every theology, he would argue, has political implications; liberation theology simply makes those implications explicit and declares itself unequivocally on the side of the politically disadvantaged.

The theologies of liberation have generated a strong response from women, blacks, Third World peoples, and others not previously a part of the theological establishment. They have brought a sociological perspective to the study of theology heretofore unknown and in the process have challenged many traditional assumptions, such as the appropriateness of patriarchal and monarchical imagery for God. Yet they have also been quite uncritical in their use of certain traditional themes, such as "God acting in history," so that many theological issues remain to be resolved.[11] Whether this bold new perspective will be developed in a fully systematic way remains to be seen. At the very least it has served a prophetic function and brought new voices into the theological discussion. Quite conceivably it could mark the

9. See especially Kaufman's *Theological Imagination: Constructing the Concept of God* (Philadelphia: Westminster Press, 1981), and Tracy's *The Analogical Imagination: Christian Theology and the Culture of Pluralism.*
10. Gustavo Gutiérrez, *A Theology of Liberation*, pp. 36–37.
11. Schubert M. Ogden, *Faith and Freedom: Toward a Theology of Liberation* (Nashville: Abingdon Press, 1979), pp. 33–34.

beginning of a major new synthesis: a paradigm shift on the order of that which occurred at the time of the Enlightenment.

ISSUES AND PROPOSALS

Systematic theology as we have come to know it did not spring forth full-blown at the beginning of the Christian era; it was built up gradually over time. Only with Augustine in the fifth century did the key elements come together to form what with justification can be called the classic paradigm. Its most distinctive feature was its historical framework: the attempt to view the whole of Christian doctrine from a history-of-salvation perspective. The result was a powerful teleology, one which has penetrated deeply into the Western consciousness yet which in the modern period has been met with severe criticism.

The Enlightenment challenged the feasibility of any kind of teleology. In particular, it exposed the mythic character of the history-of-salvation teleology. The creation story might be symbolic of God's relationship to the world; it could not be taken as a literal account of the actual formation of the world. Likewise the fall could be regarded as expressive of the human predicament, but not as an actual historical occurrence. Even the Gospel accounts of Jesus came to be seen as having mythic elements, so that there was no longer one sure point on which to fix the history of salvation. The disintegration of this long-established framework is clearly one of the major factors in the present theological crisis, though not the only one.

Platonic and Aristotelian metaphysics, on which Thomas Aquinas relied for much of his systematization of Christian belief, has also been largely discredited. The hierarchy of being, the pattern of emanation and return, and the ideal of perfection implicit in his system would be challenged by most if not all contemporary philosophers. Indeed, even the possibility of metaphysics has been questioned, so that looking to any metaphysical scheme to provide backing for a theological system would seem to be a dubious undertaking. If Christian theology is to achieve coherence and comprehensiveness it must be on some basis other than metaphysics or history.

The early nineteenth century was a major turning point for theology not only because most of the critical issues had emerged by then

25

but also because the construction of an alternative paradigm was well under way. The distinguishing features of this "new paradigm" included: the prominence given to subjectivity, the acceptance of historical criticism, a developmental view of human nature, and the presumption of a close alliance between religion and ethics. The key figure in the transition was undoubtedly Schleiermacher, for he both accepted the challenge of the Enlightenment and sought a constructive reformulation of Christian theology that would be faithful to tradition. Along with Hegel he recognized the need for a unifying principle that would hold together the disparate assortment of beliefs encompassed by traditional theology: beliefs about God, the human condition, Christ, the church, the ultimate end of life. He found that principle in the religious self-consciousness. Because the Christian self-consciousness, as he understood it, was profoundly shaped by the community and its history, he was able to incorporate into his new paradigm many elements of the old paradigm, including the teleology of redemption. But the problem had been posed. In light of the massive shift in assumptions that had occurred, what was to provide Christian theology with its overall unity, coherence, and meaning?

A century and a half after Schleiermacher this problem is still with us. The major theological systems of the modern period all address it in one way or another. Barth's Christocentricism, with its elevation of one of the traditional items of belief to the status of chief organizing principle for the system as a whole, offers one kind of solution. Tillich's method of correlation, with its appeal to the existential situation of the believer as a constitutive element in the structuring of theology, provides a quite different kind of solution. Yet important and influential as these proposals have been, none has prevailed. If there can be said to be a single overriding task for theology at the present time, it is to recover a sense of the *wholeness*, the *unity* and *integrity*, of the Christian witness. The factors that mitigate against this effort are probably as powerful now as they ever were. In some respects they may be even more powerful, for they have penetrated more deeply into our thinking. In addition, there are new factors present that challenge not only the classic paradigm, but also its modern successors.

One of these new factors is the encounter with other religions on a global scale. Traditions that were only theoretical alternatives for Schleiermacher and Hegel are live options for many present-day Christians—even traditions as far removed from Western experience as Hare Krishna and Zen Buddhism. These religious traditions challenge some of our most firmly held beliefs and assumptions. Traditions with their origins in India, for instance, are singularly indifferent to all issues relating to history. Their "theological systems," if we may speak of such, bear no trace of a historical framework—cosmological perhaps, but not historical. Zen, in particular, is very radical by our standards, challenging any sort of teleology and even calling into question the substantiality of the self. We have scarcely begun to respond to this challenge.

Closer to home there have been a number of events in this century that have served to undermine confidence in the Christian interpretation of history and the teleological framework on which it is constructed. The Holocaust is one of them, the ecological crisis another. Can we assume divine sovereignty over history when history issues in the mass extermination of innocent men and women? Can we assume that all things are ordered to human good when the relentless pursuit of human good leads to the destruction of the environment and disruption of the ecological balance in nature? Even the theologies of liberation offer no real answer to this challenge, for though they are critical of all forms of social oppression—and of the complicity of the theological establishment in that oppression—they rely for their criticism to a large extent upon a theology of history that is itself problematical.

So we may after all be in the midst of another paradigm shift. If so, the task of systematic theology will be more than ever a constructive task. The responsibility of the theologian will be to help us discern what is essential to our faith and to express it in ways that are both comprehensive and comprehensible.

AIDS FOR THE STUDY OF THEOLOGY

Collections of Sources in Translation

The following abbreviations are used throughout the book.

ACW   *Ancient Christian Writers.* Edited by Johannes and Joseph Plumpe. 55 vols. to date. Mahwah, N.J.: Paulist Press, 1952–.

ANF   *The Ante-Nicene Fathers: Translations of the Writings of the Fathers down to A.D. 325.* Edited by Alexander Roberts and James Donaldson. 10 vols. New York: Christian Literature Co., 1886–97. Reprint: Eerdmans.

FC   *The Fathers of the Church.* 85 vols. to date. Washington, D.C.: Catholic University Press, 1947–.

LCC   *The Library of Christian Classics.* 26 vols. Philadelphia: Westminster Press, 1953–66.

LPT   *A Library of Protestant Thought.* 12 vols. New York: Oxford University Press, 1964–71.

NPNF¹   *A Select Library of Nicene and Post-Nicene Fathers of the Christian Church.* First Series. Edited by Philip Schaff. 14 vols. New York: Christian Literature Co., 1886–90. Reprint: Eerdmans.

NPNF²   *A Select Library of Nicene and Post-Nicene Fathers of the Christian Church.* Second Seriers. Edited by Philip Schaff and Henry Wace. 14 vols. New York: Christian Literature Co., 1891–99. Reprint: Eerdmans.

Histories of Theology

Cobb, John B. *Living Options in Protestant Theology.* Philadelphia: Westminster Press, 1962.

Dillenberger, John, and Welch, Claude. *Protestant Christianity Interpreted through Its Development.* New York: Charles Scribner's Sons, 1954.

Gonzalez, Justo. *History of Christian Thought.* 3 vols. Rev. ed. Nashville: Abingdon Press, 1987.

Harnack, Adolf. *History of Dogma.* 7 vols. Translated from the 3d German ed. (1893) by Neil Buchanan, 1900. Reprinted (7 vols. in 4). New York: Dover Publications, 1961.

Kelly, J.N.D. *Early Christian Doctrines.* Rev. ed. New York: Harper & Row, 1978.

Livingston, James C. *Modern Christian Thought from the Enlightenment to Vatican II.* New York: Macmillan Co., 1971.

Lohse, Bernhard. *A Short History of Christian Doctrine.* Translated by F. Ernest Stoeffler. Philadelphia: Fortress Press, 1966.

McCool, Gerald A. *Catholic Theology in the Nineteenth Century.* New York: Seabury Press, 1977.

Macquarrie, John. *Twentieth Century Religious Thought.* Rev. ed. Philadelphia: Trinity Press International, 1989.

Pelikan, Jaroslav. *The Christian Tradition: A History of the Development of Doctrine.* 5 vols. Chicago: University of Chicago Press, 1971–89.

Placher, William C. *A History of Christian Theology: An Introduction.* Philadelphia: Westminster Press, 1983.

Religious Thought in the Nineteenth Century. Edited by Ninian Smart et al. 3 vols. Cambridge: Cambridge University Press, 1982–88.

Schoof, T. M. *A Survey of Catholic Theology, 1800–1970.* Paramus, N.J.: Paulist/Newman Press, 1970.

Seeberg, Reinhold. *Textbook of the History of Doctrines.* Translated by Charles E. Hay. 2 vols. in 1. Grand Rapids: Baker Book House, 1952.

Tillich, Paul. *A History of Christian Thought from Its Judaic and Hellenistic Origins to Existentialism.* Edited by Carl E. Braaten. New York: Simon & Schuster, 1972.

Welch, Claude. *Protestant Thought in the Nineteenth Century.* 2 vols. New Haven: Yale University Press, 1972–85.

Comprehensive Theologies

The following represent major inclusive interpretations of the Christian faith, classic and modern. Not all are "systematic" or "dogmatic" theologies in the strict sense.

Patristic and Medieval

Anselm. *Monologion, Prosologion, and Why God Became a Man,* in *Anselm of Canterbury,* vols. 1 and 3. Edited and translated by Jasper Hopkins and Herbert Richardson. Toronto: Edwin Mellen Press, 1974, 1976.

Aquinas, Thomas. *On the Truth of the Catholic Faith: Summa Contra Gentiles.* Translated by A. C. Pegis et al. 4 vols. Garden City, N.Y.: Image Books, 1955–57.

————. *Summa Theologica.* Translated by the English Dominican Province. 60 vols. London: Blackfriars, 1964–.

Athanasius. *On the Incarnation of the Word.* NPNF[2] 4; LCC 3.

Augustine. *The Confessions, the Enchiridion on Faith, Hope, and Love, The City of God,* and *On the Trinity.* In *Basic Writings of Saint Augustine.* Edited by Whitney J. Oates. 2 vols. New York: Random House, 1948. *Confes-*

sions and Enchiridion also in *LCC* 7, edited and translated by Albert C. Outler.

Irenaeus. *Against Heresies. ANF* 1; *LCC* 1 (selections).

Justin Martyr. *The First and Second Apologies. ANF* 1; *LCC* 1.

Origen. *On First Principles.* Translated by G. W. Butterworth. New York: Harper & Row, 1966. Also *ANF* 4.

A *Scholastic Miscellaney: Anselm to Ockham. LCC* 10. Edited and translated by Eugene R. Fairweather.

Tertullian. *The Prescription against Heretics, On the Flesh of Christ,* and *Against Praxeas. ANF* 3. *Treatise against Praxeas.* Edited and translated by Ernest Evans. London: S.P.C.K., 1948.

Reformation

Calvin, John. *Institutes of the Christian Religion.* Translated by Henry Beveridge. 2 vols. Reprint ed. Grand Rapids: Eerdmans, 1953. Also *LCC* 20–21. Translated by John T. McNeill.

Edwards, Jonathan. *Works of Jonathan Edwards.* Edited by Perry Miller et al. New Haven: Yale University Press, 1957ff.

Heppe, Heinrich, ed. *Reformed Dogmatics Set Out and Illustrated from the Sources.* Revised by Ernst Bizer. London: Allen & Unwin, 1950.

Hooker, Richard. *Of the Laws of Ecclesiastical Piety.* Edited by Georges Edelen. 2 vols. Cambridge, Mass.: Belknap Press, 1977.

Luther, Martin. *Selections from His Writings.* Edited by John Dillenberger. Garden City, N.Y.: Anchor Books, 1961.

Melanchthon, Philipp. *Loci communes theologici.* 1521 ed., translated and edited by Wilhelm Pauck, *LCC* 19. 1555 ed., translated and edited by Clyde L. Manschreck, *LPT,* 1965.

Schmid, Heinrich, ed. *The Doctrinal Theology of the Evangelical Lutheran Church.* Translated by Charles A. Hay and Henry E. Jacobs. Philadelphia: Lutheran Publication Society, 1976.

Wesley, John. *John Wesley.* Edited by Albert Outler. *LPT,* 1964.

Nineteenth- and Twentieth-Century Catholic

Adam, Karl. *The Spirit of Catholicism.* Translated by Justin McCann. New York: Macmillan Co., 1940.

Beeck, Frans Jozef van, S. J. *God Encountered: A Contemporary Catholic Systematic Theology.* Vol. 1: *Understanding the Christian Faith.* San Francisco: Harper & Row, 1989.

Fiorenza, Francis Schüssler and John P. Galvin, editors. *Systematic Theology: Roman Catholic Perspectives.* 2 volumes. Minneapolis: Fortress Press, 1991.

Gutiérrez, Gustavo. A *Theology of Liberation.* Translated by Caridad Inda and John Eagleson. Revised edition. Maryknoll, N.Y.: Orbis Books, 1988.

Küng, Hans. *On Being a Christian.* Translated by Edward Quinn. New York: Doubleday, 1976.

Lonergan, Bernard. *Method in Theology.* New York: Herder & Herder, 1972.

Lubac, Henri de. *Catholicism: A Study of Dogma in Relation to the Corporate Destiny of Mankind.* New York: Sheed & Ward, 1958.

McBrien, Richard P. *Catholicism.* Minneapolis: Winston Press, 1980.

Mersch, Emil. *The Theology of the Mystical Body.* Translated by Cyril Vollert. St. Louis: Herder Book Co., 1951.

Möhler, Johann Adam. *Symbolism, or Exposition of the Doctrinal Differences between Catholics and Protestants.* Translated by J. B. Robertson. New York: E. Dunigan, 1844.

Newman, John Henry. *An Essay in Aid of a Grammar of Assent.* Garden City, N.Y.: Image Books, 1955.

Rahner, Karl. *Foundations of Christian Faith: An Introduction to the Idea of Christianity.* Translated by William Dych. New York: Seabury Press, 1978.

———. *Theological Investigations.* 21 vols. to date from various publishers since 1961. Now all available from New York: Crossroad/Continuum.

Ruether, Rosemary Radford. *Sexism and God-Talk: Toward a Feminist Theology.* With a New Introduction. Boston: Beacon Press, 1993.

Schillebeeckx, Edward. *Jesus: An Experiment in Christology.* Translated by Hubert Hoskins. New York: Seabury Press, 1979.

———. *Christ: The Experience of Jesus as Lord.* Translated by John Bowden. New York: Seabury Press, 1980.

Segundo, Juan Luis. *A Theology for Artisans of a New Humanity.* Translated by John Drury. 5 vols. Maryknoll, N.Y.: Orbis Books, 1973–.

Tracy, David. *Blessed Rage for Order: The New Pluralism in Theology.* New York: Seabury Press, 1975.

———. *The Analogical Imagination: Christian Theology and the Culture of Pluralism.* New York: Crossroad, 1981.

———. *Plurality and Ambiguity: Hermeneutics, Religion and Hope.* San Francisco: Harper & Row, 1987.

Nineteenth- and Twentieth-Century Protestant

Barth, Karl. *Church Dogmatics.* Edited by G. W. Bromiley and T. F. Torrance. 13 vols. Edinburgh: T. & T. Clark, 1936–69.

Berkhof, Hendrikus. *Christian Faith: An Introduction to the Study of the Faith.* Translated by S. Woudstra. Grand Rapids: Eerdmans, 1979.

Braaten, Carl. E. and Robert W. Jenson, editors. *Christian Dogmatics.* 2 volumes. Minneapolis: Fortress Press, 1984.

Brunner, Emil. *Dogmatics.* Translated by Olive Wyon. 3 vols. Philadelphia: Westminster Press, 1950–63.

Bushnell, Horace. *Nature and the Supernatural, as Together Constituting the One System of God.* New York: Scribner & Co., 1858.

Cone, James H. A Black Theology of Liberation. Philadelphia: Lippincott, 1970.

Dorner, Isaac. A System of Christian Doctrine. Translated by A. Cave and J. S. Banks. Edinburgh: T. & T. Clark, 1880–82.

Ebeling, Gerhard. The Nature of Faith. Translated by R. G. Smith. Philadelphia: Fortress Press, 1961.

Evans, James H., Jr. We Have Been Believers: An African-American Systematic Theology. Minneapolis: Fortress Press, 1992.

Gilkey, Langdon. Message and Existence. An Introduction to Christian Theology. New York: Seabury Press, 1980.

Hegel, G. W. F. Lectures on the Philosophy of Religion. Ed. and trans. by P. C. Hodgson et al. 3 vols. Berkeley and Los Angeles: University of California Press, 1984–87.

Hodge, Charles. Systematic Theology. 3 vols. New York: Scribner & Co., 1872–73.

Hodgson, Peter C. Winds of the Spirit: A Constructive Christian Theology. Louisville: Westminster/John Knox Press, 1994.

Kaufman, Gordon. In Face of Mystery: A Constructive Theology. Cambridge, Mass.: Harvard University Press, 1993.

Kierkegaard, Søren. Concluding Unscientific Postscript. Translated by Howard V. Hong and Edna H. Hong. Princeton: Princeton University Press, 1986.

Macquarrie, John. Principles of Christian Theology. New York: Charles Scribner's Sons, 1966.

Migliore, Daniel L. Faith Seeking Understanding: An Introduction to Christian Theology. Grand Rapids: Eerdmans Publishing Co., 1991.

Moltmann, Jürgen. The Trinity and the Kingdom: The Doctrine of God. Translated by Margaret Kohl. Minneapolis: Fortress Press, 1993.

———. God in Creation: A New Theology of Creation and the Spirit of God. Translated by Margaret Kohl. Minneapolis: Fortress Press, 1993.

———. The Way of Jesus Christ: Christology in Messianic Dimensions. Translated by Margaret Kohl. Minneapolis: Fortress Press, 1993.

———. The Spirit of Life: A Universal Affirmation. Translated by Margaret Kohl. Minneapolis: Fortress Press, 1992.

Neville, Robert Cummings. A Theology Primer. Albany: State University of New York Press, 1991.

Niebuhr, Reinhold. The Nature and Destiny of Man. 2 vols. New York: Charles Scribner's Sons, 1941, 1943.

Pannenberg, Wolfhart. Systematic Theology. Volume 1. Translated by Geoffrey W. Bromiley. Grand Rrapids: Eerdmans Publishing Company, 1991.

Peters, Ted. God—the World's Future: Systematic Theology for a Postmodern Era. Minneapolis: Fortress Press, 1992.

Ritschl, Albrecht. The Christian Doctrine of Justification and Reconciliation.

Vol. 1, translated by J. S. Black. Edinburgh: Edmonton & Douglas, 1872. Vol. 3, translated by H. R. Mackintosh and A. B. Macaulay. Edinburgh: T. & T. Clark, 1900.

Schleiermacher, Friedrich. *The Christian Faith*. Edited by H. R. Mackintosh and J. S. Stewart, Edinburgh: T. & T. Clark, 1928. Philadelphia: Fortress Press, 1976.

Smart, Ninian and Steven Konstantine. *Christian Systematic Theology in a World Context*. Minneapolis: Fortress Press, 1991.

Sölle, Dorothee. *Thinking about God: An Introduction to Theology*. Philadelphia: Trinity Press International, 1990.

Suchocki, Marjorie Hewett. *God, Christ, Church: A Practical Guide to Process Theology*. Revised edition. New York: Crossroad Publishing Company, 1989.

Thielicke, Helmut. *The Evangelical Faith*. 3 volumes. Translated and edited by Geoffrey W. Bromiley. Grand Rapids: Eerdmans Publishing Company, 1974–82.

Thistlethwaite, Susan Brooks and Mary Potter Engel, editors. *Lift Every Voice: Constructing Christian Theologies from the Underside*. San Francisco: Harper & Row, 1990.

Tillich, Paul. *Systematic Theology*. 3 vols. Chicago: University of Chicago Press, 1951, 1957, 1963.

Troeltsch, Ernst. *The Christian Faith*. Translated by Garrett E. Paul. Minneapolis: Fortress Press, 1991.

Dictionaries and Encyclopedias

Articles on many of the topics of this book will be found in the following works.

Angeles, Peter A. *Dictionary of Christian Theology*. San Francisco: Harper & Row, 1985.

Encyclopedia of the Lutheran Church. Edited by Julius Bodensieck. 3 vols. Minneapolis: Augsburg Publishing House, 1965.

Encyclopedia of Theology: The Concise Sacramentum Mundi. Edited by Karl Rahner. New York: Seabury Press, 1975.

Hastings, James, ed. *Encyclopedia of Religion and Ethics*. 12 vols. Edinburgh and New York: T. & T. Clark and Charles Scribner's Sons, 1908–27.

Kittel, Gerhard, and Friedrich, Gerhard, eds. *Theological Dictionary of the New Testament*. 10 vols. Grand Rapids: Eerdmans, 1964–76.

Musser, Donald W. and Joseph L. Price, editors. *A New Handbook of Christian Theology*. Nashville: Abingdon Press, 1992.

The New Catholic Encyclopedia. Edited by the Catholic University of America. 18 vols. plus supplements. New York: McGraw-Hill, 1967–.

The New Schaff-Herzog Encyclopedia of Religious Knowledge. Edited by S. M.

Jackson et al. 13 vols. plus supplements. New York: Funk & Wagnalls, 1908–12.

Rahner, Karl, and Vorgrimler, Herbert, eds. *Dictionary of Theology.* Revised edition. New York: Crossroad, 1981.

Die Religion in Geschichte und Gegenwart. 5 vols. Tübingen: J. C. B. Mohr, 1909–13 (1st ed.), 1927–31 (2d ed.), 1950–65 (3d ed.).

Richardson, Alan and John Bowden, editors. *Westminster Dictionary of Christian Theology.* Philadelphia: Westminster Press, 1983.

Sacramentum Mundi. Edited by Karl Rahner et al. 6 vols. New York: Herder & Herder, 1968.

Twentieth Century Theology in the Making. Edited by Jaroslav Pelikan. Translation of selected articles from the 2d ed. of RGG. 3 vols. London and New York: William Collins and Harper & Row, 1969–70.

Creeds and Confessions

Bettenson, Henry, ed. *Documents of the Christian Church.* London: Oxford University Press, 1967.

The Book of Concord: The Confessions of the Evangelical Lutheran Church. Translated and edited by Theodore G. Tappert. Philadelphia: Fortress Press, 1959.

Book of Confessions of the Presbyterian Church (USA). Louisville: Office of the General Assembly, 1991.

Cochrane, Arthur. ed. *Reformed Confessions of the Sixteenth Century.* Philadelphia: Westminster Press, 1966.

Denzinger, Henrich, et al., eds. *The Church Teaches: Documents of the Church in English Translation.* Translated and edited by John F. Clarkson et al. St. Louis: Herder Book Co., 1955.

Gerrish, Brian, ed. *The Faith of Christendom: A Source Book of Creeds and Confessions.* Cleveland: World Publishing Co., 1963.

Leith, John, ed. *Creeds of the Churches: A Reader in Christian Doctrine.* Revised edition. Richmond: John Knox Press, 1973.

A New Catechism: Catholic Faith for Adults. Commissioned by the Catholic Bishops of the Netherlands. New York: Herder & Herder, 1967, 1969.

Schaff, Philip, ed. *Creeds of Christendom.* 3 vols. New York: Harper Bros., 1877. Reprint edition. Grand Rapids: Baker Book House, 1977.

Walker, Williston, ed. *The Creeds and Platforms of Congregationalism.* Philadelphia: Pilgrim Press, 1969.

1. THEOLOGICAL METHOD

WHERE WE ARE

As contemporary theologians grope for some new, inevitably tentative formulations of a paradigm that can guide their deliberations and inform their more modest expectations, they are confronted with the question of method. In an important sense, theological method must always be a secondary matter. It is secondary to all concrete interpretations of the concrete symbols of the tradition for the present concrete community with its experience of the Christ-event and its hopes for the future. Method—precisely as a necessarily abstract, heuristic guide—must always be secondary to the concrete stuff of each particular theological interpretation. But the secondary also serves. Reflection on method serves the common cause of concrete theological interpretation by bringing into clearer focus the principles that help to clarify the common search for a "new paradigm" for theology. The abstract not merely abstracts from the concrete; the abstract also enriches the concrete by highlighting and clarifying what is essential.

It should be helpful, therefore, to reflect on what kind of *general* theological method may be shared by contemporary theologians despite their otherwise vital differences. My hypothesis can be stated in four comments: First, whatever else is true about Christian theology, it is clearly an interpretation of the central symbols of the Christian tradition for some construal of our present situation. Second, whatever else may be true about the new paradigm, it is clearly one where the interpretations cannot be grounded in the older classicist base but must risk new interpretations of both past tradition and present situation. Third, in keeping with the eschatological thrust of the Christian gospel itself and the transformative power of contemporary feminist, liberationist, and political theologies, we also need interpretations that risk envisioning a Christian future as well. Fourth, it is also clear—and follows from the first three common characteristics—that contemporary theo-

35

logians must engage in the kinds of interpretations now known as both "hermeneutics of retrieval" and "hermeneutics of critique and suspicion." There is no innocent interpretation, no unambiguous tradition, no history-less, subject-less interpreter, no abstract, general situation, no method to guarantee certainty. There is only the risk of theological interpretation itself: the risk of interpreting the great symbols now and sharing that interpretation with the wider theological community for their criticism and their appropriation.

Such are my basic hypotheses on "where we are" for reflection on theological method. My strategy for the reflection itself is as follows: I shall claim that amidst the great differences of contemporary theologies certain methodological constants do appear. That claim can be made more specific by introducing the following definition of a shared theological method in the new paradigm: *theology is the attempt to establish mutually critical correlations between an interpretation of the Christian tradition and an interpretation of the contemporary situation.*

In an attempt to clarify this definition, the main body of this chapter is divided into three main sections: a section on interpretation, a section on the interpretation of religious classics, and a section on theological method in the new paradigm. On this reading, contemporary theology shares with the humanities, the social sciences, and, more recently, the natural sciences a turn to reflection on the process of interpretation itself. The first section will, therefore, concentrate on that turn to interpretation across the disciplines. But theology is an interpretation of that elusive, ambiguous, and transformative reality named, however inadequately, "religion." The second section will, therefore, focus on some of the major dimensions of that fact. Finally, theology is not merely a synonym for any interpretation of religion but rather bears its own methodological demands and its own criteria. The third section will, therefore, attempt to clarify the definition for theology introduced above after more general initial clarifications of what interpretation is and what a theological interpretation of religion might be.

This may seem a long route to reflection on contemporary theological method. And yet the long route is needed. For the classicist paradigm for theology is spent. We are left, therefore, with the need to reflect more exactly on what interpretation itself might be in order to clarify what contemporary theological interpretation in the new paradigm in fact is amidst all the different theologies. Such clarification is the aim of all reflection on method: not to replace substantive, topical, concrete theologies with a method become an arrogant methodologism, but to clarify what is shared amidst the differing theologies. That sharing is what helps to constitute postclassical theology as a community of shared inquiry and method.

THE TURN TO INTERPRETATION THEORY

Christianity, like any religion, is extraordinarily difficult to interpret insofar as a religion radicalizes, intensifies, and often transgresses the boundaries of those other central human phenomena to which it is necessarily related (art, science, metaphysics, ethics-politics). To interpret any religion one must also, consciously or unconsciously, end up interpreting these other phenomena as well in order to understand the differentia that are specifically religious. To read the creative theologians in the modern period alone is to find a pluralism that suggests a seemingly indeterminate creativity of interpretation. To read contemporary works in theology (or even to read one issue of one of the major journals or attend one session of one of the major conferences of scholars in the field) is to recognize a radical pluralism, indeed, an intense conflict of interpretation, from which there can often seem no honorable exit.

The clearest expression of that creativity is the pluralism of interpretation itself. Within that pluralism, how is it possible for the wider community of inquiry to reach any consensus on the better and the worse, the truly creative and the mere bright ideas among the various contenders? Here I simply suggest that the turn to interpretation theory among many scholars in theology provides one way to encourage creativity in interpretation without forfeiting the need for criteria of adequacy for interpretation.

Interpretation as a problem or even as an explicit issue becomes a central issue in cultural periods of crisis. So it was for the Stoics and their reinterpretation of the Greek and Roman myths. So it was also for the development of allegory in Christian theologies. So it is for Jews and Christians since the emergence of historical consciousness. The sense of distance that any contemporary Westerner feels in relationship to the classics of Western culture impels but need not determine the contemporary interest in the process of interpretation. But if we focus only on our sense of historical distance from the classics of our culture or on our Western sense of parochialism disclosing our cultural distance from the classics of other cultures, we are likely to formulate the problem of interpretation as primarily a problem of avoiding misunderstanding. Even Friedrich Schleiermacher, justly credited as the founder of modern hermeneutics, often tended to formulate the problem of hermeneutics in this manner. One aspect of Schleiermacher's "mixed discourse" in hermeneutics—his emphasis on empathy and divination—tended to encourage the development of romantic hermeneutics. The other aspect of Schleiermacher's hermeneutics—his emphasis on developing methodical controls to avoid misunderstanding—tended to encourage the development of strictly methodological (first historicist, then formalist) controls.

The fruits of the impasse occasioned by that mixed discourse remain with us yet. For many theories of interpretation, the central insight is into the actuality of historical and cultural distance (and hence our "alienation" from the classics). The central problem is the need to avoid misunderstanding, and the central hope is in the controls afforded by some methodology to keep us from forcing these alien texts of alien cultures or earlier periods of our own culture into the alien and alienating horizon of our present self-understanding. With some notable exceptions, most contemporary interpreters not only accept but demand the controls and the clear gains that historical methods have allowed contemporary interpreters. Clearly, the acceptance and use of historical-critical methods is one defining characteristic of the new paradigm in theology.

Interpretation as Conversation

It is impossible in so short a space to develop the complex and still-ongoing debate on hermeneutics in the modern period. For the purposes of this present analysis of the *status quaestionis* of hermeneutics within the new paradigm, I can hope only to clarify my own position and the hermeneutical tradition in which I stand. As my previous remarks suggest, I do not believe that either of the two principal strands on hermeneutics bequeathed to us by Schleiermacher's creative and, indeed, classic reflections on interpretation is adequate. More exactly, the interpreter as empathizing, divinizing virtuoso (or genius) is a romantic legacy that has yielded some fruit; yet basically romantic notions of creativity and imagination can yield the kind of intellectual havoc that has given creativity a bad name in many circles. Ultimately, the hope for methodological controls (either historicist or formalist) that will "guarantee" correct understanding seems seriously misplaced. Of course, we need historical-critical methods in theology. These controls, to be sure, do help all interpreters avoid serious (for example, anachronistic) misunderstandings of ancient texts and often help us to reconstruct the authentic text needing interpretation (for example, the present parabolic texts reconstructed into the parables *of Jesus*). Modern historical consciousness, moreover, rouses our consciousness of both the text's and our own historicity. But the belief that, by avoiding ahistoricist misunderstanding, we also somehow achieve an adequate theological understanding of the questions and responses of the classic texts seems mistaken.

In the fuller spectrum of contemporary hermeneutics, one can speak of three basic steps (not rules!) for interpretation and two correctives. In a first step, every interpreter enters the task of interpretation with some preunderstanding of the subject matter of the text. Historical consciousness (and its contemporary correlate, a sociological imagination) helps to clarify the complex reality of the interpreter's preunderstanding. Historical consciousness is, after all, a post-Enlightenment and, in some ways, even an anti-Enlightenment phenomenon. More exactly, the Enlightenment belief (still alive in many methodologies) that the interpreter can in principle and should in fact eliminate all "prejudgments" was at best a half-truth. For the truth of the Enlightenment is nothing less than the liberating demand classically expressed by Kant as *aude sapere*, that is, dare to think for yourself and free yourself from the mystifications and obscurantisms inevitably present in all the traditions. Indeed, the emancipatory thrust of critical and practical reason released anew by the Enlightenment was and is a liberating moment that forms part of the horizon (the preunderstanding) of the modern mind.

Yet the reason why this creative truth is only a half-truth can be clarified for any posthistorically conscious mind. If the expression "historicity" is not merely an ontological abstraction, if the phrases "socialization" or "enculturation" are other than disciplinary jargon, they all bespeak the other de facto truth missed by Enlightenment polemics against "prejudgments" and "traditions." The fact is that no interpreter enters into the attempt to understand any text without prejudgments formed by the history of that person's culture. No interpreter, in fact, is as purely autonomous as the Enlightenment model promised. The recognition of tradition means that as interpreters we enter into the act of interpretation bearing the history of the effects, both conscious and unconscious, of the traditions to which we ineluctably belong. Any theologian attempting to interpret the Christian tradition will surely recognize this truth.

All of us (however personally alienated from the dominant traditions of the culture) can recognize the de facto presence of the history of the effects of tradition in our preunderstanding. We can best do so by reflecting upon our own language use. For the language each of us uses carries with it the history of the effects, the traditions, of that language. The very word "religion," for example, carries with it in the English language the history of the effects of the Roman notions of "civil religion," the Jewish and Christian notions of "faith," and Enlightenment notions of "natural" and "positive" religion. No one who thinks in and through a particular language (and who does not?) escapes the history of the effects—the tradition—inevitably present in that language. We are left, therefore, with our first matter of fact for every interpreter: no interpreter enters the process of interpretation without certain prejudgments. Included in these prejudgments, through the very language we use, is the history of the effects of the traditions forming that language.

Yet the fact that we say that the interpreter "enters" the process of interpretation also allows us to recognize that a second step in that process occurs. The clearest way to see this second step is to consider our actual experience of any classic text, image, symbol, event, ritual, or person. When interpreting any *classic* text in the Western traditions, for example, we may note that these texts bear a certain permanence and excess of meaning that resists a definitive interpretation. Our actual experience of the classic texts vexes, provokes, elicits a claim to serious attention. And just this claim to attention from the classic text provokes our own preunderstanding into a dual recognition: a recognition at once of how formed our preunderstanding is and, at the same time, a recognition of the vexing, or provocation, elicited by the claim to attention of this text. In sum, the interpreter must now interpret in order to understand. The actual experience of that claim to attention may range from a tentative sense of resonance with the question posed by the text through senses of import or even shock of recognition or repugnance elicited by the classic text.

At this point, the interpreter may search for some heuristic model by means of which better to understand the complex process of interaction between text and interpreter now set in motion by the claim to attention of the text. This search for a model for the de facto process of interpretation provides the third step of interpretation. Hans-Georg Gadamer's now famous and controversial suggestion of the model of the "game of conversation" for this process of interpretation seems appropriate here. For the model of conversation is not imposed upon our actual experience of interpretation as some new de jure method, norm, or rule. Rather the phenomenon of conversation aptly describes anyone's de facto experience of interpreting any classic text.

To understand how this is the case, first recall the more general phenomenon of "game" itself. The key to any game is not the self-consciousness of the players in the game but rather the release of self-consciousness into a consciousness of the phenomenon of the to-and-fro, the back-and-forth movement that constitutes the game. The attitude of the players is a phenomenon dependent above all upon this natural back-and-forth movement of the game. When we really play any game, it is not so much we who are playing as it is the game that plays us. If we cannot release ourselves to the back-and-forth movement of the game, then we cannot play. But if we can play, then we experience ourselves as caught up in the movement of the game itself. We realize that our usual self-consciousness cannot be the key to playing. Rather we may even find, however temporarily, a new sense of the self given in, by, and through our actual playing, our release to the to-and-fro movements of the game.

This common human experience of playing a game can become the key to the basic model of conversation for the "game" of interpretation. For what is authentic conversation (as distinct from mere good feeling or debate, gossip or confrontation) other than the ability to become caught up in the to-and-fro movement of the logic of question and response? Just as the subjects in any game release themselves from self-consciousness in order to play, so too in every authentic conversation the subject is released by the to-and-fro movement of the question and response of the subject matter under discussion. It is true, of course, that conversation is ordinarily a phenomenon between two living subjects or even one subject reflecting on a question. Yet the model of conversation, as Gadamer correctly insists, is also applicable to our experience of the interpretation of texts. For if we allow the claim to serious attention of the text to provoke our questioning, then we enter into the logic of question and response of the subject matter expressed in the text. A more general model of an interaction between our preunderstanding and the claim to attention of the text may now be understood as a peculiar kind of interaction by means of this model of the conversation. If we cannot converse, if we cannot allow for the demands of any subject matter in any classic, or for any process of questioning provoked by the claim to attention of the text to take over —then, but only then, we cannot interpret. But if we have even once entered into any genuine conversation, then we are well prepared to recognize how fruitful that model is for the process of interpretation itself.

We need not retreat into the false hopes for ultimate control over that subject matter promised by the methodologies of control. We need not retreat into romantic notions of the interpreter-as-virtuoso intuiting the meaning of the text by empathizing with the mind of the author or by reconstructing the original audience or original social context. We need only converse with the formed subject matter, the questions and responses of the text. Insofar as it is we ourselves who are conversing with this classic text, moreover, we will also recognize the inevitable presence of our own preunderstanding and prejudgments in the conversation. For the claim to serious attention provoked by the text is a claim for *our* attention. It is not the case that we attempt simply to lose ourselves in the "autonomy" of the text. Rather we attempt primarily to gain ourselves by losing ourselves in the logic of questioning the subject matter disclosed by the text.

Interpretation is inevitably creative. The meaning of the text does not lie "behind" it (in the mind of the author, the original social setting, the original audience) nor even "in" the text itself. Rather the meaning of the text lies in front of the text—in the now common question, the now common subject matter, of both text and interpreter. We do not seek simply to repeat, to reproduce the original meaning of the text in order to understand its (and now our) questions.

Rather, creativity must be involved as we seek to mediate, translate, interpret its meaning—the meaning in front of the text—into our own horizon. We seek, in Gadamer's often-misunderstood phrase, to fuse the horizon (the horizon of meaning in front of the text) with our own horizon. More basically, we seek to converse with the subject matter found and expressed in the classic text. We seek, in sum, *to interpret in order to understand.*

By recognizing the actual experience of the interaction of interpreter and text as an experience of conversation, moreover, we also recognize both the creativity and the inevitable finitude and historicity of even our best acts of interpretation. For we recognize the fate of all interpretation of all classics as a fate that can become, when embraced as a conversation, a destiny. That destiny—present in all the classic conversations, especially the Platonic dialogues, and all the creative interpreters—is the recognition that we live, in and by our finitude and historicity, with the liberating insight that *insofar as we understand at all we understand differently*—differently, that is, from the original author.

The Role of Critical Theory and Explanatory Methods

Still there are, in my judgment, two crucial difficulties in this interpretation of the process of interpretation that demand correction. First, it remains an open question whether this understanding of critical reflection can really allow for the kinds of critical theories demanded to undo not error, but illusion, not normal cognitive and moral ambiguity, but systematic distortions. Here is where Gadamer's anti-Enlightenment polemic severely damages his case. His apprehension is that any move to critical theory will inevitably become yet another futile attempt to provide a mythical, "presuppositionless" interpreter. Because of that apprehension he seems to discount the necessity of critical theory in some conversations—including conversations with the classics. The basic developments in the postmodern hermeneutic tradition have in fact been developments in interpretation theories that are explicitly geared to formulating various critical theories forged to expose the latent meanings of texts—especially those latent meanings that enforce not mere error but illusion, not occasional difficulties but systematic distortions.

Gadamer's position does not really allow these necessarily suspicious moves (and their attendant critical theories) to play their limited but proper role in the dialectic of interpretation. Yet the very experience of interpretation-as-conversation should alert us to this need for critical theory. To return to the model of conversation on the interpersonal level for the moment: in the course of any conversation, if any one of us begins to suspect (the verb here is apt) that our conversation-partner is psychotic, we would be justified in suspending the conversation. In sum, the need for suspicion, as well as the need for critical theories, to spot and heal systematic distortions in our personal, cultural, and social lives, has become an indispensable aspect of any modern interpreter's horizon of preunderstanding and possibility for creative interpretation. It is true, of course, that this kind of interpretation of latent, hidden, repressed meanings unconsciously operative as systematic distortions is easier to employ (thanks to psychoanalysis) on the personal and interpersonal levels than on the social, cultural, and historical levels. However, even on these levels, various forms of Marxist "ideology-critique" and, more recently, with thinkers like Foucault, various forms of Nietzschean "genealogical methods" exist like their theological analogues in liberation and political theologies as hermeneutic aids to try to locate and undo the illusions, the hidden, repressed, unconscious distortions present in both the preunderstanding of the interpreter and the classic texts and traditions. Each one of these "hermeneutics of suspicion," moreover, cannot rest simply on the model of conversation but needs critical theories to warrant its operation.

For any interpreter who so much as suspects that there *may be* illusions or repressed systematic distortions present in any particular tradition, the need to develop this sense of suspicion becomes imperative. Whenever we suspect systematic distortion, the model of conversation becomes inadequate to describe the fuller process of interpretation. The analyst and the analysand are not, in fact, engaged in a conversation *tout simple*. Rather they are engaged in a process of interpretation whereby one conversation-partner (the analyst) employs a critical theory (psychoanalytic theory) to aid the other partner to interpret experience and thus to emancipate that other partner from the systematic distortions repressed but operative in that experience. Only after this kind of emancipation has taken place is conversation possible again.

Yet not to face that demand for suspicion as part of the demand for interpreting any tradition seems to leave us, unwittingly, without the hermeneutic resource that our postmodern era renders available, and that genuine creativity in interpretation now demands.

The second difficulty I wish to address is related not so much to the model of conversation as to the notion of the "text and its subject matter" as formulated by Gadamer. The crucial issue here is this: the subject matter that links interpreter and text in the process of interpretation is a subject matter whose claim to attention is one expressed in the form of a text. The point is worth emphasizing in order to understand the fuller process of interpretation. Insofar as we recognize that the text produces its claim to attention by structuring and forming the subject matter into a work, an ordered whole, *a text*, we must also recognize the legitimacy, even necessity, for the use of certain explanatory methods in the process of interpretation. As Paul Ricoeur insists along with Gadamer, understanding (*Verstehen*) does "envelop" the entire process of interpretation. And yet, as Ricoeur correctly insists against Gadamer, explanatory methods (*Erklären*) can "develop" our understanding of how the meaning is produced through the very form and structure of the text.

A fuller model of conversation thereby suggests itself, namely, that the entire process of interpretation encompasses the arc of initial understanding yielding to an explanation of how the sense and referent (the world of meaning in front of the text) are produced through the meanings-in-form-and-structure *in* the text. After those explanatory moments the reader has a better understanding of the subject matter (as an in-formed subject matter) than any interpreter does without them. Indeed without the use of explanatory methods like the methods of literary criticism, or semiotic and structuralist methods, it is difficult to see how, against Gadamer's own manifest intentions, the interpreter is not in danger of simply extracting "messages" (under the rubric "subject matter") from the complex, structured, formed subject matter which is the text.

Every text is a structured whole. Every subject matter comes to us with its claim to serious attention in and through its form and structure. To resist explanatory methods that can show how such expression occurs from the semiotic level of the word, through the semantics of the sentence, through the structured whole of the work as an ordered whole in the text (achieved principally through composition and genre), to the individuating power of style, is ultimately to resist both understanding and creativity (Ricoeur). Yet just this seems to occur in Gadamer's polemic against method. So apprehensive is he that explanation (or *Erklären*) may become a means to undo conversation between text and interpreter on a common subject matter (and, therefore, undo authentic hermeneutical understanding or *Verstehen*), that he is tempted to discount the necessity for explanatory methods in interpretation.

More exactly, all explanatory methods can be used by any interpreter committed to the kind of process of interpretation that Gadamer himself outlines. In fact, explanatory methods develop or challenge, even confront, one's initial understanding of how the subject matter comes to be expressed in and through its structure and form. In Ricoeur's formulation, this may be restated as the ability of these explanatory methods to show how the structured meanings and sense produce the referent of the work. Understanding and explanation (like truth *and* method) need not be implacable enemies. For any interpreter, they can become allies—albeit wary and uneasy allies. The wider conversation of the contemporary conflict on interpretation theory need not yield to the spectacle of armed camps shooting over the walls of the encampment. Rather, creative possibilities exist for the entire community of interpreters in any discipline to engage in conversation on the relative adequacy of any interpretation.

THE INTERPRETATION OF
RELIGIOUS CLASSICS

Before proceeding directly to the role of interpretation theory in theology, let us first look at its role in *any* interpretation of religion. It is important to make this detour through the interpretation of religion in order to assure that the theologian's interpretations of Christian tradition for the contemporary situation are not divorced from all interpretations of religion in the new paradigm. On the contrary, the Christian theologian performs one vital kind of interpretation of a particular religion which, precisely *as interpretation*, is intrinsically related to all other interpretations of religion. Let us see, therefore, how the steps of interpretation analyzed above are applicable to the interpretation of that puzzling, pluralistic and ambiguous phenomenon called religion. Once that is clarified, we can then turn to the particular hermeneutical character of Christian theology itself.

The first choice any interpreter of religion, including the theologian, must make is the choice of which phenomenon to interpret. The prospective interpreter may believe either that religion is one of the great creative forces of the human spirit or a deadly confusion. Whatever one's predilections on religion, interpreters must be sure that the phenomenon to be interpreted is a genuinely religious one. One way to ensure that the phenomenon will be religious is to choose one of the religious classics of a particular religion for one's interpretation. By choosing a recognized religious classic (a text, symbol, myth, ritual, person, event, doctrine), the interpreter will make two gains: first, the phenomenon, whatever else it is, will be religious; second, the phenomenon as a classic religious expression will lend itself to an interpretation theory that is designed to deal with *expressions* of experience and not directly with claims to purely unexpressed experiences. With the choice of a single religious classic from among the pluralistic ways of being religious and the plurality of religious classics expressive of those many ways, the interpretation will begin. Then the steps argued earlier as constitutive of the process of interpretation can be used to interpret this classic expression *as* a religious classic.

The interpreter is likely to note that the religious classic, like any classic, will provoke, vex, elicit a claim to serious attention. By that provocation, two steps will occur. First, if the phenomenon is religious it will ordinarily provoke some fundamental existential question for the human spirit (for example, the question of finitude or fault, the question of fundamental trust or meaning) as well as some initial comprehension of a particular response to that question articulated in this particular religious text. As soon as any provocation is recognized by the interpreter, then the second step of the interpretation process occurs. Not only are we provoked by the classic as by an other (even, sometimes, an alien other); we are also alerted by that otherness to a recognition of our own preunderstanding. The otherness, even alienness, of the religious classic heightens consciousness of one's preunderstanding of religion. The history of the effects of our cultural traditions on religion—along with the history of the effects of our own participation or nonparticipation in a particular religious community or particular cultural traditions which have been influenced, for good and ill, by particular religious traditions—now becomes clearer to us. The history of the effects does not become, contra Hegel, fully conscious but does become more conscious than the partly unconscious and partly conscious history of effects that were prior to the provocation by the religious classic itself.

This initial form of interaction of the claim to attention provoked by the religious text and the preunderstanding (including the prejudgments) of the interpreter becomes a genuine interpretation when the initial interaction takes the more specific form of a conversation. In that interaction game, the interpreter is willing to enter into the to-and-fro movement of the questions and responses of this classic text. When those questions become the interpreter's own questions, then we as interpreters find ourselves in a conversation with the now common subject matter of both text and interpreter. As in the interpretation of any other classic, this does *not* mean that interpreters must give up their own powers of critical reflection on these now common questions. It does mean, however, that if they are to interpret the religious phenomenon as a religious phenomenon they cannot simply impose their prior value judgments upon the phenomenon through such strategies as the claim that these kinds of questions are unintelligible and therefore not open to interpretation. These de jure moves crash against the matter of fact that, once the provocation of the text has elicited the interpreter to ask *its* kind of question and to consider *its* kind of response to that question, the process of interpretation-as-conversation has already begun.

The spectrum of responses of the interpreter throughout the entire process of interpretation may range from some interest or resonance through a sense that, in Dorothy van Ghent's apt words, "something else may be the case" to a fuller negative repugnance or positive shock of recognition. (In theology this latter response is recognized as the gift of faith.) In every case along the whole pluralistic spectrum of possible responses, as long as any claim to attention is allowed at all, the process of interpretation-as-conversation between the constantly shifting identities-in-difference of both text and interpreter occasioned by the to-and-fro movement of the conversation guided by the eventually common questions of the common subject matter continues. Neither interpreter nor text but the common subject matter takes over in genuine conversation. Interpretation as conversation will not occur, however, if the prospective interpreter will not allow any provocation from the religous text because one already "knows" that this conversation is hopeless. Nor will a conversation occur if the interpreter decides that the text is so autonomous that one cannot consider one's own responses as part of the conversation which is the interpretation. Nor will interpretation as conversation occur if the interpreter decides that the real meaning of the text cannot be found through the text itself but must be found "behind" the text—in the mind of the author, in the sociohistorical conditions of the text, or in the response of the original audience to the text.

And yet, as this last "textual" factor indicates, there is also need for the two "correctives" noted earlier to assure that the full arc of interpretation occurs and that a full use of explanatory methods is allowed. Since we are interpreting *expressions* (especially, but not exclusively, written texts) when interpreting the religious classics, we are interpreting a structured whole that expresses its claim to our attention through such productive strategies as composition, genre, and style. As a work the text produces its world of meaning in front of the text as a possible way-of-being-in-the-world. The text thus produces a genuine possibility for our imagination. That possibility first comes to us simply as a claim to attention. As that claim provokes our attention and pre-understanding to the point where a conversation on a now-common subject matter occurs, the interpreter will also recognize that the subject matter is always already a formed subject matter. The subject matter comes as an expression (whether in written texts, actions, styles of life, images, or symbols). The interpreter finds the need to employ explanatory methods to develop an initial understanding of that expression (in the general sense of a "structured whole" as "text") and to check, correct, or even confront that initial understanding by the use of explanatory methods. All such methods—whether historical-critical, semiotic, structuralist, or literary-critical—may serve as developments, checks, correctives, and challenges to the initial understanding. On this hermeneutic model, these methods serve these functions best by showing how the claim to attention provoked by the text is in fact produced as a world of meaning (a referent) in front of the text through the text itself.

On this reading, there is no reason to hold that a hermeneutics of religion should disallow such semiotic explanations as Louis Marin's analysis of the parables of the New Testament or such structuralist analyses as Claude Lévi-Strauss's analysis of mythic structures. It is true that a hermeneutics of religion of the kind described above will not agree that these interpretations are fully adequate. Yet it will not only agree but insist that such interpretations are legitimate moments of explanation in the process of interpretation. Any explanatory method that helps to show how the text produces its sense and referent is entirely appropriate to a hermeneutics of religion. As Schleiermacher's insistence on grammatical methods shows, as Gadamer's own recognition of the roles of structure and form demonstrates, as Joachim Wach's attention to classic religious expressions indicates, there is no reason in principle for the hermeneutical tradition to disallow the use of explanatory methods to develop, check, correct, and challenge one's initial interpretation. Creativity in interpretation is not opposed to explanation and method. The very pluralism intrinsic to the religious phenomenon itself, moreover, should encourage the use of the plurality of explanatory methods within the fuller process of interpretation. These methods may also serve to show how the religious use of *any* form—any genre or style—is a limit-use that produces the referent of the religious classic as a limit-mode-of-being-in-the-world.

In harmony with the earlier analysis of interpretation theory and in harmony with a recognition of the plurality and ambiguity internal to the religious phenomenon itself, we affirm the need for a second corrective as well. All of the great hermeneutics of suspicion (those of Marx, Freud, Nietzsche) remain relevant methods of interpretation. Each develops a critical theory (psychoanalytic theory, ideology-critique, genealogical method) to inform its hermeneutics of suspicion. The critical theories are employed to spot and emancipate the repressed, unconscious distortions that are also operative in the classic religious texts and in their history of effects through the classic religious traditions. Not only is this need for a hermeneutics of suspicion along with a hermeneutics of retrieval allowed by this general interpretation theory; it is also allowed—indeed demanded—by the nature of the religious phenomenon itself.

It is sometimes claimed that the various hermeneutics of suspicion are simply taken from the secular classics and then used by interpreters of the religious classics to interpret religion. To a large extent, of course, this is historically true insofar as such methods of suspicion as Freudian psychoanalysis, Marxist ideology-critique, or Nietzschean genealogical methods were first developed outside (indeed usually against) the religious traditions before they are employed within them. Yet, as the modern political, liberation, and feminist theologians correctly insist, these methods of suspicion are entirely appropriate to employ on inner-religious grounds. The reason for this, I believe, is clearly demonstrated in the Jewish and Christian traditions. For both major strands of these traditions—the prophetic and the mystical—include explicitly religious hermeneutics of suspicion that demand constant self-reformation and self-suspicion by the tradition on the tradition's own religious grounds.

Bultmann is correct, on purely hermeneutical grounds, to insist that the prophetic-eschatological strand of Christianity (and not merely the problematic of "modernity") demands the demythologizing of Christianity by Christianity. At the heart of every prophetic tradition is an opening and a demand for any critical theory that helps to uncover repressed illusions, including the repressed illusion (not mere errors) of sexism, racism, classism, and so forth, which are also operative in the Jewish and Christian religious classics.

Nor is it the case that the mystical strand of the religious traditions are lacking in their own form of a hermeneutics of suspicion. For the great developments of spirituality in all the traditions, including the Jewish and Christian, were developed to find not mere errors but systematic, unconscious illusions. The very use of the word "discernment" in the Christian traditions of spirituality, like the development of Cabalistic methods of interpretation in Jewish mysticism or the use of the word "enlightenment" in Buddhist traditions, is a clue that the mystical traditions also include great methods of suspicion to be applied, above all, to such religious experiences as ecstasy and vision. In short, in both the mystical and the prophetic strands of the religious traditions, explicitly religious hermeneutics of suspicion already exist. As operative, these methods of interpretation of the pluralistic and ambiguous phenomenon of religion empower an internal religious hermeneutics of suspicion while also encouraging the incorporation (now on innerreligious grounds) of any other external hermeneutics of suspicion and their attendant critical theories. As a pluralistic and ambiguous phenomenon, religion not merely allows both hermeneutics of retrieval and suspicion; it demands both.

THEOLOGICAL METHOD IN THE NEW PARADIGM

If we grant the description of modern hermeneutics outlined above, and grant, as well, the special difficulties and possibilities of interpreting that ambiguous and pluralistic phenomenon named religion, we may note the relevance of all this to the role of hermeneutics in theology proper. As suggested earlier, modern theology may be described in general terms as the attempt to develop mutually critical correlations between the contemporary situation and the Christian tradition.

It is useful to note how each of these realities—both tradition and situation—necessarily include hermeneutical elements. Theology is, in fact, a deliberately interpretive enterprise from beginning to end. For each of the two constants are not available immediately but are understood only by being interpreted. Moreover, in interpreting either of these constants, the other constant is always already present: theologians, as theological interpreters of both contemporary experience and the Christian tradition, inevitably interpret to greater and lesser degrees each reality in the light of the other. To speak of theology as the development of mutually critical correlations of contemporary experience and the Christian tradition, therefore, is simply to render *explicit* and *deliberate* the intrinsically hermeneutical character of theology itself.

It is not the case, of course, that theology only becomes hermeneutical in the modern period (see Henri de Lubac and Gerhard Ebeling). It is the case, however, that the explicit concern with hermeneutics since Schleiermacher is occasioned by the crisis of the sense of cultural distance from the religious tradition caused by the seventeenth-century scientific revolution and the eighteenth-century Enlightenment. This sense was intensified by the nineteenth-century emergence of historical consciousness (see Ernst Troeltsch and Bernard Lonergan). This same sense has been further intensified in the twentieth century by the emergence of the great liberation movements and their attendant hermeneutics of suspicion (with respect to sexism, racism, classism, and so forth). This sense has been still further intensified by the Western sense of cultural parochialism occasioned by the emerging global culture (and thereby the reality of the other world religions), as well as the tensions, conflicts, and possibilities present in the North-South and East-West relationships. All these epoch-making events have caused the need for explicit reflection on the hermeneutical character in all the disciplines (even philosophy of science).

In order to understand our present situation—indeed even to experience it—we must interpret it. Interpretation is not something added on to experience and understanding, but it is always already present as intrinsic to understanding itself. This is especially the case for any theological interpretation of our contemporary experience. For theology attempts to discern and interpret those fundamental questions (finitude, estrangement, alienation, oppression, fundamental trust or mistrust, loyalty, anxiety, mortality, and so forth) that disclose a genuinely religious dimension in our contemporary experience and language.

With Paul Tillich, we may speak of this hermeneutical task of theology as an analysis of the "situation," that is, those creative interpretations of our experience that disclose a religious dimension. It is possible to distinguish, but not to separate, the theologian's analysis of the situation from her or his analysis of the Christian tradition itself. We cannot simply separate these analyses, for like *any other* interpreter of our contemporary experience and like *any other* interpreter of the religious dimensions of that experience, the theologian too is influenced by the history of that tradition, namely, the Christian tradition. The recent retrievals of the eschatological symbols by the liberation and political theologians, for example, are not occasioned merely by the fundamental questions of a sense of alienation and/or oppression. They are also caused by the history of the effects of the Jewish and Christian eschatological symbols upon the Christian sensibilities of the theologian *as interpreter* of these contemporary experiences of alienation and oppression. In that sense, every theological act of interpretation of the situation is always already a hermeneutical act attempting to establish mutually critical correlations between contemporary experience and the Christian tradition.

Moreover, as the fuller spectrum of the fundamental questions chosen for a theological analysis of that experience in the different theologies of our period testify, there are and will continue to be real differences and really different theologies occasioned by those different

...terpretations. Consider, for example, the different kinds of theology that emerge when a profound sense of oppression and/or alienation as distinct from a profound sense of fundamental trust is explicated as *the* hermeneutical key to contemporary experience. Or note how, in the modern period of theology, the crisis of cognitive claims occasioned by the scientific revolution, the Enlightenment, and the emergence of historical consciousness led to several reformulations of the doctrine of revelation. Contrast these efforts to reformulate the doctrine of revelation with the more recent efforts to retrieve not revelation but eschatology in the liberation and political theologies. The latter theologies ordinarily interpret our contemporary experience not in the light of the crisis of cognitive claims (as do most earlier theologies of revelation) but rather in the light of the crisis of the "counter-experience" of massive global suffering.

The differences (even the conflicts) in these interpretations remain real differences of interpretation on contemporary experience. The kinds of real differences that we saw operative in hermeneutical theory itself are inevitably present in theology as well. The interpretations of the situation, therefore, will yield a conflict of interpretations of the religious dimension (and hence the fundamental questions) of "our present world of experience in all its ambivalence, contingency and change" (Hans Küng). The unity of theology will not be the unity of a particular interpretation but will be the unity of a common, deliberate, and explicit need to *interpret* this first constant and to defend any interpretation vis-à-vis alternative interpretations within the entire community of theological inquiry.

To recognize this inevitably hermeneutical character of all theology, therefore, is not to impose some single model of theology (as in some formulations of the New Hermeneutic). It is, rather, to recognize the *common* need to recognize how all theology involves the interpretation of this first constant. Thereby does the modern paradigm of theology render explicit what is implicit in all traditional theology as well. For one of the most basic *continuities* operative throughout theological paradigm-shifts is the reality of an interpretation of both tradition and situation.

This same need for explicitly hermeneutical reflection emerges when we turn to an analysis of the Christian tradition in our situation. In the light of our outline of the hermeneutical process, and in the context of recalling how any religion is inevitably pluralistic and ambiguous, it becomes imperative for theologians to render explicit their understanding of the ultimate norm of the Christian tradition. The hermeneutical enterprise thus discloses the common unity of the theological task as an agreed-upon need for each theologian to interpret both situation and tradition.

Since the emergence of historical consciousness and the recognition of the priority of praxis, there have been various candidates for interpreting the Christian message as norm (for example, "the historical Jesus," "the original apostolic kerygma," "the Christ-kerygma of Paul and John," the entire tradition, the praxis of *imitatio Christi*, "canons within the canon," "canons outside the canon," "working canons," "discrimina," the whole history of effects as tradition, and so forth). As in the case of the interpretation of contemporary experience, it is unlikely that there will be a unity based on any particular interpretation of the Christian message. Yet there remains a communal recognition of the need to *interpret* this second constant and render one's interpretation available to the entire community of theological inquiry for assessment. The emphasis on this common hermeneutical enterprise can provide some clarification of the real differences and similarities among modern theologies. For example, the theological community of inquiry could agree in principle that the often-confusing phrase "the historical Jesus" refers to that "Jesus who lived *insofar as he is known or knowable today by way of empirical-historical methods.*" On that reading, the "historical Jesus" can serve as a corrective of christologies (along with such other correctives as the "original apostolic witness") but not as the hermeneutical foundation of this second constant. That foundation would prove to be some particular interpretation of the Christian message, the gospel of Jesus Christ, which would employ this and other correctives.

An explicit hermeneutical concern oriented to this second constant not merely allows for but demands that the entire theological community of inquiry discuss its different interpretations within a shared hermeneutical commitment. Then community-wide arguments for the relative adequacy of any particular interpretation would be both encouraged and warranted. Conflict among various proposals may be our actuality, yet conversation is our hope. Hermeneutics, as itself grounded in conversation and thereby in a genuine community of inquiry, aids the possible consensus and the adjudication of the real differences among particular theologies within the shared new paradigm.

As interpretation, the articulation of this second crucial constant is also an implicit use of a method of developing mutually critical correlations between both constants. As we saw above, insofar as we interpret contemporary experience theologically, we are also interpreting the history of effects of the Christian message theologically, and we are also applying it to contemporary experience. Insofar as we perform both of these interpretations deliberately, we are correlating these two distinct but, as we have seen, not separate interpretations. We are, in short, performing the distinctly theological task of an interpretation of Christian religion, namely, developing mutually critical correlations between an interpretation of the contemporary situation and an interpretation of the Christian tradition. This formulation does, in fact, provide one relatively adequate way to describe the general hermeneutical task of all theologies in the new paradigm.

The choice of the phrase "mutually critical correlations," therefore, is a useful one for the new paradigm. As we saw above in the analysis of the inevitably hermeneutical character of any theological appropriation of either constant, every theological act of interpretation already involves some correlation of the two constants. It remains methodologically helpful to distinguish these two distinct acts of interpretation as distinct. At the same time, the interpreter cannot existentially separate the two acts. Whenever we interpret contemporary experience theologically, the history of effects of the Christian tradition is also present in the interpretation itself. Whenever we interpret the Christian message theologically, we inevitably also apply it to our contemporary experience in order to understand it at all.

To call theology a hermeneutical enterprise, therefore, is to recognize that such correlations of these two acts of interpretation are always occurring in order to produce the single act of a given theological interpretation. To add the qualifying phrase "mutually critical" to the word "correlation" highlights the hermeneutical reality that in every interpretation the subject matter itself and not any methodology must ultimately reign. In any concrete case of interpretation of any particular subject matter (like christology), the ultimate decision for the kind of correlation between the two constants must be determined not by methodological rules but by the subject matter itself. The five steps of the hermeneutical process illuminate the possibilities available —retrieval, critique, suspicion, explanation, understanding—but the concrete subject matter should decide the actual kind of correlation needed in any particular case. The word "correlation," therefore, is intended to indicate the full spectrum of logical possibilities available, namely, that the actual interpretation of the particular subject matter may prove a confrontation between the two constants (from either side), or a claim to identity between them in this particular instance, or a claim to similarities, or to those similarities-in-difference named analogies.

Theological interpretation as developing mutually critical correlations between the two constants remains a deliberately hermeneutical interpretation of that puzzling and ambiguous phenomenon, religion. Precisely as thus deliberately hermeneutical, the theologian cannot avoid the claims to meaning and truth operative in the attempt to establish the proper correlation for the concrete subject matter being interpreted. Sometimes the analysis of contemporary experience will confront earlier theological interpretations of the meaning and truth of the Christian message (for example, the confrontation of literalist and fundamentalist readings of Genesis by the development of evolutionary theory, or the confrontation of traditional theological formulations of christology by a use of the correctives provided by modern historical-critical or social-scientific methods). At other times, the analysis of the Christian message will confront reigning understandings of contemporary experience—for example, the confrontation of secularism by theologies of secularity or the confrontation of developmental theories by the retrieval of apocalyptic in liberation and political theologians, or the confrontation of the sexism and anti-Semitism operative in the tradition by the appropriation of modern movements of liberating praxis and modern critical theories of ideology-critique.

In every case of genuinely theological interpretation, therefore, the questions of both meaning and truth must be faced squarely as the theologian attempts to establish the particular form of correlation appropriate to the relationship between the two constants on any particular subject matter. Hermeneutical method informs the process, yet the concrete subject matter rules the interpretation. This hermeneutical understanding of the task of theology in the new paradigm, moreover, should increase the understanding of theology as a community of inquiry grounded in a community of commitment. In any authentic community of inquiry, pluralism is not merely tolerated but encouraged. But if that pluralism is not to decay into the mindless geniality of a "repressive tolerance" or a mere "let a thousand flowers bloom," then a conversing, responsible theological community of inquiry where all are expected to provide plausible theological warrants for their proposals becomes urgent.

The explicitly hermeneutical moment in modern theology is one way to assure the existence of a responsible pluralism in the entire theological community of inquiry. The understanding of theology as the development of mutually critical correlations between the two constants, therefore, is one way to render explicit the genuine consensus that in fact exists despite the many differences in contemporary theology. A retreat from interpretation is ultimately a retreat into a fundamentalism grounded in serious misinterpretations of both constants. The move into hermeneutical reflection in theology as in the other modern disciplines is not another imperalist declaration of a de jure methodology leveling the pluralism of contemporary theology. On the contrary, hermeneutical reflection in theology as in the other modern disciplines renders explicit the de facto basic consensus that already exists despite the real differences among modern theologies.

But if theology is to remain, in its new circumstances, a genuine community of inquiry and not a mere chaos of fads, fashions, and virtuosi, then the need to reflect upon the de facto hermeneutical character operative throughout this pluralistic community of inquiry becomes imperative for us all. For the fact is that in both practice and theory, theology in the new paradigm has become a genuine conversation among the different particular proposals for establishing mutually critical correlations between the Christian message and contemporary experience.

The modern paradigm shift, to be sure, is both new and momentous. But as I have tried to suggest throughout this chapter, this modern shift is not radically discontinuous with the great and implicitly hermeneutical tradition of Christian theology. Indeed, without a common commitment to the new general paradigm in spite of our other real differences, we may well find ourselves divorced from both that tradition and from one another. Our options, fortunately, are not exhausted by the unwelcome alternatives of chaos or fundamentalism.

Rather we find ourselves in a theological community of inquiry and commitment. In that community, we attempt, individually and communally, to work out the most relatively adequate mutually critical correlations between the Christian message and contemporary experience on the pressing theological questions of our day. In every such attempt, explicit reflection on method cannot but aid the enterprise.

SUGGESTIONS FOR FURTHER READING

Braaten, Carl E., editor. *Our Naming of God: Problems and Prospects of God-Talk Today.* Minneapolis: Fortress Press, 1990.

Bultmann, Rudolf. "The Problem of Hermeneutics." *Essays Philosophical and Theological.* Translated by James Greig. New York: Macmillan, 1955.

Congar, Yves M. J. A *History of Theology.* Garden City, N.Y.: Doubleday & Co., 1968.

Ebeling, Gerhard. *The Study of Theology.* Translated by Duane A. Priebe. Philadelphia: Fortress Press, 1978.

Farley, Edward. *Ecclesial Reflection: An Anatomy of Theological Method.* Philadelphia: Fortress Press, 1982.

————. *Theologia: The Fragmentation and Unity of Theological Education.* Philadelphia: Fortress Press, 1983.

Fiorenza, Francis Schüssler. *Foundational Theology: Jesus and the Church.* New York: Crossroad, 1985.

Foucault, Michel. *The Archeology of Knowledge and the Discourse on Language.* Translated by A. M. Sheridan Smith. New York: Pantheon Books, 1972.

Frei, Hans. *Types of Christian Theology.* Edited by George Hunsinger and William C. Placher. New Haven: Yale University Press, 1992.

Gadamer, Hans-Georg. *Philosophical Hermeneutics.* Translated and edited by David E. Linge. Berkeley: University of California Press, 1976.

———— *Truth and Method.* 2d, rev. ed. Translation revised by Joel Weinsheimer and Donald G. Marshall. New York: Crossroad, 1989.

Habermas, Jürgen. *Communication and the Evolution of Society.* Translated by Thomas McCarthy. Boston: Beacon Press, 1979.

Kaufman, Gordon D. *In Face of Mystery.* Part I.

Küng, Hans. *On Being a Christian.* Part A, "The Horizon."

Lonergan, Bernard. *Method in Theology.*

Metz, Johann Baptist. *Faith in History and Society: Toward a Practical Fundamental Theology.* New York: Seabury Press/Crossroad, 1980.

Ogden, Schubert M. "What Is Theology?" *The Journal of Religion* 52 (January 1972): 22–36.

Pannenberg, Wolfhart. *Basic Questions in Theology.* Translated by George H. Kehm. 2 vols. Philadelphia: Fortress Press, 1970, 1971.

———. *Theology and the Philosophy of Science.* Translated by Francis McDonagh. Philadelphia: Westminster Press, 1976.

Ricoeur, Paul. *The Conflict of Interpretations: Essays in Hermeneutics.* Edited by Don Ihde. Evanston: Northwestern University Press, 1974.

———. *Freud and Philosophy: An Essay on Interpretation.* Translated by Denis Savage. New Haven: Yale University Press, 1970.

———. *Interpretation Theory: Discourse and the Surplus of Meaning.* Fort Worth: Texas Christian University Press, 1976.

Robinson, James M., and John B. Cobb, Jr., eds. *The Later Heidegger and Theology.* New York: Harper & Row, 1963. Esp. the essay by Heinrich Ott, "What Is Systematic Theology?" pp. 77–111.

———. *The New Hermeneutic.* New York: Harper & Row, 1964. Esp. the essay by Gerhard Ebeling, "Word of God and Hermeneutic," pp. 78–110.

Schleiermacher, Friedrich. *Hermeneutics: The Handwritten Manuscripts.* Edited by Heinz Kimmerle. Translated by James Duke and Jack Forstman. Missoula: Scholars Press, 1977.

Segundo, Juan Luis. *Liberation of Theology.* Maryknoll, N.Y.: Orbis Books, 1976.

Taylor, Mark Kline. *Remembering Esperanza: A Cultural-Political Theology for North American Praxis.* Maryknoll, N.Y.: Orbis, 1990. Chapters 1 & 2.

Tillich, Paul. *Systematic Theology.* Vol. 1, pp. 3–68.

Tracy, David. *The Analogical Imagination: Christian Theology and the Culture of Pluralism.*

———. *Blessed Rage for Order: The New Pluralism in Theology.*

———. *Plurality and Ambiguity.*

Troeltsch, Ernst. *Writings on Theology and Religion.* Translated and edited by Robert Morgan and Michael Pye. London: Duckworth Press, 1977.

Wiles, Maurice F. *What Is Theology?* London and New York: Oxford University Press, 1976.

EDWARD FARLEY AND PETER C. HODGSON

2. SCRIPTURE AND TRADITION

WHERE WE ARE

Until recently, almost the entire spectrum of theological opinion would have agreed that the scriptures of the Old and New Testaments, together with their doctrinal interpretations, occupy a unique and indispensable place of authority for Christian faith, practice, and reflection. But this consensus now seems to be falling apart.

For one thing, biblical scholarship, increasingly influenced by history-of-religions approaches, has questioned the uniqueness of biblical writings as compared with other ancient texts. By insisting that the meaning of texts can be properly construed only in their specific linguistic and historical contexts, biblical criticism complicates the use of such texts as authorities in preaching and theology. In the second place, systematic theology has mostly freed itself from the impact of the neo-Reformation movement that dominated Protestant thinking for half a century and that subscribed to the principle of scriptural authority with great intensity. Catholic thought, meanwhile, has experienced a similar liberation from the authority of doctrinal tradition since Vatican II. Thus we are able to acknowledge that scriptural authority, while it may be in some sense indispensable to Christian theology, also has a dark underside in its potentiality for obscurantism, resistance to science, authoritarianism, and "book religion"—veneration of the "the book" as a holy object. Finally, and perhaps most important, we seem to be passing through a new wave of critical consciousness in which all authorities are being questioned, especially those associated with the dominant Western cultural and religious tradition. For example, the more radical wing of the liberation theologies has raised disturbing questions concerning the ideological abuse of scripture and tradition by the church, and some critics have wondered whether these authorities are not in fact

This chapter is based in part on Edward Farley, *Ecclesial Reflection: An Anatomy of Theological Method* (Philadelphia: Fortress Press, 1982).

61

patriarchal, sexist, indifferent to the realities of oppression, and class-oriented to the point of being no longer usable. If we are to continue to recognize scripture and tradition as authoritative, it will apparently have to be in a much more relative sense than before.

Just what does recognizing something as "scripture" entail? At this point an ambiguity emerges that may account for some of the confusion surrounding questions concerning the "necessity" and "authority" of scripture for Christian faith. In the history-of-religions sense, "scripture" refers to the existence of a normative collection of writings and their function in the origin and perpetuation of a religious faith. In this sense there are Hindu scriptures, Buddhist scriptures, and so on, with no particular theory of their inspiration, authority, or validity implied. On the other hand, a more determinate sense of "scripture" is associated historically with Judaism, Christianity, and Islam. On this view the collection of writings called scripture contains a unique deposit of divine revelation—a deposit whose special qualities are due to its inspired origins, and which is to be handed down through the ages by an authoritative teaching tradition. We shall refer to this second sense as the "scripture principle" to distinguish it from "scripture" in the first, generic sense.

On the basis of this distinction it seems clear that scripture is necessary to the Christian faith in the first sense, although saying this does not yet specify what scripture means or how it properly functions in the community of faith. It is not self-evident, however, that the scripture *principle* is constitutive of or necessary to Christian faith, even though historically this principle has characterized the theory and use of scripture predominant through most of Christian history.[1] It is our thesis that the scripture principle and the "way of authority" associated with it are actually inappropriate to "ecclesial existence" when properly understood, but this critique by no means entails a rejection of scripture as such. Our task at the end will be to sketch an alternative sense in which the biblical writings may be construed as "scripture," that is, as having a constitutive function in the shaping and nurturing of a community of faith, the "ecclesia," where redemption is experienced and individuals are transformed.

Before proceeding further we should explain that in this chapter we are using the terms "ecclesia," "ecclesial existence," and "ecclesial

1. Cf. Christopher Evans, *Is "Holy Scripture" Christian?* chap. 2.

62

community" to refer to the *ideal, distinctive,* or *essential* features of the Christian church, that is, those features which set it apart from other religious communities as a unique form of redemptive existence. Often these distinctive features are obscured in the actual historical manifestations of Christianity. "Ecclesia" is simply the Greek word for church, which we are using to signify an ideal or essential meaning, while the word "church" itself is used to signify a historical reality.

We should note, too, that while our discussion will give primary attention to the theme of scripture, tradition will not be neglected, since in both classic and modern formulations the way that scripture has been construed as authoritative in the life of the church has generally applied to tradition as well. This may appear surprising in light of the commonly perceived rivalry among Christian confessions over the primacy of scripture in relation to tradition, but the issue as so stated is, in our judgment, misplaced.

THE DOCTRINE IN ITS CLASSIC FORMULATION

Formation of the Scripture Principle in Postexilic Judaism

What we are calling the "scripture principle" originated as a solution to a major crisis in Israel's history, the dispersion of the Jewish people following the Babylonian Exile. This event significantly modified Israel's social institutions, separated a portion of the Jewish people from those institutions, and brought about an acute threat of cultural and religious assimilation. The Diaspora Jews, now lacking the land, temple, and priesthood, created two new institutions for preserving their socioreligious identity: the synagogue and the written Torah.

Under these circumstances "scripture" came to mean a written deposit of the complete and definitive revelation of Yahweh to the people, functioning as the primary source of cultic and moral regulation for the community. Three basic convictions came to be held about the Torah: (1) It is the exhaustive location of a now past divine communication, relevant to all present and future times and places, containing at least implicitly an answer for every need and crisis; (2) it is totally and equally valid in all its parts and details; and (3) it contains symbolic references to the nation, land, holy city, and temple, permitting the endurance of a people whose self-understanding remained that of a dispersed nation, a quasi-political and religious entity, having as its regulative law what was originally given for its life as a nation in possession of its own land.

Thus a *written* vehicle became the locus of revelatory divine presence. Theologically speaking, this represents a tremendous advance over the localization of divine presence in natural objects, historical places, or heroic figures. It represents a liberation and humanization of religion, which enabled Israel to survive as a distinct people. Language, the most spiritual form of human creative imagination, is probably also the most appropriate medium for experiencing and expressing God's transformative presence. At the same time, however, it is a fragile medium peculiarly susceptible to distortion—to being reduced, for example, to a fixed code or set of doctrines, taking on some of the characteristics of physical objects or fetishes (sacred things worthy of veneration, containing magic power). The constant temptation of Judaism and Christianity has been to objectify their scriptures in this fashion, although the prophetic, critical power of both religions has also resisted this temptation and to some degree overcome it.

Presuppositions and Axioms of the Classic Criteriology[2]

Before turning to the way in which Christianity accepted and modified the Judaic understanding of scripture, we shall attempt to uncover the presuppositions and axioms implicit in both the Judaic scripture principle and the developed criteriology of Christian faith. We shall distinguish two basic presuppositions and a set of axioms ingredient in each.

The first presupposition is *salvation history*, a comprehensive interpretive framework implicit in the religious thought of Israel, Judaism, and Christianity. Salvation history interprets the past, present, and future of a particular people (Israel, the church) as a sequential

2. "Criteriology" is a term used to describe ways of defining and relating the "criteria" operative in theological claims—criteria such as sources, authorities, norms, experience, canons of rationality, principles for interpreting meaning and truth, and so on. "Classic criteriology" simply means the set of criteria that prevailed during the classical period of theology, at least to the beginning of the Reformation.

story whose development and outcome is determined by God. God, the transcendent world-maker, also exercises world-governance, construed on the political model of the rule of a monarch over a realm. God exerts causality over world affairs by means of specific and decisive interventions, including not only global historical events but also specific theophanies, miracles, acts of inspiration, and punishments and rewards of individuals. The two themes of governance and interference are interconnected, since governance requires activities of governance and thus some capacity to intervene—to punish, to correct, to maintain, to inspire.

The salvation-history scheme yields certain axioms that prove indispensable to the scripture principle. One of these we shall describe as the "logic of sovereignty" or the "logic of triumph." God, the infinitely powerful world sovereign, is always able to accomplish the divine will either indirectly through the contingencies of nature and the finite purposes of human beings or, when necessary, by means of a direct causality that assures the attainment of divinely purposed ends. A second axiom has to do with the periodization of history and the fixing of the time of revelation. History unfolds through distinct stages, each of which has its place in the overarching teleology, while revelation is confined to a particular period in the past. The latter claim would not seem to be required by the salvation-history scheme, since revelation, as a concomitant of divine redemptive activity, could be construed as an ongoing process. After the Diaspora, however, Judaism *looked back* to the preexilic history of Israel as the time of the giving of Torah, which made it normative. Under the conditions of dispersal, there could be no new revelation to the people as a whole since the people no longer existed as a landed nation; thus cultic and social life must be governed by a previously given law, now continually to be reinterpreted and applied in new circumstances, while waiting for the return of the people to the land and the coming of the messianic king. Christianity adopted, uncritically it would seem, the axiom of a past epoch of definitive revelation, although it had to reperiodize salvation history in light of its belief that the Messiah had appeared. We say "uncritically" because the logic of ecclesial existence, oriented to the experience of the continuing redemptive presence of the risen Christ, would seem to require a different understanding of revelation.

The second presupposition may be described as the *principle of identity*—an identity, that is, between what God wills to communicate and what is in fact brought to expression in the interpretive act of a human individual or community. The locus of identity is sacred scripture along with the laws, doctrines, and teaching authority pursuant to it. The qualities of inerrancy, infallibility, and absolute truthfulness are ascribed both to this locus of identity and to its content. A synthesis is presumed to have occurred between the divine communicator and human recipients, a synthesis brought about by the causal efficacy of God in the form of "inspiration." Thus an identity of content is assured between what is divinely willed and what is humanly asserted. The content is primarily of cognitive character, containing information about God's nature, activity, and purposes. Clearly underlying the principle of identity is the logic of sovereignty: if God wills to communicate information about divine things, God has the means to ensure that the information is correctly received and handed on.

Three crucial axioms follow from the principle of identity: (1) *Secondary representation*. Since definitive revelation is restricted to a brief epoch of past history, a means must be found to ensure that the original deposit is preserved and handed on. The salvation-history framework justifies giving secondary representatives authoritative status comparable to the original bearers, for it sets in motion an inexorable teleological logic of fulfillment which requires perpetuation. Thus divine providence oversees the transition from charisma to tradition, from oral tradition to written deposit, from written deposit to definitive commentary, from commentary to institution. (2) *Leveling*. Originally the identity resided in the content of the message, but later the focus shifts from message to vehicle, and the distinction between vehicle and content collapses. Now the whole of the contents and the vehicle itself are regarded as divine. Divine truth, in other words, is equally distributed throughout the vehicle, and all parts of the latter are accorded equal status. (3) *Immutability*. The identity cannot be occasional or provisional; rather it is universally applicable. What was given as true for the charismatic prophet or original apostle is immutably valid for all future generations. Tradition consists in the application of an unchanging law, gospel, or teaching to new times and places, an application requiring great interpretive ingenuity (the work of rabbis, theologians, church councils, and the like).

The Christian Appropriation of the Scripture Principle

Although as an offspring of Judaism the early Christian community inherited the Jewish scriptures and soon produced a collection of writings of its own, it did not necessarily have to adopt the scripture principle. In fact, through the first century and a half of its existence, a certain tension can be discerned over precisely this issue.

For one thing, the scripture principle appears to have been modified in important respects. (1) Even though at first the Christian community faced a struggle to maintain its identity over against both Judaism and Hellenistic religious syncretism, the primary internal threat was not cultural assimilation but a multiplicity of conflicting interpretations within an already diverse cultural community consisting of Jews, Greeks, Romans, Syrians, North Africans, and the like. Thus what was called for was not community regulation and social maintenance but community confession. Besides, scripture was not *the* vehicle of duration for primitive Christianity that it was for Judaism. The ecclesial community had a norm other than scripture, namely, the living presence of the Lord and a nucleus tradition of early testimony to him. (2) The functional genre of Christian scripture shifted from Torah to gospel, and thence to doctrine. Its function was to witness to the Christ and announce to the world the salvation accomplished in him. But given the controversy between rival Christian traditions, the writings came to function primarily in the settling of doctrinal disputes. Thus they served not to provide authority for regulating social and cultic life but to authorize right teaching, belief, and confession, and their unity was not law but a gospel message intended as true. (3) In adopting the Jewish scriptures as its own, the church also relativized them, for it recognized the law to be valid only for Israel and interpreted the writings primarily in terms of the motif of prophecy and fulfillment. A reperiodization of salvation history laid the groundwork for a two-part scripture consisting of old and new covenants, with provisional validity being accorded the old covenant. (4) The new community of the Messiah was drawn from all nations to form not a new nation but a universal religious community transcending all provincial understandings of divine presence (whether localized in a people, land, temple, book, or set of doctrines).

Given these modifications, the axioms of the principle of identity would appear no longer to be valid. The person-event Jesus of Nazareth, who is believed to be the Christ, becomes the new focus of divine-human identity, which cannot be extended to any written representation, either primary or secondary. A collection of scriptural writings could serve as a control on tradition running rampant, distinguishing between early writings produced by the community of faith and containing testimonies to the founding event and, later, extracommunal imitations where the historical referent exercises little or no control. But this is not yet the scripture principle, and it does not comprise a *canon* or official collection of sacred scripture. In the second place, the focus on the gospel with its referent to the Christ is incompatible with the axiom of leveling in which every literary unit takes on the character of a divine communication. Moreover, since the content of Christian scripture is authoritative only insofar as it is universalizable, contents appropriate *only* to specific social, cultic, or ethical situations cannot be accorded redemptive significance. Finally, the fact that Jewish scripture is retained as old covenant, implying relative and provisional validity, rules out the axiom of immutability.

Despite these modifications called forth by the essentially different character of the Christian gospel itself, the mainstream of Christendom ultimately adopted the scripture principle and the apparatus associated with it: a canon of officially recognized authoritative writings, atomistic exegesis and proof-texting, and the establishment of revelation as the foundation of theology contained in human-historical deposits regarded as inspired and infallible. Under the pressure of conflicts with heresy and in the context of the institutionalization of the new religion, it was all too easy to fall back into these practices. Moreover, the Christian movement never abandoned the royal metaphor for God and God's relation to the world. The logic of sovereignty, which presumes that God employs whatever means are necessary to ensure the successful accomplishment of the divine will, eventually pervaded the total criteriology of Christendom. For the very word of God to continue to be salvifically present in the church, there must be a trustworthy reduction of the event and person of Christ to verbal testimony, a sacred deposit to be preserved and handed on by a succession of authoritative representatives.

Our account of the presuppositions and axioms of the scripture principle, and of their appropriation by the early Christian community, should in no way be construed as a history of the interpretation and use of scripture during the patristic, medieval, and Reformation periods.[3] This history is rich and variegated, with many high and low points, and we cannot hope to summarize it. Rather, we have attempted to uncover the theological and methodological presuppositions lying beneath the surface of the actual uses of scripture in liturgy, piety, and teaching. Often these uses, and the specific ways that scripture was appropriated in relation to theological proposals, stood in tension with the way in which scripture itself was intended as an authoritative deposit of revelation. Frequently a theologian's insight into the *meaning* of scripture transcended the formal scripture principle in terms of which that same theologian would have articulated the *doctrine* of scripture.

Origen, for example, was a theologian of great imaginative and speculative insight whose knowledge of the Bible and contribution to its interpretation were unrivaled in the patristic period. His use of scripture in his systematic exposition of Christian faith was richly textured, ingenious, and daring. But at the same time he was convinced that every clause of the Bible is infallible, supernatural, and divinely dictated. Because the literal sense of many texts is demonstrably erroneous if not repulsive or unedifying, each passage must also be construed in moral and mystical or spiritual senses in order to arrive at the divinely intended meaning. This opened the way to allegorical interpretation, with Origen and Clement of Alexandria as the first great Christian exponents (although they borrowed heavily from Alexandrian Judaism, notably Philo). Allegory interprets all the details of a story or text as having a figurative meaning different from and encoded within the apparent literal meaning. The task of allegory is to "decode" a text by making explicit the higher meaning of each and every unit. This procedure was necessitated by the scripture principle in order to save the principle of identity and its axioms, especially

3. For this history see in particular Robert M. Grant, *A Short History of the Interpretation of the Bible*, and Frederic W. Farrar, *History of Interpretation*.

leveling and immutability, and it had the effect of reading extraneous, excessive interpretations into texts under the control of a theological norm such as Christology.

In Augustine, as in Origen, a tension is evident between a rich and imaginative use of scripture in theology and an unsound exegetical method, allegory, which he applied in accord with two interpretive criteria: the law of love (the christological norm for deriving the figurative meaning of texts) and the rule of faith (the universally accepted truths of the Catholic faith). The same tension is found in most of the great theologians of the church down to the time of the Reformation. Martin Luther was perhaps the first seriously to challenge the allegorical method, replacing it with a "spiritual interpretation" that introduced a degree of critical freedom into scriptural interpretation, thus challenging at least implicitly the main elements of the scripture principle. By contrast, John Calvin, in many respects a more rigorous and brilliant interpreter of scripture than even Luther, would not allow any challenge to the scripture principle. There was therefore a considerable tension between his critical exegesis and his adherence to the principles of divine authorship, plenary inspiration, infallibility, supreme authority, and the like. In the period that followed, Protestant scholasticism hardened those principles even further, so that what had been largely implicit in the church fathers took the form of explicit dogma.

Tradition and the Teaching Authority of the Church

The fixing of the time of revelation to the past and the limitation of authoritative writings to that period meant that scripture was not self-sufficient but required interpretation, synthesis, and application. In fact, the Bible's own internal pluralism and historical determinacy rendered it ambiguous to subsequent generations. Thus a tradition of authoritative interpretation emerged in Christianity analogous to the Mishnah and Talmud in Judaism. It took the form first of the *regula fidei* (rule of faith) and later of the *doctrina* or *dogma* of the church, the standard of right belief.

A dogma is an officially sanctioned teaching that articulates an article of faith and is free from error. However, dogma consists not merely of individual dogmas but also of an internally coherent set of dogmatic propositions touching all the major moments of faith and

70

organized according to the salvation-history scheme. Truth is distributed in leveled fashion across the individual units of dogma and is construed in the sense of an ahistorical, immutable essence, free of error. Dogma in the strict sense was propounded in a postscriptural period of definitive commentary, the period of the church fathers and the councils, from roughly the second through the sixth centuries. Eventually almost all the attributes of scripture itself were extended to dogma, which is not theology or even the product of a theological process but a material norm presupposed by theology. Although according to Catholic teaching new dogmas are occasionally promulgated, they in fact do not have the same authority as the old ones, and for all intents and purposes the period of normative dogmatic formulation, like the time of revelation itself, is long past.

What continues is the teaching authority of the church and the theological work of individual theologians. The latter, according to the classical model, is done primarily in the genre of citation and translation rather than that of critical inquiry. That is to say, the theologian works from evidence in the form of authorities rather than immediate experience. The primary task is one of "translating" the content of scripture and dogma into appropriate modern forms, and the question of truth is limited to formal operations such as working out the internal coherence of the system of doctrine by constructing a dogmatics, a house of dogma, out of the bricks and mortar of scripture texts and church doctrines. We hasten to add that this was the *model* of what the proper theologian was about. The great thinkers of the church—Origen, Augustine, Aquinas, Anselm, Luther, Calvin—transcended it, even though they may have accepted it in principle.

The church with its magisterial or teaching authority served as the institutional guardian of scriptural interpretation, doctrinal promulgation, and theological application. The institution legitimated its claim to authority through the myth of apostolic succession, according to which a direct link was established between Jesus (more specifically, Jesus' intention to found a church), the original apostles, and their successors (the bishops of the church, among whom the Roman bishops attained primacy). Thus the episcopal college and the papacy became secondary representatives, vicars of God and Christ whose declarations expressed God's very will.

The extension of the principle of identity reached its logical culmination with the dogma of papal infallibility propounded at the First Vatican Council, although the claim had been implicit for centuries. Ironically its promulgation occurred at a time when the claim had already lost much of its credibility. In fact it was an overextension that could not be sustained and that called forth internal criticism demanding more authentic ways of understanding ecclesiastical authority in the Catholic tradition.

The primary issue of the Reformation concerned this third locus of authority in the classical criteriology: the institutional church. The Reformers challenged certain external features of Catholic institutionalization, yet the Protestant churches generally believed themselves to be providentially sanctioned as the form of the church willed by God, even when splintered into hundreds of rival sects. Furthermore, even though primacy was accorded scripture as opposed to tradition, an authoritative interpretive key to scripture was created in the form of the Lutheran and Reformed confessions, which took on the character of inspired, inerrant documents—an ersatz teaching authority in Protestant dress. And of course the patristic dogmas were never questioned, nor was the authority of the church fathers, or the ecumenical creeds. Thus despite the norm of *sola scriptura* (scripture alone), the differences between Protestant and Catholic versions of authority were more apparent than real, especially when viewed in light of the presuppositions and axioms of the classical criteriology operative in both. The negative impact of *sola scriptura* was to turn Christianity into a book religion—a logical extension of the scripture principle not unlike the logical extension of institutional authority in the dogma of infallibility. The positive insight behind the assertion of *sola scriptura* (as well as *sola fide, sola gratia*, and ultimately *sola Christus*) was the critical questioning of all authorities. This insight did not, however, really bear fruit until the Enlightenment.

CHALLENGES AND CONTRIBUTIONS OF MODERN CONSCIOUSNESS

The Collapse of the House of Authority

David Friedrich Strauss once wrote: "The true criticism of dogma is its history."[4] There is a sense in which giving a historical account of

---

4. D. F. Strauss, *Die christliche Glaubenslehre in ihrer geschichtlichen Entwicklung und im Kampfe mit der modernen Wissenschaft dargestellt* (Tübingen: C. F. Osiander, 1840), 1:71.

the classical criteriology as we have done is its own critique. It is unnecessary to describe in detail how and why the "house of authority" has collapsed. Our purpose in any case is not destructive, as was Strauss's; rather, we want to understand how scripture and tradition can continue to function as criteria for church and theology outside the house of authority. We shall therefore limit ourselves to a brief look at how various levels of criticism brought about the collapse of a structure that already was tottering from within.

The first and still the most important is *historical criticism* in its various forms. The beginnings of historical consciousness may be traced back to the Renaissance, but they came to fruition in the Enlightenment and its aftermath. Historical consciousness assumes that every entity occurs in a specific but ever-changing context and is itself always fluid. No exceptions to the principle of historicity can be allowed. While this insight was fully grasped by Johann Gottfried Herder and others in the eighteenth century, its impact was experienced only gradually. Criticism seemed to arrive in successive waves until finally all aspects of scripture and doctrinal tradition were engulfed. Because it was easier to assume a critical stance toward the Old Testament, methodological breakthroughs generally occurred first in Old Testament research and were only later applied to the Christian scriptures.

The first and most basic historical-critical level at which investigation was carried out was *text criticism*, developed already by such Renaissance scholars as Nicholas of Cusa. It tested the authenticity of received texts and established the first principles of critical editions. It was followed by *literary* and *source criticism*, which showed that the authors to which many books of the Old and New Testaments were traditionally attributed were not the actual authors, and that in most cases a complex process of oral and written tradition underlay the writings in their present form. The documentary hypothesis regarding the Pentateuch and recognition of the central role played by oral tradition in the formation of Israel's scriptures led to similar discoveries in the area of New Testament. Concurrently, various forms of *content criticism* emerged. The rationalists attacked the miraculous elements in the sacred history and attempted to replace them with a "purely natural" explanation. Then the so-called "mythical interpretation" came along to argue that these elements are ingredient in the structure of biblical mythology and cannot be removed without destroying its meaning. Strauss in particular advanced the thesis that much of the biblical material is actually not historical but mythical or legendary in character, reflecting the religious interests of the author or community that produced it. With this went a challenge to the truth claims mediated by such material. The effect of such criticism on the gospel history of Jesus was especially devastating.

These three forms of criticism tended to predominate in the eighteenth and nineteenth centuries. In our own century, *tradition criticism* has played a major role, beginning with the form criticism of Rudolf Bultmann, who showed that a developmental trajectory of the units comprising the synoptic tradition can be established, permitting a reconstruction of the earliest, preliterary forms of the tradition. Bultmann's successors, the so-called redaction critics, stressed the importance of understanding the function of a text in the literary and theological framework established by the editor or author. Within current biblical studies, two new methods have come to be increasingly influential: *structuralism*, concerned with a depth dimension of grammatical and linguistic relations, and a second level of *literary criticism*, concerned with literary genres. By attending to the function of symbol, myth, legend, narrative, poetry, parable, epistle, and other literary forms, critics have come to the realization that scripture does not contain "doctrine" or "deposits" of revealed truth at all. Biblical language portrays new ways of being in a world transformed by grace; its meaning is a function of symbolic and metaphorical uses of language that cannot be directly translated into conceptual terms.

Obviously these various layers of historical and literary criticism seriously complicate the traditional way in which scripture was understood to contain the content of revelation—as divinely inspired, infallibly expressed, equally distributed to all its parts, available for translation into theological concepts, immutably valid for all generations. Similar types of criticism were applied to the history of doctrine. The historical myths underlying doctrinal legitimation of dogma and papacy were exposed, and the whole process by which an authoritative tradition originated and developed was grasped in a thoroughly historical manner. Here the great master was Adolf Harnack, but he had many eminent predecessors, notably Johann Salomo Semler and Ferdinand Christian Baur.

A second level of criticism is neither historical nor literary but *social-phenomenological*. It argues that the scripture principle does not offer a vehicle of duration corresponding adequately to ecclesial existence. This sort of criticism has rarely been advanced explicitly, but it is implicit in the ecclesiology and theological method of certain theologians such as Friedrich Schleiermacher. We have already touched on a number of its themes. A community whose actual social duration is based on testimony to the gospel, the experience of salvation mediated by the presence of the risen Christ, and the inauguration of God's promised eschatological rule cannot have a literature construed as an atomistic collection of authoritative texts containing a deposit of revelation confined to a special time in the past. The ecclesial community, moreover, is nonethnic, universal, and culturally pluralistic, so that purely ethnic, provincial, and culturally relative elements of scripture cannot be authoritative. On this view it is altogether possible that features logically attending the form of social and religious existence represented by Christian faith have never been fully actualized or even perceived, and in their place forms have been adopted that contradict Christianity's own immanent ideal. The question of scripture and tradition is therefore closely intertwined with that of ecclesiology, as we shall attempt to show.

The third level of criticism is *theological*. It addresses the themes or presuppositions that underlie the scripture principle, namely, salvation history and the principle of identity. While this theological critique has been widespread during the past two centuries, it has rarely been perceived as undercutting the scripture principle. Yet clearly it does. The patriarchalism, monarchialism, and triumphalism of the classical salvation-history scheme, for instance, have been widely discredited. Triumphalism in particular founders on the rock of theodicy, for it has proven very difficult to sustain the logic of sovereignty in the face of massive evil experienced during the past century. If theology shifts from the model of causality to that of influence, and acknowledges the contingencies of world process—as in various forms of existentialism, process thought, and political theology—then salvation history and the logic of triumph dissolve. This is also the case with the principle of identity. Since the Adamic myth rules out an ontological identity between Creator and creation, this identity has usually been construed on the model of causal efficacy as an identity between what God wills to happen or make known and

75

what in fact happens or is known in history. Apart from the discrediting of the logic of triumph, the chief difficulty with the principle of identity is that it is a literalized myth. In folk religion everywhere, God is represented mythically as thinking, willing, reflecting, and accomplishing in the mode of an in-the-world-being who intervenes selectively in world process. There are enormous problems with this sort of mythology. It mundanizes the divine and sacralizes the non-divine. It violates finite human freedom and the contingency of the natural world. And it is hard pressed to avoid attributing specific evils as well as goods to the divine will. With the end of mythological thinking about God, the theological foundations of the scripture principle evaporate.

The house of authority has collapsed, despite the fact that many people still try to live in it. Some retain title to it without actually living there; others are antiquarians or renovators, attempting in one way or another to salvage it; still others have abandoned it for new quarters or no quarters at all. During the past century and a half, a spectrum of possible theological responses to this "shaking of the foundations" may be sketched as follows. Clearly at one extreme are those who abandon the biblical writings as in any sense scripture, regarding them as obscurantist, provincial, no longer authoritative for life in the modern world. This was seen as an option in the Enlightenment and was taken up explicitly by certain forms of historicism, modernism, and relativism. At the other extreme are those who continue to defend the scripture principle more or less uncompromisingly: Protestant scholasticism, Catholic orthodoxy, the Princeton theology, modern evangelicalism.

In the middle ground, two groups may be distinguished. One seeks to modify the principle by displacing the locus of revelation from the canon of scripture as such to specific events, figures, concepts, or subsets of texts—something like a canon within a canon. An identity is no longer maintained between the written document and revelation, but the authority of scripture continues to derive from its revelatory substratum, which might or might not be presumed to be beyond the reach of historical criticism. The other group, without always acknowledging it, *uses* scripture in relation to constructive theological proposals in such a way as to negate the presuppositions and axioms of the scripture principle, and thus to construe scriptural authority in functionalist rather than revelationalist terms. This group may continue to espouse a rather traditional *doctrine* of scripture, yet clearly they are doing something quite different. We shall examine these options more closely in the next section.

The Doctrine of Scripture and the Uses of Scripture in Modern Theology

While modern theologians have continued for the most part to regard scripture as the source of a specific revelatory content to be translated into theological concepts, their actual *use* of scripture often belies this assumption. The tension between the *doctrine* of scripture and its *uses* that we observed to be already present in classical theology has become especially acute in modern times. This is clearly shown by David H. Kelsey in his *The Uses of Scripture in Recent Theology* (1975).[5] Although he distinguishes seven different uses, the uses fall roughly into two main groups, possibly with one type mediating between them.

At one extreme, scripture may be construed as containing inspired, inerrant *doctrine*. Kelsey's representative theologian of this type is the Princeton theologian and traditional Calvinist, B. B. Warfield, but it is also a position espoused by Catholic orthodoxy and Protestant evangelicalism with little change. What is authoritative about scripture is its doctrinal content, and this content *is* revelation itself—of direct divine origin, inspired fully in all its parts, infallible with respect to matters of doctrine or belief, to be translated without alteration into theological propositions. Here we have the standard scripture principle with one minor adjustment. When offering reasons for adopting this view of plenary inspiration, Warfield advanced a functionalist argument: As *used* in the church, the Bible is a holy or numinous object experienced as such by members of the community who bow and tremble before its awesome power and supernatural illumination.

In the second place, scripture may be construed as containing distinctive *concepts*. This is the position of the so-called biblical theology movement, epitomized by the Lutheran New Testament scholar, Hans-Werner Bartsch. Scripture is authoritative because of the intrinsic revelatory power of its concepts. Using critical methods, the

---

5. In "The Bible and Christian Theology," *Journal of the American Academy of Religion* 48 (September 1980): 385–402, Kelsey summarizes the constructive proposals developed from his earlier analysis. We shall draw heavily upon both these sources in the present section.

task of biblical scholarship is to set forth the system of technical concepts that comprise the essence of Hebraic and Christian scriptures.

Third, scripture may be construed as the *recital* of salvation history. Revelation is understood no longer as contained in verbal deposits but as consisting in certain distinctive "acts of God in history," to use terminology popularized by G. Ernest Wright and others. These distinctive acts comprise salvation history, a subset of events within world history from which, when confessionally recited in scripture, the concept of God may be inferred and then translated into theological proposals.

These first three types hold in common the view that scripture is authoritative by virtue of its *content*, a content in some sense identical with divine revelation. However, in the second and third types the content has been displaced from the actual words of scripture, the writings as such, to something that must be critically reconstructed from the writings, namely, a system of technical concepts or a set of distinctive events. All three continue to understand the role of theology to be primarily that of translation and citation. At best they allow for certain modifications in the scripture principle but do not question its underlying premises.

The fourth type, epitomized by Karl Barth, may be viewed as transitional. Like Wright, Barth regards the authoritative aspect of scripture to be its function as narrative or recital. But what is recited is not a content. Rather, *scriptural narrative renders an agent* by setting forth the distinctive pattern of intentions and actions through which the agent's identity is constituted. In Barth's view, the whole canon of scripture renders the same subject, Jesus Christ, whose identity is that of God with us. This subject may reveal himself through our encounter with the texts. The texts are authoritative by virtue not of any inherent property they may have but of a *function* they fill in the life of the Christian community. As Kelsey summarizes Barth's view: "To say that scripture is 'inspired' is to say that God has promised that sometimes, at his gracious pleasure, the ordinary human words of the biblical texts will become the Word of God, the occasion for rendering an agent present to us in a Divine-human encounter."[6]

6. David H. Kelsey, *The Uses of Scripture in Recent Theology*, pp. 47–48.

The final three types share a common perspective. They construe scripture as *expressing* a past revelatory event and *occasioning* its present occurrence. The expression may be in the form of poetic *images* having to do with a cosmic creative process (Lionel Thornton), or religious *symbols* concerned with the manifestation of the power of new being (Paul Tillich), or *kerygmatic statements* expressive of God's word of personal address by which a new self-understanding is evoked in the hearer (Rudolf Bultmann). The images, symbols, and statements are not identical in content with the event, power, or word they express (although they may "participate" in them). "Express" is a slippery term that enables these theologians to acknowledge the con-ditioned character of biblical writings while holding that some sort of revelatory occurrence is nonetheless mediated by them, albeit in noninformative ways. The actual authority of scripture derives not from its content but from its power to occasion new occurrences of revelation and new experiences of redemptive transformation when used in situations of proclamation, theological reflection, and per-sonal self-understanding. Finally, images, symbols, and kerygma may not be directly translated into theological concepts. Theology rather has the task of "redescribing" what has been expressed biblically in symbolic or mythic language, employing, for these theologians at least, a philosophical conceptuality (whether process, idealist, or exis-tentialist) and an "imaginative construal" of what Christian faith is all about. Only in that way can it be set forth intelligibly to the modern mind.

Looking back over this typology, we realize that a full correspon-dence between the classic *doctrine* of scripture and the actual theo-logical *use* of scripture is found only in the first type. Already in the second and third types certain tensions appear as a result of relocating the content of revelation from scripture as such to something that must be critically reconstructed from it. In the last four types there is a clear disparity between the ways in which scripture is actually construed as authoritative for church and theology and what Kelsey calls the "standard picture." Ironically, though, whenever theologians such as Karl Barth, Paul Tillich, and Rudolf Bultmann espouse a doctrine of scripture, they do so primarily in terms of that standard picture. They understand scripture to be authoritative because it mediates, in the form of narrative, image, symbol, kerygmatic myth, and so on, a normative revelatory occurrence that in some fashion is to be occasioned anew and translated into modern conceptualities. In other words, the doctrine of scripture continues to be subordinated to the doctrine of revelation.

Under these circumstances what seems called for are fresh theological understandings of scripture that attempt to overcome the disparity between doctrine and use. Several such attempts have been made recently, but for the most part they represent modifications of the options we have just explored.

For example, certain evangelical theologians such as G. C. Berkouwer and Jack Rogers, while retaining the traditional principle of divine inspiration, are prepared to concede that the human instruments of this inspiration are finite and contingent, thus to qualify the doctrine of infallibility and acknowledge the legitimacy of certain forms of criticism. But they still view scripture as containing a divinely given revelatory content. Another option is represented by Schubert Ogden, who proposes that the authority of scripture derives in fact from "a canon within the canon," the "Jesus-kerygma" of the earliest apostolic community, accessible only by means of historical-critical reconstruction.

In his own constructive proposal, Kelsey develops an explicitly functional understanding of scripture. Scripture, he says, has authority to the extent that it functions in the church to shape new human identities and transform individual and communal life.[7] It can be understood theologically to function this way because it is God who is active in scripture—not God "saying" or "revealing" (the classic images), but God "shaping identity," "using" the uses of scripture toward a specific end: the actualization of God's eschatological rule. James Barr, while sharing this functionalist perspective, attributes the Bible's relevance in the modern world to its offering a "classic model for the understanding of God." This model is a product of creative human imagination, but it has the power to evoke fresh disclosures of the reality of God and the meaning of human existence.

Within the confines of this chapter we cannot do justice to any

---

7. A striking antecedent of this view is found in S. T. Coleridge's *Confessions of an Inquiring Spirit* (1840). The basis for the authority of scripture is not some abstract and implausible doctrine of plenary inspiration and verbal infallibility. Rather, Coleridge contends, scripture is self-authenticating to the extent that it has a transformative, redemptive effect upon those who hear and read it. "Whatever *finds* me, bears witness for itself that it has proceeded from a Holy Spirit" (p. 42). The ultimate test is pragmatic and functional.

of these proposals. While finding the work of Kelsey and Barr especially helpful, we do not believe that an adequate reformulation of the doctrine of scripture has yet been achieved by contemporary theology. We certainly cannot offer such in the concluding section of this chapter. Instead we shall consider several specific, unresolved issues and conclude by offering some tentative suggestions of our own.

ISSUES AND PROPOSALS

The specific issues are ones that for the most part we have been unable to treat, because our concern has been focused at a more fundamental level. One of these has to do with the question of the canon. "Canon" by traditional definition signifies an officially sanctioned collection of writings containing divine revelation—supernaturally inspired and inerrant, the ultimate authoritative rule of faith, doctrine, and life. Obviously, with the collapse of the house of authority this way of understanding "canon" must be given up. The question is whether there are other senses in which the concept of canon may continue to be valid or helpful. Kelsey suggests that it represents a way of ascribing some kind of "wholeness" or inner unity to a set of writings. While the quest for wholeness is unavoidable, a variety of kinds of wholeness may in fact be ascribed to the texts, leading to several competing versions of the canon. Theologians, he says, may have a "working canon," or a "canon within the canon," to which they appeal in construing the wholeness or essence of Christian faith, but none of these may be endowed with divinely sanctioned authority. In our judgment continued use of the concept of canon, however modified, is not helpful and should be abandoned. We acknowledge, however, that there remains a question as to how those writings that are constitutive of the faith of Israel and early Christianity can best be identified.

Another specific question concerns the relation of scripture and tradition to each other and to other ecclesial authorities. We have tended to view the issue of scripture versus tradition as a false one, since in the classic criteriology most of the qualities attributed to scripture were eventually extended to the doctrinal tradition as well. Obviously both scripture and doctrinal tradition are part of an ongoing "traditioning" process, which is to be understood in historical-critical terms, not in terms of successive stages of salvation history. But at the same time we acknowledge that differences exist between writings that attest the origin of a religious faith and those that help to perpetuate it—differences both in the character of these writings and the uses to which they are put by church and theology. A further question concerns the relation of both scripture and tradition to other elements of theological criteriology such as the role of experience, the function of norms in relation to sources and authorities, the kind of reality-reference implicit in religious faith, and finally the adjudication of truth claims or the making of theological judgments.

A third persistent issue concerns the use of biblical exegesis in church and theology. Implicit in our entire discussion is the contention that the exegesis of biblical texts must be critical, whether employed in preaching, instruction, or the doing of theology. The alternative to critical exegesis is proof-texting, which brings with it all the paraphernalia of the old scripture principle. However, we acknowledge that preachers, theologians, and lay people cannot be expected to be biblical scholars, and we recognize that biblical scholarship itself has tended to complicate the theological use of biblical texts by showing how dependent their meaning is on determinate historical, literary, and linguistic contexts. Theologians and preachers work with their own sets of criteria, employing biblical texts in quite different frames of reference while at the same time seeking not to do violence to them. They must start with the principles of critical exegesis and historical consciousness, yet they need to move beyond them in ways that are fitting. As Kelsey points out, while the results of biblical scholarship are clearly relevant to doing theology, they are not ultimately decisive, since every theological proposal and every sermon is shaped by a prior imaginative construal of what Christian faith is all about, a construal that determines how biblical texts and other sources will be selected and interpreted, while at the same time being controlled by close attention to the patterns, nuances, and details of the texts.

Finally, we may point to some new interpretive issues that raise questions about the authority of scripture and tradition or that offer additional possibilities for their appropriation. These may be put into two groups. The first has to do with new theories of religious language, including British analytic philosophy, French structuralism and deconstructionism, German and French hermeneutic phenomenology, and American linguistics and literary criticism. Obviously we can say nothing about these theories here other than to observe that our understanding of how language functions, especially in texts of religious, poetic, and narrative character, has been greatly enriched in recent years. The reality-reference of biblical symbols, metaphors, and stories is quite different from that presupposed by the old scripture principle, concerned as it was with the communication of revealed truths and doctrines. Freed from the first naiveté of the old doctrine of scripture, we are now able to enter into the intentionality of the writings with a kind of second-order or postcritical naiveté, in that way sharing in their evocation of the power of being and the new ways of being in the world associated with it.[8]

The second group of interpretive issues reflects the concerns of feminist theology, black theology, and liberation theology in general. We touched on this issue at the outset, noting that all authorities associated with the dominant Western cultural and religious tradition have become problematic in the eyes of those who have suffered oppression within Western society. The theological movements associated with these oppressed groups have raised searching questions and offered new interpretive insights. To what extent, for instance, do patriarchalism, the acceptance of slavery, the logic of sovereignty, the royalist metaphors, and a predominantly Western orientation discredit scripture and the doctrinal tradition? Are black, feminist, and liberationist hermeneutics now the only valid ones? How do they relate to the critical consciousness that had its birth in the Enlightenment?

These are difficult, persistent questions that we cannot hope to resolve here. Rather, in conclusion, we return to the underlying theological problem with which we have been concerned all along, namely, how to reconceive scripture and tradition after the collapse of the house of authority, and how to understand their function in the constitution of ecclesial existence. Our thesis is that scripture and tradition are *vehicles of ecclesial process* by means of which the originative event of Christian faith is able to endure as normative and to

8. See the works by Paul Ricoeur cited in Suggestions for Further Reading; also Paul Ricoeur, *The Symbolism of Evil* (Boston: Beacon Press, 1967), pp. 10–19.

function redemptively in the transformation of human existence. Implicit in this thesis is a rejection of the traditional way of understanding the church as primarily a community of *revelation* that endures by means of deposits of revelation in scripture, dogmas, and institution. In contrast, we view ecclesial existence as the redemptive presence of the transcendent, transforming any and all provincial spaces, whether based on ethnic, geographical, cultic, racial, sexual, political, social, or doctrinal considerations—transforming them in the direction of a universal community, yet without losing the determinacy intrinsic to human being. The problem is to discern the sort of *origination* and *duration* that attends this kind of redemptive community, as well as the *vehicles* of duration. Remembrance of the events in which Christian faith originated will not be for the sake of the events themselves—a purely antiquarian interest—but for the sake of redemption.

The originative events are "sedimented" in the literatures by which they survive—in the case of Christianity the literatures of Israel, kerygma, and interpretive tradition. Consider first the "kerygma," using the Greek word for "proclamation" to designate the literatures comprising what is usually called "New Testament." For Christian faith the paradigmatic figure Jesus of Nazareth is the decisive nucleus of the transition to ecclesial existence. Yet in order for this paradigmatic figure to be redemptively efficacious for subsequent generations, his "story" had to assume linguistic embodiment. This occurred first orally, in the apostolic witness, but then expanded to a body of writings whose function was to contribute to the upbuilding of ecclesia. The determination of what is properly to be included in this normative literature cannot be settled on the basis of an official canon of inspired writings. Rather, we have to look to the character of the writings themselves as comprising a unique witness to the originative event and as containing intrinsic literary and theological power to evoke a fresh disclosure of God and consequent redemptive transformation of human existence. Writings having these qualities came to be regarded as "scripture" within the Christian community, just as other writings have become "classics" for the wider human community. Obviously no hard and fast line may be drawn between the writings called "scripture" and other early Christian literature.

The writings of Israel are also an essential vehicle of ecclesial process. That is because the faith of Israel is immanent in and constitutive of Christianity as well as Judaism. Faith in Jesus Christ is not a substitute for Israel's faith but a new universal availability of divine presence. With respect to many motifs of Christian faith, the literature we are calling "kerygma" is itself inadequate. Compared to the fuller, more profound treatment in the literature of Israel of such themes as creation, providence, idolatry, sin, wisdom, worship, justice, it is clearly deficient. The interpretive problem in using these writings is that of disengaging the implicit universality of Israel's faith from its landed-national paradigm. Israel's rich imagery must therefore be probed for its *own* potentially universal layers of meaning. It is not a matter of linking the two "testaments" as promise and fulfillment under the motif of salvation history, or of treating the law as propadeutic to the gospel, or of merely claiming that without the Old Testament the New Testament can scarcely be understood. All these represent an interpretation alien to Israel's faith and a subordination of it to Christianity.

Finally, there is the interpretive tradition to consider. Communities are shaped not only by events of origin but also by the controversies, crises, and interpretations that comprise their ongoing tradition. Such events gain shaping effect only through embodiment or sedimentation in linguistic and institutional forms. What ordinarily has been called doctrinal and theological tradition we are calling "sedimented interpretation." Living interpretation becomes sedimented in ways that comprise the self-identity of the community and contribute to redemptive transformation. Disclosures can and do attend the ongoing history of the ecclesial community; revelation is not exhausted at the outset. Indeed, the act of interpretation may itself be disclosive, and the new disclosures may in time obtain sedimentation.

Thus far we have provided a rather formal descriptive account of how the literatures of Israel, kerygma, and traditional interpretation function as normative vehicles of ecclesial process. If it should be asked why this is the case, what empowers them to function redemptively, then, with Kelsey we should want to advance a theological proposal concerning God's "use" of these literatures in the shaping of a new kind of corporate existence in which human beings are redemptively transformed. To speak in this way does not imply any kind of special divine intervention or supernatural inspiration. Rather, ecclesial process as such *is* the salvific work of God in history. It is an utterly historical process, subject to the contingencies, failures, and unfinished character of all such processes. God saves *through* the historical manifestation of human possibility, not *from* history or in spite of it. God does not "cause" or "control" these manifestations, nor does any sort of direct identity exist between what God wills and specific historical occurrences. Rather, like Kelsey, we must speak of God "shaping," "transforming," "occasioning," "making use of the uses" of scripture and tradition. The unpacking of these metaphors would require a reformulation of the doctrine of providence and new ways of thinking about the church, sanctification, and the spiritual presence of God. These are matters to which other chapters of this book attend.

SUGGESTIONS FOR FURTHER READING

Barr, James. *The Bible in the Modern World.* London: SCM Press, 1990.

————. *Holy Scripture: Canon, Authority, Criticism.* Philadelphia: Westminster Press, 1983.

————. *Old and New in Interpretation.* London: SCM Press, 1966.

Barth, Karl. *Church Dogmatics.* Vol 1/1, chap. 1; vol. 1/2, chap. 3.

Berkouwer, G. C. *Holy Scripture.* Grand Rapids: Eerdmans, 1975.

Bultmann, Rudolf. *Jesus Christ and Mythology.* New York: Charles Scribner's Sons, 1958.

Childs, Brevard. *Biblical Theology in Crisis.* Philadelphia: Westminster Press, 1970.

Coleridge, Samuel Taylor. *Confessions of an Inquiring Spirit.* Stanford: Stanford University Press, 1957.

Congar, Y.-M. *Tradition and Traditions.* London: Burns & Oates, 1966.

Ebeling, Gerhard. "The Significance of the Critical Historical Method for Church and Theology in Protestantism." In *Word and Faith*, pp. 17–62. Philadelphia: Fortress Press, 1960.

————. *The Word of God and Tradition.* Philadelphia: Fortress Press, 1964.

Evans, Christopher. *Is "Holy Scripture" Christian?* London: SCM Press, 1971.

Farley, Edward. *Ecclesial Man: A Social Phenomenology of Faith and Reality.* Philadelphia: Fortress Press, 1975.

————. *Ecclesial Reflection: An Anatomy of Theological Method.* Philadelphia: Fortress Press, 1982.

Farrar, Frederic W. *History of Interpretation.* New York: E. P. Dutton & Co., 1886.

Frei, Hans. W. *The Eclipse of Biblical Narrative.* New Haven: Yale University Press, 1974.

————. *Scriptural Authority and Narrative Interpretation.* Philadelphia: Fortress Press, 1987.

Grant, Robert M. *A Short History of the Interpretation of the Bible.* 2d ed. Philadelphia: Fortress Press, 1984.

Johnson, Robert. *Authority in Protestant Theology.* Philadelphia: Westminster Press, 1959.

Käsemann, Ernst. "The New Testament Canon and the Unity of the Church." In *Essays on New Testament Themes,* pp. 95–107. London: SCM Press, 1964.

Kelsey, David H. "The Bible and Christian Theology." *Journal of the American Academy of Religion* 48 (September 1980): 385–402.

————. *The Uses of Scripture in Recent Theology.* Philadelphia: Fortress Press, 1975.

Loades, Ann and Michael McLain, editors. *Hermeneutics, the Bible, and Literary Criticism.* New York: St. Martin's Press, 1992.

Marxsen, Willi. *The New Testament as the Church's Book.* Philadelphia: Fortress Press, 1972.

Ogden, Schubert. *On Theology.* San Francisco: Harper & Row, 1986.

Rahner, Karl. *Inspiration in the Bible.* New York: Herder & Herder, 1964.

Ricoeur, Paul. *Biblical Hermeneutics.* Semeia 4. Missoula: Scholars Press, 1975.

————. *Interpretation Theory.* Fort Worth: Texas Christian University Press, 1976.

Rogers, Jack B., and McKim, Donald K. *The Authority and Interpretation of the Bible.* New York: Harper & Row, 1979.

Sanders, James A. *Torah and Canon.* Philadelphia: Fortress Press, 1972.

Strauss, David F. *The Life of Jesus Critically Examined.* Translated by George Eliot. Philadelphia: Fortress Press, 1972.

Tavard, George H. *Holy Writ or Holy Church: The Crisis of the Protestant Reformation.* London: Burns & Oates, 1959.

Thiel, John E. *Imagination and Authority: Theological Authorship in the Modern Tradition.* Minneapolis: Fortress Press, 1991.

Tillich, Paul. *Systematic Theology.* Vol. 1, Introduction.

Wilken, R. L. *The Myth of Christian Beginnings.* New York: Doubleday, 1971.

3. GOD

WHERE WE ARE

The idea of God is at once the most important and yet the most questionable of all religious doctrines or "symbols" in the West. This idea or symbol points to the central object of both Christian and Jewish faith, the sole "subject" of their revelation, and the final principle of both reality and meaning throughout human existence. Nevertheless, of all concepts in modern cultural life—and in varying degrees for "believers" and "doubters" alike—the idea of God remains the most elusive, the most frequently challenged, the most persistently criticized and negated of all important convictions. Is there a God? Can such a One be experienced, known, or spoken of? Is such experience testable, such knowledge verifiable, and such speech meaningful? Or is all such experience illusory, such seeming knowledge in fact a projection, such speech empty? These issues represent the primordial issues for philosophy of religion, for philosophical theology, and for confessional theology alike.

Almost every dominant motif and movement in modernity—its expanding scientific inquiry, its emphasis on what is natural, experienced, and verifiable, its persistent search for the greater well-being of humans in this world, its increasing emphasis on autonomy and on present satisfactions—has progressively challenged the concept of God and unsettled both its significance and its certainty. This challenge has been on two fronts: (1) The traditional concepts of God, inherited from the premodern cultures of medieval, Renaissance, and Reformation Europe, revealed themselves in almost every aspect to have anachronistic elements and to be unintelligible in the light of modern knowledge and modern attitudes toward reality, with the consequence that these concepts have had to be reformulated on a fundamental level. (2) More important, these same aspects of modernity have challenged the very possibility of an idea of God, its knowability, its coherence, and its meaning; to much of modernity such an idea is on a number of grounds an impossible idea and, as a consequence, the whole enterprise of a theistic religion appears as a futile, expensive, and even harmful activity.

Because of this second point the prime problematic connected with the symbol of God has in modern times differed noticeably from earlier problematics. Our fundamental questions in religious reflection are not about the *nature* of the divine and the *character* of God's activity or will toward us, which represented the main questions of an earlier time. The question now is the *possibility* of God's existence in a seemingly naturalistic world, the possibility of valid knowledge of God and meaningful discourse about God, and the possibility of any sort of "religious" existence, style of life, or hope at all. As a result, the efforts of religious thinkers in our century have by and large been directed at these two interrelated problems: (1) a justification of the meaning and the validity of the concept of God in relation to other, apparently less questionable forms of experience—scientific, philosophical, social political, artistic, psychological, or existentialist; and (2) a reformulation of that concept so that it can be meaningful and relevant to the modern world.

Despite the new and sharper edge to the question of God in modern times, certain continuing issues characteristic of the traditional discussion of this concept have also been present, albeit in specifically modern form. In the concept of God, as in the reality experienced in religious existence, dialectical tensions have appeared and reappeared as the center of theological discussion. It is a strange notion filled, as we shall see, with paradoxes and polarities. These perennial problems *internal* to the concept of God (whether orthodox or reformulated) also characterize modern discussions and manifest themselves with each option characteristic of modern theology and philosophy of religion. In the following, we shall seek to explicate their career in modern theologies as well as to show the way modern views of God have handled the question of the reality of God and of the possibility of such a concept.

THE DOCTRINE IN ITS CLASSIC FORMULATION

The General Idea of God

In Western culture, dominated as it has been by the Jewish and the Christian traditions, the word or symbol "God" has generally referred to one, supreme, or holy being, the unity of ultimate reality and ultimate goodness. So conceived, God is believed to have created the entire universe, to rule over it, and to intend to bring it to its fulfillment or realization, to "save" it. Thus as a functioning word in our own cultural world, God in the first instance refers to the central and sole object of religious *existence*, commitment, devotion, dependence, fear, trust, love, and belief—and to the center of worship, prayer, and religious meditation. Secondarily, "God" has been the object of religious and philosophical *reflection*, the supreme object of theology and of most (though not all) forms of speculative metaphysics.

So understood, God represents a puzzling and elusive notion by no means easy to define, as the traditions of Jewish, Christian, and Islamic religious thought have clearly recognized. As the supreme being or ground of being, the Creator and ruler of all, God transcends (exceeds or goes beyond) all creaturely limits and distinctions, all creaturely characteristics; the reason is that the divine, so conceived, is the *source* and therefore not simply one more example of those limits, distinctions, and characteristics. As Creator of time and space, God is not *in* either time or space as is all else; as the source of all finite realities and of their interrelations, God is transcendent to all experienced substances, causes, and all ordinary relations; as that on which all depends, God is neither essentially dependent on nor a mere effect of other things. Thus deity can hardly be spoken of as simply "a being" among other beings, changeable as is all else, dependent and vulnerable as is every creature, in time and passing as we are, or mortal as is all life—lest the divine be a mere contingent creature and thus not "God." For these reasons the concept of God inevitably tends toward that of the transcendent absolute of much speculative philosophy: necessary, impersonal, unrelated, independent (*a se*), changeless, eternal. And for these reasons as well as others, the customary reference to God as "he" is now seen to be extremely problematical!

On the other hand, as we shall see, God in Jewish and Christian witness, piety, and experience is also in some way personal, righteous, or moral, the ground or base in actuality of value, concerned with all creatures, with people and their lives, impelled and guided by important purposes for them individually and collectively, and deeply related to and active within the natural world and the course of history. The reflective problems in this concept of God, illustrated by debates throughout Western history, therefore have a dual source: in the fact that God, however described, is *unlike* ordinary things of which we can easily and clearly speak, and in the fact that inherent in the religious reality itself and in its reflected concepts are certain dialectical tensions or paradoxes—absolute-related, impersonal-personal, eternal-temporal, changeless-changing, actual yet potential, self-sufficient or necessary and yet in some manner dependent. Such dialectical tensions stretch, if they do not defy, our ordinary powers of speech, definition, and precise comprehension. However one may approach the divine, religiously or philosophically, therefore, one first encounters "mystery," and with that encounter appear, among other things, special procedures and special forms or rules of speech—a characteristic as old as religion itself.

Biblical and Early Christian Concepts of God

Let us now discuss briefly the diverse origins of the "paradoxes" or "dialectical tensions" in this notion we have noted earlier, before we trace the development of these polarities in Christian history. The origins of this understanding of God lie in the Hebrew and Christian religious traditions, especially in their sacred scriptures. In what we call the Old Testament, God or Yahweh is "undeniably" and "jealously" one, and transcendent to all the limited and special forces and powers of our experience of nature, society, or self. On the other hand, Yahweh's central characteristic or, better, mode of experienced being or self-manifestation is a concern for and relation to history and especially to a particular people in history—Israel. Although God manifests power and glory throughout the vast scope of nature, the main arena for the divine "works" is the particular sequence of historical events related to the calling, establishment, nurture, and protection of the chosen people. In this activity in history, moreover, God is revealed as a moral or righteous God, the source of the law, and quick to punish those, even chosen ones, who defy this law. Yahweh is, however, also a God of mercy, patience, faithfulness, and grace, since according to the prophets, despite Israel's obvious unworthiness and continued betrayal of her covenant with God, God promises to redeem Israel in the future. This God of history, covenant, judgment, and promised redemption is throughout assumed to be, and often clearly affirmed to be, the ruler of all events. All agree that the divine purposes shape, reshape, and in the end will complete history. Finally, by inevitable implication, this sovereign lord of history is seen to be also the creator and ruler of the entire cosmos.

These themes in the notion of God are continued, albeit with modifications, in the New Testament: God is one God, a God concerned with history, judgment, and redemption, the God who is Creator and Redeemer, alpha and omega. Only now the central manifestation of the living God of Abraham, Isaac, and Jacob is in the "Son," Jesus of Nazareth, through whom the divine righteous and loving will for human beings is revealed, the divine judgments made known, the divine power to save even from death effected, and in whose speedy return God's sovereignty over all creation will be fully and visibly established. The presence of God, moreover, is now less in the temple and in the law as in the Spirit, dwelling in the minds and hearts of the Christian community and in their witness and hopeful expectation. Thus appears a new set of Christian symbols helping to define "God" and the divine activity; not only creation and redemption, covenant, law, and messianic promise, but now also Son/Logos, incarnation, atonement, Holy Spirit, parousia, and, as a summation of these "new" concepts, Trinity.

In briefly tracing the development of this complex notion from the beginning of the Christian era to our own times, we should recall that once Western culture became Christian (A.D. 325), the concept of God became the symbolic center for every aspect of life and for the understanding of nature, society, and human existence generally. Consequently, it became not only the object of endless philosophical and theological speculation but also the foundation for every special discipline of thought, every representative mode of action, and all important social institutions. Thus, inevitably, this notion and the modes of thinking that expressed it made union with the sciences, with ethical, legal, and political theories, and, above all, with the philosophy of each epoch.

During the crucial formative centuries of Christendom, the dominant intellectual inheritance through which Western life understood itself and its world was that of Greco-Roman philosophy. Thus it was natural that during this long period the biblical notion of God outlined above was given its main conceptual shape with the help first of Platonism and Stoicism and then, during the High Middle Ages, of Aristotelianism. In this classical philosophical tradition, especially in its later Hellenistic stages (200 B.C.–A.D. 400), the sense of the reality, value, or meaning of the changing, temporal, material world, and of earthly human and historical life in time noticeably weakened. Correspondingly, for this tradition the divine was precisely that which infinitely transcends change, time, matter, flesh, and history. As a quite natural consequence, those transcendent and absolute aspects or implications of the biblical creator and ruler were, in the developing conceptualization of God from A.D. 150 to 400, enlarged and extended: God became eternal in the sense of utterly nontemporal, necessary in the sense of absolute noncontingency, self-sufficient in the sense of absolute independence, changeless in the sense of participating in and relating to no change, purely spiritual instead of in any fashion material, unaffected and thus seemingly unrelated and even unrelatable to the world. It would, however, be false to conclude that the absoluteness of the patristic conception of God stemmed entirely from Hellenistic philosophy, though it was expressed in the latter's categories. It also stemmed from the character of patristic piety. Since that piety emphasized, as did most Hellenistic spirituality, the victory of the incorruptible, immortal, and changeless principle of deity over the corruptible, mortal, and passing character of creaturely life, the divine is and must be that which transcends and conquers the passingness of mortal flesh.

The Symbol of the Trinity

In the early patristic period, for example, with Justin Martyr, Clement of Alexandria, and Origen, this *absolute* aspect of God was unequivocally affirmed and regarded as designated by the traditional biblical symbol of the "Father," the utterly primordial, unoriginate, changeless, eternal, and unrelated source of all else. The *related* aspect of God, equally central to the life and piety of Christian faith, was consequently expressed through the symbol of the "Son" or the Logos, the principle of divine outreach and self-manifestation (almost a "second God," as Justin and Origen put it) through which the transcendent Father, changeless and inactive, created the world, was revealed in it, and acted to redeem it. The Holy Spirit completed

93

the relationship by assuring the presence of the divine in the community and in persons. Thus at the outset of the philosophical career of the Christian God, the symbol of the Trinity served to provide conceptual expression for the dialectical polarity of the Christian God as at once the self-sufficient creator of all, transcendent to all finitude (Father), and as the active, revealing, loving redeemer (Son), present in grace and power to God's people (Holy Spirit).

By the inexorable and possibly ironic logic of events and ideas, however, this important *mediatorial* role of the symbol of the Trinity soon disintegrated. As the doctrines of the Arians quickly made evident, a Son or Logos that genuinely mediates between the absolute and the relative and that is related to the creaturely, the temporal, and the changing in time can be itself neither ungenerate, eternal, changeless, nor fully "God" *if* God is defined solely by the traits of a transcendent absolute. An originate, related, mediating principle is by that token hardly God; but in monotheism such a subordinate, semiabsolute, and partly divine being, however "good," is inadmissible as representing incipient polytheism. Besides, if Jesus Christ is not fully God, how can he save? These unanswerable arguments of Athanasius pushed the conception of the entire divine Trinity in an absolutist direction; Father, Son, and Holy Spirit were at Nicaea and again later at Constantinople *all* defined as fully divine, that is, as essentially negating every creaturely attribute: temporality, potentiality, changeableness, relatedness, and dependence. As a consequence, the Trinity ceased to be the central symbolic expression of the polarity of the divine relatedness. To put this point more precisely, a distinction now appears in post-Nicaean theology between the *essential* Trinity (the "three-in-oneness" characteristic of the eternal God's inner life) and the *economic* Trinity (the "three-in-oneness" manifested and expressed externally in God's creative, revealing, and redemptive activity in relation to the world). Clearly this distinction, in contrast to the pre-Nicaean concept of the Trinity, where a "halfway absolute" Son mediated between the absolute Father and the world, covered over rather than resolved the fundamental problem or dialectic of the Christian concept of God, namely, how the absolute God can be related to the relative world. Now in the new form the same old question arises: How can the essentially trinitarian God in whom Father, Son, and Holy Spirit are alike eternal, changeless, *a se*, and impassive participate in all the actions and reactions in relation to changing temporality entailed in the economic Trinity?

As the appearance of this distinction makes plain, at no point did Christian theology allow itself to deny God's continual relatedness to and activity in the world of change. How could it, since the entire corpus of Christian belief from creation to redemption, every aspect of its ritual of word and sacrament, its entire sacred law and its sanctions, and every facet of its piety of prayer, miracles, and special angelic and saintly powers depended on the reality in past, present, and future of that divine presence and divine activity? Nevertheless, that a deep theological problem remained for the classical theological conception of God is also evident. Once God was defined in theology as "pure actuality," "eternal being," "changeless," and thus quite void of potentiality, alterability, passivity, or temporality, it became virtually impossible, if not contradictory, to express intelligibly the obvious relatedness and mutuality of God to the changing world necessitated by the scriptural witness and by the structures of the Christian religion itself.

Although with the Reformation the philosophical or metaphysical definition of God as absolute, changeless, eternal being or actuality radically receded in prominence in theology, the same problem remained. In the "biblical" theology of the major reformers, God is conceived centrally through personal rather than metaphysical categories: as almighty or sovereign power, as righteous or holy will, as gracious and reconciling love. The "ontological" concepts of self-sufficiency (aseity) and eternity remain, but what now determines the shape of the doctrine of God in each reformer is the center of Reformation piety or religion, namely, the new emphasis on the priority and sole sovereignty of divine grace in redemption, on the utter unworthiness and inactivity of the recipient of grace, and finally on the absolute priority and decisiveness of divine election.

What is here eternal and changeless is the divine decree destining, yes *pre*destining, each creature to grace or to its opposite. The first cause of *being* that led Thomas to the concept of pure actuality has become, if I may so put it, the first "cause" of *grace*, leading to the concept of the eternal and changeless divine decrees. Thus for primarily religious rather than metaphysical reasons the same paradox tending toward contradiction appears: an eternal, hidden, and yet all-sovereign divine electing will on the one hand, and the affirmation of the presence and activity of God in relation to a real and not sham sequence of historical events and of human decisions on the other hand. Although it was Calvin especially who drew out most clearly the implications of this new paradox based on Reformation piety rather than on traditional philosophy, still the same paradox in this new form is evident and fundamental for the theologies of Luther and Zwingli as well.

CHALLENGES AND CONTRIBUTIONS OF
MODERN CONSCIOUSNESS

At the start of the post-Reformation period there were two dominant conceptions of God, one Catholic and the other Protestant. They differed markedly in the categories with which God was described, yet to our twentieth-century eyes they exhibited the same paradoxical (not to say contradictory) character: the Catholic conception of an absolute, purely actual, changeless being "illegitimately" (so to speak) related to the world, and the Protestant conception of an eternal, sovereign, divine will ordaining and effecting all temporal events from eternity, thus again "illegitimately" related and even responsive to historical crises and human needs. Understandably, subsequent modern reflection on the issue of God has, at least since the seventeenth century, been largely constituted by sustained philosophical and theological criticism of these two inherited conceptions, and thence characterized either by humanist and naturalist rejection of the concept entirely or by a more or less radical theological reformulation of it. Perhaps the best way to cover this extensive process is to remind ourselves first of the grounds in modern (Enlightenment and post-Enlightenment) sensibility for this criticism and, second, to describe some of the characteristic forms of these reformulations as those forms appear in the present theological discussion.

The Enlightenment Critique

The grounds for the modern critique of the idea of God have been essentially three: (1) the new emphasis on *experience* as the sole relevant and dependable source for valued and meaningful concepts and the sole ground for the testing of those concepts; (2) corresponding shift to the *subject* as the sole seat of legitimate authority in all matters pertaining to truth and as the sole originating source of significant moral and/or personal action; and (3) finally, since the principle of authority in matters of truth and morals has moved radically inward to the subject, all external forms of authority are radically questioned, especially those coming from church traditions or scripture.

Thus, as we have already noted, the question of the reality of God, even of the possibility of the concept in any of its forms, has been sharply raised in modern culture. On the one hand, a powerful "naturalistic" viewpoint, which finds belief in God anachronistic and incredible and thus a religious relation to God either offensive or irrelevant, has arisen and spread pervasively throughout the Western and Communist worlds into almost every class. From this viewpoint "nature," as understood by science, is the seat and source of all that is real; men and women are the source of values, and their needs and wishes are the sole criterion of values. Thus this world and its history represent the sole locus of hope. Whether in socialistic or capitalistic form, or as theorized by Karl Marx, Sigmund Freud, Jean-Paul Sartre, or Albert Camus—or by most if not all the leaders of the scientific and philosophical communities—this naturalistic humanism has dominated the cultural scene. As a consequence its powerful presence has posed the central intellectual issues for theologians concerned with the defense and reformulation of the concept of God.

Whether or not "naturalistic humanism," a nonreligious understanding of reality generally and of human history and existence, is a lasting possibility has also become problematic in the modern period. This possibility of a totally "secular" world view was assumed in the French Enlightenment and taken for granted by most of the nineteenth-century critics of religion (e.g., Auguste Comte, Ludwig Feuerbach, Karl Marx). However, recent history has seemed to show that as traditional religion wanes as the symbolic center of a community's life, "ideology" tends to take its place, an ideology with important religious aspects or dimensions. Thus even if God has receded from the center of Western consciousness, "the religious" has apparently not—for the political and social worlds of Western culture are structured ideologically, and thus its major conflicts are still inspired by competing forms of religiosity.

Insofar as thinkers have sought to defend and retrieve a concept of God, these new emphases on the authority of experience and the human subjects of experience have slowly but effectively reshaped that concept. First, the traditional concept of the divine self existing alone, a notion essentially and necessarily quite out of relation to any human experiences of the divine, became understandably a most questionable concept: How could there be experience and knowledge of any such unrelated object? Thus most modern "doctrines" of God remain within the parameters of possible experience and speak of the divine (as of anything else) only on the basis of our experience, in terms of either God's metaphysical relations to the world, our immediate experience of God, or God's special activities of revelation in history. Second, if all that is real for us must be within the area of our experiencing, then inevitably the sense of the reality and value of the changing, temporal world of process will increase, for this is the world we experience and know. Thus, however much or little the transcendence of God may be emphasized in modern doctrines, we find now that the *relatedness* of God to the world, to the events of history, and to temporality itself has become the starting point for discourse about God rather than an embarrassment to it. Most concepts of God in modern times are therefore dynamic, related, even sharing in some aspects of temporality and dependence, whatever sorts of categories (personal and biblical, or ontological and metaphysical) they may choose to use. In our subsequent treatment we shall discuss in more detail the various options available in our day for a concept of God, and the issues around which present discussion of this subject centers. It will be evident, however, that whatever the option or issue, it is a God related to us and to our experience, and so a dynamic, active God, who is known, affirmed, and described and not a wholly transcendent, independent, and changeless God.

Modern Reformulations

Knowledge of God

The question about how God is to be known—by rational inquiry of some sort, through religious experience, or through a revelation responded to by faith—has been a traditional and recurrent question throughout Christian history. In that history there have been those who, while denying neither the efficacy nor the significance of mystical experience or of revelation, have insisted that the existence of God can be established by philosophical argument, and so the nature of God known and defined, at least in part, by reason alone, that is, by "natural theology." On the other side have been those who distrusted philosophical reason as "pagan" or at least as misguided; correspondingly they have argued that the true and living God, the God of Abraham, Christ, and the church, can be known only in revelation. As a consequence for them a valid understanding of the nature and intentions of God must proceed alone from revelation and not also from philosophical reasoning. While the developments in modern culture we have just traced have not effaced this traditional issue and its contesting parties, still these developments have to some extent effected changes in the way each side argues its case. I shall mention briefly three points of difference.

1. The question of the possibility of a concept of God, the most radical question about God's reality, has come to the fore. Thus each side, the natural theologians and the revelationists, find themselves more concerned than their predecessors were with the source or point of origin (in a "godless" natural and historical world) of this idea in philosophy or in the experience of revelation respectively, that is, with the question "How do we *come* to know God?" as well as with the question "*What* do we know about God in the way we do know it?"

2. Though the sharpness and difficulty of the question of the reality of God and of the intelligibility of that concept has made a natural theology eminently desirable if not necessary for modern believers, still the drift—not to say flood tide—of modern rationality away from metaphysical speculation has raised increasing difficulties for that enterprise in modern culture. Whereas in many epochs only orthodox members of the church might be scornful or ungrateful at the use of philosophy in theology and especially at the idea of a natural theology, now it is the philosophical community more than the theological community that raises questions about the possibility of metaphysics and of natural theology of any sort. In modernity (as possibly at the end of the Hellenic era) natural theologians have had to contend with philosophical resistance to their speculative, meta-

physical labors as well as with religious-theological resistance, and they face the bizarre and arduous task, not forced upon their predecessors, of presenting a reasoned defense of metaphysical reason even before they begin their quest via such reason for God.

3. The modern critique of authority, the emphatic denial of absolute authority to any document or institution, has transformed the interpretation of revelation and its cognitive meaning. Prior to this the "revealed faith" could refer to sets of propositions in the scriptural corpus or the dogmatic tradition, and how one "knew God" via either one could be plainly and intelligibly stated. With the modern critique of scriptural and dogmatic authority and of a "propositional view of revelation," at best revelation comes *through* the words of scripture and tradition and is received not in terms of objective propositions but on the "religious" level as an experiencing or "feeling" (Friedrich Schleiermacher), as an "encounter" resulting in a personal acknowledgment or a decision of faith (dialectical theology), that is, as an existential reality and activity, so to speak, below the conceptual and ordinary cognitive level. The obvious problem of a cognitive event (not only of certainty *that* its object is but also of knowledge of *what* it might be) taking place via such a prelinguistic, preconceptual, and preexperiential "experience" thus plagues contemporary revelationists as it did not their predecessors. We should note that neither one of the traditional avenues to the knowledge of God, metaphysics or revelation, is in the least straight and smooth in our own day!

Despite these added difficulties, each answer has in our own time had its powerful and persuasive adherents. Those who emphasize the knowability of God by reason have offered one version or another of the classical "proofs" of God: the cosmological, from the existence of the finite world (mainly the neo-Thomists); the teleological, from the order of the finite world (note especially the brilliant use of this argument by Alfred North Whitehead as well as by a variety of evolutionists such as F. R. Tennant and Teilhard de Chardin); the ontological, from the implications of the concept of God itself as a concept of a perfect and so necessary being (the quite original work of Charles Hartshorne is unique at this point); and the moral argument, from the implications of moral experience. These widely variant forms of philosophical approach have been united in arguing that any theology intellectually respectable enough to speak to modern, intelligent people must re-present its religious heritage in the intellectual form of such a rationally grounded philosophical theology. Without such a philosophical base for our knowledge of God, our certainty of the divine reality and our comprehension of the relation of this concept to our other concepts will be seriously lacking. As a consequence, the idea of God will increasingly be regarded as merely subjective and idiosyncratic, a private matter of "feeling" and therefore unreal, a private image unrelated to the width of all experience, vacant of content and in the end "meaningless." Powerful recent examples of these arguments for a philosophical basis for our knowledge of God have been the Hegelian idealists, the neo-scholastic and now the transcendental Thomists, and perhaps most notably the growing and flourishing school of process or neoclassical theologians.

On the other side have been those who have shared a more jaundiced view of culture's reasoning and of its philosophical "proofs"; on religious grounds they have emphasized the transcendence and mystery of God and the actuality and sufficiency of revelation as the source and norm for the concept of God. They are not at all unaware that most contemporary philosophy has come to regard metaphysical speculation and all proofs of a divine reality as representing a dubious and uncritical use of reason, and therefore itself devoid of certainty, objectivity, or meaning. They also have sensed the ideological and invalid character of much "modern" thinking. For them modern thought, far from providing an objective and valid ground for our ultimate faith, itself represents a significant aspect of the modern problem, needing itself new principles of illumination if it is to help our religious existence.

Most important, the main problem of the knowledge of God, they insist, is not that we cannot know God with our finite minds, but that in fact secretly we do not at all wish to know God. Thus, as Barth argued, natural theology represents the persistent and systematic attempt of self-sufficient people to create a "God" of their own and so to avoid relationship with or knowledge of the real God. A philosophical God, the product of our own metaphysical thinking and the construct of our own wayward modern wisdom, may be infinitely more comfortable for us to live with; nevertheless, such a "God" is a far cry indeed from the real God who confronts us in judgment and may confront us therefore also in grace. Furthermore, the very center of Christian promise resides in the *re-creation* of what we are and of how and what we think, not in their mere extension and solidification. Thus God—not "our own words to ourselves"—must speak to us in revelation. Such an event of revelation provides the sole basis and the sole norm for the religious existence of the Christian community from which and for which valid and legitimate theology speaks. To be sure, theology does speak to the world as well as to the church, but in its speech it must seek to represent not the wisdom of the world but the message of the gospel, not the word of humanity but the word of God. Theology may use philosophy—it cannot avoid that—in explicating this message in coherent and adequate form. Its primal obligation, however, is to be faithful to revelation and not to the pressures of public rationality as the world defines rationality. Faith therefore precedes and controls the use of reason in theology; *credo ut intelligam* rather than *intelligo ut credere*.

Language about God

A second issue, characteristic of the whole tradition yet vital to recent theology, is concerned with the question of the nature of the categories or concepts fundamental to or appropriate for Christian speech about God. Should these be "personal," "historical," and "ontic" in character, as they surely are in scripture, or should they be ontological, metaphysical, and therefore "impersonal" in character, as in almost every speculative philosophical system, even an idealistic or a panpsychistic one?

As in the first debate, there are compelling reasons on both sides, reasons apparently intrinsic to the character and claims of the Christian religion. In its fundamental symbolic content, exemplified in its belief in God as creator and providential ruler, in its view of human beings as finite, temporal, and yet "real," and in its idea of history as the arena of God's activity, Christian faith cannot avoid making assertions about the character of ultimate reality and about the essential structures of natural, human, and historical existence. Thus inescapably it must employ ontological or metaphysical as well as ontic or existential words to express its own deepest meanings. As intrinsically related to reality as, so to speak, the anchor of value within reality, God therefore must be expressed in categories appropriate to the discussion of the structures of reality as a whole, that is, in ontological or metaphysical categories.

On the other hand, there is little question that the center of Christian piety, its religious center, has classically been expressible only by means of personal, that is, anthropomorphic language. Just as a description of a human being devoid of any personal inwardness, decision, action, and so responsibility would subvert all that Christianity has to say about human nature, so a description of God void of all personal categories (intentions, purposes, mercy, love, and so on) can hardly express what Christians intend to say about God. While, therefore, the ontological or philosophical theologians seem (initially at least) better able to explicate conceptually the symbols of creation and providence, the biblical theologians, using personal categories, seem only to gain in strength when they speak of sin, the law, and the gospel, and especially when they speak of God's "judgment" and God's "love."

The Concept of God:
Agency, Temporality, and History

While the following three issues are not completely new to Christian discussion of God, the characteristic emphases of modern culture have nevertheless intensified each of them, shifted their focus and balance, and thus reshaped these issues dramatically. As a consequence, so it seems to me, the contemporary doctrine of God in Christian theology appears in undeniably new forms, whatever particular symbol (e.g., creation, providence, eschatology) in systematic theology we are discussing. Let us first mention what we might call the limitations in God's agency characteristic of recent theology.

For a variety of reasons we have briefly described (especially in this case the centering on the subject), the sense of human autonomy and of the depth, reality, and "awfulness" of evil have grown with the rise of modern culture. On both counts theologians are less and less able or willing to say blandly that God wills, intends, or even effects whatever happens, including those actions and events that we assess to be evil. Apparently, to deny human freedom and to saddle God with evil (e.g., the rise to power of Adolf Hitler) runs counter to all we believe about ourselves, history, and God. This has in turn led to two typical theological moves in the present far less prominent in the classical tradition. The first is the denial of the absoluteness and aseity of God in every respect: God's perfection and even God's necessity do not involve God's absoluteness, says Hartshorne; and in order that God be good and we be free, says Whitehead, God must be radically distinguished from the principle of ultimate reality, from the force and power of reality, that is, from what he calls "creativity." Thus the finitude of God, in the sense that God is not the *source* of finite reality in all its aspects but rather that God is only one of a number of correlated and primal ultimate "factors" constitutive of finite actuality, is now asserted by a most important school of contemporary Christian theology. Needless to say, this is new in the tradition.

Another kind of move, occasioned by the same issues but implying a quite different theological viewpoint, emphasizes the "self-limitation" of God in the creation of a contingent, relative, and dependent creature, but a creature that within limits is genuinely autonomous. Thus is this creature capable of and called to *self-constitution*, to becoming itself through its own commitments, decisions, and actions; as a consequence this creature is capable of original, novel action and so is "free" to sin and/or to accept grace, that is, free to act in ways neither determined nor predetermined by God. This "Arminian" position (which, whatever its denials, it seems to be) has been, I think, shared by most nonprocess theologians in the present century with the possible exception of Barth. Some of the most dramatic changes in the concept of God in modern times have, therefore, occurred in new interpretations of God's relation to natural evil and mortality on the one hand, and of the symbols of providence, election, predestination, grace, and eternal damnation on the other. In all these loci creaturely freedom or autonomy now plays a role much larger than before, qualifying the absolute sovereignty of the divine will and the divine power. Correspondingly the goodness of God and so God's separation from evil have been much more jealously guarded—whether this be achieved metaphysically through the concept of the finitude of God or theologically through the conception of the divine self-limitation.

Again, for the variety of reasons we have mentioned, the sense on the one hand of the reality and value of temporal passage, of change, and of the new and, on the other hand, of the reality and value of relatedness has vastly increased. To the Hellenic and Hellenistic epochs the divine was both more real and more good to the extent that it was *not* involved in change and in relatedness. In our epoch we tend to reverse this apprehension. A changeless and unrelated God probably would seem to most of us not only a compensatory chimera of the imagination, unexperienced and so unknown, but even more a notion void of all real content and value since such a deity would lack relatedness to the changing world where initially all reality and value reside. Thus the most prominent characteristic of contemporary theologies of all sorts is what may be termed their "war with the Greeks." There is hardly a conception of God from Hegel onward that is not dynamic, changing, and in some manner intrinsically related to the world of change—and almost the worst thing any school can say of its opponents is that they are in this or that regard "Greek." The instance of this dynamic view of God currently most influential is of course the Whiteheadian, where God is an example of process rather than its negation. God thus shares in the metaphysical categories of process: temporality, potentiality, change, relatedness, development, and dependence or passivity.

With quite different tactics the biblical or neoorthodox theologians have carried on *their* war with the Greeks. Although they retained the symbols of the absoluteness and aseity of God, the transcendent creator of an essentially dependent creature—so that their views were deeply differentiated from a "process" God—nevertheless, in using the personal and historical categories of biblical speech, they too produced a conception of a dynamic and related God. And like their rivals in the process school, their main conscious opposition was to "the Greek concept of God" as changeless, unrelated, aloof. Theirs then was a "God who acts in history"; who "comes" or "is coming"; who effects "mighty deeds" of revelation and redemption, and so on. All these clearly are temporal as well as personal words expressive of actions over time and within time, of relatedness, of a relative dependence ("encounter," "judge")—words implying temporality, change, passivity, and potentiality as well as "personality" in God. The neoorthodox did not draw out explicitly the ontological implications of this their central language about God. Often they left the obvious puzzles in the "dialectical" or "paradoxical" forms they thought appropriate to the divine mystery. Or, as Barth was wont to do, they simply stated that this apparent contradictoriness is precisely what is implied by the divine freedom. Nevertheless, it is clear that their view too entailed radical changes from any recognizably "orthodox" conception of God. These changes have been even more evident in the post-neoorthodox eschatological theologies in which, for some, God is so temporal that, far from representing an eternity beyond time, the divine being is now said to be only "future."

As is well known, a major theme in modern culture, practically its defining feature or essence, has been the theme of historical development or progress, a theme asserting the supreme meaningfulness of history as a whole as a steady advance toward higher and higher forms of social life. Insofar as the liberal theologies of the nineteenth and early twentieth centuries accommodated themselves to this pervasive modern theme (myth?), God was interpreted as the immanent spiritual and moral force underlying the historical development of society; the kingdom was interpreted as that social order which is history's goal; and the Christian community was viewed as having its raison d'être in the political implementation of this historical progress toward the divine kingdom of justice and love.

Amid the turmoil of twentieth-century history, this vision of a developing historical progress rapidly dissipated. The dominant theologies of the continent—Barthian, Bultmannian, Scandinavian—therefore tended to separate the Christian message of salvation and the redemptive activity of God from questions of political and historical development. In the most extreme form of this theology (e.g., Bultmann), the gospel breaks into an individual's historicity as an "eschatological event," challenging that individual's basic "world," freeing him or her from the past, and giving him or her the new prospect of an open future. Appropriate for any time or place, this message has nothing directly to do with the ups and downs of social history; coming vertically into life, it touches and heals only that which can receive it, namely, the individual spirit which can welcome it with decision, commitment, and faith. Although he remained an active socialist throughout his life, Karl Barth was interpreted theologically (rightly, I think) all during his lifetime as in *this* sense also propounding a nonsocial and nonpolitical interpretation of the gospel. Social history and "God's history" are two different, if interrelated, histories, and Christian salvation in Christ remains at best only indirectly connected with or relevant to improvements in the social order.

In the last two decades a very strong reaction in the other direction has occurred. A number of liberationist or political theologies have appeared, calling upon Christian action and Christian theology to turn again toward the wide spectrum of social history's crises and oppressions as their main if not exclusive area of concern. The new theologies stress their identity with a given oppressed community, call for revolutionary action or praxis, and recognize only theological reflection that arises out of both. Thus we have black theologies, feminist theologies, and Third World theologies. As a consequence of this identification with groups oppressed by Western social reality, they tend to make alliance with Marxist thought rather than with Western philosophy and social theory in general. And finally they see the divine action as itself adversarial to all that is the case in the sorry present; while they are also utopian, they are markedly antidevelopmental in the essential themes of their thought.

Such adversarial theologies understandably wish to deny the relation of God to all that characterized the dominant and oppressive past or present of Western history. Yet as socially centered theologies they wish also to identify God in some important sense with history. Thus for them God is neither the God of the past nor the God of the present; nor is God a God beyond time, a God vertically above or below each moment, the ground and determiner of all being. Rather, God is "eschatological," the one who is coming, the "God of the future," the one who from the future will master the present and establish the divine sovereign rule in future history. This conception of God, as one might expect, tends to puzzle theologians still mired in capitalistic and/or male society; but professorial proponents of such praxis-oriented theologies who are also still mired in high-ranking academic positions in that society (and drive a Mercedes) puzzle us even more. Nevertheless, the power with which this movement has redirected the concentration of theology back to history and forward into the future—hopefully not Heilbroner's future—has been impressive and marks this as a most creative form of contemporary theology.

The sharpest theological debates in the last decade and a half (at least outside the United States) have centered on the issues summarized here: whether theology can be carried on apart from revolutionary action; whether God has been active and sovereign in the past and the present, and will be in the future; whether the gospel is a promise of redemption for the individual soul or only for historical society; whether that promise is to be fulfilled here and in eternity or solely in a kingdom characterizing the historical, social future; and whether in Christ, God's redemptive action was once and for all accomplished and manifest (even if its effects remain fragmentary), or whether in Jesus are to be found solely promises for a future social parousia of the kingdom.

ISSUES AND PROPOSALS

In summing up, it may be helpful briefly to present the author's way of addressing some of the issues we have discussed.

Basic to a monotheistic conception of God in my view is the conviction that God is the source of the totality of being. This affirmation is fundamental both to the main thrust of scripture and to our experience of the reality, goodness, and possibility of finite life in time. It is also the inescapable precondition for any Christian understanding of our experience of estrangement or sin, for any valid Christian interpretation of history, and for any understanding of reconciliation and redemption that is in accord with scripture and experience—though these are issues far too complex to resolve here. Thus my own constructive view differentiates itself as sharply as it can from any of the "process" views of God which deny that God is the source or ground of finite reality and give to "creativity" that status of ultimacy traditionally accorded to God. On the other hand, I also disagree with those forms of "orthodoxy" which have insisted on the active omnipotence or total sovereignty of God in the coming-to-be of finite events—whether they be the events of natural process or the thoughts, decisions, and actions that characterize the events of history. As always, the central problem for the doctrine of God is how to unite intelligibly the *absoluteness* of God as the unconditioned source of our total being with the dynamic *relatedness* and the *reciprocal activity* of God as the ground, guide, dialogical partner, and redeemer of our freedom.

To the modern consciousness, reality—both personal and historical as well as natural—is in passage, deeply and inescapably temporal. It is therefore in terms of temporality or process that the world and God must be reconceived if the relatedness of God to the world as creator, preserver, judge, and redeemer is to be explicated. Radical temporality implies the *becomingness* of all things, the movement of whatever is from its former givenness to its present state—where briefly it "is" and constitutes itself in freedom—thence into new as yet unrealized possibilities. Correspondingly it implies the *vanishing* of all possibilities that are to come and all actualities that presently are into the "has-beenness" of the past. Past, present, and future unite in each creative present, but every creative present itself recedes into the relative and ineffective nonbeing of the past, making room for not-yet possibilities from the future to become actual in each subsequent present.

In such a situation of radical passage, where the not-yet future becomes real in the freedom of the present, and each present in turn vanishes into the nonbeing of the past, there is required some deeper reality that is itself not in passage—that does not vanish into the nonbeing of the past—and yet is intrinsically related to that passage. This deeper reality, experienced in the *continuities* present in changing time, in the *freedom* also present in time, and in the *novel possibilities* impinging on time, is the initial referent for the word "God." God so conceived is active in the coming-to-be of our temporal being, in its preservation over time, and in its movement through time into the future.

God is first experienced as the unconditioned ground of the movement from a vanishing past (the recent past) into the new present that constitutes our "reality." Such a movement, essential both to present reality of any sort and also to its continuity with the past (and so to substance, causality, sensing, and knowing), can be provided neither by the past itself, which is gone, nor by the new present, which is just coming to be. There must therefore be an unconditioned ground of each which does not pass away and yet which is in creative relation to the movement of temporal being.

God is also experienced as the source of our freedom in the present, as the ground of that act of self-constitution that unites the given from the past with the new actuality of the present in the light of the possibilities open to it in the future. Freedom does not ground itself; it experiences itself as *given*—something to be actualized by us but not created by us. It cannot be given to us merely from the past or merely from the future, for in relation to both we experience freedom. It too is therefore of God and can realize itself only in a dependent relation to God. God in turn is *unconditioned* in relation to finite past, present, and future, not arising out of the past or dependent and vulnerable in the present or, finally, in danger of ceasing to be in the future. Nevertheless, in relation to each mode of time God is self-limiting, making room for the finite freedom which God grounds and establishes in each present. Needless to say, the ontological distinction between God and the finite world thus established and preserved—as well as God's continual relatedness to it—is vast and, as in all traditional discourse about God, calls for an *analogical* rather than a univocal mode of speech. This also means that God is in some important sense "hidden" within temporal passage and that the divine presence is to be recognized and acknowledged more through a religious discernment than by means of objective inquiry.

Finally, God is experienced as the source or ground of new possibility and of the impingement of the future on the present. These novel possibilities are not produced out of the past, out of preceding actuality—else they could not embody the genuinely new. Nor are they produced by any creatures or set of creatures in the present—else there would be no subsequent order among the near infinity of present creatures. Rather, they are "held" in the envisionment of some unconditioned reality that spans past, present, and future and that views these possibilities *as* possible, as "not-yet" and still as relevant to and in harmony with past and present actualities. Thus God, as the ground of future possibility, is at the same time the ground of order and intelligibility, the divine principle of *logos*—a traditional symbol now reconceived in a dynamic, temporal mode. God is both *being* and *logos*, the abyss of reality as the dynamic ground of the actuality of each present and the principle of possibility and order as the ever-moving source of novelty and harmony. Although God so conceived is unconditioned, infinite, and absolute, clearly God so conceived is also self-limited, temporal (the future is also for God possibility and not actuality), changing (in relation to a self-constituting world), and reciprocal (in relation to the freedom of the creature).

God, however, is more than being and *logos*; God is also *love*. In order for there to be genuine historical possibility, more than possibility is needed. We historical creatures corrupt our possibilities in enacting them, and so we warp if we do not destroy them—and also we die. The reconciling, reuniting, and redemptive love of God is essential for the fulfillment of possibility in human life and history, and it is the reality of that love which is the essence of the Christian gospel. The recreative and reuniting power of the divine love is, like the divine being and the divine *logos*, manifest universally, appearing everywhere in history, especially in history's religions where redemptive forces are at work. For Christians, however, it has its central locus, its deepest reality and power, and its final criterion in the Christ and the community which lives in his Spirit.

This brings us to what may be the most important *new* issue confronting Christian theology at the present time: the encounter with other religious traditions. In our present situation, religious faiths, like political and economic systems, encounter one another regularly and intimately. Since this encounter of the religions, especially in the past two or three decades, has become an omnipresent reality, the relation of Christian theology to other, non-Christian modes of "theology" has emerged as a burning issue. Not only have Christianity and Christians "encountered" other religions, they have also encountered these religions as bearing *power* and as embodying vital, healing, redemptive forces providing unique illumination and grace to our ailing cultural life and our somewhat impoverished existence. No longer, therefore, is it possible for Christians to declare other faiths either devoid of truth (as did orthodoxy) or primitive or less developed steppingstones to the absoluteness of Christianity (as did the early liberals). The suggestion that within other religions the promise of grace and salvation is present and also the truth is experienced is now admitted by most and affirmed by many. But if that be so, what does it mean for the uniqueness of Christian revelation, for the finality of Christ's incarnation and atonement, for the salvation of non-Christians—and a thousand other important theological questions?

Understandably, most of the new debate on these matters has centered on the crucial questions of special revelation and Christology. And many have assumed that, were these christological doctrines to be liberalized or toned down, the issues vis-à-vis other religions would dissipate. This is, I believe, not so. Important divergences (say, with Hinduism and Buddhism) appear in connection with *every* significant theological or philosophical question, from that of the nature of reality and our knowledge of it, through the nature of human being and its "problem," to the understanding of history and final salvation. And not least of all, significant divergences appear in connection with the symbol of "God." This is not only because there are some important religions which witness to no reality equivalent to the referent of the symbol "God." It is also because whatever it is that differentiates philosophical and theological systems from one another permeates the entire system and not just some of its doctrines. A Christian theism with a minimal Christology—whether deist, unitarian, low liberal, process, or whatever—is as "Western" and Christian in its philosophical conceptuality, its thematic style and emphases, and its religious implications as a typically neoorthodox theology centered on biblical symbols and on Christology—and so just as divergent (though perhaps at different points) from a Hindu or Buddhist "theology."

In conclusion, it is safe to say that the encounter of religions with one another and their subsequent dialogues with one another will effect radical changes in the discussion of God carried on by every present form of Christian theology. To predict what new directions these changes will represent is really only to state what my own preferences are, where I think the understanding of God "ought" to go, granted this encounter. As for the direction it will in fact go, I have no insight except to suggest that, even more than in connection with the new rapport between Catholicism and Protestantism, a close encounter with the nothingness of Buddhism will effect noteworthy changes in every recognizable form of contemporary discourse about God.

SUGGESTIONS FOR FURTHER READING

Anselm. *Monologion* and *Prosologion.*
Aquinas, Thomas. *Summa Contra Gentiles.* Book 1.
———. *Summa Theologica.* Part 1, questions 1–43.
Augustine. *The City of God* and *On the Trinity.* In *Basic Writings of Saint Augustine,* vol. 2.
Barth, Karl. *Church Dogmatics.* Vol. 2/1.
———. *The Humanity of God.* Richmond: John Knox Press, 1960. Chap. 2.
Boff, Leonardo. *Trinity and Society.* Translated by Paul Burns. Maryknoll, N.Y.: Orbis Books, 1988.
Brunner, Emil. *The Christian Doctrine of God.* In *Dogmatics,* vol. 1.

Calvin, John. *Institutes of the Christian Religion.* Book 1.

Cobb, John B. *God and the World.* Philadelphia: Westminster Press, 1969.

Farley, Edward. *The Transcendence of God.* Philadelphia: Westminster Press, 1960.

Gilkey, Langdon. *Naming the Whirlwind: The Renewal of God-Language.* Indianapolis: Bobbs-Merrill, 1969.

———. *Reaping the Whirlwind: A Christian Interpretation of History.* New York: Seabury Press, 1976.

Hartshorne, Charles. *The Divine Relativity.* New Haven: Yale University Press, 1964.

Hegel, G. W. F. *Lectures on the Philosophy of Religion.* Vols. 1, 3.

Hocking, William Ernest. *The Meaning of God in Human Experience.* New Haven: Yale University Press, 1912.

Hodgson, Peter C. *God in History: Shapes of Freedom.* Nashville: Abingdon Press, 1989.

Johnson, Elizabeth. *She Who Is: The Mystery of God in Feminist Theological Discourse.* New York: Crossroad, 1992.

Jüngel, Eberhard. *God as the Mystery of the World.* Grand Rapids: Eerdmans, 1983.

Kasper, Walter. *God of Jesus Christ.* New York: Crossroad, 1984.

Kaufman, Gordon D. *In Face of Mystery.*

McFague, Sallie. *Models of God: Theology for an Ecological, Nuclear Age.* Philadelphia: Fortress Press, 1987.

———. *The Body of God: An Ecological Theology.* Minneapolis: Fortress Press, 1993.

Marion, Jean-Luc. *God Without Being: hors-texte.* Translated by Thomas A. Carlson. Chicago: University of Chicago Press, 1991.

Niebuhr, H. Richard. *Radical Monotheism and Western Culture.* New York: Harper & Row, 1956.

Ogden, Schubert. *The Reality of God and Other Essays.* New York: Harper & Row, 1966.

Origen. *On First Principles.* Esp. Book 1.

Pannenberg, Wolfhart. *Systematic Theology.* Vol. 1.

———. *Theology and the Kingdom of God.* Philadelphia: Westminster Press, 1969.

Rahner, Kar. *Foundations of Christian Faith.* Chaps. 2, 4, 5.

———. *The Trinity.* New York: Herder & Herder, 1970.

Schleiermacher, Friedrich. *The Christian Faith.* Pp. 194–232, 325–54, 723–51.

Tertullian. *Against Hermogenes.* ANF 3.

Tillich, Paul. *Systematic Theology.* Vol. 1.

Whitehead, Alfred North. *Process and Reality.* New York: Macmillan Co., 1929.

———. *Religion in the Making.* New York: Macmillan Co., 1926.

4. REVELATION

WHERE WE ARE

Traditionally when Christians have attempted to explain what they know about God and how they have access to that knowledge, they have appealed to something called "revelation." In most versions of Christianity, revelation has served as the epistemological basis for theology; that is, an appeal often has been made to revelation in order to account for knowledge of God. Today, however, it is no longer clear what revelation means or how it provides knowledge of God. Revelation is sometimes understood to refer to dramatic moments, such as Paul's experience on the road to Damascus or highly emotional events of the sort that take place at revivals. While these interpretations of revelation are not uncommon, they are unfortunate because they obscure what revelation traditionally has meant and the important role it has played in Christian faith and theology. Furthermore, these misinterpretations of revelation are symptomatic of much deeper problems besetting any attempt to reinterpret revelation in the contemporary world.

Revelation has generally been understood to be correlative with faith. Christians feel compelled to talk about faith in terms of "revelation" because they believe that faith is not the result of human inquiry or discovery. Faith does not discover its object; it is, on the contrary, constituted by it. Christian faith is human response to what has been unveiled or disclosed by faith's object. The unveiling or disclosure is what theology refers to as "revelation."

Three aspects of this broad interpretation of revelation are worth noting. First, revelation means an unveiling or, to use a more contemporary idiom, a "disclosure." When revelation takes place a veil is dropped, and that which had been masked or hidden from view is disclosed. Second, the event in which this unveiling occurs cannot be initiated by human activity. The initiator of the event is not the individual who witnesses the disclosure but the agent disclosed or

114

unveiled in the event. The very use of the words "unveiledness" and "disclosure" suggests that what makes itself known in a revelatory event is the stuff of mystery. Revelation yields not the solution to a problem, the answer to a difficult question, but the unveiling of a mystery. Third, although faith is a human act, revelation is not. Because revelation refers to an event in which what is made known exceeds the grasp of human inquiry, the event is attributed to God's grace. Whatever else the doctrine of revelation is about, it is a statement about the grace of God. Revelation is not at the disposal of human inquiry and control, and consequently it becomes an event only by means of grace.

While most interpretations of revelation share at least some of these formal features, there are also important differences between the classical descriptions of revelation and various contemporary forms of the doctrine. These differences are so severe that in many respects contemporary interpretations of revelation bear only a formal resemblance to their classical predecessors, and sometimes not even that. One reason for the sharp differences between classical and contemporary interpretations of revelation and for the present disarray in contemporary theology is that revelation, the traditional foundation for knowledge of God, has become problematic; it is no longer clear what revelation means and whether revelation provides theology with an adequate basis for its claims about God. Why this alteration in the interpretation of revelation has taken place and what it implies about the future of theology are the major concerns of this essay.

THE DOCTRINE IN ITS CLASSIC FORMULATION

There is no "doctrine" of revelation as such in the Bible, and many of the problems addressed by recent interpretations of revelation were simply unknown to the writers of scripture. Indeed, there is considerable evidence for one biblical scholar's argument that for the writers of Hebrew scripture, "apart from some quite limited concessions, there is no stage at which God is not known."[1] The writers of Hebrew scripture do not offer arguments for the existence of God and do not discuss the plausibility of claims about God in relation to competing alternatives, whether those of natural science or the human sciences. The Bible simply assumes knowledge of God. The issues that have

1. James Barr, *Old and New in Interpretation*, p. 89.

come to constitute the "problem" of revelation—the relation of reason to revelation, the limits of reason, and the historicity of human understanding—are not issues in scripture. That does not mean, however, that the Bible is not used as a resource in later discussions of revelation. As we shall see, both classical and contemporary discussions of revelation appeal to themes in scripture as warrants for their interpretations.

A Morphology of Revelation

Although in the first seventeen centuries of the church's history theological reflection on revelation assumed various forms, it is still possible to identify certain formal features that characterize most interpretations of the doctrine. Usually revelation is interpreted as having both an objective and a subjective dimension. The objective dimension refers to *what* is revealed, while the subjective dimension refers to *how* revelation is received. The precise way in which revelation is interpreted often depends on which of these dimensions is given primary emphasis.

The objective dimension of revelation (what is revealed) may be construed in various ways. It may be understood to be a proposition, an infallible teaching of scripture, the gospel or word of God, God's will toward the world, the personal being of God, or the moral order. These different interpretations of what is revealed yield distinctive doctrines of revelation and, not surprisingly, different interpretations of Christian faith. If the object of revelation is understood to be the word of God in the person of Jesus Christ, faith will take a different form than if the object of revelation is understood to be a proposition or doctrine, regardless of where it is found (in scripture or in tradition). Some versions of the former interpretation tend to emphasize the effect of revelation—the Spirit's gift of saving faith—while some versions of the latter seek a more objective basis for faith in an inspired scripture or church.

In addition to the objectivity of revelation, there is also the subjective dimension (how revelation is received). Apart from this subjective dimension, what is revealed would remain unrelated to those who witness it. The subjective dimension refers to the appropriation of what is objectively revealed. In most of the classical interpretations of revelation this subjective dimension is described as some form of illumination. God illumines the mind so that it can see what it cannot see by means of reason alone. In its typical Protestant form the subjective dimension refers to the inward testimony of the Holy Spirit whereby the external word of God becomes an inward word in the heart of the believer due to the activity of the Spirit.

Some of the significant differences among various interpretations of revelation in both classical and contemporary theology can be understood in terms of the relation between the objective and subjective dimensions of revelation. The two extremes on the theological spectrum are, on the one hand, a highly subjective interpretation, such as is found in some forms of mysticism, in which revelation has no mediated forms or concepts and refers only to immediate experience; and, at the other end of the spectrum, a strongly objective interpretation, such as is found in some forms of sacramental theology and fundamentalism, in which the objective content of revelation can be established apart from its representational imagery or subjective appropriation.

Most interpretations of revelation can be found somewhere between these two extremes. Some interpretations of revelation, however, stress the objective side of revelation to such a degree that the subjective side is minimized or ignored. If the object of revelation is found in scripture or the teaching of the church, then the subjective reality of revelation may be treated merely as a means for explaining the exalted status of the church's scripture or tradition. On the other hand, if undue emphasis is given to the subjective dimension, the noetic content of revelation may become obscure or ambiguous to the point of meaninglessness.

These differences will become clearer as we sketch two models of revelation in classical theology: revelation as illumination of the intellect, and revelation as encounter with the Word and Spirit of God. In both these models, we will discover some interpretations that lean in the direction of the objective and others that lean in the direction of the subjective.

Revelation as Illumination

Because of the Christian mission to the Gentiles, Christian apologists in the second century were drawn into conversation with Hellenistic culture. Like many theologians after him, Justin Martyr, the premier apologist of the period, appealed to the prologue of John's Gospel and its description of Jesus Christ as the *logos* or the Word of

God made flesh for a common ground with Hellenism, especially Platonism and Stoicism. In his *Second Apology*, Justin argued the superiority of Jesus' teaching to that of Socrates and all other human wisdom on the basis that Jesus alone was the entire Word of God. Justin did not argue that the Word of God could be found only in Christ. On the contrary, he believed that the teaching of Plato, along with other Greek writers, was not different from that of Jesus but only a dim intimation of him who was the Word incarnate. The *logos*, as he conceived it, is implanted in all people, but although it can be found in various places, it is fully embodied only in one place or person—in Christ, who in turn "illumines" all others.

Justin was only one of many theologians who have used the prologue to John's Gospel as a warrant for interpreting revelation as divine illumination. The claim that it is God who enables the believer to come to a knowledge of deity was a major theme in the theologies of Augustine, Bonaventure, and Thomas Aquinas. In his commentary on the Gospel of John, for instance, Augustine sounded a theme that is to be found throughout his theological writings: the identification of Jesus Christ as the light which illumines the darkness of the human intellect and overcomes the blindness created by human sin. "We, too, have been born blind of Adam, and have need of him [Christ] to enlighten us."[2] Augustine's description of illumination is strikingly similar to Plato's comparison of the idea of the good with the sun, except that for Augustine the Word of God is not only that which illumines the darkness of the intellect, evokes faith, and makes understanding possible, but also that which is itself illumined and made known to the believer. In order to make this point, Augustine drew a distinction between the Word's illumination of the intellect and what the intellect knows when it is illumined. In his treatise *On the Trinity* he maintained that the light which illumines the intellect is not the intellect itself, but the intellect cannot know what is true apart from this illumination. What remained unclear in Augustine's theology was the precise nature of this "light" and its relation to the intellect.

This problem received considerable clarification in the theology of Aquinas in the thirteenth century. Aquinas modified and extended Augustine's description of the divine illumination of the intellect. He

---

2. Augustine, "Homilies on the Gospel of John," *NPNF*[1] 7:203.

began by describing the human intellect in terms of two powers: the passive intellect and the agent intellect. The latter, he argued, has its origin in the divine light but is not the divine light itself. In order for human beings to attain ultimate happiness—which Aquinas understood to be the supernatural vision of God—they must first be taught by God, as pupils are taught by their master. Faith, for Aquinas, was an act of assent by the intellect to those things "taught" or revealed by God. But the intellect cannot even assent to what has been revealed unless it is illumined inwardly by God's grace. When grace makes faith possible, the object of faith is that set of truths taught in scripture and the tradition of the church.

What Aquinas achieved was a synthesis between reason and revelation in which the two were understood to be distinct but complementary realms of understanding. While Augustine described the relation between reason (or intellect) and revelation in such a way that it was not clear where the one began and the other ended, Aquinas clearly separated them. What the intellect knows on the basis of sense experience is not contradicted by what is revealed to faith, though it is also the case that the intellect can never know God unless it is illumined by God's grace. Unfortunately Aquinas's carefully constructed synthesis did not long endure. John Duns Scotus and William of Ockham firmly separated reason and revelation, and by the middle of the fourteenth century the synthesis of reason and revelation had been sundered. In some quarters an interpretation of revelation as divine illumination survived, but that interpretation no longer dominated theological reflection. One form of the illumination theory which did continue to exert influence is that represented by medieval mysticism, a tradition that extends from the Pseudo-Dionysius in the fifth century to such fourteenth-century figures as Meister Eckhart and John Gerson. For many of the mystics there is something in the human soul with which God unites in an ineffable manner. As a result of this "mystical union," the human soul is joined directly to God and radically transformed thereby.

Revelation by Word and Spirit

During the Reformation, subtle but significant shifts took place in the interpretation of revelation. Both Martin Luther and John Calvin took the position that there is knowledge of God apart from revelation but that this knowledge is of little or no consequence. The general knowledge of God derived from the created order is for all practical purposes useless. What is decisive is knowledge of God's will toward the world, and that cannot be known apart from Jesus Christ.

For Luther the Word of God is Jesus Christ, but we have access to that Word only in the words of proclamation and scripture. Luther does not simply identify the Word of God with the external words of proclamation and scripture, since these words only become God's Word (that is, become revelatory) when the Holy Spirit makes Christ present in them. The Word of God is both what is revealed to faith and what does the revealing, but the Word can never be separated from the Spirit, since it is the Spirit who enables the external words to become internal words.

The gospel is the living Word of God, Jesus Christ, and it is this Word which is the sole content, center, and unity of scripture. This Word is the criterion for determining what is law and what is gospel in scripture, but this external clarity cannot be separated from scripture's internal clarity, which is the illumining work of the Spirit "required for the understanding of scripture, both as a whole and in any part of it."[3]

Like those theologians who advocated an illumination model of revelation, Luther also found considerable warrant in the Gospel of John for his interpretation of revelation in terms of Word and Spirit. It was not the Gospel of John, however, but the Pauline epistles, especially Romans and Galatians, which provided Luther his primary referent in scripture for his interpretation of revelation. The Pauline distinction between the "righteousness of faith" and the "righteousness of the law" enabled Luther to argue that the center of scripture and the true meaning of revelation is the *gospel* of Jesus Christ, as constituted by God's Word and Spirit, and everything else must be understood in relation to that gospel.

John Calvin adopts a model of revelation that is similar to Luther's. Because human vision has been blinded by sin and cannot perceive God in the work of creation, Calvin describes scripture as the spectacles through which God may be seen in the world. Apart from scripture there is no proper knowledge of God, and there can be no sound doctrine in theology unless the theologian becomes a pupil of

3. Martin Luther, "On the Bondage of the Will," *LCC* 17:112.

scripture. There is little difference between Luther and Calvin on the question of the Word's relation to Spirit. The words of scripture remain external to the believer and will not become revelatory and salvific unless they receive the inward testimony of the Spirit. It is this inward testimony of the Spirit that confirms the authority of scripture.

Where Luther and Calvin differ is in their interpretation of the relation between scripture and the Word of God. For Luther, as we have seen, Jesus Christ is the center of scripture, and scripture is gospel only insofar as it points to him. Although Calvin's theology seems to have the same center as Luther's—the Word of God in Jesus Christ—at times the object of faith (what is revealed) seems to be the formal authority of scripture rather than scripture's witness to Jesus Christ. Where Luther is able to make emphatic judgments about which parts of scripture do and do not preach Jesus Christ (the Letter of James, for example, does not do so to the extent that the Letter to the Romans does), Calvin is much more likely to engage in extensive attempts at harmonization and accommodation.

The left wing of the Reformation produced such figures as Carlstadt, Kaspar Schwenkfeld, and Thomas Müntzer, who offered interpretations of revelation which differed significantly from those of the magisterial reformers. Revelation for these thinkers was the revelation of the Word in the heart of the believer. Müntzer, for example, emphasized the importance of the inner word and the work of the Spirit almost to the point of denying the positive function of scripture and the external word. In the Word and Spirit model of revelation, the radical reformers play a role not unlike that of the medieval mystics in relation to the illumination model. Both represent a movement in the direction of a total concentration on the subjective dimension of revelation.

In the late sixteenth and early seventeenth centuries both models of revelation—illumination and Word and Spirit—were given decidedly objectivist interpretations. In 1546 the Roman Catholic Church, gathered at the Council of Trent, declared that saving truth and moral discipline are contained both in the written books of scripture and in the unwritten traditions given to the apostles from the mouth of Christ and preserved in the teaching of the church. Furthermore, the council affirmed that no one should pretend to interpret scripture contrary to the church. On the Protestant side, the Westminster Confession of 1647 declared that God was the author of scripture and that everything necessary for faith and life could be found in scripture or deduced from it. In both cases, revelation referred to a series of propositions which were understood to be objectively true because they were taught by a divinely inspired church or could be found in a book authored by God.

Although there are important differences between these two models of revelation, there are also some important similarities, not the least of which is that both models describe the content of revelation as truths about God, who is presumed to transcend the empirical world and be externally related to it. In the course of their development, both the illumination model and the Word and Spirit model made use of different philosophical schemes, yet what was claimed to be revealed—truths about God—reflected a common metaphysical view of God. God stands outside the created order, which depends on God for its order and being. Statements about God, however, have the same cognitive status as human statements about other empirical realities. When the Enlightenment challenged this metaphysical description of God's relation to the world and this epistemological account of the cognitive status of statements about God, both classical models of revelation were shaken at their foundations. It was this challenge from the Enlightenment that brought about the collapse of the classical models of revelation and that constitutes the continuing "problematic" for contemporary interpretations of revelation.

CHALLENGES AND CONTRIBUTIONS OF MODERN CONSCIOUSNESS

The Enlightenment's Attack on Revelation

The period from the seventeenth through the nineteenth centuries marks a watershed in the interpretation of revelation. During this period several developments occurred to create an intellectual climate in which it became increasingly difficult to defend the classical models of revelation. Francis Bacon's discovery of "the new science," Isaac Newton's formulation of a mathematical physics in which nature is conceived of as a rational and unified order, the emergence of reason as the primary authority for the interpretation of experience, the distrust of tradition and superstition—all these created an environment in which classical theology found itself under attack and on the defensive against the dominant intellectual movements of the day. Three developments in this period were especially important for subsequent discussions of revelation: the emphasis given to human reason as the chief interpreter of reality and the final arbiter of conflicting claims; the denial that revealed truths about God (or, for that matter, any statements about God) bear a necessary relation to empirical reality; and the discovery of the historical character of human reason and understanding.

The content of the classic models of revelation was confined to revealed truths about God. Although these objective truths could not be known by a human intellect marred by sin, they could be known through the work of the Spirit in illumination or in scripture. In these classic models the primary criterion for the interpretation of experience and reality was revealed truth. In the Enlightenment, however, the focus shifted dramatically. No longer were revealed truths the final arbiter; now human reason became the final court of appeal for the interpretation of reality. Even though God remained the primary substance in Descartes's metaphysics, Cartesian method began with a search for clear and distinct ideas, a search which led Descartes to the *cogito*—the human being's existence as a thinking being—as the primary datum for reflection. Descartes's significance is not tied to the success of his method or his philosophical proposals; rather, his philosophy represents a bench mark in human thought. Human reason rather than tradition or established authority is now to be seen as the ultimate measure of truth.

One can trace the development of the autonomy of human reason during the period of the Enlightenment. At the beginning of this period, John Locke in his *Essay Concerning Human Understanding* drew a distinction between those truths that are according to reason, above reason, and contrary to reason. Christian faith, he argued, is "reasonable" in that its propositions are either according to reason (for instance, that God exists) or above reason (the resurrection of the dead), but not contrary to reason. Locke, like René Descartes, argued the case for the "reasonableness" of Christian faith, but the argument itself is not as important as the fact that "reasonableness" had become the measure of truth.

Locke's distinction between reason and revelation was vigorously rejected by the deists in England (John Toland, Anthony Collins, and Matthew Tindal) and by the neologians in Germany (J. J. Spalding, J. S. Semler, and A. F. W. Sachs). For many of the deists there was nothing in "revealed religion" that could not be found in a "natural religion" cast in moral categories. Indeed, the gospel or revealed truth is nothing but a "republication" of what can be found in natural religion. While Locke still worked with a model in which revelation and reason were complementary, the deists dismissed the category of revelation altogether as superfluous to the meaning of religion. By making moral categories rather than revelation the basis for religion—a common motif in "Enlightenment religion"—the deists planted the seeds for a reinterpretation of religion and Christian faith which has continued to bear fruit in nineteenth-century Protestant liberalism and in some forms of contemporary theology.

While the deists' attack on revealed religion represented a major development in the Enlightenment, deism did not become the universally accepted religion of the age as its proponents thought it would; and the reason it did not points to a second feature of the Enlightenment's critique of revelation—the denial that revealed truths about God bear any necessary relation to empirical reality. Although the deists argued that revelation was a superfluous category, they still understood natural religion to include a creator God about whom certain truths could be affirmed. The deists, like the classical theologians who preceded them, presupposed a metaphysical structure in which God was externally related to the world. Truths asserted about God had the same cognitive status as truths asserted about other beings in the world. What makes the philosophical programs of David Hume and Immanuel Kant of such overwhelming importance is that they attacked the metaphysical assumptions which undergirded both the classic doctrine of revelation and the deists' alternative of natural religion, thus raising profound questions about the cognitive status of *all* statements about God.

In his investigation of the nature of causality, Hume argued that there is no necessary relation between cause and effect other than the habit or custom of association; therefore, any concept of causality, including that of a first or primary cause such as God, is at best a hypothesis which cannot be demonstrated. Of course, if God is at best a hypothesis, then statements about God do not have the same cognitive status as statements about empirical facts, and a distinction must be drawn between statements that purport to be revealed truths about God and those that can be demonstrated empirically. Statements about God which claim some necessary relation to empirical fact invite, on this view, a skeptical response.

While Kant's analysis of the nature of reason and the possibility of metaphysics did not lead him to Hume's extreme skepticism, Kant did conclude that human reason cannot claim to know things as they are in themselves, only as they appear to reason. Furthermore, he argued that although reason makes use of certain ideas, what Kant called "transcendental ideas" (including the transcendental ideal— God as absolute perfection), these ideas are neither innate nor derived empirically. They enable reason to discern a larger pattern of meaning in experience, but the ideas themselves have no necessary relation to empirical objects. Transcendental ideas, including the idea of God, serve an important "regulative" function, but they do not constitute objects, nor can it be demonstrated that they correspond to anything in the empirical world. Kant did not deny the possibility of revelation, but he did insist that reason could never affirm the actuality of revelation and that "all attempts to employ reason in theology in any merely speculative manner are altogether fruitless." That did not mean that nothing could be said about God. Rather, he maintained that "the only theology of reason which is possible is that which is based upon moral laws or seeks guidance from them."[4]

The consequences of Kant's philosophical program for classical theology and for the natural religion of the Enlightenment were nothing less than revolutionary. If the existence of God could not be demonstrated, and if statements about God (derived either from reason or from supernatural revelation) bore no relation to any empirical object, then the rug had been pulled out from under theology. The metaphysical structure on which classic models of revelation had been erected was thereby destroyed, and an apparently unbridgeable chasm was created between theology and the world accessible to reason.

---

4. Immanuel Kant, *Critique of Pure Reason*, p. 528.

Finally, the Enlightenment witnessed the emergence of history as a critical science and the first signs of what in the nineteenth century would become a challenge to theology every bit as serious as that posed by Hume and Kant. The classic models of revelation presuppose a metaphysics blissfully unaware of the problem which historical relativity poses for religious claims to universality. In the eighteenth century, however, Gotthold Lessing raised precisely this issue in his now famous dictum: "The accidental truths of history can never become the proof of the necessary truths of reason."[5] There is an "ugly broad ditch" between the two which, he concluded, could not be bridged. Since the revealed truths of classical theology refer to God's activity in historical events, this separation of historical event from universal truth threatened the central convictions of Christian faith. The full import of the separation was, however, not comprehended until a century later, when Ernst Troeltsch posed the problem in its most acute form.[6] Troeltsch argued that all assertions which appeal to historical events are at best probable, and that historical inquiry is predicated on the assumption that every event is analogous to and correlative with other events, else the historian would have no basis for judgment or interpretation. From this depiction of the texture of historical events, it followed that all interpretations of events, including those of Christian faith, are relative to the location and perspective of the interpreter and cannot serve as the basis for claims of universality and uniqueness. This argument clearly undermined traditional Christian claims, based on revelation, that Christianity was the only true or absolute religion.

The combined effects of these three developments—the authority given to reason, the redefinition of the limits of reason, and the recognition of the historicity of knowledge and understanding—made it difficult, if not impossible, for any theologian sensitive to the climate of the day to continue to advocate a theology grounded on classic models of revelation. It is not surprising, therefore, that the overarching concern of theologians in the nineteenth century was to establish a new foundation for Christian theology.

---

5. Gotthold Lessing, "On the Proof of the Spirit and of Power," in *Lessing's Theological Writings*, p. 53.

6. For Troeltsch's significance for the doctrine of revelation see the essay by Hans W. Frei, "Niebuhr's Theological Background," in *Faith and Ethics*, pp. 9–64.

Nineteenth-century Responses
to the Enlightenment

In the nineteenth century, several reinterpretations of revelation were offered in response to the impasse created by the Enlightenment. Two of them appeared in the first third of the century and overshadowed subsequent discussions of revelation. The first was the theology of Friedrich Schleiermacher, who argued in *The Christian Faith* that doctrines are reflections of the piety that emerges from the experience of redemption in the Christian community. Christian piety articulates the experience of redemption as it is lived in the church and attributed to Jesus Christ, the founder of the community. By making the experience of redemption the basis for theological reflection, Schleiermacher proposed a new foundation and method for the critical explication of Christian faith. Neither knowing nor doing but that form of feeling Christians refer to as "redemption" became the basis for theology. Schleiermacher's turn to the experience of redemption created a new theological paradigm which escaped the Kantian critique of classical metaphysics and theology and also suggested a new interpretation of the meaning of revelation.

In the introduction to his major theological work, Schleiermacher denied that revelation has primarily to do with intellectual assent to revealed truths, since that would imply that revelation can be limited to the cognitive dimension of human existence. He readily acknowledged that revelation leads to the formulation of doctrines; nevertheless, he contended that revelation refers primarily not to the apprehension of propositions but to "the *originality* of the fact which lies at the foundation of a religious communion." This original fact shapes the life of the community and "cannot itself be explained by the historical chain which precedes it."⁻ In the Christian community, of course, this original fact is Jesus Christ and the redemption accomplished by him. This original fact, which is the foundation of the community's life, cannot be explained wholly in terms of the natural forces and causes that precede it. Appeal must therefore be made to divine causality as its ultimate source. It is the necessity of this appeal to divine causality in order to account for the originality of Jesus

7. Friedrich Schleiermacher, *The Christian Faith*, p. 50 (sec. 10).

Christ that compels Schleiermacher to use the category of revelation. What is revealed is not so much truths about God as the reality of redemption, which in turn becomes the basis for indirect discourse about God. For Schleiermacher, God cannot be known directly. Redemption, however, does provide a legitimate basis for language and knowledge about God. What is known as a consequence of redemption is that God's nature is love.

The second major proposal for the reinterpretation of revelation came from G. W. F. Hegel, who used the term "revelation" in a twofold sense to describe Christianity as "the absolute religion." On the one hand, Christianity is revelatory *(offenbar)* because it is the religious representation of the very nature of God or Spirit. What is revealed is that Spirit makes itself known in a process whereby it freely becomes an object for itself and is eventually reconciled with itself at that point at which it is also most alienated from itself. The Christian symbols of incarnation and crucifixion are the religious representation of the nature of Spirit as self-revealing. On the other hand, Christianity is also a revealed *(geoffenbart)* religion because it is what Hegel called a "positive" religion, that is, it refers to a particular, historical religious community.

The category of revelation allowed Hegel to capture both dimensions of Spirit and to describe Spirit from two different but interrelated perspectives. His early work, *The Phenomenology of Spirit*, describes Spirit's self-revealing movement without any necessary reference to particular historical events. In his later *Lectures on the Philosophy of Religion*, however, he attempts to show a necessary relation between the self-revealing nature of Spirit and the historical reality and religious imagery of Christianity. Hegel's description of Spirit allows no disjunction between reason and revelation. There is not a natural world susceptible to rational inquiry and some other world which can be known only by revealed truths. Spirit is internally related to the world and is its essential meaning. The natural order (including nature and history) is the self-manifestation of Spirit. As Hegel uses the term, revelation reflects both the sense in which Spirit is self-disclosing and the sense in which the world and its history are the manifestation of that self-disclosure.

The reinterpretations of revelation by Schleiermacher and Hegel were not the only proposals that appeared in the nineteenth century.

The last third of the century witnessed the emergence of that movement commonly referred to as Protestant liberalism. Theologians such as Albrecht Ritschl and Adolf Harnack sought to interpret Christian faith so that it would be intelligible to a culture that had accepted the Enlightenment's attack on classical metaphysics and that had consequently found classic Christian affirmations meaningless or irrelevant. Ritschl and Harnack accepted Kant's revision of the limits of reason and his distinction between pure and practical reason. Ritschl argued that there is a fundamental difference yet also an interdependence between judgments of fact and judgments of value. Furthermore, he attempted to correlate historical inquiry about the Jesus of the New Testament with the faith of the Christian community. The result was an interpretation of Christian faith which eschewed classical metaphysics and emphasized instead the doctrines of justification and reconciliation and a moral interpretation of the biblical symbol of the kingdom of God. Neither Ritschl nor Harnack simply reduced Christian faith to morality, but they did understand the kingdom of God to be an ethical ideal. For some of the theologians in the generation that followed Ritschl and Harnack, the interpretation of the kingdom of God as an ethical ideal raised serious and far-reaching questions. Had a cultural and philosophical (in this case Kantian) ethic become normative for the interpretation of Christian faith? If so, what had become of the Christian claim that the God known in Christian faith transcends every cultural and philosophical system—and not only transcends it but stands in judgment of it?

Contemporary Discussions of Revelation

With the collapse of nineteenth-century liberalism around the time of World War I, the doctrine of revelation again became a major topic for theological discussion. Theologians in the postwar period attempted to reconstruct theology on grounds they considered more secure than those they inherited from Schleiermacher, Hegel, Ritschl, and Harnack, and they turned largely to revelation as providing those grounds. Thus, much of the history of twentieth-century theology could be summarized by examining the various attempts to interpret Christian faith by some version of the doctrine of revelation. Such a summary would be difficult to execute because the discussion of revelation in twentieth-century theology is so diverse and complex that it does not readily lend itself to capsule formulas. It is possible, however, to identify some of the major themes in the discussion: revelation as God's self-disclosure, revelation and human existence, and revelation and the meaning of history.

Revelation as God's Self-disclosure

As a corrective to what they understood to be an undue emphasis on human subjectivity by theological liberalism, those theologians sometimes grouped together under the label of "neoorthodoxy," but more appropriately classified as neo-Reformation, stressed the objectivity of Christian faith. For Karl Barth and Emil Brunner, in particular, the object of Christian faith is God's self-disclosure in Jesus Christ. In Barth's *Church Dogmatics* the objective reality of revelation is always given precedence over any discussion of its subjective possibility, and the objective reality that is the basis of Christian faith is God's self-disclosure as Word. By the Word of God, Barth means that event in which God speaks, which is none other than Jesus Christ.

Neo-Reformation theologians did not attempt to return to a pre-Enlightenment interpretation of revelation. Barth, for example, responded to the "problematic" of the Enlightenment by making the category of the Word of God the foundation for theology. Theology cannot speak directly of God, but Jesus Christ as God's Word becomes the basis for Christian knowledge and language about God. God's Word, for Barth, is God's activity of self-revelation. Like Luther, Barth understood revelation to be tied to the category of Word, and like Hegel he claimed that what is revealed in God's Word is God's "name," or identity, as Father, Son, and Holy Spirit (which is to say, as revealer, revelation, and revealedness). Consequently, the prolegomenon to Barth's *Church Dogmatics* consists of the doctrine of revelation and its correlate, the doctrine of the Trinity.

The Word of God, for Barth, has three forms. The first and primary form of the Word is the historical event of the incarnation. First and foremost, revelation means "the Word became flesh." God's Word cannot be separated from Jesus Christ and the reconciliation that becomes a reality in him. The second and third forms of the Word are those events in which God's Word (which is an unmediated reality in the incarnation) becomes a mediated reality in the human words of scripture and proclamation (preaching and the sacraments). God's Word may appear in the midst of human words, making those human words an occasion for God's self-revelation. When this event takes place, human words are exalted and transformed because God speaks through them.

Barth developed the doctrine of revelation in such a manner that he avoided what has become a major issue for contemporary theology—hermeneutics (the task of interpreting and understanding artifacts and statements which come to the interpreter from a different culture or period of history). In the manner of the Reformers, Barth appealed to the Spirit as a sufficient explanation of how the event of the incarnation becomes a present reality in the life of the church. That response has not been considered adequate by most contemporary theologians who understand the problems of hermeneutics and historical relativity to be serious issues which cannot be resolved simply by the invocation of the Spirit.

Revelation and Human Existence

In the first half of the twentieth century, Rudolf Bultmann's theology represented the most important alternative to Barth's. There were some striking similarities between Barth and Bultmann despite the differences that separated them. Both understood revelation to be the foundation for theology, and both linked revelation to a christological interpretation of the Word of God. Revelation, for Bultmann, was not simply the communication of knowledge, but also an event or occurrence in which a person is addressed by the Christian kerygma and summoned to respond in obedience, which for the Christian constitutes authentic freedom. The alternative is to respond in sin, which is the boasting and self-confidence of inauthentic existence.[8] The event character of revelation was particularly important to Bultmann, and it is one reason he insisted that revelation takes place in preaching, in that event in which a person is addressed by God's Word.

Although Bultmann, like Barth, links revelation to the Word of God, the primary emphasis in Bultmann's discussion is the faith which revelation evokes rather than what is revealed. Indeed, there is

8. Rudolf Bultmann, "The Concept of Revelation in the New Testament," in *Existence and Faith*, pp. 58–91.

some ambiguity in Bultmann's theology with regard to the precise reference of both Word of God and the kerygma. At times they appear to be identified with specific biblical texts, but elsewhere they seem to have a highly formal character with uncertain content. Because he believed that the content of revelation is not God or even knowledge about God but the event of revelation—the event of address and response in which human existence is constituted in its relation to God—Bultmann argued that in order to speak of God one must first examine human existence. On this issue there is clearly a close relation between Bultmann and Schleiermacher with his claim that theology is based on the experience of redemption.

Bultmann's theological program set the stage for a new approach to the doctrine of revelation—one that attempts to identify what it is in human existence that makes revelation possible if not actual. This approach has taken various paths and has come to be known as "foundational" or "fundamental" theology. In most of its forms, fundamental theology searches for that basis in human being which prompts claims about transcendence and the experience of grace. Different philosophical resources have been appropriated in order to locate the possibility and meaning of revelation in human existence. In several cases, such as Langdon Gilkey's *Naming the Whirlwind* and Ray Hart's *Unfinished Man and the Imagination*, contemporary phenomenology has been used to uncover the foundation of revelation in human existence.

Some of the most impressive attempts to use contemporary existentialism and phenomenology to determine the conditions that make possible Christian language about revelation have come from Roman Catholic theologians such as Karl Rahner and Bernard Lonergan. Rahner's *Hearers of the Word* offers a description of revelation in the context of traditional Roman Catholic theology (that is, theology congruent with Thomism), but it does so by employing an "existential" analysis of human being derived from Martin Heidegger and a "transcendental method" derived from Kant. Rahner's use of transcendental method is indicative of the acceptance by most contemporary theologians of Kant's view that God is not an empirical object about whom we can speak directly. Fundamental theology begins with humankind and its constitutive experiences and asks the transcendental question: What must be the case in order for human experience to take the form it does? The essence of humankind, according to Rahner, is spirit, the "openness" of humanity to being itself. It is this openness to being which is the basis for the possibility, if not the actuality, of revelation. God's Word encounters human beings in the midst of their transcendence (their openness to being) and their historicity.

Revelation and History

Christian theologians have often appealed to history as a demonstration or illustration of the reality of revelation. Irenaeus' *Against Heresies* and Augustine's *City of God* are classic attempts to construct a theology of history. In the nineteenth century, Hegel and some of his interpreters, such as J. C. K. von Hofmann, also attempted to correlate revelation with history. And in the twentieth century, biblical theologians such as G. Ernest Wright and Oscar Cullmann have propounded a concept of "salvation history" based on the distinction between secular and sacred history. According to Cullmann, the Bible contains a history that is something more than a series of separate stories, a history of God's redemptive activity in the world; at the center or midpoint of this history is Jesus Christ, who discloses the final meaning of both sacred history and secular history.

One of the most important attempts to develop the doctrine of revelation in relation to the category of history in this century has been H. Richard Niebuhr's *The Meaning of Revelation*. Torn between Troeltsch's discovery of the relativity of all human knowledge and a neo-Reformation understanding of revelation as God's self-disclosure in history, Niebuhr reconstructed the doctrine of revelation by means of a distinction between external (or objective) history and internal (or subjective) history. External history is concerned with an impersonal account of events, a quantitative concept of value, a serial interpretation of time, and an understanding of community as a set of objective forces. Internal history, on the other hand, is concerned with the personal disclosure of subjects, a qualitative concept of value, history as remembered time, and community as a collection of selves. Revelation, then, belongs to internal history; it is that part of a person's or a community's internal history "which illumines the rest of it and which is itself intelligible."[9] Although Niebuhr's description of revelation avoids some of the problems of "salvation history," he does

9. H. Richard Niebuhr, *The Meaning of Revelation*, p. 68.

not provide a convincing account of how events in external history become part of a person's internal history.

Recently some systematic theologians have turned their attention from the notion of a special or sacred history to the category of history itself or universal history as the proper sphere for understanding revelation. Although this turn to universal history conjures up images of Hegel, the move also has been tempered by a heavy dose of eschatology. For Wolfhart Pannenberg and Jürgen Moltmann the category of eschatology is an essential part of the structure of Christian faith and should play a major role in any discussion of revelation. Pannenberg has argued that neo-Reformation descriptions of revelation (particularly Barth's) do not cohere with scripture and are closer to Gnosticism than to Christian faith. The claim that revelation refers to God's full self-disclosure, he argues, has little if any warrant in scripture. God's "self" is revealed never fully and directly but only indirectly in the fate of Jesus of Nazareth. The full and direct revelation of God is eschatological and can be understood only in terms of history as a whole or universal history. For Moltmann as well, revelation is based on an eschatological interpretation of the resurrection of Jesus Christ. The resurrection is an event of promise and as such refers to the as yet unfinished future of Jesus Christ, a future which "is not merely the unveiling of something that was hidden, but also the fulfillment of something that was promised."[10] In that sense, it is "revelatory."

ISSUES AND PROPOSALS

In the first half of the twentieth century the doctrine of revelation became such a prominent feature on the theological landscape that questions began to be raised as to whether modern theology did not suffer from an "inflation of revelation." Questions also were raised about the intelligibility of these new interpretations of revelation. If modern theologians emphasized revelation only in order to sidestep the critical questions of the Enlightenment and to affirm an objective basis for Christian faith, then some critics questioned whether revelation could serve as a foundational principle and the basis for further theological reflection.

10. Jürgen Moltmann, *Theology of Hope*, p. 88.

Questions have also been raised as to whether modern concepts of revelation have any basis whatever in the Hebrew scriptures or the New Testament. James Barr, for example, argues that a sophisticated concept of history (history used as an organizing and classifying principle) is foreign to Hebrew scripture. In a sense, however, this criticism may be beside the point, for most modern theologians would not say that revelation is simply the repetition of a biblical concept. What really gives rise to the prominence of revelation in modern theology is the emergence of critical history and with it the problem of hermeneutics. Although most contemporary interpretations of revelation are concerned with *what* can be said about God, they are even more concerned with *how* it is possible to speak intelligibly of "God." This may not have been a problem for the writers of scripture, but it is an urgent problem for theologians who recognize the historicity of human understanding and the cultural relativity of all human assertions. Most of the major proposals in twentieth-century theology concerning the interpretation of revelation include not only a foundation for knowledge about God (revelation's objective referent) but also, and most importantly, a hermeneutical description of how revelation takes place.

Because of the emphasis on hermeneutics in contemporary interpretations of revelation, it seems likely that future descriptions of revelation will focus on the historicity of human understanding and the role of scripture and tradition in the Christian community as the locus for revelation. If revelation were interpreted in this context, special attention would have to be given to the importance of history for an understanding of human identity and the crucial role of memory in the construction of personal identity. The life, language, and texts of the community would be seen as the medium for revelation, with the hermeneutical encounter occurring in the collision between personal identity and the language (or tradition) of the community. The emerging discussion of narrative theology offers at least one proposal for how revelation might be interpreted in these terms.

In narrative theology, revelation refers to that process in which the personal identities of individuals are reinterpreted and transformed by means of the narratives which give the Christian community its distinctive identity. What might be called "Christian narrative" is the confessional narrative that results from the collision between an individual's personal identity narrative and the narrative identity of the Christian community. A narrative theology developed in this manner properly recognizes that the identities of persons and communities cannot be separated from an interpretation of their respective histories, and that in most cases it is the narrative identity of the community (articulated in its scripture and traditions) which provides the context for the reinterpretation of personal identity.

In most forms of narrative theology the focus is on what we have referred to as the subjective dimension of revelation. The category of Christian narrative is used to describe how the faith of the community is appropriated by individuals. The narratives of the Christian community (which are rooted in scripture but not confined to it) become the occasion and the context for the reinterpretation of personal identity or what might also be called "conversion." This emphasis on the subjective dimension of revelation does not mean that narrative theology ignores the question of the objective content of revelation. Narrative theology acknowledges the relational and personal character of Christian faith and its claim that when revelation takes place the identity of the individual is shown to be in relation to that personal reality Christians call "God." God cannot be identified with the narratives of the Christian community, but there also can be no knowledge of the reality Christians call "God" apart from those narratives and the history they recite.

Clearly narrative theology is indebted to both Schleiermacher and Hegel and to more recent theologians such as Barth and H. Richard Niebuhr. From Schleiermacher narrative theology borrows its emphasis on the communal context for Christian faith and the experiential base for revelation; from Hegel it takes the category of history as the sphere in which the reality of God is self-disclosed. And although Barth's description of the three forms of the Word of God provides a basic structure for the interpretation of the objective and subjective dimensions of revelation, it is Niebuhr's development of the category of "story" or narrative that has most decisively influenced narrative theology's reinterpretation of revelation.

But whether revelation is interpreted in the context of narrative theology or by some other idiom and method, any attempt to interpret revelation that hopes to be persuasive must come to terms with a number of extremely difficult issues that remain unresolved in contemporary theological discussion. Four of these are especially important: the agency of God, the role of the imagination, the question of truth claims, and the encounter with other religions.

1. Both classical and contemporary interpretations of revelation have assumed that revelation is not something initiated by human discovery, ingenuity, or reflection. Revelation refers to an event in which God, or that which is ultimately real, is disclosed in the midst of human finitude. God is traditionally understood to be the primary agent in this event, but for some time theologians have recognized that a host of difficult theological issues surround any attempt to speak of God as an agent and a particular event as "God's act." Future discussions of revelation will have to deal with this problem if theologians are to persist in their claim that revelation is a gracious event and as such attributable to the agency of God.

2. The hermeneutical focus of recent theological discussions raises the question of the role of the imagination in the process of revelation. Revelation is never simply the objective fact of God's self-disclosure. Most appeals to revelation are attempts to interpret the meaning of those events in which individuals and communities believe the identity of God is disclosed. There can be no such thing as a doctrine of revelation which is limited to what we have referred to as the objective dimension of revelation. Revelation always entails the interpretation and appropriation of those events or "facts," and the imagination plays an essential role in this process of interpretation. Contemporary theology, however, has not yet provided a compelling description of the nature of the imagination and its role in the interpretation and appropriation of revelation. It also remains unclear what the relation is between the agency of God in revelation and the role of the imagination in the acts of interpretation and appropriation.

3. Like several other major doctrines in Christian theology, revelation has often been interpreted solely in terms of its meaning for Christian faith. The perennial issue that lurks in the background of any discussion of revelation is the question of the criteria for determining the truthfulness of revelation. Is an image, symbol, or tradition revelatory simply because it illumines existence and imbues it with meaning? Or is it revelatory because it contains what is true in itself? There are really two problems here. The first issue is whether there is any sense in which revelation is true because of the nature of

its object (that which is revealed). The second issue is whether there are criteria for determining the proper interpretation and appropriation of what is revealed. Future discussions of revelation must attempt to develop criteria that will distinguish between legitimate interpretations of disclosure events and interpretations which reflect distortion and self-deception. While there clearly can be no guarantees against self-deception, and while every interpretation necessarily involves a form of distortion, theological interpretations of revelation must develop criteria that at least signal the possibility of self-deception.

4. Future discussions of revelation also will have to deal with the new situation in theology created by cultural and religious pluralism. Classical interpretations of revelation were often used to establish the imperialism of Christian faith in relation to other faiths and religious traditions. Since the Enlightenment, however, Christian theologians have become increasingly aware of the legitimacy and importance of other religions. Christian theology must now reassess not only the content of its revelation but also what it understands revelation to mean in relation to other religions. This "new situation" in theology does not mean that Christians will discard their tradition and its various interpretations of revelation, but that this tradition must now be brought into dialogue with other experiences of God's grace.

In light of these difficult problems, why do theologians continue to speak of revelation? Why do they not simply acknowledge the Enlightenment's devastating criticisms of classic models of revelation and dispense with the category altogether? As we have seen, most contemporary theologians do indeed accept the validity of the Enlightenment's critique of classical Christian theology; but, like their predecessors in the tradition, they find themselves unable to dispense with revelation. There is something about the nature of God as understood by Christians, something tied up with the category of grace, that requires the use of this term. Both what is known about God and the way in which that knowledge occurs requires some appeal to revelation in order to reflect the active agency of a reality other than the human intellect in the self-disclosure of what is ultimately real. Any contemporary theologian who attempts to reconstruct the doctrine of revelation in a manner that will be intelligible to the modern world faces a formidable task, but the nature of what it is that Christian faith claims to know demands that theologians continue the effort.

SUGGESTIONS FOR FURTHER READING

Augustine. "Homilies on the Gospel of John." *NPNF*[1] 2.

Baillie, John. *The Idea of Revelation in Recent Thought*. New York: Columbia University Press, 1956.

Barr, James. *Old and New in Interpretation: A Study of the Two Testaments*. New York: Harper & Row, 1966.

Barth, Karl. *Church Dogmatics*. Vol. I/1, pp. 51–283.

Brunner, Emil. *Revelation and Reason: The Christian Doctrine of Faith and Knowledge*. Philadelphia: Westminster Press, 1946.

Bultmann, Rudolf. "The Concept of Revelation in the New Testament," in *Existence and Faith*. New York: Meridian Books, 1960.

Calvin, John. *Institutes of the Christian Religion*. Esp. book 1, chap. 1.

Dowey, Edward A. *The Knowledge of God in Calvin's Theology*. New York: Columbia University Press, 1952.

Dulles, Avery. *Revelation Theology: A History*. New York: Herder & Herder, 1969.

Farrer, Austin. *The Glass of Vision*. London: Dacre Press, 1948.

Frei, Hans. "Niebuhr's Theological Background," in *Faith and Ethics*. Edited by Paul Ramsey. New York: Harper & Row, 1957.

Gilkey, Langdon. *Naming the Whirlwind: The Renewal of God-Language*. Indianapolis: Bobbs-Merrill, 1969.

Hart, Ray. *Unfinished Man and the Imagination: Toward an Ontology and a Rhetoric of Revelation*. New York: Herder & Herder, 1968.

Haught, John F. *Revelation of God in History*. Wilmington, Del.: M. Glazier, 1988.

Hegel, G. W. F. *Lectures on the Philosophy of Religion*, Vol. 3.

Kant, Immanuel. *Critique of Pure Reason*. Translated by Norman Kemp Smith. New York: St. Martin's Press, 1965.

Kaufman, Gordon. *Systematic Theology: A Historicist Perspective*. New York: Charles Scribner's Sons, 1968. Esp. pp. 3–80.

Lessing, Gotthold. *Lessing's Theological Writings*. Edited by Henry Chadwick. Stanford: Stanford University Press, 1956.

Locke, John. *The Reasonableness of Christianity*. Edited by I. T. Ramsey. Stanford: Stanford University Press, 1958.

Lonergan, Bernard J. F. *Insight: A Study of Human Understanding*. New York: Harper & Row, 1978.

Luther, Martin. "On the Bondage of the Will," in *Luther and Erasmus on Free Will and Salvation*. Edited by Philip S. Watson and B. Drewery. *LCC* 17.

Moltmann, Jürgen. *Theology of Hope*. Translated by James W. Leitsch. Minneapolis: Fortress Press, 1993. Esp. chap. 1, pp. 37–94.

Niebuhr, H. Richard. *The Meaning of Revelation.* New York: Macmillan Co., 1941.

Pailin, David. *The Anthropological Character of Theology.* New York: Cambridge University Press, 1990.

Pannenberg, Wolfhart, ed. *Revelation as History.* London: Macmillan & Co., 1968.

Rahner, Karl. *Hearers of the Word.* New York: Herder & Herder, 1969.

Rahner, Karl, and Ratzinger, Joseph. *Revelation and Tradition.* London: Burns & Oates, 1966.

Schleiermacher, Friedrich. *The Christian Faith.* Esp. pp. 44–52.

Schüssler Fiorenza, Elisabeth. *Revelation: Vision of a Just World.* Minneapolis: Fortress Press, 1991.

Thiemann, Ronald F. *Revelation and Theology.* Notre Dame: University of Notre Dame Press, 1985.

Tillich, Paul. *Systematic Theology.* Vol. 1, esp. pp. 71–159.

5. CREATION AND PROVIDENCE

WHERE WE ARE

Traditional Christian beliefs about the divine origin, governance, and final disposition of the world were for many centuries foundational components of the dominant world view in Western culture. Residues of these beliefs can be found today in various places, in arguments advanced by the pro-life camp in the abortion controversy, for instance, and in such quasi-religious sentiments as "Life is a gift" and "Things tend to work out for good in the long run." But the powerful convictions once expressed in traditional formulations of the doctrines of creation and providence do not now have a vivid and compelling life in the churches. In secular thought the convictions and the doctrines have been in deep recession for several centuries.

One cause of this inclusive decline is to be found in a tendency of the doctrines to distort or obscure the convictions and passions of the religious life. But many important elements of doctrine and conviction have been powerfully challenged, if not overthrown, by views inspired by modern science. The traditional teaching of the doctrine of creation is that the world as a whole had an absolute beginning: before creation nothing but God existed; everything begins when God said, "Let there be. . . ." Modern scientific theories concerning the origin of the physical universe have virtually nothing in common with traditional Christian teachings. The life sciences offer explanations of the origin and development of human beings which are strictly incompatible with historic creation. So also for the doctrine of providence. The theological tradition holds that events great and small, cosmic and historical, faultlessly operate to serve a divine ordination. This exaltation of purpose controlling—indeed defining— every entity and every set of entities in the cosmic spread runs afoul of the decision made very early in the modern world, and powerfully reinforced at critical junctures thereafter, to drop the category of purpose altogether from scientific explanation. So the conviction that

God the Creator has oriented human beings toward a perfectly fulfilling good beyond nature and history, and makes all things conspire to
this end, has fallen into a deep and persistent recession—but not
simply because the facts, none of which is more appalling than the
Holocaust, ruinously assault the Christian view. It is also because
hardly any large and potent intellectual current in the modern world
seems to support Christian teaching about providence.

Thus many Christian theologians have made systematic rather than
marginal adjustments in the traditional doctrines of creation and
providence. The large intent in this activity has been twofold: (1) to
recover the authentic pulse of Christian experience and (2) to respond
appropriately and creatively to the religious pathos of contemporary
existence. Accordingly, we must note that the commanding theological posture has not been simply defensive, as though the faith of our
ancestors had to be protected against the assaults of a secularism
determined to destroy it. To the contrary, many theologians believe
that there is much that is creative in modern life, much that offers
enrichment for humanity; and, by no means least in proper reckon-
ing, much that offers release from archaic and mordant prejudice
skulking behind conventional pieties.

Theological efforts to preserve a significant measure of continuity
with a Christian past, and to make a sympathetic and convincing
response to the challenges of the modern and postmodern world, are
treated in the third part of this chapter. Here we must be content to
note that profound ambiguities surround the doctrines of creation
and providence as elements in the message of the contemporary
churches. Modern philosophies have raised havoc with the traditional doctrines. Are there things working on the convictional and
experiential levels that theologians might well grasp for the reconstruction of creation and providence as integral components of Christian faith? Suitable answers to that question must first reckon with the
rise and decline of the tradition.

THE DOCTRINES IN THEIR CLASSIC FORMULATION

Root Images of Creator and Provider
in Scripture

The general connection between doctrinal propositions and religious convictions much more deeply embedded in experience surely

obtains in the case of creation and providence. On the convictional level, Christian expressions of experience are indissolubly linked with images rather than with concepts; doctrinal formulations tend largely to operate with concepts and often function as theories. We have therefore to review in brief compass the convictional-imaginal substructure of the doctrines of creation and providence.

God is the maker of heaven and earth. As creator, God depends upon nothing but the divine power and wisdom (Genesis 1; Job 38). Even if something is there before God acts, it is thoroughly insignificant, barely worth mentioning—darkness, formlessness, chaos—and biblical writers exhibit little theoretical concern with it. God has no rivals in wisdom, power, and righteousness before or after the act of creation.

Human beings are special projects of divine creativity (Gen. 1:26, 27; 2:7; Ps. 8:5) whether or not Adam is the first living creature God fashions (Gen. 2:4ff.) or the last in the series (1:26ff.). The great point is expressed as *image, likeness* (1:26). The New Testament greatly expands and enriches this conviction with images of family life: God is the Father,[1] we are members of the divine household (Rom. 8:14ff.), sons and daughters. Jesus Christ is the firstborn among many sons (Rom. 8:29); in eternity he is appointed to be the head of the household (Col. 1:15ff.); he is the one alone in whom the divine will is perfectly manifested (John 5:19ff.). So while the majesty of the Creator is displayed in countless ways throughout heaven and earth (Job 38ff.) and is so overwhelming that earth's inhabitants are like grasshoppers before God (Isa. 40:22), and though human beings are made from earth's dust (Gen. 2:7), nevertheless the manifestations of God's concern for human life override all other disclosures of that being, that life.

Just as God provides food for the beast and bird (Job 38:39–41; Matt. 7:26), takes note of the death of a sparrow (Matt. 10:29), and spreads a mantle of glorious beauty across the fields (Matt. 7:28–30), so above all the divine Provider looks after the chosen of humankind. God is their shepherd (Isa. 40:31; Psalm 23; Luke 15:3ff.). For them God controls the formidable forces of nature (Matt. 8:26) as well as the ferociously wicked nations (Hab. 3:12, 13). Thus God stands forth as the one who orders the seasons for humankind's benefit and

1. But see Ps. 103:13; Jer. 31:9; Hos. 1:1ff.

governs the course of cosmic and historical events to an indescribably glorious consummation (1 Cor. 2:9; Rev. 18:22).

The Theological Consensus from Origen to Calvin

The meaning of the classic doctrines of creation and providence can be set out in a series of propositions that we shall treat hereafter as the teachings of "the consensus." This theological consensus reaches from the second century through the seventeenth and includes such luminaries as Origen, Augustine, Aquinas, and Calvin. While these luminaries had their differences, on our two topics they exhibited remarkable agreement.

1. In creating the world and all that is therein, God made something to exist where nothing was, not even the abstract possibility of something: *ex nihilo*, from nothing God created whatever is. No other being is endowed with divine power, goodness, or wisdom. The divine act of origination has no proper analogies in any act of any creature; God does not need an antecedently existing "material" or a medium in which to work or an idea to be expressed in the medium. All things are from God and everything that any being is. A great seventeenth-century philosophical theologian put it thus: God creates both essence and existence; nothing creaturely exists in any mode before the divine creative act.

Those who contributed most to this doctrinal formulation of biblical teaching were philosophically trained and knew that there were problems for philosophical reflection implicit in that "nothing" from which God creates. Early and late, Job has been taken to be a kind of philosophical work. But are we really to suppose that when Job says God "hangs the earth upon nothing" (26:7) the author is making a *philosophical* claim about what there was or was not before God created? Or should we say that the "nothing" of Job is very like the "void" of Genesis 1 and of the Psalms and Isaiah—a condition so blank, sterile, and uninteresting that it is cited only to set off the majesty of the creator God? The consensus thinkers do not let the matter rest there. They are aware of philosophical alternatives: perhaps God created the world out of nothing but the divine self; perhaps nothing names a reality co-eternal with God, something-we-know-not-what, entirely characterless until God imprints it, but *there,* accordingly, to be used by God. Such are not merely idle though harmless speculations. They are religiously suspect. They corrode the sense of God's absolute distinction from the world; they dim or weaken the conviction that God's creative action is purely gratuitous as well as all-constituting.

2. The inclusive effect of God's all-constituting action is the creation. It is a closed order of finite beings. It is a world in which the essential relations of the classes of entities to one another and to the whole order do not change throughout the life history of creation. Within this order each suborder has its own determinative laws, and each class of entities has a particular good it is bound to seek and to attain. On this point the consensus is virtually unanimous from start to finish. Indeed, very few non-Christian thinkers during the ascendancy of the consensus quarrel with the general notion of a closed, finite cosmos.

Thus the work of Creator flows into the work of Provider. But the second proposition, like the first, appears to move us beyond the biblical conviction that "for everything there is a season" (Eccles. 3:1). Now we are dealing with the formal teaching that the wisdom and power of God are manifested in a perfection of teleological organization embracing alike the lowest orders of beings and the highest—from earthworms to angels. God is the provider; every order of being has what it needs fully to be itself and to contribute to the harmony of the whole. Other things being equal, this is true for every member of every order.

3. A fundamental and unalterable law of the entire created world calls for superordination/subordination—*hierarchy*. Materiality is the lowest rung on the ladder, spirituality the highest. Sense experience is at best the crude beginnings of cognition; pure mental activity runs far beyond the stirrings of sense. Carnal pleasure may well link us with the animals, while mystic rapture may move us close to God. To this we must add that the power of being as well as moral authority—the right to rule—always flows from the higher to the lower: the more "eminence" (power plus value) a being has as a cause, the more it ranges above any and all its effects.

In their wholehearted support of this element in the doctrine of creation, the consensus theologians are remarkably close to Platonic views—rather too close for the comfort of some parties, quite acceptably close for others. Origen, for example, seems to have felt that materiality is nothing real in itself. Body is an illusion, really, a painful lesson God inflicts upon peccant souls. With this view Augustine sharply disagrees (*City of God* 12). But such disagreements do not diminish general assent to the hierarchical scheme, nor do they reduce or deflect significantly the powerful tendency to discover the pure reason for the existence of the lower in the interests of the higher. So human beings are free to use creatures lower in the hierarchy as suits human interests with only instrumental concern for their well-being. Many generations of Christian people have so construed Gen. 1:26ff. It remains to be seen whether the massive destructiveness of that conviction will become clear and urgent enough in the perceptions of Christian peoples to change the pattern and course of Western civilization before the planet is rendered uninhabitable for other forms of life as well as for humankind.

4. Since God created the world, it cannot lack anything God intended for it to be and to have. The divine purpose and the divine management cannot be violated or even momentarily frustrated by the behavior, intentional or unwitting, of any part of creation. God did not and presumably could not have made a faulty part.

Here the consensus experiences stresses and strains. Obviously God's performance as Creator and Provider cannot be faulted. On the other hand, is not God the only being who is really perfect? The world is a creature. It cannot rival the Creator. But can it not have a reflected perfection, an integrity, a perdurability and intelligibility derived from God, of course, but really invested with such splendors by God?

By the time of the High Middle Ages an important division in the consensus was evident. The Augustinians insisted that the contingency of created being must be construed as meaning absolute dependence on God. Just as the sun gives life to all that lives and is the light in and by which all things are known, so God is the life in all that lives and the truth through which all truths are comprehended. A different view was held by Thomas Aquinas and his followers. "Autonomy" is not the right word for their account of the world's ontological integrity or for the native capabilities of the human mind, but it looks in the right direction. Their view is that God, in the perfection of divine wisdom and benevolence, imparts to creation an ability to function according to what might be called a charter which is at once authorizing and energizing. Each order of being has an inherent stabilizing and fructifying formality (or determining purpose). These forms are available to the natural mind. They are the basis of authentic natural knowledge.[2]

5. The question concerning the perfection of God's creative and sustaining activities has a more existential bite than this conflict seems to suggest. This is felt most acutely as the problem of evil. Creation and providence embrace what we experience as evil. Evil then is not a freakish occurrence. It is not something unexpected, unforeseen, unplanned-for in God's creation and management of the world.

The consensus is firm on this point just so long as the operating terms are ambiguous. It is agreed that God cannot be the direct and determining cause of human wickedness. It is agreed that God knows in eternity that wickedness will appear in history beginning with Adam's fall. God knows that monstrously evil persons will go through life unhindered by the forces of righteousness and go down with worldly honors to quiet graves.[3] So *why?* For the sake of a greater good, that is, greater than would otherwise have been attainable.

In the consensus, tension builds up along the line of "greater good." It is agreed that the benefits God in Jesus Christ secures to humankind are incalculably rich. But is the awful history of "man's inhumanity to man" thereby justified? That depends largely on what reality and reach human freedom has. Origen and Irenaeus held that human sin is the price paid for the freedom essential for the fulfillment of the divine plan for creation, that is, the emergence in history of the divine-human community. In Western Christianity much more emphasis is placed on juristic concepts and images. Human beings can be held fully responsible, that is, truly culpable, for their horrid condition, their sin and guilt. God did not *make* Adam fall, but God made the Adam who fell of his own weight. There are

2. It has been argued that the Thomist-Aristotelian view is the natural and indispensable foundation of modern science. See Alfred North Whitehead, *Science and the Modern World* (New York: Macmillan Co., 1953), p. 14.

3. A set of persistent problems circles around the doctrinal formulations of the eternal God's knowledge of historical-temporal events. High doctrine denies that God's self-being is in any sense temporal and yet insists that the divine knowledge necessarily embraces every event in cosmic and human history. The reason for this latter claim runs through the consensus. It is rendered systematic by Aquinas: that by which God knows the world is the same as that by which God creates the world.

indeed important differences in the West between, say, Aquinas and Calvin. Aquinas holds out for a semiautonomy in human beings that persists through and beyond the fall. Calvin finds no trace of that degree of independence in scripture. But they agree that human freedom is nothing for which a price is exacted from God's own being; we must not suppose that God's perfect righteousness compelled God to choose, from among possible worlds, the one which offered the greatest good.

6. One way or another, evil is part of providence. For humankind, pain has an ordained educative function. In Jesus Christ and through the tutelage of the Holy Spirit, suffering is salvific as well. History proves that sin has terrible consequences. Monstrous wickedness is perceived in its true colors in the magnitude of the suffering it inflicts on the human community. Thus we learn that in good and evil humanity is an inclusive community. Thus we discover that its essential being and value are preserved by God throughout the vicissitudes of history.

7. Miracles are the extraordinary things God does to preserve and enrich the life of humanity. Some miracles involve a local and temporary suspension of the laws of nature, such as the miracles of healing. In others God intervenes in the play of historical events, such as the deliverance of Jerusalem from the Assyrians. The resurrection of Jesus Christ is the absolutely crucial miracle. It embraces the natural forces of life and death, on the one hand, and such historical realities as the demonic pride of Israel's messianism and the imperial might of Rome, on the other. In the resurrection of Jesus Christ the ultimate salvation of the people of God is guaranteed. The life everlasting of traditional doctrine presupposes the miracle in which soul and body are reunited.

We must note in passing that the miracle of liberation from human oppressors plays a comparatively small role in the New Testament even though it is expressly stated in the inaugural sermon of Jesus, "to set at liberty those who are oppressed" (Luke 4:18). This providential activity plays an even smaller role in the consensus. It makes a great deal of salvation from supernaturally potent "principalities and powers," disguising themselves in earthly empire. But the ultimate transhistorical destiny of the soul dominates, though it certainly does not extinguish, concern for earthly freedom and happiness. The consensus supplies little inspiration or justification for social revolution, no matter how massive the spiritual corruption produced by systematic physical deprivation and psychological terror.

8. The divine purpose in creating and sustaining the world and in preserving the community of the faithful includes a full termination of the world and its history. It is sometimes conceded, for instance by Aquinas, that time might consistently be thought to have no end, but revelation grounds and sustains the Christian confidence that it does in fact end at God's command. Then God creates "a new heaven and a new earth." In that realm of perfect peace the blessed of humankind shall know God and enjoy forever the fullness of that life. Thus God is Alpha and Omega. From God the world springs. In God's good pleasure the world exists for its full course, thus realizing every potentiality with which divinity has endowed it. At God's signal the world gives up the ghost. God creates in its place an everlasting duality: a blessed realm, paradise; an accursed one, hell.

Persistent Tensions in the Consensus

The consensus intends to eliminate anything that would compromise the perfect freedom of God in creating and disposing of the world. Nonetheless, the existence of the world follows *in some sense* from the timeless perfection and absolute self-existence of God. It is philosophically conceivable (whether or not it is religiously intolerable) that such a God might have gotten along eternally without a world, but this eternally and essentially self-complete being chooses to have a world after all. The consensus insists that the divine motive in this choice is entirely beyond human comprehension. They say also that it is unimpeachable.

The picture is even more complicated. Early in its career the consensus worked out a philosophical distinction between necessary and contingent being. Necessary being is that which cannot conceivably fail to exist. It is rational to conceive of a contingent being as not existing, though in a given case such a being might in fact exist. Now God alone is necessary; the world is contingent in whole and in every part or member. Thus the world depends absolutely upon God. That is the religious conviction at the heart of the traditional view.[4] It is closely tied to belief in God as Lord in and over history. But a

---

4. Anselm builds his famous ontological argument on and around this distinction. The same distinction is used systematically by Aquinas (see his third proof for God's existence), though he rejects Anselm's argument.

lord must have a people; one cannot be a ruler without a kingdom. Should we say, then, that God did not need to be Lord, but having decided to be Lord, God had to have a people? Such questions were felt to be vexatious long before the dawn of the modern age.

In scripture the word *cosmos* has many meanings. For our purposes the two most important ones are "earth" and "world," this planet and the entire created order. The consensus is faithful to scripture in teaching that God is sole creator of the world and of the planet earth. It also teaches that God has a special relation to earth. Is this because sin has not corrupted any other part of creation? There are ambiguities in the consensus. Did one or more angels fall before humankind was created? If so, sin and retribution and salvation are played out on a cosmic stage. There are strong hints of this in the New Testament, but not many of them are largely featured in the Western consensus. This inspires a narrow and provincial reading of God's interest in humanity and a correlative downgrading of the value of other creatures. Doctrine and liturgy in the East preserved the cosmic scale of creation, fall, and redemption.[5]

How and why is evil incorporated in the divine purpose? The consensus does not deny that there is evil on earth; its denial would reduce the work of Jesus Christ to providing assurance that evil is an illusion. On the other hand, the consensus will not say that God was powerless to create a world free from evil start to finish. God was not bound to create this world, but the world God created was bound to have evil in its life history. The presence of evil, however, does not flaw the perfection of the divine creative and sustaining activity. All things work for good; ultimately only goodness endures. The truth of this grand affirmation is available only to faith. Faith itself is God's free gift.

Is this faith prevented from seeking empirical attestations? Does either nature or history bear such witness to God that even the most stubborn disbelief is compelled to testify against itself and confess that it cannot give even a dubiously intelligible reading of experience in the round?

---

5. Perhaps the persistent and pervasive interest of college students and seminarians in C. S. Lewis is due in part to his portrayal of the engagement of cosmic powers in confining the depradations of wickedness to planet Earth, and also to his anticipation of scientific efforts to colonize beyond this planet. On the other hand, his *Problem of Pain* shows a thoroughly Western side.

On such questions the consensus lived in tension with itself and with the convictional/imaginal levels of Christian existence. Even Calvin insists that the experiential sense of a creator God was inextinguishable in the human spirit. But are there evidences of providence in human history? Specifically, what is there to show that the risen Christ is now and forever the Lord of history? The consensus holds that grace alone avails to convert disbelief on this all-important point.

How is divine causality related to what appears to be causal efficacy in finite beings? Here part of the problem for the consensus is to keep belief in God as the absolute cause of the being and behavior of all things from erasing in principle the distinction between God and the world. If no creature is endowed with causal efficacy, it would seem to follow that the world is a passive if not lifeless medium in which deity expresses itself. That would reduce human beings to the order of curiously lifelike puppets. But on the other hand, can the consensus say that God shares creativity with any other being? Genesis could be read as a warning against any such concession. In 3:22–24, God is represented as acting to prevent forever any human incursion on divine prerogatives. In a latter-day idiom, a caretaker had better not aspire to become a policy maker.

The internal tensions of the consensus are exposed and exploited by the modern age. This does not mean, however, that incoherence is the most formidable threat the traditional faith has had to face in the modern world.

CHALLENGES AND CONTRIBUTIONS OF MODERN CONSCIOUSNESS

The consensus doctrines of creation and providence constitute a systematic teleological explanation of reality. God's will is the ultimate explanation of all existents and all events. To know a thing's purpose is to know its essential reality. So to know what a thing is good for and why events occur is at once the loftiest and most practical of human cognitive activity. All things exist in such articulation that the lower orders of being serve the interests of the higher, and the activities of the higher conform to laws that transcend the laws of the lower. As Paul says, "the glory of the celestial is one, and the glory of the terrestrial is another" (1 Cor. 15:40). So it is clearly absurd, if not blasphemous, to try to subsume the spiritual under the laws of matter; heavenly bodies—stars, planets, the moon, and the sun—cannot be subject to laws governing earth.

The modern scientific age can fairly be said to have begun with a direct challenge to the teleological explanation of nature, and with a stunningly successful generalization of the laws of motion to include celestial bodies as well as earthly. Thus religious and antique scientific lore about the heavens begins to lose its persuasiveness. Before long it will seek asylum in poetry and vulgar superstition.

These victories are commonly attributed to the seventeenth-century astronomer Galileo. He did not venture to banish teleology from the explanation of human being, but it is nonproductive, otiose, in the explanation of nature. Thus the way is opened to a clean if not fatal division between objective reality, describable and explicable in exact mathematical laws, and the ineffabilities of subjective consciousness. When this view triumphs, humankind has either to be assimilated without significant remainder into nature or appear as the eternal outsider, an alien dubiously present anywhere anytime.[6]

Rationalism and Idealism

What the church did to defend the geocentric and anthropocentric consensus against this powerful assault is an often told story. The defense very early gave off symptoms of radical deficiency. René Descartes's rescue operations were not received with enthusiasm by church authorities. They may have sensed that his protestations of orthodoxy concealed a readiness to revise consensus doctrines in order to enhance their plausibility for an age in which radical doubt seemed more rational than traditional faith.

Descartes, a younger contemporary of Galileo, provided systematic ratification of the distinction the latter drew between objective (scientifically manageable) sense qualities and subjective ones. But it was no part of Descartes's intention to downgrade the reality of the mental world. Quite to the contrary, the mind behaves much more as *substance* (self-subsistent activity) ought to, whereas physical entities can

---

6. The alien ought not to be confused with the biblical image of the pilgrim. Pilgrim is a blessed creature, having a real and beautiful home in a native country; and God guarantees a safe arrival after ordained test by earthly vicissitude. But the alien has a homeland only in fantasy. Persistent effort to live in it is bound to make this forlorn creature an unsuccessful animal.

boast only geometrical properties. Nevertheless, endowed with those properties and those alone, nature emerges as a great and sublimely articulated machine to which God originally imparted its motion— for how can geometrical properties generate motion?

So Descartes's God is quite literally a deus ex machina. As Creator, God's prime function seems to be to set the cosmic machine in motion. But Descartes's view of providence has astonishing echoes of Augustinianism. He holds that the world depends for its existence at every moment upon God. So there is no real distinction between creation and providence; it is as though the world were re-created in every successive moment. In Descartes's view time is a succession of point-instants rather than a "flow" or a continuum upon which the mind imposes abstract divisions. Thus the dependence of all that exists upon the Creator-Preserver is absolute. The will of God answers only to itself, not to any nondivine power or to any creaturely criterion of rationality and goodness.

Descartes's views had little effect upon the course of science already slated for triumph after triumph in the empirical world. And no one knew this any better in the seventeenth century than Gottfried Leibniz. Committed as he was to the consensus ("God is the creator of essence and existence alike"), Leibniz nonetheless ventured where the tradition had feared to tread; he specified the motive of the Creator. Being perfectly good, God cannot do other than create the best of all possible worlds. The world of God's creation operates, moreover, as a perfectly designed and constructed machine, every part acting with every other in a harmony that reflects the wisdom and benevolence of the Creator. Furthermore, the laws of nature are precisely formulable.

These efforts to preserve if not to improve upon consensus doctrines proved to be an ambiguous legacy. For one thing, Leibniz's program involved a metaphysical idealism. In his view the space-time world is a complex though benign illusion. Can this be reconciled with scriptural conviction about the material basis of human existence? Furthermore, Leibniz's account of the perfection of order of nature gives strong support to deistic views. There had been many arguments in the consensus about the relative perfection of the created order. But there was very large agreement that the God of creation and providence is hardly a remote deity content to contemplate the mechanical perfection of divine craftsmanship, unperturbed eternally by any need or desire to adjust it or to fiddle with it.

In the Leibnizian view, the moral world manifests a perfection analogous to the order of nature. That does not mean evil is an illusion. It means that evil serves a divine purpose; it provides for a greater good than would otherwise have been possible. It is rational to believe, thus, that all things work together for good, for this is the best of all possible worlds. So the door is opened to an unqualified humanistic optimism about the true course and ultimate outcome of history.

The Leibnizian affirmations of the consensus merit close attention not simply because Leibniz is one of the seminal religious thinkers in the modern world. What we have here is a system profoundly sympathetic to the consensus but worked out in ways quite as profoundly congenial to the spirit of the Enlightenment. Other currents move powerfully against the rationalistic theism of the Leibnizian school and finally against any philosophically serious form or fragment of the consensus doctrines of creation and providence.

Pantheism, Deism, Skepticism

The Cartesian rescue of creationism tended strongly to translate God's motive in creation as benevolence with a low interference factor. Thanks to the genius of a man who rescued himself from Cartesianism, a persistently attractive alternative to traditional Christian views was developed in the seventeenth century. The man was Spinoza, and the system was pantheistic naturalism. In that view there is no substantial difference between God and the cosmos. There is only one substance. It is infinite and eternal. It lacks no ontological perfection (*moral* attributes all express human biases). It is deficient in no power of being. Everything that exists is an expression of this being. Viewed one way, it is a geometrically perfect order of things; viewed another, it is an inexhaustibly creative being from which an infinite number of things necessarily follows. There may be a *religious* reason for calling this being God. Philosophically it may properly be called nature.

Thus there is no place for talk, either religious or philosophical, about God's freedom in creation. There are no rational appeals to the sovereign will of a transcendent Creator. There is no teleology built

into the nature of all things. There is no appeal to a might-ha
except as a human-all-too-human excuse for acting from men
fusion and unruly passion. That person is truly blessed who achieves
rational understanding and acceptance of his or her place in the
perfectly determined order of things. Then and there religious wisdom and rational truth are mutually supportive.

In this view the world runs absolutely unerringly on its rails. The
true and ultimate order of things has all the perfections the consensus
had ascribed to God alone. So "providence" is only a religious word
for the necessity linking every entity and every event with every other.
Right perception of this necessity and assent to it is freedom.

Despite the widely felt influence of Spinoza's thought, the most
successful alternative to the consensus outlook in the eighteenth century was deism. Its success was guaranteed by Newtonian science.
There, for the time being, a place was preserved for the Creator, the
divine mind that made a perfect or nearly perfect machine—nature
functioning according to unerringly precise laws. Miracle, the providential suspension of the laws of nature, was squeezed out of the
world. Isaac Newton himself thought that God's wisdom and power
were needed occasionally to correct cosmic slippages. Newtonians
proved him wrong—mathematically, of course.

This attenuated teleological scheme, designed to make a nice philosophical fit with a natural religion delivered once and for all from
bondage to supernatural revelation, was subjected to a severely pun-
ishing attack by David Hume. Even if the order of nature were in fact
like a perfectly constructed and flawlessly functioning machine (why,
he asks, a machine rather than an organism?), it is still a finite order,
and only in the eyes of faith is it full of positive value. How then can
it supply unequivocal evidence for the existence of an infinitely
perfect Creator? But are we so sure, is our confidence really rational,
that the world is a perfect order of any kind? What of the prodigious
spread of pain in nature? What is the experiential or rational basis for
believing that moral evil is a transitory phenomenon?

What makes the evocation of such ancient metaphysical and religious quandaries so effective is Hume's systematic and subtle skepticism. Within the terms thus established, neither the consensus nor
deistic thinkers had much success in arguing their cases. Thereafter,
"Enlightenment" comes largely to mean skepticism about traditional

beliefs and values, and a marked cynicism about the origin and necessity of religion.

The Contributions of Historical Consciousness

Help for the doctrines of creation and providence came from the emergence and flowering of the historical consciousness in the last half of the eighteenth century. There it appears that humankind is essentially historical. From Johann Herder on, it is made clear that humanity makes its own history. Human beings are the real subjects-agents of the historical process. The "divinity that shapes our ends" is inherent and immanent in the life story of humankind. God is not an eternally (timelessly) self-complete being who manipulates the human community like a puppet master. So creation and providence are in a fair way to become symbols expressing the mysterious unity of spirit and nature and the ultimate union of divinity and humanity as the inclusive goal of history.

What keeps theologians imbued with historical consciousness from the embrace of pantheism? Friedrich Schleiermacher certainly did not intend to bend the Christian faith toward a vulgar pantheism, the view that God is in all things. He meant to preserve a distinction between God and the world. This is a cardinal principle of the consensus. But is the distinction between God and world one of substance, as the consensus had insisted? Hardly. Schleiermacher rejected the dualism inherent in the consensus view in favor of monism, which is a powerful if not dominant tendency in romantic religious outlooks. Schleiermacher's rejection of the consensus distinction between creation and providence, however, was partly inspired by other things. As the supreme architect of the theology of religious experience, Schleiermacher found little warrant in the historically conditioned Christian consciousness for that classic distinction, and in fact none at all in the generic religious reality, the feeling of absolute dependence.

G. W. F. Hegel and his followers did nothing to slow down or redirect the theological drive toward philosophical-religious monism. This view provides no place for traditional distinctions between God and world or between God and human being. Nature is spirit not yet aware of itself and thus for the moment alienated from itself. That is one illustration of the way in which the all-absorbing categories for the interpretation of reality are those appropriate for a historical being altogether engaged in self-discovery and self-expression, and thus to the perfection of self-consciousness.

The cardinal concepts of Christianity are preserved in Hegelian systematics as perennially valid symbols in which the divine reality, absolute Spirit, is expressed. So creation and providence survive, only now they have nothing to do with a God who plans out and governs a cosmic reality from a situation beyond the historical world. Here we are close to collapsing religious truth-claims into myths. The question whether the myths are benign or not is left open for the time being.

The theologians imbued with historical consciousness created still another problem for defenders of the consensus: historical relativism. According to this view, the great matter in the interpretation of history is to make the meaning of the past intelligible for life and thought as they are now constituted. Yet since every epoch has its own unique parameters that make existence meaningful for it, we have no way of grasping the reality of any thought world except our own.

These theories of historical knowledge and historical reality have formidable consequences for the Christian faith. They are especially vexatious for theologians who adduce scriptural testimony in support of creation as absolute origination. For example, grant that scripture represents God as creating the world in time. How can the meaning of that be shown to be timelessly true without by that very stroke showing it to be altogether unhistorical? The historical consciousness offers a way out. Creation and providence alike symbolize the dependence of the finite upon the infinite. Above all, they symbolize the dependence of any particular history, that is, the career of a given community, upon an overarching and universal meaning—the career in time and space of the all-inclusive divine-human community.

Liberal Reconstructions of the Doctrines

The philosophy of Immanuel Kant, coming at the close of the eighteenth century, offers little comfort or assistance to consensus sentiment. Some of the central elements of his philosophy became part of the fabric of liberal reconstruction. This is particularly true of the theological program built upon Kantian agnosticism both about nature in itself and deity in itself. The pure essence of true religion is revealed in the ethical realm. The consensus carried far too much speculative baggage. Creation is a case in point; it was made into a philosophical, scientific absurdity. It makes as much sense (which is to say none) to deny that the world had a beginning in time as to assert it. Gone also is the consensus doctrine of special providence, or miracle. God does not need to tinker with nature. Authentic deity would not impose arbitrary rules upon the moral self. God cannot make a human being moral. God would not treat an immoral person as though that person were virtuous. Nonetheless, some of the prime insights of Christian faith go to render intelligible the constitutive tensions of the moral consciousness. They offer a transcendent hope for the resolution of the most fundamental of those tensions beyond history—the everlasting conflict between obligation and happiness. So it is not unreasonable to look forward in good faith to a realm where the righteous under God shall be made perfectly happy. To bring that to pass is God's business. On Kantian grounds it is exceedingly hard to show that God has any other.

The Kantian liquidation of the consensus investment in metaphysics did not capture the entire liberal movement. After the middle of the nineteenth century, liberalism was in considerable part a tug of war between monistic idealism (inspired by Hegel) and personalistic idealism (inspired by Kant). Each party claimed to be the legitimate beneficiary and faithful defender of everything salvable in the collision of the consensus with modern consciousness. The monists collapsed any substantial distinction between God and the world. For them, history is the irresistible unfolding of a purely immanent divine Spirit; such Christian concepts as creation symbolize this all-inclusive process, which can be said to be personal only in its effects. Personalists contended that there is a divine purpose which could be fairly made out. That purpose is well expressed in the words of a great nineteenth-century poet: the world is a vale of soul-making. For the personalists, creation has very little to do with cosmic origins. The true import of the doctrine bears on the divine value-creating and value-preserving process immanent in the world. God is not a being self-defined, self-contained, and infinitely valuable apart from the world and history. God is the supremely personal being who provides the conditions for the emergence of finite and free persons. So conceived, God is the perfect master of the arts of moral suasion.

Creation thus moves inexorably to merge again with providence. Enlightened persons do not look to God for what they themselves alone can and must do, that is, in the proper exercise of freedom to make virtue the goal of life for self and society. The forces of history are not supernaturally orchestrated for the realization of this goal. Nevertheless, the liberal thinkers believed that an ultimate frustration of the ethical aim of reality was unthinkable. The moral flow of the world may suffer momentary checks, but it is irresistible. That is the manifest and ultimate will of God.

The liberal theologians were already partly prepared for the irresistible progress of Darwinian evolution in the last quarter of the nineteenth century. They believed that theological competition with science was as unnecessary as it was unproductive. Moreover, evolution did not really eliminate in principle rational appeal to a mind of transcendent wisdom and creativity. Denial of this appeal was a philosophical issue, not a scientific one. The activity of the Creator could as easily be conceived to cover millions of years as the biblical six days. The hand of providence could as fairly be discerned in the evolution of moral sensibility as in the destruction of Sennacherib or the fall of pagan Rome. Liberal theologians wanted nothing to do with efforts to convert scripture into a manual of science-before-science. The truly inspired minds in biblical history are those grasped by the vision of ethical monotheism. The alpha and the omega of the cosmic-historical process is the realm of ends, the enduring community of persons united in the bonds of love, the kingdom of God realized in the time and space of this world.

The development of physics in the nineteenth and twentieth centuries has brought to rich fulfillment an important part of the seventeenth-century dream of nature. This is a science liberated from the long domination of the concepts of substance and eminent cause. These concepts are linchpins of the consensus. As substance, God is timelessly perfect, beyond any change, and totally insusceptible to being affected or influenced by any other being. So understood, God is the real and true cause of every change in every being.

After science disposed of substance and eminent cause, it was only a matter of time before philosophy would follow suit. So inevitably the question was put to theologians: Can the concepts of creation and providence be at last liberated from ancient and blind allegiance to substance and eminent cause?

Liberal theologians of idealist persuasion responded with subject as the replacement for substance and with immanent moral teleology in the place of the theological determinism of the consensus. An alternative has opened up in more recent times: process theology, in which God is the supreme instance of creativity. Creativity itself is an all-pervasive factor in reality. So what God supplies to the world is not energy or being, but aim and relative order. And God participates in the life of every being, great and small. God's caring is inexhaustibly resourceful as well as infinitely tender. The Creator is not a world starter. God savors the achievements of every entity. The divine enjoyment preserves every value-creation no matter how trivial human self-absorption might think it to be. Thus the consensus doctrines of the transcendence and timeless perfection of the Creator and Preserver drop out of liberal response to revolutionary novelties in the modern world.

Attempts to Revive the Consensus

This does not mean that the consensus has had no strong voices raised in its behalf or, more accurately, raised in behalf of traditional convictions no longer adequately served by consensus strategies or liberal reconstructions. World wars and the Holocaust effectively terminated the dominance of liberalism in the Protestant world. We shall not attempt a general characterization of postliberal thought. Rather, we shall briefly consider several efforts to reinterpret creation and providence. These may be viewed as so many theological efforts to make productive contact with the convictional depth and experiential vividness of Christian tradition.

Karl Barth reinstated the distinction between creation and providence. Creation is God's singular act by which the world—all that is not triune God—comes to be. The reality of God's action is set forth in saga, Barth's term for the foundational narrative of scripture. Barth admits that there are mythical and legendary elements in the Bible, but he insists that saga is neither myth nor legend. Scriptural saga reveals Jesus Christ as the creative and redemptive Word of God. Scripture everywhere and always manifests God in Christ, creating, preserving, and perfecting personal relationships with humankind, God's covenant-partner. God is indeed the Creator of heaven and earth; essentially, God is Lord of history. The Creator and Preserver is Reconciler. Everything else known about God is derived from Jesus Christ. In him divine and human history are perfectly copresent.

More than a slender residue of the consensus persists in Barth's theology. Granted that the definiteness and inclusiveness of the traditional hierarchy has disappeared, a superordination/subordination scheme nonetheless persists. It is there in Barth's view of the relationships of man and woman. It is there also, though less obvious and less distressing, in Barth's distinction between what science says about humankind and the real and ultimate truth. Science is unable to grasp the essential nature of this creature; science cannot penetrate the phenomenal order of existence and history. Normative humanity is disclosed only in Jesus Christ, true divinity and true human being. There alone God's design for our history is manifested and achieved.

Rudolf Bultmann's readiness to embrace an existentialist philosophy for his theological work stands in sharp contrast to Barth's refusal to accept assistance from any systematic philosophy. In fact, both Bultmann and Barth accept some kind of philosophical distinction between appearance and reality. Bultmann makes a great deal of the triumph of the scientific world view; it is an indissolvable fact of our historical situation, and, even though it is not the last word on the human situation, it is a very important word. So belief in God the Creator, the unconditioned cause of the world, can claim no warrants from the empirical order. Nor can history as it is prosecuted by modern methodologies render traditional doctrines of providence plausible. Nevertheless, the right interpretation of the fundamental and universal problematic of human existence brings to light a relationality in which transcendence is implicated. Not that God thus becomes an object of knowledge; the revelation of Jesus Christ does not bring God transcendent into the orbit of human cognition. Jesus Christ confronts us with an unconditional command and an unqualified summons to assume the burden of authentic existence. So just as faith in the Creator cannot be supported by an appeal to modern science and scientific world views, so also the unique human possibility for the individual is not ascertained or actualized by any humanistic science. Faith as decision-to-be for God and other persons springs from an inwardness, a unique subjectivity of personal existence.

Paul Tillich's response to the challenges of modernity differs in fundamental ways from Barth's and Bultmann's. He agrees with them that the knowledge claims of the consensus must be systematically revalued. No perusal of nature, scientific or otherwise, can yield knowledge of the Creator. No objective investigation of history can render persuasive the Christian conviction that God acts redemptively in history. But Barth believes that scriptural teachings about creation, providence, and reconciliation are true, once and for all. And Bultmann believes that a nonmythical gospel of Jesus Christ can be made out in the New Testament. Against both of them Tillich holds that all religious language is symbolic. So the real and valid intent of the doctrines of creation and providence is to give symbolic expression to the heights and depths and the continuities and discontinuities of experience. It is still possible and important to raise the question of the truth. Symbols are true, accordingly, insofar as what they symbolize shines through them and generates appropriate responses to the realities. So "creator" does not name or conceptualize a specific being that acts upon other beings. Rather, it is a historically conditioned symbol of creativity as a root power of being as such: the one who is God beyond the gods of theism and atheism.

Today many people express sadness over the passing from the scene of all the commanding theological figures of Protestantism. No giants, it is acknowledged, have appeared to take their places. Yet we are not as likely to acknowledge another fact, namely, that a shift is occurring in the theological agenda itself. In the concluding section we shall consider some of the large questions concerning the doctrines of creation and providence affected by this shift.

ISSUES AND PROPOSALS

1. Can Christian thought about creation take seriously the notion of a world-originating divine act? For many centuries now, scientific and philosophical difficulties have been building up around this notion. In recent years big-bang scientific theories have stirred hopes for the successful revival—perhaps we ought to say resurrection—of the consensus view. But even if "big-bang" blew all opposition off the astrophysical board, there would still be ample room to doubt that such a theory affords substantial solace to the consensus mind. Scientific theories about cosmic beginnings have little to do with the place of human beings in the vast time-space spread of the universe. The

consensus has been fundamentally concerned all along with the question about the place of humankind in the divine creative activity, as Barth in our time and Aquinas in his epoch testify.

Contrasting views of language permeate such discussions in our time. "Origin" in science means something very different from what it means in Christian discourse. Religious language is much closer to the full round and texture of existence than the language of science or of systematic philosophy. So Christian employment of "creation" begins on the experiential and convictional levels, where it gives expression to the sense of radical contingency and absolute dependence upon God. Accordingly, modern theological treatments of creation run strongly toward the relationship in which creaturely existence and divine power and righteousness are interlocked. What does it mean to be rooted and grounded in finiteness and yet to have the "sense and taste of the infinite" (as Schleiermacher expressed it) ineradicably present? Perhaps this duality of experience is the generic religious sense to which historical religions in splendid variety of liturgical and doctrinal accouterment give particular expression.

2. So today there are thinkers who believe that systematic theology must employ a set of concepts valid for dealing with the full spread of reality; it must sweep up God and everything else that exists. In this view creativity is a fundamental category for the all-inclusive continuum of being from the lowest life-pulse of infinitesimal physical particles to God, and back. On the other side are those who hold that theological categories cannot rise above the human situation. In this view, creativity has no valid cosmological application unless it is in the mode of poetic-mythological celebration of life. Within the compass of humanity, creativity is the mark or perhaps the essence of the realized ethical person.

3. Thinking and rethinking the doctrines of creation and providence must go on today in a situation in which the open universe overshadows the closed universe of traditional world views, religious and scientific. The consensus was wedded to the closed universe; God had so created it. Newtonian science seemed to confirm this religious bias toward a closed, bound, and determined nature. But already in the seventeenth century the universe of scientific and philosophic imagination began to show signs of opening up and expanding to infinity. The visionaries of the Enlightenment could see

no limit to the development of human potentialities once humankind was liberated from political tyranny and religious superstition. Then Darwinism revealed nature as committed to inexhaustible novelty. Thus nature slipped the leash of ancient preconceptions of order and rationality bound into finite and everlastingly insurmountable limits.

What then of nature's God? Is God another infinite alongside infinite nature? What does God create? What in fact needs God's preserving power and wisdom? Theologians early in modern times were constrained to ponder the question whether God's omniscience would be intolerably strained by a cosmic-temporal spread actually (rather than analytically) infinite. Now the problem moves into the constitution and behavior—the life story, so to speak—of any and every entity. Is it simply an effect of antecedent causes? Or is every entity self-caused, self-generated, self-projected across its environment? Is freedom thus coupled with causal efficacy throughout the cosmos? If so, what is God's role in such a world? Is God the one who orchestrates an innate, underived, and unpredictable spontaneity in all things in order to produce at any given moment the richest possible effect compatible with coherence? On this front the conviction that all things are God's because of the eminence of the Creator and Preserver seems to have been blunted.

4. Christian theology has generally evinced much livelier interest in the human dimension of perennial philosophical questions than in the universal ones: human nature rather than nature, history rather than cosmos. So even if self-causation (freedom) is distributed throughout the universe, what is to be made of *human* freedom? But in the dominant scientific world view, nature is an unbroken causal continuum, a realm of pure necessity.

Ever since Kant, a considerable body of Protestant theologians have persisted in setting humankind over against nature, but not in the manner of the consensus. That nature is the realm of causal necessity is a principle rather than a discovery of modern science. On the other hand, the moral consciousness has its own structure, its own laws *sui generis*. As participant in spiritual reality, humanity is geared into the transcendental order of being. In that order ethical imperatives carry their own authority; they are neither legislated nor enforced by God, but they do manifest the true and everlasting divine purpose to realize a pure ethical community.

5. Liberal theology here seems to have doubled back to pick up an important theme in the consensus, namely, that the communication of goodness is God's purpose in creating the world and sustaining it unto its perfection. That God is good and cannot do evil is a religious sentiment powerfully expressed in Plato's dialogues. Plato hints that the more goodness a being has the stronger is the inclination of that goodness to communicate itself without stint. We have seen that Spinoza drew the conclusion that the world, the all-inclusive cosmic system, necessarily exists and is necessarily perfect. That conclusion is totally unacceptable to the consensus.

But it is not just the consensus that finds such a conclusion unacceptable, perhaps even abhorrent. Total war obliges us to be acutely aware of the magnitude of historical evil. What is to be made of a providence that allows the Holocaust to happen—not only allows it but also incorporates it in the original and comprehensive plan of creation?

Here the great theological task seems to be to render something very like a cost-benefit analysis of the contractual grant of freedom in which humankind is inextricably situated by God's will. Not that the Holocaust can be deduced from the terms of the contract (or covenant). The scheme—should we now say scenario—of freedom-in-creation does not allow for the deductive method in the interpretation of history. So the Holocaust, for our time the paradigm case of historical evil, could have been avoided; it need not have happened. Does this mean that if it was foreseen and not prevented, the advance knower must have been deficient either in goodness or in power? The question contains a famous theological dilemma. We have a question about the dilemma: Is it *real*? Should God have *made* Britain's prime minister take a firm stand against Hitler's bluff in remilitarizing the Rhineland in 1936? The appearance of the Holocaust rode on the outcome of that bluff. Should God have *made* the average American citizen aware of the magnitude and virulence of evil in fascism before 1940? The creation of the Holocaust rode on that indifference, that passivity, that willful ignorance. It is difficult to give such notions of divine coercive action any content that is both Christian and intelligible. That all things work for the good is at least as much an eschatological vision as it is an empirical-descriptive principle. But it must retain something of the latter.

The Christian faith is intelligible insofar as it provides a comparatively clear purchase on the actualities of nature, history, society, and personal existence—which is to say that the core empirical element in providence is awareness of how the process of good-coming-out-of-evil can be infused into any historical situation for its creative transformation. But this process is anything but a mechanical one. There are no guarantees that such a process once begun will be sustained unto its envisaged consummation. Human envisagements are incurably fragmentary. They are also prone to corruption. But the truly immense, the all but wholly imponderable complications in the process of creativity—here understood as making good to come from evil—come from the side of God. "God's ways are not your ways nor God's thoughts your thoughts." Only God is able to endure the full spread of the consequences of human folly and wickedness, and to make it as telling a part of the cosmic weave as the evolution of the galaxies.

SUGGESTIONS FOR FURTHER READING

Aquinas, Thomas. *Summa Theologica*. Part 1a, questions 22–23, 44–49, 65–74, 103–19.

Augustine. *City of God*. Books 11–12.

Barth, Karl. *Church Dogmatics*. Vols. 3/1, 3/3.

Bultmann, Rudolf. *Existence and Faith*. New York: Meridian Books, 1960. Pp. 23–34, 171–82, 206–25.

Calvin, John. *Institutes of the Christian Religion*. Book 1, chap. 3.

Descartes, René. *Meditations*, in *Discourse on Method and Other Writings*. New York: Penguin Books, 1970.

Hegel, G. W. F. *Lectures on the Philosophy of Religion*. Vols. 1, 3.

Kant, Immanuel. *Religion within the Limits of Reason Alone*. New York: Harper & Row, 1960.

Leibniz, G. W. *Monadology*, in *Discourse on Metaphysics/Correspondence with Arnauld/Monadology*. La Salle: Open Court Publishing Co., 1979.

Neville, Robert C. *Creativity and God: A Challenge to Process Theology*. New York: Seabury Press, 1980.

Origen. *On First Principles*. Book 2.

Schleiermacher, Friedrich. *The Christian Faith*. Pp. 142–93, 233–56.

Spinoza, Benedict de. *Ethics*, in *The Rationalists*. New York: Anchor Books, 1974. Part 1, including Appendix.

Tanner, Kathryn E. *God and Creation: Tyranny or Empowerment?* New York: B. Blackwell, 1988.

Whitehead, Alfred North. *Process and Reality*. New York: Free Press, 1929.

6. HUMAN BEING

WHERE WE ARE

As a distinct topic, "theological anthropology" is relatively new to the theologian's agenda. It is doctrine about "human nature" or what it is to be "person." Christian thinkers have always had things to say on that topic, of course, but for most of the history of Christian thought, they have said it in and with discussion of other topics. Thus they have always made claims about human beings as part of creation, about human beings' ability to know God, about the "fallenness" and "sin" of human beings, about the dynamics by which people are "redeemed" from that sin and made new beings, and about the ultimate destiny to which they are called. Each of these was a theological topic in itself. In the process of discussing these matters, theologians traded on conceptual schemes designed to describe what it is to be a human being, what it is to be the sort of being of whom all those things concerning creation, revelation, sin, and so on, were claimed.

Theological anthropology in the narrow or strict sense has tended to focus on either or both of two major guiding questions: (1) What is it about human beings that makes it possible for them in their finitude to know the infinite God? (2) What is it about human beings that makes fallenness possible in such a radical way as to require the kind of redemption to which Christianity witnesses? In the classic theological tradition these questions were addressed not directly in and of themselves but in the process of discussing other topics. Theological anthropology became a topic in its own right only in the modern period. And perhaps not by accident the basic conceptual scheme used to analyze humankind changed radically. As we shall see, what had been in the classic tradition an often implicit discussion of "human nature" became in the modern period an explicit discussion of "subjectivity." Our principal task in this chapter is to explore the significance of this shift.

THE DOCTRINE IN ITS CLASSIC FORMULATION

The classic formulation of theological anthropology was largely based on the story of the creation and fall of Adam in Genesis 1–3, interpreted through conceptual schemes borrowed from Greek philosophical traditions. The focus was on Adam, who was understood in a double way. On the one hand, he was taken to be the historically first individual human being. On the other hand, he was taken to be the scriptural ideal type or paradigm of "human nature" as such (after all, the Hebrew word from which "Adam" comes is the generic term for humankind). It is not logically necessary that the first human being should also be normative for what it is to be human. The assumption that he is creates a problem: Ideal types are highly general. Which features of the concrete individual man Adam, as depicted in the Genesis story, are part of the ideal type that is normative for human nature? And by what principle does one select them?

The view of human nature generated by this story had two major themes: (1) a picture of the place that human nature has in the unchanging structure of the cosmos God created and (2) a picture of humankind's unique capacity for communion with God—what has traditionally been called the *imago dei* (image of God.)

The Structure of Human Nature

The story of the creation of Adam is part of the larger story of the creation of the world. Accordingly it is the classic formulation of the doctrine of creation that provides the context in which human nature is understood. The created realm is a *cosmos*, a single, structured, harmonious whole. More exactly, it is a hierarchy of kinds of beings, a hierarchy of "essences." Following a pattern of thought at least as old as Plato, an essence is conceived on analogy with an abstract form or pattern. Just as the form a sculptor imposes on the clay is what makes it determinately a statue of a person or of a horse, instead of being a formless blob of clay, so an essence is the form that makes one actually to be the determinate kind of being one is. Human nature is one of those kinds of essences. It is the "humanness" of every individual human being, that which makes him or her genuinely human. Since it makes them all equally and fully human, it is identical *in* them all. But it is not identified *with* any one of them.

Within the overall hierarchy of the cosmos, it is located near the top because it is more like God's kind of being than are other creaturely natures.

Interpreting human nature in the context of creation has several important implications. For one thing, it expresses an extraordinary sense of fundamental security: a harmonious relationship to the rest of creation is part of the unchangeable structure of human nature. One is truly "at home" in this world. This is poles apart from the familiar modern way of understanding ourselves as isolated spirits arbitrarily thrown into a world lacking purpose or intrinsic value. In the classic view, to be sure, we do encounter terrible physical suffering and abysmal moral horror, which the human mind cannot explain. Nevertheless, because the world is a structured cosmos it is ultimately intelligible (at least to God!); because it is harmonious it is ultimately beautiful and good.

To understand oneself this way can be liberating as well as comforting. Pagans too believed that humankind was at home in a cosmos. But they often saw its structure as a prison cage governed by impersonal and implacable fate. By contrast, to understand oneself as an integral part of a cosmos freely created and governed by the biblical God was to understand the world as a home ruled by a divine love that worked for the fulfillment of humanity.

Moreover, on this view a relationship to God is essential to human nature. Creatures are finite precisely because they depend on the Creator for their continuing actuality. If they had no such relation, they simply would not be. Call it the creature's "ontological" relation to God, its relationship of dependence for being. In this regard, human nature is essentially related to God in exactly the same way as all other creatures. This has two religiously important consequences. Human nature, along with all creation, is radically secularized. The relation between creatures and God is a relation between two really different and radically different kinds of realities. It is in no way even partially a relation of "identity" between finite and infinite being. There is no respect in which "human nature" contains a part of God or is in any way intrinsically divine. Human nature is of immeasurable value, but it is not sacred in the sense of being worthy of worship. Second, finitude is not human nature's religious problem. Finitude is God's good creation, not a predicament from which human beings need to be "saved." Whatever it is, salvation will be an affirmation of the essential finitude of human nature, not an escape from it.

As an integral part of the cosmos fundamentally related to God, human nature has four major dimensions.

1. Body and Soul

Human beings, as traditionally conceived, are constituted by two quite different kinds of reality related to each other in a hierarchical pattern. The Genesis story says God formed Adam "from the dust of the ground and breathed into his nostrils the breath of life. Thus the man became a living creature" (Gen. 2:7 NEB). Human nature is constituted by a complex relationship between "dust of the ground" and "breath of life." Classic formulations explicated these two notions respectively by using a traditional philosophical distinction between body and soul. "Dust of the ground" seemed to cohere with the traditional understanding of body as *material*, that is, a mode of reality that is distributed over space, can be experienced by the senses, and is subject to all manner of physical disintegration. "Breath of life" seemed to cohere with the traditional understanding of soul as *spiritual*, that is, a mode of reality that is not distributed over space, cannot be sensed, and cannot disintegrate. When the biblical images "dust" and "breath" are interpreted using the considerably more precise concepts "body" and "soul," the contrast between them is heightened. They are hierarchically related. In a living creature the soul animates the otherwise inanimate material body; thus the soul rules the body. Death is the separation of the soul, that is, the life principle, from the body. Nothing brings out more sharply the difference between them. In death the body, as material, undergoes disintegration; the soul, as spiritual, cannot undergo disintegration and so continues in existence (is "immortal").

Traditional philosophical doctrine has noted that, in contrast to all other forms of life, human life is distinguished by the capacity to know truth (through the use of "reason") and by the capacity to regulate its own behavior so as to be morally responsible for it. It therefore concluded that the human soul is the principle not just of mere "livingness" but also of rational and free life. Furthermore, a distinction was often drawn between two kinds of rational capacities: the ability to collect and analyze evidence, build inferential arguments, and solve problems (call it "discursive thinking"), on the one hand, and the ability to apprehend unchanging and universally valid principles of truth, goodness, and beauty (call it "understanding") on the other.

In adopting the concept "soul," theologians also took over these notions. Human nature is essentially free and rational. This makes it enough "like" the rational and free God that it belongs near the top of the hierarchy of created being. More than that, to some degree it inescapably knows God. There are importantly different classic formulations of just how this happens. Augustine held that in understanding, the mind has an immediate intuition of God in and along with its immediate apprehension of the unchanging criteria of truth, beauty, and goodness that one constantly uses in making judgments about what is relatively more true, beautiful, or good than something else. This intuition of God admits of many degrees and may often be no more than a sense of responsibility before higher norms. However dim, it is the "light" within which we do all our "thinking." It is uncreated, the very presence of God to the mind. In contrast, Aquinas seems to have held that the "light" in which we do all our thinking is created; it is itself part of our creaturely mental capacities. He denied that we have any immediate intuition of God, but he held that in discursive thinking, in which we come to grasp the causes of things, we implicitly come also to grasp the reality of God. And he proposed arguments through which this implicit knowledge of God's reality can be brought to explicit acknowledgment. Either way, it is part of classic doctrine to affirm in human nature an essential cognitive relation to God in addition to the ontological relation.

A great danger in the body/soul conceptual scheme is that it may foster a dualism in regard to value: the body may be worth less than the soul. Traditional formulations rejected such suggestions. Origen, for example, moved into dualism when he speculated that Adam was originally created as a disembodied soul who was subsequently, on account of his disobedience, punished by a "fall" *into* a body. In this view, bodies are a punishment and are part of what we need to be saved from. This view was rejected. It is wrong to say Adam *is* a soul (who happens to be stuck with a body). No, Adam is an embodied soul. Embodiedness is essential to being a human soul. But what kind of body? Scripture complicates the discussion, because the apostle Paul distinguishes between the "animal body" of the first (and fallen) Adam and the "spiritual body" of the second (and resurrected) Adam, which is to say, Jesus Christ (1 Cor. 15:44–45). Augustine's mature position, which is representative of classic formulations, was that the creation story teaches that God created Adam with an animal body like the ones we have. A material body is not a punishment; it is good, and having it is good, as part of God's good purposes in creation. Only at the general resurrection will we have spiritual bodies.

Classic formulations never gain clarity about what a spiritual body is. But the distinction is important because of the nuance it introduces concerning the goodness of material bodies. Having a body is essential to human nature. Having a *material* body is not essential; at the general resurrection we shall still have human nature complete even if we come to have another kind of "body." But—and this is theologically crucial—*having had* a material body at some time *is* essential to human nature. Being part of a material cosmos is not an evil, and it is not a punishment. It is neither part of the discipline of our redemption nor what we need to be redeemed from. Precisely because it is a nuance, however, and a rather subtle one at that, it undoubtedly failed to stem a strong drift in Christianity toward negative attitudes concerning the human body. In particular, this way of describing the relationship places the body in the position of a seducer. It is always possible that the proper hierarchical relationship between soul and body will be reversed if the appetites of the body, in their own way perfectly good, prove so attractive to the soul that they displace the soul's own "higher" appetite for truth in moments when the soul must choose between the two. If the soul is "seduced" by the body this way, then the body is still governed by the soul and, more basically, the soul is governed not by its own rational capacities but by the body's interests. No doubt there were many other powerful causes for this suspicion of the body, quite outside classic doctrine. Nevertheless, it must be acknowledged that the body/soul conceptual schema employed in classic formulations permitted and probably suggested such attitudes.

2. Social Being

Human nature has a social dimension. According to the story, Adam, the paradigm of human nature, was created a social being.

He is not complete as himself unless he has a human partner: "'It is not good for the man to be alone. I will provide a partner for him.' So God formed out of the ground all the wild animals and all the birds of heaven. . . . But for the man himself no partner had yet been found. And so the Lord God put the man into a trance, and while he slept, he took one of his ribs and closed the flesh over the place. The Lord God then built up the rib, which he had taken out of the man, into a woman" (Gen. 2:18–22 NEB). This has led classic formulations of the doctrine to place a high stress on the social character of human nature. Humankind is characteristically conceived as the one family of Adam, so tightly knit that somehow it is a single reality "in Adam."

At the same time, the decision to take an individual man as paradigm for human nature, the hierarchical patterns of thought in which the doctrine is elucidated, and the dualistic way "body" and "soul" are related have conspired to make this feature of classic theological anthropology enormously destructive for women. The story says that a male figure was created first as the paradigm for human nature and that a female figure was created second, and was created *for* the male. Does this mean that maleness is, by God's intent, paradigmatic of human nature and that femaleness is somehow inferior and subservient to it? By and large the classic tradition has understood it that way, teaching women to perceive themselves as inferior to men and rightfully subject to them.

There have been important variations on this theme. Gregory of Nyssa held that Adam was created with a "glorious" (which is to say, "spiritual") body that was androgynous. Ideally, sexual differentiation is not essential to human nature. However, foreseeing that Adam would sin and have to die, God introduced sexual differentiation in a second creative act to prevent the race from dying out once Adam sinned. This has the effect of stressing the parity of male and female sexuality, but parity in that both are deficient modes of human nature. Sexual differentiation is simply a necessary compromise of original creation to fend off an even greater evil.

Augustine developed two lines of thought that have dominated the classic tradition, though they stand in some tension with each other. The subordination of women to men is a hierarchy of status and role in the material cosmos, but not a hierarchy in regard to being or intrinsic worth. Men and women are souls that have animal bodies. As souls they are equally fully human. It is only as *embodied* souls that they are hierarchically related, and that is a hierarchy of roles, not of being. Women, because their bodies are female, are to fill roles associated with child-rearing and are dependent on men. Men, because their bodies are male, are to fill roles associated with protecting women and children by laboring to provide food and shelter. But when we come to have spiritual bodies at the general resurrection, that differentiation will disappear. This is to say that the hierarchical pattern may be ordained by God for the time being, but it is not strictly speaking essential to human nature as such. We can still be fully human in its absence.

This softening of the view, pale as it is, is undercut by a second theme. Augustine shares the view that the body, while good, must be viewed with suspicion because it is a potential seducer of the soul. For him, this is especially true with regard to sexual pleasure. The fact that the Genesis story depicts Eve as tempting Adam to disobey gave Augustine biblical warrant for interpreting his own male struggles with sexual temptation as paradigmatic of that seduction. Seductiveness is asymmetrical. As embodied souls, women are seductive to men in a way in which men, as embodied souls, are not seductive to women. Consequently women are more to be feared morally than men. It is not that to be female is intrinsically evil but that it is morally more dangerous. Aquinas hardened this position into the view that women are not only hierarchically subordinate to men in status and in role but also, precisely as embodied, deficient expressions of human nature. He held this view not for any theological reason but on the authority of some of Aristotle's views about the respective roles of men and women in procreation.

At this point both moral and theological considerations raise radical doubts about the adequacy of the classic formulation of the doctrine of human nature. One has to ask whether it is moral to hold a view that has caused so much human anguish. Theologically one has to ask whether by this point the classic view has not come into such conflict with other basic Christian convictions as to suggest that there is something fundamentally wrong in the very way the doctrine has been formulated.

3. Teleology

Human nature has a teleological dimension. That is, while it is itself an unchangeable structure, it is essentially ordered to the completion of two purposes that are not yet fully accomplished.

Within the structure of the cosmos, Adam was created with a role to play in relation to the rest of creation: "Be fruitful and increase, fill the earth and subdue it, rule over the fish in the sea, the birds of heaven, and every living thing that moves upon the earth" (Gen. 1:28 NEB). Accordingly, it is part of the structure of human nature that we have a calling, a role to play in and for creation. The role has been variously understood in the tradition, sometimes as "caring for" and "tending" a partner, far more often (and with disastrous ecological results) as "mastering" and "dominating" an opponent. Either way, human nature is understood in terms of a purpose to be realized.

Second, the Genesis story makes it clear that Adam was created to fill a role in relation to God. He was created to live in unending communion with God. It was to be an immediate and intimate relating to God, but in obedience to rather than in parity or mutuality with God. And the unendingness of the communion depended on the obedience: "You may eat from every tree in the garden, but not from the tree of the knowledge of good and evil; for on the day that you eat from it, you will certainly die" (Gen. 2:17 NEB). It is part of the structure of human nature that it is oriented toward this relationship of obedience to God. Several things depend on it: The unendingness of the communion depends on obedience. Adam is told that if he disobeys, he will die. And classic formulations add that preserving the correct relation of body to soul and properly caring for the rest of creation also depend on obedience.

4. Temporality

Finally, human nature is essentially involved in time. This point needs to be made carefully. Human nature itself is nontemporal. No event in time could cause it to change its structure (that is, cease consisting of a free and rational soul that has been embodied, or cease being social, or cease being ordered to caring for creation and communing with God). Time cannot get *into* it to change it. On the other hand, it is part of the structure of human nature to be *in* time. This follows from its being part of its structure that the soul has been *at some time* materially embodied. It also follows from the soul's freedom. Freedom means the possibility of change in action. Change and time are correlative: Time is the measure of change; no change, no time. If freedom is essential to human nature, then the temporality of human action is too.

So human nature is the nontemporal *basis* of temporal acts. The classic tradition has typically expressed this with the philosophical distinction between "being" (what a thing is) and its "operations" (its acts). In the order of reality, being precedes operations. That is, operations depend on a being for their reality (no action, say running, could be going on without the presence of a being who does them) in a way in which a being does not depend on its operations for its reality (in monumental sloth, a human being might be present without performing any actions and nonetheless be "real"). Thus human nature is a kind of being and is the nontemporal basis of (human) acts; human acts are temporal operations whose ontologically prior basis is human nature. So human nature is essentially involved in time, but time does not get into human nature.

The last two dimensions of human nature taken together provide the possibility for radical failure or "fall" in human beings. Human beings cannot fail to exhibit an orientation toward caring for creation and communing with God, and when they act they cannot fail to act in time. These are aspects of the unchangeable structure of human nature. But precisely because they are free, human beings can fail actually to perform the concrete acts of caring and of obedient communion to which human nature orients them. Moreover, failure to act in obedient ways that constitute actual communion with God leads to a deformity outwardly in one's actual relationship with creation and to a deformity inwardly in the way soul and body are interrelated. Failure to commune with God in obedience is not just one more mistake; it brings with it a radical deformity of oneself.

Image of God, Freedom, and Fall

This radical deformity is what early church theologians called "fallenness." But how can human beings suffer a truly radical deformity and still retain their human nature intact? Augustine suggested the two-part answer that largely shaped medieval and Reformation views on this matter. The first part is to stress that what is deformed is the image of God, not human nature. Adam was created "after" or "according to" the image of God (Gen. 1:26–27). Only the Logos, the Word of God, *is* the *imago dei*. Failure to live according to the ends for which we were created can damage the *imago*. That is because human nature is understood as a static structure, whereas the *imago* is understood in largely dynamic terms. It consists in my actively taking up right relationship both to myself and to God. More precisely, it consists in taking up a cognitive relationship in which I simultaneously and inseparably know myself rightly and know God rightly. In this relationship people know themselves as creatures and implicitly know God by virtue of the light provided by God's immediate presence to them. To know God and oneself in this way is actually to bear the *imago dei*. The image is always at least potentially present, so in one way it is a permanent capacity of human nature; yet it is not something simply given. In this case, knowing properly depends on loving truly. I can know myself, and know God in knowing myself, only if I care enough to attend properly to God and myself. So to bear the image of God is freely to relate to oneself as a being *in* God. To cease to do that is to cease imaging God properly. Then the image is damaged.

In what way is this a *radical* deformity? The second part of Augustine's answer is to insist that when the *imago dei* is damaged, human will falls into bondage to sin. While remaining human, one becomes unable to avoid sinning. This is a truly *radical* deformity. It confronted Augustine with a paradox, since freedom of the will is essential to unchanged human nature. He resolves the paradox by distinguishing between two quite different senses of "will." Free will as free choice among alternatives (call it *arbitrium*) is essential to human nature and is never lost. But all choices are made for the sake of some value. Basically we all will to be happy. Augustine contends that our decision about what makes for happiness is a special kind of act of will (call it *voluntas*). To pick something as the basis of our happiness is to love it. As created, Adam exercised will as *voluntas* in freely loving God. He was related to himself in the way that images God. That provided the basis on which he exercised will as *arbit-*

rium. Every choice among alternatives was made in service of God. Then Adam chose (*voluntas*) a creature (himself!) instead of God as the basis of his happiness. Thereby he constituted himself in a new way. He retained the capacity for free choice among alternatives, but the chooser was now defined by a new way of relating to himself. He was constituted as a non-God-lover, a self-lover. He chose freely, but every free choice was chosen in service to himself as the basis of his happiness. And that is a situation one is not free to change. When one ceases to image God, one's immediate intuition of God is so weakened that one cannot be conscious enough of God to start loving God anew. The dynamics of the *imago dei* are such that if the image is distorted, the person is radically deformed and in bondage.

CHALLENGES AND CONTRIBUTIONS OF MODERN CONSCIOUSNESS

The Turn to the Subject

One hallmark of the modern period in Western cultural history has been the rise of a distinctive set of root convictions about personhood. They developed slowly and from different sources, but by the start of the nineteenth century they had become a widely shared and unquestioned set of beliefs. To be a person is to be a center or "subject" of consciousness who is at once a knower of "objects," a knower of the moral law, and a possible enactor of moral duties. Both as knower and as doer, a subject is autonomous, historical, and self-constituting.

Take the subject as knower. It has a kind of autonomy in that it is not dictated to by a world of already determinate "objects" that is over against it and simply given to it. Immanuel Kant was believed to have shown in the *Critique of Pure Reason* that the "objectivity" of the objects we know is not a given. Rather it is largely constituted by the knowing consciousness. All that is given is sense experience. Consciousness organizes that experience into objects. It does so on terms it itself provides, and not on terms dictated by how reality is "outside" consciousness. It is consciousness that organizes experience into an intelligible field of individual objects. So there is a way in which the subject as consciousness is "behind" or "outside" the world as a field of knowable objects. It is not an item in the world. Like God, it orders and transcends a world. Moreover, since what can be known is restricted to what can be ordered out of sense experience, neither the knowing subject (or "transcendental ego") itself nor any other trans-empirical substance can be a possible object of knowledge. As the study of history and of non-Western cultures progressed during the nineteenth century, it came to be widely held that the categories in which consciousness organizes sense experience may themselves change from culture to culture and from one historical period to another. So far as that is true, the subject as knower is historicized. Not only does consciousness know objects in history, but the movement of history can change consciousness.

Take the subject as morally responsible doer. Its autonomy is deeper than mere freedom of choice. It was generally accepted that in his *Critique of Practical Reason*, Kant had made his point that a subject is truly moral only in following a law (*nomos* in Greek) that is grounded not in something other than itself and not even in the will of God (which would be "hetero/nomy"), but rather in itself as subject (which he called "auto/nomy"). As the nineteenth century passed, it became clear that there was room for considerable difference of opinion about which aspect of the subject is the basis of moral norms and about their actual content. But the principle of moral autonomy has become an unquestioned assumption of modern consciousness.

The principle of autonomy brings with it another principle. Moral subjects are self-constituting. There is an ambiguity in the phrase "moral subject." It may mean that the subject's behavior is actually moral. Of course, that is never a given. But moral subject may mean "a subject whose behavior is rightly open to moral assessment." In that sense, animals are not moral subjects; they can behave neither morally nor immorally. The principle of moral autonomy brings with it the view that being a moral subject in this second sense is also never a given. What *is* given is an array of physical and emotional hungers that, in their pressure for immediate gratification, tend to motivate behavior. It has also been common to say that, in contrast to these "desires," subjects have a qualitatively different kind of yearning for fulfillment as subjects. It has been variously characterized as a yearning for happiness (following classical philosophy) or for "authenticity." A subject will satisfy the yearning for fulfillment only when it constitutes itself as a moral subject. It constitutes itself a subject when it actively takes charge of itself so that its behavior is guided not by desires but by the moral law grounded in the very structure of its subjectivity (however that law may be spelled out in detail).

More precisely, the subject is constituted by the *history* of its relating to itself in this way. Here again the basic historicity of the subject of consciousness becomes apparent. The fact that moral subjectivity is never a given means that it is open to threats. Once achieved, it may be lost. The "act" of self-constitution may need to be repeated. As the nineteenth and twentieth centuries have unfolded, there have been different opinions about the sources of the threat. For much of the nineteenth century it seemed that the threat stemmed from the fact that the subject is embodied. The Enlightenment and the rise of modern science had left a mechanistic picture of the body as a set of cogs in the machinery of the physical world. The autonomous, self-constituting character of the subject makes it at once wholly other than this mechanical system and yet involved in it and threatened by it. Later in the century, Darwin's powerful hypothesis that evolution of the species, including homo sapiens, is driven by a battle whose only law is the survival of the fittest posed the threat differently. In this instance the moral subject was threatened by the fact that, as embodied, it is part of a basically amoral biological system.

To many other thinkers late in the nineteenth century and early in the twentieth, the threats to the moral subject seemed to stem more from its cultural dimensions than its physical dimensions. The process of self-constitution, for all its radical autonomy, always takes place in a social context. But social contexts always involve a material culture. One did not need to be a Marxist to acknowledge the force of Karl Marx's contention that the economic structure of cultures can profoundly distort the consciousnesses of subjects living in them. Nor did one need to be committed to existentialism to recognize the cogency of Martin Heidegger's analysis of ways in which the routines and language of everyday conventional technological culture can deform subjectivity into "inauthenticity." In any case, whether they are rooted in the body, culture, or elsewhere, it is the threats that focus the autonomy, historicity, and self-constitutingness of a moral subject: One is a moral subject only as a *history* of a struggle autonomously to constitute oneself a morally responsible subject in the face of threats to one's status as moral subject.

This set of root convictions about personhood deprived any theologian who shared them of the major assumptions on which the classic theological view of human nature had been based. Given the modern view of the subject as knower, it is impossible either to claim a cosmic structure of being in which human nature has its proper place or to claim that each individual human being is a rational substance. Consciousness can only know what is in sense experience, and that does not include either a cosmos "out there" to be known or a rational substance "in here" to do the knowing. The secure cosmic home in terms of which the classic view understood human beings is gone. Furthermore, given the modern view of the subject as moral subject, it is impossible to view the unique acts of individual human beings as secondary to some underlying being, identically the same in all subjects. The very idea of human nature became unintelligible. What constitutes one a subject is precisely what is most unique to each one: the history of one's own struggle autonomously to constitute oneself as a subject. And precisely because that history is seen as a struggle, human life is seen no longer as "at home" in a beautiful and intelligible cosmos but instead as cast into a world at best indifferent to human values and at worst antithetical to them.

A great many Protestant and Roman Catholic theologians in the nineteenth and twentieth centuries have refused to share modernity's assumptions about personhood, preferring to conserve the classic theological views of human nature. They view the root assumptions of modernity about personhood as dubious philosophical theses which they reject. Some theologians, however, consider efforts to disavow these assumptions a kind of self-deception. They view them as inescapable aspects of the identities of modern Christians simply because they live in *this* culture. It seems to them intellectually more honest explicitly to affirm these new convictions about personhood and to try to use them in addressing the same agenda of questions about persons that earlier theologians faced. Recall that the agenda had two points: What is it about finite persons that makes it possible for them to know the infinite God? And what is it about persons that makes it possible for them, while remaining persons, to undergo so profound a "fall" that it requires the sort of "redemption" to which the church witnesses? The convictions about personhood that modern consciousness brings present these theologians with this challenge: How can one affirm the autonomy, historicity, and self-constituting-ness of persons as subjects and still affirm not only that they know and are redeemed by God, but that in this they are radically *dependent* on God?

Strategies for Theological Reconstruction

Six major strategies have emerged in nineteenth- and twentieth-century theology to meet this challenge. Most of them continue to be influential. Before sketching them singly, it is worth noting two features they share. None of them is alleged to be based on the story of Adam. As an explanatory account of the coming into existence of homo sapiens and of the fall, the story is rejected. As a paradigm of what personhood ought to be, it is replaced by the story of Jesus who, it is now common to stress, is at once the truly actualized person and the image of God. If the story of Adam figures at all in this theology, it is as a paradigm of the movement from innocence through temptation to sin. And here, instead of personhood being understood in terms of the biblical story, the story is interpreted in terms of analyses of consciousness developed independently of the story. Second, they share the theme that theologically the central thing to say about subjects is that they do stand in a relation to God of radical dependency. In classic theology there had been a clear conceptual distinction between two modes of relatedness to God: the human being as "knower of God" (the invariant), and as "sinner redeemed by God"—both of which may admit of different modes and degrees at different times in a person's life. In "modern" theologies, by contrast, there is a marked tendency to collapse these into one relationship.

1. Structure of Consciousness

The first strategy for reconciling a relation of radical dependence on God with the subject's history of autonomous self-constitution relies on an analysis of the *structure* of subjectivity as embodied consciousness. It is within the framework of that structure that self-constitution takes place. Consciousness has several levels or grades. By virtue of its embodiedness it is flooded at one level by sense experiences and by hungers and desires demanding immediate gratification. At another level, consciousness as "theoretical reason" can order sense experience into a world of objects whose interrelations it can then analyze and explain; and as "practical reason" it can grasp the moral law and assess which actions count as doing one's moral duty even if it requires subordinating or suppressing desire. But what Christians mean by the God-relation can be neither a cognitive relation with an object of theoretical reason nor a relation of moral commitment by practical reason to a good maxim. There is, this strategy urges, a third level of consciousness distinct from sense consciousness and consciousness of a world of other objects and persons. It is an immediate consciousness of God. It is a relationship to God in *consciousness*. Friedrich Schleiermacher characterized it as a "feeling of absolute dependence." Paul Tillich calls it "ultimate concern." Karl Rahner calls it a "preapprehension of being" or of "mystery." However it is put, it honors the turn to the subject by being a claim about consciousness, not about substances. It is a relation of *immediate* consciousness. It is a "consciousness-of," but it is not mediated by concepts and so has no determinate "object" (since objects are conceptually formulated). Tillich makes this point by insisting that this is a consciousness that transcends the subject-object structure of knowledge, and Rahner characterizes it as a "pre-thematic" apprehension. Thus the God-relation is a structural feature of every consciousness.

And it does not violate autonomy. It is at once a dependency relation on God and the necessary condition of the subject's autonomy. On the one hand this strategy argues that the subject is unintelligible apart from God-consciousness. As knower and as moral subject, it is dependent on the God-relation to be precisely what it is. On the other hand it is clear that a subject's true actualization is not a given. The subject must actualize itself. In that act of self-constitution is its deepest autonomy. The God-relation, far from violating that autonomy, is rather its necessary condition, for self-constitution consists in either allowing or prohibiting immediate God-consciousness to dominate consciousness as a whole. Without the consciousness of God there would be nothing to allow or prohibit.

2. The Subject in Nature

The second strategy relies on an analysis of the situatedness of subjects in nature. Consciousness intrinsically "intends" or is consciousness-of natural and social phenomena that are other than itself and that provide it a kind of context. The subject always constitutes itself in a situation that has natural and social dimensions. On this strategy, the God-relation is emphatically not an intrinsic part of the structure of each consciousness. The theological reason for this denial is important: The God-relation in redemption to which Christianity witnesses is an unpredictable gift of grace and not a universal feature of consciousness that can be taken for granted as something simply given. The God-relation consists rather in faith, a gift that some have and others do not. Faith is a particular mode of subjectivity whose distinctive features are determined by that which it intends and to which it is a response. As such, the God-relation is only one possible way among many in which a subject may be related to its situation as it constitutes itself.

The focus here is on the moral subject. This strategy accepts Immanuel Kant's contention that the subject as knower is restricted to sense experience. So the God-relation cannot be a cognitive relation. It also rejects the thesis of the first strategy that distinct from knowing and doing is a deeper level of consciousness which, as "feeling" or "intuition," is consciousness of God, for that contradicts the theological claim that the God-relation is grace and not a structural feature of consciousness. As put by Albrecht Ritschl, whose formulation was immensely influential in the last quarter of the nineteenth century and the early part of the twentieth, the moral subject is situated in a contradiction. It is both "a part of the natural world and a spiritual personality claiming to rule nature." Its involvement in nature is a threat to its status as a moral subject that knows values and knows an obligation to make them actual. We constitute ourselves as moral subjects by taking responsibility for our behavior. This may be done in many ways. The theological claim is that there is only one way of constituting oneself that will sustain one's difference from "nature." That is to act in the faith that deeper than amoral nature is a reality that sustains the actualization of values in history. More exactly, faith is the trust that the historical life of Jesus discloses the nature of this reality as a love that forgives our failures to act in this trust and motivates us to love one another more deeply. This faith is the God-relation. It does not violate the autonomy of the subject who has it; rather, it sustains that subject precisely in its autonomy against the amoral mechanisms of nature.

3. The Subject in Time

The third strategy focuses on the subject's situatedness in time rather than in nature. Every subject has a relationship to itself. Following Martin Heidegger, Rudolf Bultmann (whose use of this strategy has been very influential in mid-twentieth-century theology) characterizes this self-relation as a "self-understanding." It is the concrete "how" of the subject's life, the unique way in which in actual practice it takes or treats itself. All of the subject's transactions with its natural and social setting and with the contents of its own psychological states are done in terms of its self-understanding. The question of how it will understand itself is always open and must be decided anew in every moment. The hallmark of authentic self-understanding is freedom. In it a subject is free to respond to each new situation that history brings in terms of its novel possibilities and demands. But there is always the possibility that a subject will understand itself "inauthentically." That happens when it understands itself on terms set by a given situation. It loses itself in nature or in society's current status quo and therewith loses its freedom to respond *to* the new situations that the passage of time brings. A subject thus falls into bondage to a cultural situation that immediately becomes part of the past. It is tied to the past and closed to the future. The theological claim is that all subjects do in fact understand themselves inauthentically. This is fallenness: a bondage to ideals and norms in terms of which one has chosen to understand oneself, living according to the works of some "law." Here culture and society pose the threat to true self-actualization. However, the objective fact of the proclamation of the gospel of God's loving acceptance of humankind in Jesus Christ provides the concrete possibility of recovering authentic self-understanding. It is grace. If one decides to understand oneself as one affirmed and forgiven by God, one is set free from defining oneself in terms of any status quo. This self-understanding is faith. It is given its particular form by that to which it is a reponse, the gospel of Jesus Christ. Since the word "God" means "the power that can restore us to authenticity," this *is* the God-relation. It does not violate but rather creates the subject's autonomy.

4. *Dynamics of Self-Making*

A fourth strategy for reconciling our dependence on God with our autonomy in self-constitution rests on an analysis of the dynamics of situated self-making. Rooted in G. W. F. Hegel's thought, it was very influential on mid-nineteenth-century theology. Its influence on twentieth-century theology has come through inverted and reversed versions.

Ironically, this strategy embraces the turn to the subject as a way to recover a cosmic context in which to understand the subject. The central thesis is that knowing consists of a dialectical process having three moments. Out of sense-experience one constructs a concept, a truth (thesis); then, experience being what it is, another truth is called forth that seems to contradict it (antithesis); but genuine understanding comes only when the two are united and transcended in a more embracing truth (synthesis) which will itself come into conflict with a contradictory truth (antithesis again), and so on. Absolute knowledge would come when all individual truths are embraced in one grand synthesis.

This dialectic is for Hegelians the principle of knowledge. If the broadly Kantian thesis is correct that the knowing subject "constitutes" the objectivity and order of the reality it knows, then this dialectical principle of knowledge is also the principle of reality. Each individual subject (spirit, *Geist*) is constituted by a dialectical process of self-making which is situated in nature and history. On the one hand this means that each subject is limited by the fact that there are others with whom it must interact. It is not unlimited; it is finite. On the other hand it means that each *Geist* is constituted by a dialectic between two aspects of itself. It is an autonomous center of consciousness, a "subjective spirit" that manifests itself as a center of both natural energy and moral agency, in this way becoming "objective spirit." These two aspects of finite spirit—the subjective and the objective—are dialectically related. Finite spirit is constituted by the process of objective self-manifestation. Yet every objectification of itself, that is, every one of the political, social, and moral roles and structures it creates for itself, is inadequate to express its autonomy. So history is the story of subjective spirit's progressive overcoming of successive modes of objective spirit and their forms of bondage in the direction of greater freedom. Conversely, history is the story of objective spirit, persons as social and moral agents, giving subjective spirit concrete placement in some culture and historical tradition that defines its very identity. Finitude includes radical cultural and historical relativity.

The fact that spirit knows all this about itself, however, means that in some other respect it transcends its situatedness and is nonsituated or infinite. It is *absolute* spirit. As such its reality is constituted by the same dialectical principle. Absolute spirit is a process of *nonsitu-ated* self-making. The world and its history are not really other than absolute spirit. Rather, history as a whole is the second moment in the three-moment dialectic in which absolute spirit (thesis), by manifesting or objectifying itself (antithesis, world history) comes to ultimate self-reconciliation in self-knowledge (synthesis). But that is to say that finite spirits have their reality in a larger cosmic context. Being so situated *is* their God-relation. Furthermore, that context is one in which God comes to ultimate actualization precisely through the process in which finite spirits come to their own actualization. So the God-relation is the condition, and not a violation, of their autonomy.

5. *Dynamics of Self-choosing*

A fifth strategy rests on the dynamics of the subject's situated self-choosing. Søren Kierkegaard provides the classic formulation of this strategy, and it has been very influential in mid-twentieth-century theology, especially in Reinhold Niebuhr's *Nature and Destiny of Man*. The subject is constituted by three relations: (1) It is a relation between "finitude" and "infinity." Niebuhr takes this to mean that it is a relation between a determinateness imposed by the subject's actual setting in nature and history (it has this body type, these physical and mental endowments, this particular cultural heritage, and not others) on one hand, and a freedom unendingly ("infinitely") to transcend this givenness and entertain possible alterations and alternatives to it on the other. (2) It is a relation that relates itself to itself. It may relate to itself as the bipolar reality it is ("finite" and "infinite," "nature" and "freedom") by so living as either to deny one of its poles or to affirm them both. "Fallenness" is to conduct one's life as though one were not free (sin as sensuality) or as though one were not nature (sin as pride). (3) A subject is a relation that relates to itself truly only as it stands related to God. It is only in consciousness of and trust in God's gracious power that one is *able* so to relate to oneself that in one's living one affirms both one's finitude (nature) and one's infinitude (freedom), and keeps them in their rightful balance. At least a dim consciousness of the presence of this divine power is present in every subject (general revelation). Vivid and focused consciousness of it through particular historical events (e.g., the crucifixion of Jesus) is saving special revelation, for it engenders the trust that pulls one out of fallen denial of one aspect or the other of oneself.

In this strategy the threat to the subject is rooted not in something, whether nature or history, other than and outside the subject, but rather within the very dynamics of the subject itself. That it is constituted by deciding how to relate to itself means it is always possible that it will decide wrongly and misconstitute itself. This strategy has generally been seen as the polar opposite of the fourth strategy, designed to affirm the irreducible individuality of the finite subject. Yet it is a kind of reverse image of it as well. The crucial difference between them is that the moments in the dialectic of self-constitution are related to one another by free decisions and not by an inevitable process. Each subject must make its own decisions by which the dynamics of its self-constituting move along on their dialectical way. Self-constituting is a self-choosing, not a self-making. The possibility of a God-relation is a part of the dynamics of every subject. Its actualization is the basis of the subject's fully actualized autonomy, not a violation of it. But its actualization itself depends on the subject's free decision and is not a function of a cosmic process in which the subject is but a moment.

6. God as Subject

A sixth strategy has been controversial because it rests on a rejection of the agenda of questions that classic and modern theology have shared. In his *Church Dogmatics*, Karl Barth proposes to reconcile the subject's autonomy and dependence on God by grounding both in God's free decision. In his view, Christian theology, precisely because it is finally about God, cannot discuss human beings by addressing these questions: What is it about finite subjects that makes possible knowledge of God? And what is it about them that makes radical fallenness possible? Rather the question should be: What is it about *God* that makes these things possible?

For Barth, a seriously theological point of view will see God as subject (or, in Barth's terminology, "person") in the proper sense of the term. It will see us as persons only in a qualified and extended sense of the term. Barth is faithful to the turn to the subject, insisting that God as person has being only "in God's acts" and not in an essence or substance lying behind God's acts. The "acts" in which

God has being constitute a dialectic of self-relatedness having three moments. God's reality as person is triune. The theological claim is that God "decides" to enter into relationship with persons other than God. The best image for that relationship is covenant. Implicit in this is God's further decision to be known to covenant partners: revelation. It takes place in a very concrete way: incarnation. In Jesus, God comes into the closest covenant fellowship with a finite subject. This is the end to which the creation of a world of finite subjects is ordered. All creaturely subjects are involved in this covenant relationship with God by virtue of being related to Jesus. It is simply a matter of objective fact that Jesus is part of human history to which we are all related. All subjects are "elected" for this relationship. It is this relationship to God, which is created by God's decision, that constitutes us as persons.

So the God-relation is universal, but it does not consist of a mode of consciousness and cannot be discovered by an analysis of the structure of consciousness (against the first strategy). Because it nonetheless involves all subjects, the God-relation is not just one possible relation among many (against strategies two and three). Because it is the fulfillment of that to which creation was ordered in the first place, the covenantal relation that constitutes us as subjects is a relation that places us in a cosmic setting. But the God-relation is not a moment in a cosmic process. It is free grace, the final redemption of God's primordial purpose (against strategy four). And in this view, subjects are constituted by a free decision by God and not by themselves (against strategy five). In a way this is strategy four turned on its head. Instead of the history of interactions among finite "spirits" being the process through which absolute spirit is known and actualized, God's decision to enter into covenant fellowship with a finite "other" (i.e., "to reveal God") is the basis of history. Whereas strategy five connects the necessary moments of the dialectic through which each subject constitutes itself by its own free decisions rather than by an inevitable process, Barth's strategy connects the moments in the cosmic dialectic through which God realizes God's primordial decision for covenant fellowship, including the constituting of finite subjects, by God's own free decision. This focuses the major theological objection to this strategy. While it allows for full stress that the God-relation is grace and that the ones begraced are irreducibly finite subjects dependent on grace, what happens to their autonomy? In many places it is clear that Barth intends to affirm our autonomy. But it is not clear that this strategy will permit one to affirm it consistently.

ISSUES AND PROPOSALS

There have been at least three persistent issues bedeviling Christian theological anthropology since the turn to the subject.

1. Can its stress on the *autonomy* of the subject in its self-constituting be reconciled with the ways in which modern consciousness in other moods seeks to *explain* human behavior? The explanations come in at least three broad types. One kind of explanation is cast in terms of psychological analyses of consciousness, both from experimental psychology and from various kinds of psychoanalytic theories. Another kind of explanation is based on the study of the behavior of more or less "social" animals. Still another type of explanation is grounded in neurological research, especially study of the brain. The conceptual framework theologians have relied on seems simply inadequate to engage these forms of explanation of behavior. "Emotions," "animal behavior," and "brain processes" presumably all belong in the theologians' category of nature. Even when nature is not treated as something other than the subject and as a threat to it and is instead incorporated into the subject as one pole in the dialectic by which it is constituted, it is still treated as somehow inferior to and a threat to the glory of the subject's other pole (freedom, spirit, or self-transcendence). "Nature" is altogether too abstract a category to use in trying to come to terms with these explanations that seem to deny the subject's autonomy. To use it in describing the subject is to distort the description of the subject by abstracting it from its very physical or material concreteness.

2. Can the stress on the autonomy of the subject's *self-constitution* in modern theology do justice to the material bases of human life? Stress on self-constitution, as we have seen, places high value on the cultivation of highly refined sensibilities, intense levels of self-awareness, and unique individuality. In practice this is possible for people whose economic, social, and political power relative to the rest of society gives them a remarkable degree of leisure. They are next to

impossible for people to attain whose poverty, powerlessness, or ignorance makes life itself precarious. The rise of liberation theologies expressing the theological perspective of oppressed blacks, women, and Third World people insistently raises this question: Is not the concept "subject" in modern theology fatally flawed for the purposes of Christian theology precisely because it reflects a Western, male, bourgeois status that has the requisite surplus of time beyond what is needed to sustain life, but only as the fruit of other people's oppression? Once again the charge is that the concept of subject that theologians have used is abstract. But in this case it is "abstract" in the Marxist sense: abstracted from the *material* economic, social, and political power structures that in actual life are ingredient in a subject's concreteness.

3. Have theologians evaded the hard question about reconciling finite human autonomy with radical dependency on God? They have attempted to reconcile the two by thinking of persons as patients and recipients of influences from nature, society, or God. Or they have taken persons as centers of inwardness that engage in self-making or self-choosing by "acts" that are entirely interior and utterly private. In either case, persons are considered as actors in a public world only secondarily, and in ways somehow derivative from what consciousness receives or inwardness "does." The one apparent exception we found to this comes from the fourth strategy, which stressed that person as "objective spirit" has a dialectical parity with person as "subjective spirit." And there it is unclear whether the finitude of finite spirits is ultimate, or whether it is but a moment in a process culminating in an undialectical unity of all spirits in absolute spirit. In regard to the other strategies, we have seen that it is possible to show ways in which consciousness' autonomy is compatible with dependency on God. But surely the hard questions come when one considers persons not as patients but as finite agents—active concrete powers in a shared and public world—and when one tries to reconcile the autonomy of finite agency with dependency on God. Again, exquisite analyses of subjectivity turn out to be misleading because they are abstract, that is to say, abstracted from the concrete reality of persons as finite energy systems, causal agents (perhaps self-causing?) in a public world.

At least two sorts of theological development seem to be called for.

In classic theology claims about the material dimensions of human life were made in a doctrine of creation that declared the actual physical contexts and dimensions of human life, whatever they may in fact be, to be fundamentally good and supportive of human freedom. This was true even when theologians played down or dropped any effort to explain the origin of the physical universe by their doctrines of creation. The claims about the material dimensions of personal existence could be made in terms of an ontological relationship between all reality and God. This unchanging and unchangeable relationship, we saw, was logically distinct from the relations constituted by knowledge of God and by fall and redemption, which could be understood as varying in degree or ceasing altogether. However, as we have also seen, in modern theology these two kinds of relationships between persons as creatures and God have consistently been collapsed into one kind of relationship, consisting in a mode of consciousness or in a conscious decision, and admitting of degree. It may be that theological anthropology will be unable to do justice to the material dimensions of human life until it has recovered a full-blown doctrine of creation as a mode of relation to God other than relationships in consciousness.

In addition, theological anthropology may be able to deal with persons in their genuine concreteness only by a second "turn," from the person as patient or subject of consciousness to the person as agent. There are at least two quite different kinds of movements that may promise a new turn to the agent. On one side, in liberation theology and political theology the Marxist tradition has begun to influence Christian analyses of the human predicament and God's engagement in it. These movements have not yet perhaps fully articulated the conceptual schemes on which they rely. But it is already evident how much they depend on an analysis of personhood in which the concept "praxis" is central, a concept that focuses on persons as agents before they are subjects of consciousness, taken precisely in their concrete material contexts. Second, there is a revival in Anglo-American philosophical theology of a modest sort of metaphysics that tries to sketch a conceptual scheme central to which is an analysis of "action" and of persons as "agents." This too is a varied phenomenon, no single school of thought at all, and certainly not yet the fount of a highly articulated set of proposals. But, like the first movement, it promises to be fertile for new consructive proposals of better ways in which to elucidate the Christian witness to the liberating and humanizing effect of personal dependence on God.

SUGGESTIONS FOR FURTHER READING

Aquinas, Thomas. *Summa Theologica*, Part 1a, questions 90–101; Part 1a2ae, questions 81–85 (Blackfriars edition, vols. 13, 26).

Augustine. *City of God*. Books 12–14.

Barth, Karl. *Church Dogmatics*. Vol. 3/2, secs. 44–45.

Bultmann, Rudolf. *Existence and Faith*. Edited by Schubert M. Ogden. New York: Meridian Books, 1960. "The Concept of Revelation in the New Testament," "The Historicity of Man and Faith," "Romans 7 and the Anthropology of Paul," "History of Salvation and History."

Burrell, David B. *Aquinas: God and Action*. Notre Dame: University of Notre Dame, 1979. Chaps. 8, 9, 10, 13.

Farley, Edward. *Good and Evil: Interpreting a Human Condition*. Minneapolis: Fortress Press, 1990.

Farrer, Austin. *The Freedom of the Will*. New York: Charles Scribner's Sons, 1958. Chaps. 1–5.

Gregory of Nyssa. "On the Making of Man." *NPNF*[2] 5.

Hegel, G. W. F. *Phenomenology of Spirit*. Translated by A. V. Miller. Oxford: Oxford University Press, 1977.

Keller, Catherine. *From a Broken Web: Separation, Sexism and Self*. Boston: Beacon Press, 1986.

Kierkegaard, Søren. *Fear and Trembling* and *The Sickness unto Death*. Translated by Howard V. Hong and Edna H. Hong. Princeton: Princeton University Press, 1983, 1980.

Moltmann, Jürgen. *Man: Christian Anthropology in the Conflicts of the Present*. Philadelphia: Fortress Press, 1971.

Niebuhr, Reinhold. *The Nature and Destiny of Man*. Vol. 1, chaps. 6–8.

Origen. *On First Principles*. Books 1:8; 2:8, 9.

Pannenberg, Wolfhart. *Anthropology in Theological Perspective*. Philadelphia: Westminster, 1985.

Rahner, Karl. *Foundations of Christian Faith*. Part 1.

Rist, John. "Augustine on Free Will and Predestination." In *Augustine: A Collection of Critical Essays*. Edited by R. A. Markus. New York: Anchor Books, 1972.

Ruether, Rosemary Radford. *New Woman/New Earth*. New York: Seabury Press, 1975.

Schleiermacher, Friedrich. *The Christian Faith*. Chap. 1.

Segundo, Juan. *Evolution and Guilt*. Maryknoll, N.Y.: Orbis Books, 1974.

7. SIN AND EVIL

WHERE WE ARE

The doctrine of sin and evil occupies a somewhat anomalous position in Christian doctrine. On the one hand, there is no positively stated orthodox doctrine of sin comparable to the soteriological doctrines of Trinity and Christology. The ancient church agreed with Augustine that certain views of sin and evil are incompatible with Christian faith. Accordingly, the church condemned the Manichean heresy for its theological pessimism and the Pelagian heresy for its anthropological optimism concerning evil. But the church stopped short of officially adopting Augustine's own positive formulation of original sin. Instead, it came closer to adopting his teachings concerning grace. Yet these soteriological doctrines presuppose some concept of the human condition, including responsibility for evil. There is, as Augustine well knew, a systematic connection between the concept of salvation and the concept of sin, so that neither concept can be formulated in complete separation from the other. Consequently, while the church did not officially adopt Augustine's teachings concerning sin, his formulation of the doctrine of original sin has been highly influential—so much so that it can almost be said to have attained semiofficial standing.

The reason for its only being semiofficial is that it has always been controversial. It was forged in the Pelagian controversy. Despite the church's siding with Augustine against Pelagius, its refusal to adopt the entire doctrine of original sin indicates that Pelagius's objections to certain aspects of the doctrine had some sting. Even modern scholars concede that most of the important objections to the doctrine were raised in Augustine's time by his opponents. Nonetheless, Augustine's doctrine of original sin constituted a substantial and undoubtedly the major view of evil in Christian thought until the modern period, when it came under its most severe criticism as a result of the impact of historical-critical consciousness. The Adam story of Genesis 2–3, for instance, is no longer credible as actual history. The concept of original righteousness as a historical period of human perfection and sinlessness prior to the fall is problematic. And the concept of original or inherited guilt is rejected by many as intellectually and morally offensive.

In modern secular culture, moreover, the Christian concept of sin has been eclipsed and virtually displaced. Secular culture perceives evil no longer as a theological problem but rather as a problem of *human* institutional and social arrangements. Divine aid is felt to be either unnecessary or not among the real possibilities available to resolve the problem. Instead, evil calls for intelligent human action. There are present in modern culture, however, quite different views concerning the meaning and results of human action. Some take a rather optimistic view in which the problem of evil is capable of human management and therefore amenable to control. Science and technology are regarded as the instruments by means of which we will eventually eliminate evil as a problem. Whether evil is seen as a resistance of nature to human manipulation and exploitation or as a recalcitrance on the part of human beings to social planning and conditioning, it is at least viewed as a "problem" which will sooner or later yield to an appropriate technological "solution." So runs the "myth of progress."

The twentieth century, however, has seen widespread disenchantment with the belief in progress. Two world wars, the Holocaust, and the ever-present threat of nuclear annihilation are grim reminders that despite technological progress evil has not disappeared from modern culture. Nor is it likely to do so. Major intellectual movements such as Freudian thought and existentialist philosophy (Camus, Sartre) have rediscovered the tragic side of human life and culture. In these views evil is perceived to be coincident with the human condition. Since it is structural, there is no solution to the problem of evil; evil simply defies all explanations and solutions. Hence these views suggest that human beings must learn to resign themselves to evil, learn to live with it. Moreover, by 1970 the global problems of overpopulation, environmental pollution, and resource depletion had led some to argue that the very science and technology on which modern industrial societies so heavily depend presents the ultimate threat to the human prospect. Instead of being instruments of progress, science and technology—the central creations of progressive and enlightened Western culture—may turn out to be the instruments of human self-destruction. Such visions of impending doom have led one existential philosopher, Martin Heidegger, to wonder whether only a god can save us now.

From a theological perspective, the contemporary situation is marked by the eclipse of the classical Christian doctrine of sin and by interest in and concern for the problem of evil. Modern culture presents a generally secular view of evil with optimistic and pessimistic variations. It is of particular theological interest that the *types* of views concerning evil against which classic Christian thought struggled—the optimistic Pelagian view and the pessimistic Manichean view—have tended to displace the Christian doctrine of sin. Hence the ancient debate goes on, and theological reconstruction is necessary in order to join in the debate and seek constructive alternatives.

THE DOCTRINE IN ITS CLASSIC FORMULATION

The classic doctrine took shape in reflection on the legacy and meaning of the scriptures and in response to the external challenge of Gnosticism and the internal challenge of the Pelagian heresy. Accordingly, we shall first examine the scriptural legacy, which theological reflection sought to articulate, and the problems attending such reflection. Then we shall turn to the classic Augustinian doctrine itself.

Scriptural Warrants of the Doctrine

There is no doctrine of original sin to be found in scripture—a point urged against the Augustinian view by the Pelagians. Nevertheless, the doctrine took shape in part through reflection upon the meaning of scripture. An important Old Testament passage is the Adam story in Genesis 2–3. The Adam story is not primarily a speculation concerning the first human being who commits the first sin. Following Paul Ricoeur, we should rather begin by noting that the story is fundamentally penitential in motivation. That is, it reflects and portrays the Jewish penitential spirit manifest in the prophetic literature and the Psalms. From this vantage point the significance of the Adam story lies in its separation of the origin of evil from the origin of being. The origin of evil is not located in a precosmic primordial chaos in which the gods struggle against chaos to be born. Nor is evil older than the creation, or even coincident with it. The creation is not evil but good. Evil is something that occurs within a creation already completed and good. Thus evil is traced not to God or to the world but to human beings. The Adamic myth presents an anthropological approach to the origin of evil. The penitential motivation of the story can be expressed as follows: God is good and therefore not responsible for evil. Human beings, although created and destined for good, have committed evil and thereby have become corrupted. It is through the action of human beings that evil enters the world. The passage from innocence to sin is narrated in the Adam story as something that has happened, an event which was not necessary but rather free and contingent. In this contingent happening lies the anthropological origin of evil as something which ought not to be and which does not have to be but nevertheless is. It must be stressed, however, that the Adam story is not yet a myth of the "fall" of the first human being. The conditions of Adam are homogeneous with those of everyone else; Adam is representative of all of humanity. To be specific, the Adam story portrays the collective penitential experience of ancient Israel.

One additional feature of the Adam story deserves mention. Although it presents an anthropological approach to evil, it does not concentrate evil entirely in the Adam figure. While Adam is the protagonist of the story, he is not alone. He has a companion, Eve, and an adversary, the serpent. The figure of the serpent furnishes two important qualifications to the anthropological approach to evil: (1) Adam and Eve together do not absolutely originate evil; they find it "already there" in the form of temptation and freely yield to it. Hence the serpent symbolizes a mysterious depth-dimension of evil that cannot be fully rationalized or fully absorbed into self-conscious, deliberate freedom. (2) While the serpent is Adam's adversary, he cannot compel or coerce, for he is a fellow creature. He can only provide temptation, or the occasion for sin. The yielding to sin is therefore not necessary or coerced; it is a free, contingent act for which the human agent is responsible.

The New Testament as a whole does not use the Adam story. Evil is acknowledged and the concept of sin radicalized (cf. Matthew 5), but evil appears largely in the form of supernatural powers and demons that have invaded the creation and the human soul. It was Paul who took up the Adam story again and elaborated it as an anthropological theory of evil. Perhaps the most important passage is Rom. 5:12–21. In the interest of soteriology, Paul is led to formulate a type-antitype contrast between Christ and Adam, the new being and the old: "By one man's disobedience many were made sinners, so by one man's obedience many will be made righteous" (Rom. 5:19). In this soteriological argument, Paul appropriates and extends the Adam story as an anthropological theory of evil: "Sin came into the world through one man and death through sin, and so death spread to all men because all men sinned" (Rom. 5:12). Significantly, but not without ambiguity, Paul connects human sinfulness with Adam. Just as redemption originates in and through Christ, so sin originates in and through Adam. From Adam it spreads to all of humanity, as indicated by (1) the empirical universality of death and (2) the conflict between flesh and spirit (Rom. 7:14–25). Thus Paul advances the concept of an original or first sin in Adam, which has universal human and even cosmological significance, for not only does death originate in Adam's fall, but creation itself is affected by being subject to bondage, futility, and decay (Rom. 8:18–25).

The Augustinian Doctrine of Sin

Augustine did not invent the doctrine of sin, but he did give it classic articulation and systematic expression. He drew upon the scriptural legacy, Christian thought, Platonic philosophy, and his own experience, weaving all these elements together into an imposing structure of thought. Central to this system is a fully developed anthropological view of evil. Augustine's anthropology is beyond the scope of this essay. It should be noted at the outset, however, that for Augustine creation is good, and hence human beings are created good and set within a good creation already completed. Human beings are created good, desire good, and are not satisfied with anything short of the eternal supreme good, or God. Given the supremacy and primacy of good, evil has no place within the created order. Indeed, evil has no positive ontological status at all; it is not a being, but rather a privation or corruption of being. Every being, insofar as it is, is good. Hence there is no ontological foundation for or explanation of evil. Nevertheless, evil may be described (but not explained) as a voluntary defection of humankind from the natural order of creation.

According to this natural order, human beings are most free and fulfilled when they grasp and are ruled by the highest good, God. Then the various orders and powers of the soul and body are harmoniously bound together. The self is unified, centered. Evil consists in a turning away from God, the supreme good, and a turning toward the world or changeable goods in an inordinate way. Humanity, in turning away from God, refuses to be governed by any authority save itself; hence in rejecting God human beings are led to absolutize themselves. Thus they exchange a life of freedom and fulfillment for another which holds out the prospect of "liberation" but actually delivers the self into bondage to inferior mutable goods. Humanity is no longer oriented and disposed toward its true good, which is necessary for the proper internal life of the soul. The lower powers of the soul are thus deprived of guidance and become disordered, that is, their respective goods are identified as the true good. The human being falls into a condition of bondage to desire. Desire (or concupiscence), while a natural tendency, now becomes drawn into the circle of the self-absolutization of human beings, and so becomes inordinate. Thus sin concretely takes the form of a self-imposed bondage, a free will that binds itself.

From this general position, Augustine is led to oppose two alternative views of evil: the Manichean or Gnostic view for its theological pessimism, and the Pelagian view for its anthropological optimism. Although Augustine's position has a basis independent of both Gnosticism and Pelagianism, it will be convenient to structure our discussion in terms of a twofold negation of Gnosticism on the one hand and Pelagianism on the other. Against the Gnostics, Augustine maintains that the sin is not identifiable or coincident with human finitude. It occurs not from ontological necessity but freely and contingently. Consequently it must be distinguished from the essential features of humanity and the human condition. Against the Pelagians, Augustine maintains that sin is not merely accidental or simply contingent in the sense that it might be avoided altogether, but rather a corruption of human nature, a self-imposed bondage of the will which is empirically universal in scope. Hence, although evil is not synonymous with essential human nature, it nevertheless appears as a kind of "second nature" which is manifest in inordinate desire, a positive inclination toward evil. The twofold negation of Gnosticism and Pelagianism leads to three central elements or concepts in the classic doctrine as Augustine presents it: original perfection, original sin, and original guilt.

The Negation of Gnosticism: Original Righteousness

Gnosticism is a type of thought that takes its point of departure from a sense of the incommensurability of self and world experienced as a primordial disruption, and is expressed in antagonistic dualistic concepts. Evil consists in being incarnated in the midst of an alien hostile cosmos, which threatens to claim and annihilate the self. Hence the dualism of self and world leads to the dualism of soul and body on the anthropological level, and to the ultimate dualism of God and world. The self is identified with the soul, mysteriously confined within the body, which is the medium of the soul's incarceration in an alien world. Evil is thus equated with finitude, and the hope of salvation is to escape from the evil cosmos to the transcendent alien God. Further, the ultimate dualism between God and world means that the knowledge of God is not a natural human condition. In the Gnostic scheme, evil is identical with finite mundane existence; being in the world is the primal disruption and alienation. Although individuals participate in evil, they are not responsible for it; on the ultimate ontological level, evil is a second principle opposed to the transcendent God.

Augustine rejects such cosmic pessimism on both philosophical and theological grounds. Metaphysical dualism is incoherent. If there is one supreme being or principle, then there is nothing which can oppose or limit it. Hence it follows that being is good. Further, if being is good, its goodness implies that the supreme being is not a hostile power; in short, God is not jealous. As supreme good, divinity tends to communicate itself and share its goodness. Hence the existence of the world is not evil but good. Even though finite being may be characterized by both being and nonbeing, insofar as it is, it is good. Neoplatonic metaphysics and the Genesis creation story agree in ruling out the Gnostic equation of evil with finitude or the world. It follows therefore that evil has no ontological status. It is not a being or substance, but must rather be understood as the corruption of being, the privation of good.

These general metaphysical principles are exhibited and rendered determinate in Augustine's treatment of Genesis 1–3. Augustine adopts these passages as literal history and proceeds from them to develop his anthropological approach to evil with its radical distinction between the origin of being and the origin of evil. The Platonic thesis that being is good is concretely manifest in the goodness of creation. Human being is created good and placed in a creation already completed and good, a paradise. Hence, God is the author not of evil but of being, and being is unqualifiedly good. Moreover, the human being in its totality is good, and sustained in its paradisiacal condition by immediate knowledge and fellowship with God. Evil enters the picture only after history has already begun. Adam's and Eve's turning away from God is a historical event, the "fall." Our first parents refused to accept their creaturely status and so defected from the divinely established order of creation. The origin of evil therefore lies in the misuse of a created good, namely, freedom. Adam's rebellion and defection constitute the first sin. This account clearly separates the anthropological origin of evil from the theological origin of being. The noncoincidence of sin with finitude is maintained by the historical scheme of original righteousness and a historical fall or first sin. Against Gnosticism, Augustine elaborates an anthropological theory of evil in which evil is not necessary but contingent, a defection of freedom from divine order.

The Negation of Pelagianism: Original Sin and Guilt

Pelagianism may be characterized as an anthropological theory of evil with a moralizing, rationalistic distortion. Augustine had established that sin is contingent, a voluntary act. The Pelagians added to this an indeterminate conception of human freedom: human beings are born without virtue, but also without vice. Virtue and vice are acts freely committed by the person in the course of a historical career. Human beings are capable of acting in either way. If the essence of sin is a voluntary act, it follows that human beings must be able not to sin. Each human being is considered in the same position relative to sin as Adam prior to the fall. It is possible to avoid sin and, in fact, some exemplary individuals have done so.

Sin is thus conceived as a purely contingent, morally reprehensible act; it is a deliberate, conscious choice of evil in the face of known good. The contingency of the sin implies that while it is widespread it is not a universal condition or state of humankind. Adam corrupts only himself, not his offspring. He sets a bad example, which is imitated and thus socially transmitted. But such transmission implies nothing more than a socially acquired bad habit. In short, there is no inescapability and no universality of sin in this account. Furthermore, evil acts do not take away or alter the ontological features and conditions of human freedom, namely, its indeterminacy and neutrality with regard to good and evil. These essential features of freedom persist unaltered and unaffected by sin.

In rejecting the Pelagian account, Augustine draws upon his view of human freedom as dependent on union with the eternal. Human beings are essentially disposed toward the good and dependent on union with the eternal for their true happiness and satisfaction. Therefore, when they turn away from God and toward the world, they do not merely choose another way of being human on a par with every other. Rather, their turning from God contradicts the essential disposition and tendency of human nature. Such a contradiction is not neutral or innocuous, for it results in a corruption of that nature. When the self turns from the eternal good, the original righteousness of the human constitution is lost, and the self is plunged into disorder. After the fall, humankind is no longer oriented toward the eternal good, but rather has become disordered, a prisoner of its own vain efforts at self-absolutization. The self exists in a state of self-imposed bondage. Consequently Augustine rejects the Pelagian reduction of sin to a deliberate, conscious choice of evil in defiance of good. Humanity is no longer in the state of indifference imagined by the Pelagians. The disordering of human nature by sin means that human beings are predisposed and inclined toward evil. The bondage of sin means that there is now a bias toward evil which precedes and shapes conscious and deliberate choices. Since such bias is inescapable in the light of the fall, it is empirically universal.

This ensemble of claims constitutes the doctrine of original sin. Augustine distinguishes two elements in this doctrine: the *vitium* (fault, blemish) and the *reatus* (legal penalty). The *vitium* refers to the positive corruption and diminution of essential human nature, which Augustine identifies with concupiscence or inordinate desire. This propensity or bias toward evil is present in human beings prior to any act and manifests itself in actual sins. Since it is present prior to any action, its presence in human beings requires explanation. The explanation is the fall of Adam, interpreted as a historical event which vitiates not only Adam himself but all subsequent human life. Through his disobedience and rebellion, Adam introduces a corruption into the human race such that when human nature is propagated, sin is propagated with it.

The *reatus* of sin refers to the legal-juridical dimension of sin as a transgression of law for which God holds the transgressor guilty and punishable. Since all human beings have the *vitium* of sin by natural propagation, all human beings fall under the *reatus* of sin as well. All are violators of the divine law, and so all deserve punishment. This claim is not without problems. First, if sin is a hereditary taint, this appears to undermine human responsibility for sin and the anthropological explanation of evil. Second, the claim that all deserve punishment is somewhat plausible in the case of adults, in whom original sin breaks forth freely in actual sins, but would not seem to apply to infants. Augustine is led to extend this claim to all without exception on the basis of the ecclesiastical practice of infant baptism. All baptism is for the remission of sins. But what sins could a newborn infant have committed? No voluntary acts of sin for which the person is responsible seem possible in this case; yet the church baptizes infants. This can only mean, he concludes, that such baptism is for the removal of the stain and corruption inherited from Adam's fall. The abstract character of such an argument makes the doctrine vulnerable to criticism along Pelagian lines.

Catholic and Protestant Variations

Both Catholic and Protestant theologies have much common ground in Augustine, although they interpret this common ground somewhat differently, largely under pressure of disputes about grace. Thomas Aquinas refined the Augustinian doctrine into a highly influential Catholic position. He agrees with Augustine concerning the literal-historical interpretation of Genesis 2–3. However, the Garden of Eden in his view was not a paradise and so was not fundamentally different from present world conditions. The wolf would devour the sheep even if the first parents had not sinned. Adam and Eve, although created good, had to withstand hardships and even temptation. Moreover, withstanding temptation was within their power, for they were sustained in the condition of original righteousness by God's grace (habitual grace). They were able to withstand sin, able not to sin, and if they had preserved themselves intact in the state of original righteousness, they would have passed into a still better, final state of constitutive immortality and beatific vision. In turning away from God, however, Adam and Eve lost the gift of habitual grace on which original righteousness (the unity of the self) depends. Thus essential human nature became disordered, wounded, and weakened; henceforth human beings would not be able not to sin. For Aquinas the essence of sin is *formally* the loss or privation of original righteousness and its divine support (habitual grace) and *materially* concupiscence, or the inordinateness of desire into which the human nature is plunged by its fall from grace. Aquinas settles the question of the transmission of sin that Augustine had left open: The sin of the first parents (original sin) is transmitted to their descendants by natural generation. All are therefore sinners, not by actual or personal sin but by a sin of nature which is inherited and present in each individual prior to personal (or actual) sins.

The Protestant Reformation, in certain respects a rediscovery and revitalization of Augustine's thought, reacted against the Catholic position. The Reformers, however, construed the Catholic position not so much according to the formulation given by Aquinas as in terms of the modifications introduced by Duns Scotus. Since Scotus interpreted concupiscence as a lower natural power of the soul, he could not identify the essence of sin with concupiscence. So he dropped the claim that concupiscence is the material element in sin and retained only the formal element, the lack of original righteousness. The Reformers—notably Martin Luther and John Calvin—took this to be the "Catholic position" and concluded that it was anti-Augustinian inasmuch as it defined sin as a mere defect (*privatio*). It failed, in their judgment, to acknowledge the bias toward evil inherent in human nature. Against this construal of the Catholic position, the Protestants advanced the Augustinian concept of concupiscence and formulated it as "total depravity." Sin, they maintained, is more than a mere defect or privation; it is a depravity or corruption of the entire human nature. There are no faculties or aspects of human being not corrupted by sin. Thus, although human beings are created in the image of God, this image is lost in the fall.

Catholic theologians, and many others, interpreted the Protestant thesis of total depravity to mean that essential human nature was not just corrupted, weakened, and wounded by the fall, but entirely lost. Hence the Protestant view appeared to border on the Manichean position in which evil has positive ontological status. However, as far as this writer can tell, the Protestant thesis of sin as total depravity is virtually indistinguishable from the essence of sin stated by Aquinas. The confusion and much of the polemics arise from a failure to distinguish the various senses of concupiscence. Considered *apart* from the fall, concupiscence is acknowledged by both sides to be one of the lower powers of the soul and as such natural to humankind, namely, the faculty of desire. No theologian ever maintained that concupiscence in this sense is sin, because that would be Manichean. On the other hand, concupiscence is also used to refer to the entire human being *after* the fall, to designate the inordinateness of the soul resulting from its loss of original righteousness. The fundamental sense of concupiscence here is inordinate self-seeking. In this sense, concupiscence is crucial to the efforts of both Protestant and Catholic theology to distinguish sin from an evil nature (Manicheanism) and from a mere accident or bad choice (Pelagianism).

CHALLENGES AND CONTRIBUTIONS OF MODERN CONSCIOUSNESS

The Reemergence of Rival Viewpoints

The doctrine of original sin has been controversial from the time of Augustine; hence critical disagreement with Augustine, and even the displacement of certain features of the Augustinian doctrine, are not peculiarly modern phenomena. However, the doctrine as a whole came under attack in the eighteenth and nineteenth centuries because it appeared to contradict two central convictions of modernity: (1) the conviction of essential human goodness and (2) the supreme value accorded human freedom and autonomy. Even sympathetic defenders of Augustine, such as Reinhold Niebuhr, have conceded that the form in which the classic doctrine is expressed makes it appear self-contradictory. On the one hand original sin is not regarded as belonging to essential human nature; therefore it is not outside the realm of human responsibility. On the other hand original sin is an inherited corruption, and therefore inevitable. Sin is natural for human beings in that it is empirically universal, but it is not natural in the sense of being necessary.[1]

There are reasons for the apparent contradiction between the inevitability of human sin and human responsibility for sin despite its inevitability. Ricoeur has pointed out that the Augustinian doctrine is expressed in terms which unite a juridical category (voluntary punishable crime) with a biological category (the unity of the human species by natural generation).[2] It is the attempt to mix such categorically disparate, even exclusive elements that produces the tensions and absurdities to which Niebuhr rightly refers. Augustine fuses and unites these disparate elements as he articulates the central point of the doctrine, namely, humanity's self-imposed bondage to sin. The juridical element in the classic doctrine derives from Augustine's opposition to Manicheanism and his insistence on separating the origin of evil from the origin of being, or finitude. The existence of evil in a good creation is an indictment against human beings, not God. The biological element in the classic doctrine derives from his negation of Pelagianism and his attempt to present human prevolitional solidarity in sin as deriving from natural generation. Thus even though the basic insight may be sound, as a concept original sin appears to be paradoxical and incoherent.

These internal tensions in the forms of expression of the classic doctrine make it susceptible to reduction to or displacement by its rival views of evil. For example, Ricoeur notes that while the concept of original sin is anti-Gnostic in intention, it appears Gnostic in its rationalized doctrinal form. The anti-Gnostic intention of the doctrine is to express the conviction that human beings are created good but have freely become corrupted and evil. The concept of original sin is supposed to integrate the scheme of inheritance (human solidarity) with the voluntariness and contingency of evil. However, when the concept of original sin is taken literally and rationalized, the result is often the opposite of the original intention. There is crystallized instead the idea of an inherited corruption and inherited guilt. Thus the rationalistic form of the doctrine makes it appear indistinguishable from its Gnostic rival in that sin appears to be

1. Reinhold Niebuhr, *The Nature and Destiny of Man*, 1:242.
2. Paul Ricoeur, "Original Sin: A Study in Meaning," in *The Conflict of Interpretations*, ed. D. Ihde (Evanston: Northwestern University Press, 1974).

identified with an essential or inescapable aspect of the human condition for which no human being is or could be responsible. The doctrine then appears reducible to its Gnostic rival. This apparent indistinguishability in turn calls forth the other rival, Pelagianism, with its attempt to discard the pessimistic metaphysical baggage and to bring sin into focus as a conscious, deliberate act. In both cases the central intention of the doctrine—the self-imposed bondage of the will—is lost.

The Challenge of Historical Criticism

A second problem posed for the classic doctrine in the modern period also has to do with the conceptual form in which it is expressed. The classic doctrine rests upon a literal interpretation of Genesis 2–3 as actual history. The terminology and conceptuality of the classic doctrine—original righteousness, original sin, and original guilt—clearly presuppose and reflect a historical structure and framework. The Bible is thought to provide divinely guaranteed, infallible information concerning the creation of the world, the pre-fall condition of human beings, and the fall itself. Moreover, Augustine's major moves against Manicheanism and Pelagianism are made in terms of this historical scheme and framework: (1) The noncoincidence of sin with finitude is maintained by the separation of creation and fall as distinct historical events. Hence evil is not older than creation or even coextensive with it; evil is rather referred to human beings. (2) The universality of sin and human solidarity in sin is maintained against Pelagianism by regarding all human beings as natural descendants from a common ancestor through whom the taint and corruption of sin entered the world.

The cosmological and scriptural presuppositions of the classical doctrine are no longer shared by theology insofar as it reflects critical and historical consciousness. The biblical narratives are not scientific accounts of natural-cosmological history. Attempts to extend biblical authority into the scientific sphere have been fruitless and counterproductive. When the biblical-theological symbols and narratives have been interpreted literally as history, science, or law—such as occurs in the later stages of doctrinalization—the original and profound insights they provide into the anthropological origin of evil have been inevitably obscured. Insight tends to be replaced by dogmatic mythology as, for example, in Augustine's speculations about human procreation before the fall. The doctrine tends then to disintegrate into its Gnostic rival on the one hand or its Pelagian rival on the other. For this reason Paul Tillich concludes that the entire classic doctrine is pervaded by literalistic absurdities arising from its form of expression, and that the only course open is to abandon the classic doctrine of original sin—terminology, historical framework, and all.

The Basic Antinomy in the Classic Doctrine

We have found that the classic doctrine follows the Adamic myth or story in presenting an anthropological theory of evil. Given the literal interpretation of Genesis, however, the classic doctrine accounts for all evil by asserting a historical fall of the first human being. It transforms the Adam story from a dramatic narrative of the sin of Adam and Eve into a historical account of the fall of humanity generally. Thereby the classic doctrine is led to suppress and distort crucial elements of the biblical narrative. Specifically, the doctrine of the fall suppresses the crucial point symbolized by the serpent: the presence of temptation in the creation prior to the fall. The serpent points to an evil "already there," not absolutely originated by humans but to which humans yield. The fact that evil is already there prior to the sin of Adam and Eve points toward a recognition of the tragic depth of evil. The latter element is suppressed in the classic doctrine, which traces all evil to the first man and woman.

The classic doctrine distinguishes finitude from sin and evil by asserting original righteousness. Thereby it postulates a state of historically actualized perfection prior to the fall. Adam and Eve were in a state of intellectual and moral perfection, free from anxiety, pain, and suffering. Most important, they dwelt in the immediate presence of God and were sustained directly in this relationship. Such a postulate is incomprehensible in view of present knowledge concerning the historical and evolutionary origins of human beings. Moreover, it contains a serious contradiction first pointed out by Friedrich Schleiermacher: the contradiction between original righteousness and the fall.

The more the original righteousness and perfection of humankind is stressed, the less plausible and less intelligible the fall appears. For is it conceivable that under the conditions postulated by original righteousness—where humans are directly sustained by the immediate presence of God, the supreme end and good—humankind would turn away from God, disrupt this fundamental relationship on which its very existence depends, and deliver itself into corruption? If the conditions postulated by original righteousness had actually obtained, it would seem that no fall could have taken place. The postulates of the classic doctrine do not explain or illuminate the nature of the human relationship to God or human sin but rather render sin completely incomprehensible. If one accepts such presuppositions, one is forced to assume either that the sustaining presence and care of God was for some reason withdrawn, which makes God responsible for sin, or that sin is a sheer malevolent rebellion on the part of humankind, which makes the first humans appear totally irrational and malevolent. Neither alternative is compatible with the biblical narrative or with the central assumptions of Christian faith. Therefore the only alternative is to reject the classic doctrine of the fall and its postulate of original righteousness.

The dilemma has yet another aspect: either sin is rendered *impossible* by the created perfection of human beings, or sin is made *inevitable* by the recognition that even though human beings are created good, nevertheless there is present in humans some flaw which makes possible their temptation and sin. Moreover, to acknowledge the presence of some flaw in humanity seems to point in the direction of making God ultimately responsible for sin and evil. The classic doctrine is impaled on the first horn of the dilemma (original righteousness excludes sin), while modern theological reconstructions are confronted with the other (to acknowledge a flaw seems to equate finitude with sin).

Issues in Modern Reconstructions

The classic doctrine concentrates evil in the Adam figure and traces all evil to the fall. From Augustine onward this doctrine was closely linked with a pessimistic, even tragic, conception of humankind and the human condition. Moreover, it was also linked with a view of salvation as limited and restricted to the elect. Hence the universality of sin was stated more clearly, powerfully, and elaborately than the universality of salvation: All have sinned, whether personally or in Adam, but divine grace subsequently redeems only some. There has been increasing recognition that such formulations obscure and possibly undermine the soteriological center of Christian faith. The condemnation of sin is not the ultimate word of the Christian gospel, which is rather God's forgiveness and salvation. Hence many theologians, ranging from Robert Bellarmine in the sixteenth century to Karl Barth and Karl Rahner in the twentieth, have suggested a revision of the classic doctrine which logically derives human solidarity in sin from human solidarity in redemption through Christ. In effect, the doctrine of sin becomes a secondary derivation from the doctrines of salvation and Christology. Original sin is a postulate derived from redemption and may be defined as a privation of redemptive grace. This move has two advantages: (1) It clarifies the center of gravity of Christian faith as soteriological rather than punitive, and thus corrects the anthropological pessimism of the classic doctrine of sin, and (2) it sets the doctrine of sin into a more comprehensive christological-soteriological scheme and derives the distinctive meaning of sin from that scheme. In this way the distinctive character of sin is emphasized in contrast to Manichean and Pelagian views of evil.

Although the above revision provides an important corrective, it also creates some problems of its own. For example, it runs the risk of becoming an abstract fideism. Fideism is present in the attempt to derive the meaning of sin entirely from soteriology and Christology, for if the meaning of sin is entirely generated out of the symbols and concepts of soteriology, no real insight is obtained into sin and evil as aspects of human experience. It was precisely its genuine existential and phenomenological insights into the human experience of evil that made the Augustinian tradition so persuasive and powerful. Augustine's and Aquinas's discussions of concupiscence, for example, provide brilliant insight into the human condition. Moveover, their discussions of concupiscence can be appreciated to a considerable extent apart from soteriology and Christology. It is one thing to assert that soteriology provides the ultimate context and clarification of sin as an anthropological reality, and quite another to assert that the entire meaning of sin consists in a privation or absence of saving grace. In the latter case, no insight into the human condition as pervaded by evil is actually obtained. Fideism runs the danger of abandoning a genuine anthropological account of evil and leaves the exploration and analysis of actual human evil to its Manichean and Pelagian rivals.

Assuming that Christian theology remains committed to an anthropological account of evil, the problem is how to reconstruct the anthropological account in view of the difficulties in the classic doctrine. Modern attempts to carry out such a reconstruction have brought to light several important issues which must be faced and satisfactorily dealt with.

1. When theology acknowledges modern critical consciousness, it must also recognize that modern science and cosmology have brought to light universal conditions of evil—disease and death, for instance—which antedate the emergence of humankind. Hence, not all evil can be explained by the theory of a historical fall or first sin of a first human. This means that there has emerged a category of evil which is wider than and not reducible to human sin and human evil. This does not mean that modern science returns to the Gnostic vision of the cosmos and existence as evil, but it does involve the recognition that the cosmos is not and never has been a paradise. The question is: What is the relationship between the flawed cosmos, its natural evil, and human evil? From the larger cosmological perspective, sin may be but one type of evil.

2. If the category of flaw and natural evil is broader than sin, and cannot be derived from the historical fall of Adam and Eve as the Augustinian tradition sought to do, then it must be conceded that the fall or human sin does not occur within a wholly good world or paradise. Again, this is not to affirm that the world is evil, but it must be recognized that the goodness of the world does not exclude the presence of a tragic aspect. And human beings are not responsible for this aspect; they find it already there. In short, not all evil can be assumed by or absorbed into humankind in any contemporary anthropological theory of sin and evil. Fortunately, Paul Ricoeur has shown that this recognition is already present in the serpent figure of Genesis 2–3. This crucial recognition is obscured and lost in the patristic assumption of an original perfection. Paul Tillich is among the few contemporary theologians who recognized this element of the Adam story and saw the necessity of incorporating it as the tragic aspect of all existence into his own reconstruction.

3. The flawed character of created existence extends to humans

themselves. Immanuel Kant saw human nature as essentially good, yet flawed by the inexplicable presence of "radical evil." Later figures such as Friedrich Schelling, Søren Kierkegaard, and representatives of existential phenomenology drive the point home in their analysis of humanity as constituted by a fundamental ontological insecurity arising out of the very nature of freedom itself. Freedom is the capacity for self-transcendence; as such it requires that humanity not coincide completely with itself, but rather choose itself in the face of its possibilities. The essence of the human self is not given in advance, but must be concretely chosen and brought about by projecting, selecting, and actualizing possibilities. The freedom of the self prevents its identification with anything actual or given; rather, the self is identified with its possibilities and choices. Precisely because freedom has no given nature, it is inevitably accompanied by and gives expression to *Angst*, or a constitutive anxiety. Freedom and anxiety are thus the specifically human way of being fallible, which is to say, vulnerable and susceptible to sin and evil. Such fallibility is acknowledged by theologians such as Reinhold Niebuhr and Paul Tillich, among others. Fallibility, anxiety, and the like are, however, not sin; nor are they to be identified with sin. Neither does fallibility simply displace sin, as in certain existentialist anthropologies (Jean-Paul Sartre), for fallibility is an aspect of the transcendental structure of the self which makes possible both faith and unfaith—or sin.

Contemporary Alternatives to the Traditional Formulation

The foregoing elements—the rejection of the literal historical scheme of creation and fall, the acknowledgment of evil as a generic category distinct from and irreducible to sin, the recognition of a flaw or fault in human nature which may dispose it toward sin—constitute the central problem facing modern reconstructions of the doctrine of sin. If creation and fall are no longer separate historical events, how can the origin of evil be separated from the origin of being? How can theology claim that sin is not coincident with finitude? To reject the historical fall in which the corruption of human nature occurs is to posit that human nature is everywhere the same. This implies that each person is in the same position concerning good and evil as Adam and Eve. And this moves in the direction of Pelagianism. On the other hand, to acknowledge that there is a constitutive ontological insecurity and flaw in universal human nature seems to move in the direction of Manichean dualism. Tillich confronted the question boldly. If theology gives up the historical scheme of creation and fall as separate events, he concluded, the only alternative is to say that creation and fall coincide. "Creation and fall coincide insofar as there is no point in time and space in which created goodness was actualized. This is a necessary consequence of the rejection of the literal interpretation of the paradise story. . . . Actualized creation and estranged existence are identical."[3]

To some, including Reinhold Niebuhr, Tillich's assertions appear speculative and Manichean in tendency in that they appear to subordinate human freedom to the tragic estrangement present in all existence. Given Tillich's existential ontology, sin appears to be necessary, that is, identical with finitude. His response is to affirm that there is a tragic depth dimension of human freedom, but that this becomes Manichean or Gnostic only if the tragic element is entirely separated from personal freedom. Then the ultimate ground of sin would be wholly outside the human activity.

The problem is that if the fall as a historical event is rejected, and if a constitutive fault or flaw in human nature is acknowledged, then finitude and evil appear to coincide. The contingency of sin and the accompanying human responsibility for sin appear to be lost, and with them goes the anthropological theory of evil. Given these appearances, some theologians conclude that the essential features of the Christian doctrine of sin cannot be preserved or stated if the doctrine of the fall is given up. Thus N. P. Williams, after an examination of the various theories of a transcendental (nonhistorical) fall, came to the conclusion that every attempt along these lines results in the virtual identification of sin with finitude and ends up in the Manichean dualism that Augustine rightly rejected. Williams held that it is impossible to maintain the distinction between sin and finitude in anything other than a historical scheme which includes the fall as an actual event. The postulate of a historical fall is an essential requirement of the anthropological view of evil set forth by Christian faith, even if the fall as a historical event can no longer be located in the Adam story interpreted as literal history.

Williams retains the historical-fall doctrine as a postulate of Christian faith. However, his proposal presents at least three difficulties.

---

3. Paul Tillich, *Systematic Theology*, 1:50.

The first is the problem of the location of the fall as a historical event, especially in view of the discrediting of the Genesis narratives as actual history. To Williams this appears to be a cosmological-biological question. Therefore, he locates the fall in a precosmic revolt of the life-source. But the content of this postulate, if not the necessity of making the postulate, is wholly speculative. The content has the effect of making human beings troubled spectators of something else's misdeeds but not sinful themselves. Williams has merely exchanged one myth for another, and it is difficult to determine whether his preference is theologically more satisfactory than the myth of the fall of Lucifer. The second problem concerns the transmission of the *vitium* of sin, with which Augustine struggled. A biological-hereditary transmission through propagation appears to reintroduce the very Manichean fatalism that the fall doctrine was supposed to obviate. The third problem has to do with the tragic depth of human freedom. It is not clear whether the revised doctrine of the fall acknowledges the presence of a tragic flaw in human nature or whether, like the classic doctrine, it derives all evil from the fall. For example, in existential ontologies of finitude, autonomous freedom is essentially accompanied by and expressed in anxiety. This is the tragic element in freedom. It cannot be the case, therefore, that autonomy and anxiety are the *results* of the fall since they are ontological and constitutive of freedom.[4] On the other hand, if autonomy and anxiety really are due to the fall, then the pre-fall condition of humankind must exclude the tragic flaw. The antinomy previously noted in the classic doctrine is not avoided. The recognition and acknowledgment of a tragic depth of human freedom requires an alternative to the Augustinian scheme and framework if the anthropological account of evil is to be retained.

ISSUES AND PROPOSALS

Enduring Accomplishments of the Classic Doctrine

To the extent that the doctrine of sin is identified with its classic terminology and conceptuality, it is vulnerable to displacement by its

---

4. See his *Systematic Theology: A Historicist Perspective* (New York: Charles Scribner's Sons, 1968), p. 366.

modern rivals and in fact has ceased to inform the contemporary consciousness of evil. Fortunately there is more to the doctrine than the dogmatic mythology of some of its vehicles of expression might suggest, for the classic doctrine succeeded in portraying sin as a reality present in human experience—not synonymous with essential human nature but a corruption of it. Phenomenologically sin presents several constitutive features. First, sin is a turning away from the transcendent, a refusal of finitude and dependence on the transcendent. Hence sin begins with *unbelief.* Second, to refuse one's proper dependence and subordination to the transcendent is to desire oneself inordinately. Refusal of the transcendent absolute is one side of the self's attempt to render itself absolute. Hence there arises an inordinate self-centeredness and self-seeking, or *pride.* Third, unbelief and pride alter the self's mode of being in the world from a life lived in communion with and dependence on the transcendent to an inordinate desire of finite goods. The latter are drawn into the self's inordinate self-seeking, and so *avarice* and *idolatry* arise as additional essential features of sin.

Unbelief, pride, avarice, and idolatry are not only particular sins, they are also essential features present in all sin. They constitute the fundamental structure of human evil which in turn is manifest in several different modalities of evil (e.g., the seven deadly sins: pride, envy, anger, sloth, avarice, gluttony, and lust).[5] Such sins are not specific acts or deeds (or violations of rules) so much as they are structures of behavior and habits which serve the fundamental corruption of humankind. With the exception of sloth, each of the deadly sins describes inordinate attachments of the self to some finite good, a perverse devotion of one's entire being to that good, and hence a making of it one's god. Since this "god" is a projection of the self's own efforts at self-securing and self-absolutization, the result is idolatry. Sloth, on the other hand, is more closely related to the element of unbelief; it is a turning away from the transcendent, from the struggles of life, even from life itself.

Note that in any of its forms and modalities, sin is not a pure seeking of evil for its own sake. Sin is not sheer malevolence; rather,

5. See Thomas Aquinas, *Summa Theologica,* Part 1a2ae, question 84, answer 4; see also the renewal of interest in the seven deadly sins in Kaufman, *Systematic Theology;* Henry Fairlie, *The Seven Deadly Sins Today* (Notre Dame: University of Notre Dame Press, 1978); and Sanford Lyman, *The Seven Deadly Sins: Society and Evil* (New York: St. Martin's Press, 1978).

sin is a perverted, corrupted seeking of genuine good. Hence sin is not an evil substance but a voluntary defection of humankind from its proper good and order. On the other hand, since unbelief and turning away from the transcendent is the initial and fundamental element in inordinate self-seeking, sin is not a merely anthropological problem. It involves the estrangement and alienation of humankind from the transcendent, and it results therefore in the self-imposed bondage of humankind to false gods created by inordinate desires. This phenomenology of sin is one of the most enduring accomplishments of the classic theological tradition; its importance has scarcely diminished in the contemporary situation. This existential phenomenology of sin reveals important aspects of the classic doctrine of sin which are not part of or dependent on its discredited dogmatic mythology.

Beyond Augustinian Theodicy

Theodicy is here taken in the sense of a comprehensive framework including and ordering the totality of Christian doctrines. Specifically, theodicy is the systematic attempt to discern the proper relationship between the themes of sin and salvation and the relative emphasis to be accorded each within the whole. The classic Augustinian theodicy presents several problems. First, the doctrine of original sin is oriented toward the past, toward creation and fall as determining historical events. This orientation has the effect of making the universality of sin and evil clearer and relatively more dominant than the universality of hope and salvation. Compared to the universal creation and fall, election to salvation is limited in scope; out of the mass of humanity meriting punishment, God redeems only a few. To be sure, the Augustinian theodicy employs the principle that God allows sin and evil to exist in order to bring greater good out of evil. However, the very existence of those consigned to eternal punishment shows that God is apparently content to leave some evil not transformed into good. This suggests, in turn, divine malevolence or divine inability and casts doubt upon the ultimacy of God's salvific will. The aesthetic explanation—that the eternal punishment of the reprobate maintains a cosmic balance and serves the requirements of divine justice—is an unsuccessful attempt to evade these obvious difficulties. Invariably it lapses into Manichean dualism. Second, the classic doctrine derives all evil from the fall and so fails to acknowledge the tragic depth and flaw in human freedom. Hence it ends in an irresolvable antinomy. Further, the classic doctrine distorts its scriptural warrant by suppressing the recognition of the tragic depth of human freedom recognized and portrayed symbolically in the serpent figure of Genesis 2–3. For these reasons Christian theology requires a more adequate theodicy, one which does not distort or suppress the depth elements of freedom, which is not impaled on the antinomy of the classic doctrine, and which does not allow the universality of sin to overwhelm or compromise the central soteriological theme.

Sin and Evil in the Context of Universal Redemption

Recently interest has been shown in a type of theodicy that is different from and earlier than the Augustinian. This theodicy has been identified by John Hick as the Irenaean type, after the second-century theologian Irenaeus of Lyons.[6] In this theodicy there is no fall and therefore no doctrine of the fall. Rather, the starting point is the ontological *imperfection* of creation manifest in the instability and ethical-religious immaturity of humankind. Human beings as initially created are not perfect, but they are perfectible. The ethical-religious perfection of humankind is capable of being actualized only in a temporal-historical career. Such ethical perfection cannot be ready-made even by God, for growth in maturity of freedom requires purposive action carried out over a period of time. Under the conditions of ethical-religious immaturity, sin is virtually inescapable. However, the center of the Irenaean theodicy is not creation and fall but redemption. Irenaeus develops a theodicy in which soteriology is the center and pivot of the argument. The redeemer recapitulates the faulty and sinful development of the old man and brings it to fulfillment. In this scheme the actualization and fulfillment of human perfection are located not in the beginning but in the end. The temporal orientation is not toward the past but toward the future.

In the modern period the Irenaean scheme was taken up by Schleiermacher, who developed it in relation to modern philosophical

6. John Hick, *Evil and the God of Love*, pp. 207–76. See also Austin Farrer, *Love Almighty and Ills Unlimited* (New York: Doubleday, 1961), esp. chap. 4.

anthropology on the one hand, and in relation to soteriology on the other. His reconstruction is the most inclusive and systematic treatment to date. Following Kant, Schleiermacher acknowledges radical evil or a tragic flaw in human existence, coextensive with its essential goodness. Since Schleiermacher rejects the classic doctrine of the fall, he posits the antagonism of these two elements as the initial general human condition. Human beings are thus initially posited in a state of ontological instability and imperfection (the antagonism of flesh against spirit, in which spirit has not yet attained supremacy). Despite such initial antagonism, however, humankind is capable of freely developing and of realizing its essential goodness in its temporal-historical career. But the ontological imperfection and instability, and the epistemic distance from the transcendent which this condition entails, make sin a virtually inescapable accompaniment of free human development. Sin is thus empirically universal, a collective concept anchored in collective historical-cultural experience. Hence sin has a tragic historical inevitability. Since even God cannot create a human being with ready-made ethical-religious perfection, and must sustain humanity in its free development and temporal career in which sin inevitably arises, God shares responsibility for sin. The tragic dimension of sin is acknowledged and taken seriously, but it does not provide the ultimate or final theological perspective.

Although divine goodness appears to have a tragic aspect in this view, God is not a "tragic god," nor does God's ordaining of sin posit sin as an independent end in itself. In Schleiermacher's scheme, God ordains sin relative to redemption, as that which is to disappear through redemption. The ordaining of sin is a subordinate aspect of God's ultimate salvific will for humanity. The Augustinian axiom, that God allows evil in order to bring greater good out of evil, is here given a clear soteriological foundation and thereby becomes central to the systematic argument. The Irenaean scheme actually posits two stages of creation. The first stage is marked by the tragic inevitability and universality of sin, but this is included within a larger salvific plan and arrangement: Redemption is the completion of the creation of humankind. As the second stage of creation, redemption completes and fulfills the first. The second stage of creation is thus more than and greater than the first. The whole scheme has a highly eschatological orientation.

Although this Irenaean type of thought acknowledges the tragic depth and flaw of human freedom, it avoids Manichean dualism and remains essentially anti-Gnostic. That is because sin, though made possible by finitude, does not completely coincide with finitude. Sinless human development is possible because such has occurred in the redeemer figure, Jesus the Christ. More important, however, sin is ordained to *disappear* through redemption, hence it cannot be a necessary element of existence. At the same time, Pelagianism is avoided because redemption, as the second stage and completion of creation, is not derivable from the first stage and so is not a simple, autonomous human possibility.

The Irenaean type of theodicy is dominant among contemporary theologians and would appear to represent a clear advance over previous proposals. It should be noted, however, that as a general scheme of developmental creation, the Irenaean proposal is not without some potential pitfalls of its own. If Schleiermacher's explicit soteriological foundation and eschatological orientation are passed over, and the scheme mistakenly identified as a cosmology, problems quickly emerge. It may, for instance, be misconstrued as propounding a superficial "evolutionary optimism" of the sort which maintains that evil will gradually and naturally disappear. Conversely, it may appear as a resurgence of tragic pessimism, holding out no possibility of salvation, inasmuch as good is inevitably accompanied by evil. Taken in its completeness, however, Schleiermacher's formulation of the Irenaean scheme need not lead to either outcome, for it transcends the framework of both speculative cosmology and theodicy while articulating the deepest convictions of Christian faith.

SUGGESTIONS FOR FURTHER READING

Anselm, "The Virginal Conception and Original Sin," "On the Freedom of the Will," and "The Fall of Satan." In *Theological Treatises*. Edited by Jasper Hopkins and Herbert Richardson. Cambridge, Mass.: Harvard Divinity School Library, 1965–67.

Aquinas, Thomas. *On the Truth of the Catholic Faith: Summa Contra Gentiles*. Book 4, chaps. 50–53.

———. *Summa Theologica*. Part 1a2ae, questions 71–89.

Arminius, Jacob. *Writings*. Translated by James Nichols and W. R. Bagnall. Grand Rapids: Baker Book House, 1956.

Augustine. *The Anti-Pelagian Writings*. NPNF¹ 5.

———. *On Free Will*. LCC 6.

Barth, Karl. *Church Dogmatics*. Vol. 4/1.

Berdyaev, Nikolas. *The Destiny of Man*. Translated by Natalie Duddington. London: Geoffrey Bles, 1954.

Berkouwer, G. C. *Sin*. Translated by Philip C. Holtrap. Grand Rapids: Eerdmans, 1971.

Bonhoeffer, Dietrich. *Creation and Fall: A Theological Interpretation of Genesis 1–3*. Translated by John C. Fletcher and Kathleen Downham. New York: Macmillan Co., 1959.

Brunner, Emil. "The Christian Doctrine of Creation and Redemption." In *Dogmatics*, vol. 2. See esp. chaps. 3, 4.

Buber, Martin. *Good and Evil: Two Interpretations*. Translated by Ronald Gregor Smith and Michael Bullock. New York: Charles Scribner's Sons, 1953.

Bultmann, Rudolf. *Theology of the New Testament*. Translated by Kendrick Grobel. New York: Charles Scribner's Sons, 1951–55. Seep esp. vol. 1, chap. 4.

Calvin, John. *Institutes of the Christian Religion*. Book 2, chaps. 1–3.

Davis, Stephen T., editor. *Encountering Evil: Live Options in Theodicy*. Atlanta: John Knox Press, 1981.

Edwards, Jonathan. *Original Sin*. In *Works*, vol. 3.

Farley, Edward. *Good and Evil: Interpreting a Human Condition*. Minneapolis: Fortress Press, 1990.

Farley, Wendy. *Tragic Vision and Divine Compassion: A Contemporary Theodicy*. Louisville: Westminster/John Knox Press, 1990.

Griffin, David. *God, Power and Evil: A Process Theodicy*. Philadelphia: Westminster Press, 1976.

———. *Evil Revisited: Responses and Reconsiderations*. Albany: State University of New York Press, 1991.

Gutiérrez, Gustavo. *On Job: God-Talk and the Suffering of the Innocent*. Maryknoll, N.Y.: Orbis Books, 1987.

Hick, John. *Evil and the God of Love*. New York: Harper & Row, 1966.

Kierkegaard, Søren. *The Concept of Anxiety*. Translated by Reidar Thomte. Princeton: Princeton University Press, 1980.

———. *The Sickness unto Death*. Translated by Howard V. Hong and Edna H. Hong. Princeton: Princeton University Press, 1980.

Luther, Martin. *Bondage of the Will*. Edited by E. Gordon Rupp. LCC 17.

———. *Lectures on Romans*. Translated by Wilhelm Pauck. LCC 15.

Niebuhr, Reinhold. *The Nature and Destiny of Man*. Vol. 1, chaps. 7–9.

Pagels, Elaine. *Adam, Eve, and the Serpent*. New York: Random House, 1988.

Pailin, David, editor. *The Anthropology of Evil*. New York: B. Blackwell, 1985.

Rahner, Karl. "Concupiscence." In *Theological Investigations*, vol. 1.

Ricoeur, Paul. *Fallible Man*. Translated by Charles Kelbley. Chicago: Regnery, 1965.

Rondet, Henri. *Original Sin: The Patristic and Theological Background*. Translated by Cajetan Finegan. New York: Alba House, 1972.

Schleiermacher, Friedrich. *The Christian Faith*. Pp. 259–370.

Schoonenberg, Piet. *Man and Sin: A Theological View*. Translated by Joseph Donceel. Notre Dame: University of Notre Dame Press, 1965.

Suchocki, Marjorie. *The End of Evil: Process Eschatology in Historical Context*. Albany: State University of New York Press, 1988.

Tennant, Frederick. *The Origin and Propagation of Sin*. Cambridge: University Press, 1902.

Tillich, Paul. *Systematic Theology*. Esp. vol. 2, pp. 44–78.

Wesley, John. "The Doctrine of Original Sin According to Scripture, Reason, and Experience." In *Works*, vol. 9. Grand Rapids: Zondervan. Reprint of 1872 edition by the Wesleyan Conference Office of London.

Williams, N. P. *The Ideas of the Fall and Original Sin*. London: Longmans, Green & Co., 1927.

8. CHRIST AND SALVATION

WHERE WE ARE

Christology is reflection upon the one whom the Christian community confesses as Lord and Savior. Historically this reflection has not been a merely theoretical matter. The effort has been informed by the keenest of human interests—the interest in salvation. It is therefore fitting that soteriology (the doctrine of salvation) be considered at the same time as Christology.

In testifying to Jesus Christ, the community points to a particular person who lived at a specific time and in a specific place. This reference gives Christianity its distinctive identity, its specificity. But Christian thought throughout its history has oscillated between questions of identity and questions of relevance,[1] and if Christology is located at the first pole, that of identity, then soteriology would seem to gravitate to the second pole, that of relevance. One might say that the role of soteriology is to show why this person Jesus Christ is understood to be significant.

The modern period, however, experienced the polarity as a tension. Linking soteriology to Christology has seemed to many to be odd and even presumptuous. After all, it amounts to gathering up the most fundamental of human concerns—the concern with salvation, however defined—and linking it, focusing it, and somehow making it contingent upon a Jewish prophet in a minor Roman dependency some two thousand years ago. The sense of anomaly and tension this creates is often termed "the scandal of particularity."

In view of this concern, modern theology has tended to reverse the classic order of the doctrines. In classic dogmatics one felt free to begin with Christology and then proceed to soteriology. One might talk about who Christ is, then about what he has done. For many in the modern period, however, to begin with Christ seems to presume too much, to risk being irrelevant if not intolerant. Thus modern

1. Cf. Jürgen Moltmann, *The Crucified God*, p. 7.

theologians have generally preferred to start with soteriology, to begin by establishing a common ground with their audience on the basis of common humanity. It has been said, after all, and only half in jest, that sin is the one Christian doctrine which can be empirically verified. And if sin should seem too harsh a term to serve as a point of contact, one may speak in a more positive vein, invoking the human search for peace and meaning. Whatever the particulars, this pattern of argument appears and reappears throughout the modern period in the rhetoric of conservative preaching no less than in the proposals of liberal revision. In this broad sense the modern temperament has been preoccupied with apologetics—depicting some human need or experience, then speaking of salvation in relation to that need or experience, and finally presenting Jesus Christ as the one through whom such salvation comes.[2]

Few would deny the fruitfulness of the modern strategy. Further, one may claim on its behalf that it simply brings to light a method already implicit within the classic Christologies. The best of the tradition, as we have already remarked and as we shall see in greater detail, was never merely theoretical; it was animated from first to last by a deep soteriological interest. At the same time, however, the shape of theology does make a difference. To reverse the classic paradigm generally entails a reinterpreting of content as well. When the soteriological interest is converted into a topic of reflection in its own right and becomes itself a sort of doctrine (and a decisive one at that), then the modern approach, as we shall also see, produces problems of its own.

THE DOCTRINES IN THEIR CLASSIC FORMULATION

Biblical Foundations

Our knowledge about the historical Jesus is slight, but certain essentials are generally recognized. There was such a person; he preached a message summarized in the words "The time is fulfilled, and the kingdom of God is at hand; repent, and believe in the gospel"

---

2. For the sake of simplicity I refer to the Christology-soteriology pattern, exemplified in the early creeds, as "the" classic paradigm. This is not to say that the period was confined to a single pattern, but merely to underline the fact that thinkers of the classical period felt at liberty to use the Christology-soteriology pattern, and did so extensively, whereas many leading figures of the modern period have not. Cf. Dietrich Bonhoeffer, *Christ the Center*, pp. 37–39; Wolfhart Pannenberg, *Jesus: God and Man*, pp. 38–49.

(Mark 1:15). He exercised a ministry directed particularly to the poor and the outcast; and he was crucified under Pontius Pilate. Of his preaching it is clear that he did not proclaim himself; his gospel was not itself a developed Christology. But neither did he set forth a collection of truths, a series of ethical principles, unrelated to his own person. His attention was fixed upon "the kingdom of God," a radical turn in history which was immediately at hand. To this in-breaking event he bound his person and his ministry.

For the Jews to whom Jesus spoke, the coming of the kingdom was a matter of the greatest significance. One could not remain neutral before it. Jesus himself showed little interest in the specifics of historical prediction; his attention was fixed instead upon the necessity of decision. This necessity was heightened by the distinctive element in his preaching, the element of utter immediacy. Others had preached the coming of the kingdom, but with a view to what must be done in preparation. Now no time was left to prepare—the kingdom was already at hand! The human schemes we devise for having a hand in our salvation, and thus for keeping God at a comfortable distance, had all collapsed. The only question was whether one would repent and receive the kingdom as a child.

This person, the one who preached this message, was crucified. Precisely because Jesus had so bound his ministry to history, the execution was a crisis for the community that had gathered about him. The events themselves, it seemed, had refuted him. In the face of this reversal there arose within the community the testimony that Jesus was nevertheless alive—that he had risen from the dead. Here was the final confirmation of his ministry, God's vindication of him. And here was the assurance of his abiding presence: It was he himself who reigned. And if this was so, then all that went before was seen in a new light; all the events, Jesus' actions and words, had now to be reinterpreted.

Thus "the proclaimer became the proclaimed, and the implicit Christology of Jesus becomes the explicit Christology of the church."[3] The New Testament itself is at once the product of this process of reinterpretation and a testimony to it. Beginning with what they had witnessed, the community reached back into their thought world,

---

3. Reginald H. Fuller, *The Foundations of New Testament Christology*, p. 143.

which was informed by both Judaism and Hellenism, in search of ways of understanding. Jesus was variously proclaimed as the Son of Man, the Son of David, and the Son of God. He was proclaimed the Messiah, the Anointed One, the Christ. These titles were rooted in the worship of the church and specifically in the practice of praying to Jesus as the one present and active in the life of the community. The function of each title was to take Christ's activity, both present and past, and place it in some crucial relationship, through a pattern of promise and fulfillment, to the saving activity of God. Each of the early titles, that is to say, was already implicitly soteriological.

This also meant that Christ's saving activity was not confined to his death. For the New Testament community, salvation was already present in his life—in his preaching and healing, his pronouncing of forgiveness, and his compassionate identification with the outcast and the oppressed. Thus his death must be seen as related to his entire ministry and yet as representing a decisive turn. The earliest interpretation of his death may well be the simple statement that Christ "died for our sins in accordance with the scriptures" (1 Cor. 15:3). The term "for," appearing repeatedly in such contexts, contains in germ a major strand of New Testament soteriology. The effect of such passages, once again, is to depict Jesus' death as the culmination of *God's own* saving activity. This point must be stressed, for there is no place in the New Testament for the notion that God stands aloof from human affairs or stands only in a posture of judgment until after Christ's death has made reconciliation possible. On the contrary, "God was in Christ reconciling the world to himself" (2 Cor. 5:19). God was supremely active in that life and death, and it is for precisely this reason that they have saving significance.[4]

This conviction was infinitely more important in the eyes of the early community than any particular theory of how it had come about. Accordingly, the images which attach to Christ's death must be interpreted in light of this testimony and not the reverse. Of the various depictions, a number elaborate the understanding that Christ died "for our sins"—for instance, the images of ransom, punishment, and sacrifice. Christ is portrayed as the Paschal Lamb; his blood is efficacious. Simultaneously another cluster of images, interwoven

4. See George S. Hendry, *The Gospel of the Incarnation*, pp. 115-47.

with the first, portrays the death as a cosmic victory over powers of death and darkness, forces inimical to God. Here the cross is a triumph in which the reign of sin is ended. Death itself is overcome.

Classic Christology:
Nicaea and Chalcedon

Central to the thought of the second-century Apologists was the conception of Christ as the divine Logos. Through this conception the Apologists sought to establish lines of contact with the surrounding Jewish and Hellenistic cultures. At the same time, the conception clearly marked out the uniqueness of the Christian claim, for the Apologists understood Christ not simply as a great prophet or teacher, a second Moses or Socrates possessing the *logos* to a certain degree, but as *being* the very Logos. Further, the conception of Christ as Logos displays the Christian community's early recognition that if salvation is to be secure, then the one who redeems must be the one who created as well. Salvation cannot simply be, as it was in some early theologies, salvation *from* the created order. On the other hand, the modes of thought fashioned by the early Apologists did create certain problems for later theology. It remained possible on their premises to think of the Logos as subordinate to God and thus as a lesser divinity; in addition there was the uncertain status, in the Apologists' soteriology, of Jesus' suffering and death. The first issue was to be addressed at Nicaea, the second at Chalcedon.

The thought of Irenaeus, particularly the importance he accords to the incarnation, provides a striking example of the way in which Christology is informed by the interest in salvation. According to this second-century theologian, Christ "became what we are in order to enable us to become what he is" (*On Heresies* 5.pref.). Irenaeus is representative of Eastern Christian thought in holding, contrary to much of Western soteriology, that the incarnation is not just a necessary prelude to the death on the cross. Rather, the incarnation itself is of a piece with Christ's saving activity, conceived as active obedience to God in identification with humankind. With the incarnation there is initiated a process which extends throughout Jesus' life whereby he embraces all aspects of human experience excepting sin. In the course of this process, Christ "recapitulates" not only the whole of human experience but also the entirety of the created order. Thus Irenaeus receives with full seriousness Paul's declaration of God's intent "to unite all things in him [Christ], things in heaven and things on earth" (Eph. 1:10). Once again, as with the Apologists, a link is forged between Redeemer and Creator. But now there is something more: In redemption, creation itself is brought to completion.

Questions implied but unresolved in the early Christologies came to a head in the fourth century. The theology of Arius made it impossible to ignore the fact that one could speak of Christ as the Creator of the world and yet consider him subordinate to God. In the name of a strict monotheism, Arius contended that in the last analysis the Logos must be considered a creature; he asserted in deliberately provocative terms that there was a time when Christ was not. It is significant that one indication of the inadequacy of Arius's position was that it did not square with the universally accepted practice of worshiping Christ.

In opposition to the Arian position, the Council of Nicaea (325) spoke of Christ as being *homoousios*—of the same nature—with God. In interpreting this formula we may take the thought of Athanasius as representative of what came to be acknowledged as the Nicene position. His thinking springs not from detached metaphysical speculation but from a specific soteriological concern. Athanasius reasons that if Christ were but a creature, he could not save us, "for how could a creature, by a creature, partake of God?" (*Against the Arians* 2:67). We were created out of nothing, and in sinning we had turned back toward that nothingness. What Christ achieved in saving us was to reverse this process; once again salvation was conceived as a virtual re-creation. It followed therefore that salvation could not be accomplished by one who was himself a creature—anymore than creation could be. That required, precisely, one who was "of the same nature" as God.

The achievement of Nicaea was considerable. The council made it clear that Christ's obedience did not make him less divine. This had profound implications for conceiving of divinity not simply as power but also as love.[5] Further, the council made it clear that Christ's role as mediator did not mean that he was a sort of *tertium quid*, more than human but less than God, hovering somewhere between the

5. See Arthur C. McGill, *Suffering: A Test of Theological Method* (Philadelphia: Geneva Press, 1968), pp. 58–76.

two. But in laying these matters to rest, the council made another set of inherited questions all the more acute.

We noted that already at the time of the Apologists there was the question of the status of Christ's suffering and death; indeed, as Paul asserts, the cross has always been the great stumbling block. Now, with the Nicene clarification of Christ's oneness with God, this question had to be addressed: How could one so exalted be crucified and die? The question was complicated by the fact that Christian thinking had taken over from Greek philosophy the concept of the divine "impassibility." The root of this concept is the recognition that the things of this world flourish and then perish, while God alone abides. From this it is concluded that change of any sort implies transience; thus God, to be God, must be unchanging. This unquestioned assumption placed enormous pressure upon Christian thought to regard Christ's suffering and death as somehow unreal or as having no bearing upon his divinity.

To erect a barrier against such misconceptions, the Council of Chalcedon (451) spoke of Christ as "one person in two natures." The debates surrounding Chalcedon are notoriously complex, for reasons both political and metaphysical, but once again the soteriological intent is unmistakable. Chalcedon held that Christ did not simply take on the appearance of humanity—he became truly human. And becoming human meant, as prior debate had served to clarify, that more than a human body was involved. The incarnation of the Logos involved a human mind and will as well. Gregory of Nazianzus was well aware of what was at stake when he wrote that "what has not been assumed cannot be restored; it is what is united with God that is saved" (Ep. 101). Salvation, on this reasoning, requires Christ's full and distinct humanity. But salvation also requires that the human be somehow united with the divine, since what is not united with God is not yet saved. A careful balance must therefore be struck, affirming both distinctness and unity. And it was such balance that Chalcedon sought in the formula "one person in two natures."

It must be stressed that this formula was never meant to be an exhaustive and self-sufficient account of the person of Christ. Specifically it may be suggested that the framers of the creed conceived the formula in relation to a long-standing tradition of Christ's preexistence, self-emptying, and exaltation, which was embodied in the liturgy and preserved in the great christological hymn of Phil. 2:6–11.[6] This tradition portrayed Christ not by a formula but by a narrative—a story which is moral in its implications and yet cosmic in its scope. The significance of this tradition had been implicitly reaffirmed in the very shape of the Nicene Creed. When Chalcedon is reinserted in this context, its static language regarding two "natures" is balanced by a language of process, and it becomes easier to make the soterio-logical point, for the narrative encourages us to speak not simply of two realities united in one person, but also of a saving process of *exchange*. In a manner characteristic of liturgy, the narrative revels in paradox. Hilary of Poitiers is fully within this tradition when he writes, "We were raised because he was lowered; shame to him was glory to us" (*On the Trinity* 2.25).

This point is crucial because the occasion which had necessitated the council in the first place was at least in part a perplexity over the status of Christ's suffering and death. Here in the tradition of preexis-tence, *self-emptying*, and exaltation was an account that gave to those events a central and irreducible place. Seen in this context, the aim of the council was intentionally indirect. It sought to stake out a conceptual space in which this kenotic tradition and others like it might continue to develop and flourish. The council wished not to create a rival account in competition with the others but to set down certain *rules* regarding the existing accounts and all future accounts, indicating which fell within the acceptable bounds and which were apt to prove irreconcilable with the proclamation of salvation.

Understood in this way, the Chalcedonian definition merits its position as the classic statement of Christian orthodoxy regarding the person of Christ. Nevertheless, it must be acknowledged that there are aspects of Chalcedon which stand in an uneasy relationship to the very traditions it sought to protect. The language of the creed, impos-ing in its terminology and reinforced by a certain conciliar authority, might lead one to believe that this was "real" theology. In compari-son, other theological modes, such as those of the liturgical narratives, may seem of little significance. Further, the creed established the pattern for a way of talking about Christ which began with the duality

---

6. Jaroslav Pelikan, *The Christian Tradition: A History of the Development of Doctrine*, 1:256–66; cf. Robert Victor Sellers, *The Council of Chalcedon: A Historical and Doctrinal Survey*, pp. xiii–xviii.

of the divinity on the one hand and the humanity on the other. Once we begin in this way, all we may subsequently say about the unity of Christ's person has something of the air of an afterthought, as if we were gluing the two natures together. Besides, beginning with the duality—as if the two terms were already understood in their own right and needed only to be united—provides an open invitation to import into Christology our prejudices and preconceptions. When this occurs we are apt to find, as subsequent theology often found, that the old debates return unabated, dividing our very notion of Christ's person.

Classic Treatments of Salvation:
Anselm to Luther

For the West, Chalcedon represented a point of relative closure regarding Christology and thus freed subsequent thinkers to turn their attention to a more direct consideration of soteriology. At the same time, the new task was profoundly shaped by the earlier achievement. The very title of Anselm's seminal work on the atonement, *Cur deus homo?* (1098), poses the question of why God united with humanity. The answer, to Anselm's mind, would have to be one which showed that the incarnation was in some sense a logical necessity.

Anselm found the grounds for this necessity in the moral order of the universe. It was this order, disturbed by human sin, which required a setting right. But to meet this requirement was beyond human doing, first because human powers had been vitiated by sin, and second because the debt owed was infinite. Anselm secured this latter point, the infinite character of the obligation, by interpreting the moral order in terms of a certain conception of *honor.* Because the one offended is of infinite worth, there is infinite liability. The debt is owed by humankind, but it is beyond all human paying. It is not, however, beyond the reach of God. Here the same logic works from the other side: If there should be offered a gift which had been of cost to God, then the worth of the gift would reflect the worth of the giver, which is to say, it would be infinite. What was needed, therefore, was a gift from God offered by a human being on behalf of all humankind. Hence the necessity of the incarnation.

It only remained for Anselm to specify the precise nature of the gift, and in doing this he introduced another portentous innovation. Anselm took Christ's suffering and death to be an instance—indeed, the primary and originative instance—of the practice of penance, which was coming to prominence in the church of Anselm's time. What is crucial here is that penance be understood as distinct from punishment: It has the character not of something undergone but of a gift freely offered. So understood, it comports well with the notion of an offering given to God's honor and with a theory of merit, for when one suffers a punishment, the act is self-contained, a requirement has simply been met. But when one makes a payment or offers penance, a certain merit may accrue, and if the offering be precious enough, it may create a kind of reservoir upon which others in turn may draw. In this manner Anselm established the foundations for much of the medieval church's self-understanding as the custodian of grace.[7]

Another medieval understanding of salvation quite different from Anselm's is the "moral influence theory" of Peter Abelard. Abelard held that Christ's work is best understood as a manifestation of God's love, which has the purpose of awakening a corresponding love in the hearts of humankind. It is this awakening of love, neither more nor less, which constitutes salvation. Against Abelard it is often argued that his interpretation is unduly subjectivistic; but the simplicity of his account, together with its sensitivity to the divine love and human experience, has won for it many advocates within the modern period.

For the understanding of Christ and salvation, as for much else, the high medieval period was outwardly a time of consolidation rather than innovation. But there did occur during this period a profound shift in the conceptual context within which the doctrines were conceived. It was a cultural transformation from a broadly "realist" to a predominantly "nominalist" world view. The bearing of this development upon our own concerns is twofold. First, the notion of a unitary human nature came to seem less real and more a matter of convention. This created difficulties regarding the solidarity which had been presumed to bind humankind together and, in turn, to Christ. Throughout the classical period, this concept of human solidarity had provided the crucial link between Christology and soteriology. If

---

7. Robert S. Franks, *The Work of Christ: A Historical Study of Christian Doctrine*, pp. 114, 135.

the concept of an underlying human nature is now regarded as a fiction, how can the act of God in becoming human—that is to say, in becoming one particular person—be efficacious for all? This unsettling question was made the more acute by a second, related factor: the waning of confidence in the notion, so basic to Anselm, of an independent moral order. It can be argued that with regard to this pervasive transformation, the thought of Thomas Aquinas represented a precious moment of judicious, insightful balance. In any case it is certain that, for better or for worse, the emergent nominalism succeeded in setting the terms for much of subsequent discussion. In the questions it raised, it anticipated the Enlightenment. In the answers it gave—dissolving the apparent quandaries by appeal to the freedom and finality of God's sovereign will—it presaged the Reformation.

Most classic treatments of salvation, and many modern treatments as well, have taken as their task determining how it is that through Christ humankind is restored to fellowship with God. The aim of Martin Luther's doctrine of justification by faith, in contrast, was less to answer this question than to overthrow it. For the question presupposes a two-step process: first, the state of humankind is in some way transformed in order to render it acceptable to God; second, and as a consequence, divine fellowship ensues. For Luther, by contrast, there is no such preparation. Christ is given to us as free gift, and he *is* our fellowship with God. Then, as a result, we come to know that he is our righteousnesss, that his righteousness is imputed to us. Arguably, this all-decisive event in which we encounter God in Christ is for Luther the true meaning of the Nicene *homoousios*, and the divine exchange whereby Christ took our place in order that we might take his is the meaning of Chalcedon.

Salvation is thus constitutive of Christ's very being. Luther conveyed this formative conviction by an endless variety of images. Christ is the Word, the Victor, the King. Salvation is Christ's triumph over sin; it is his suffering of our punishment in our place. The richness of Luther's imagery and the sweep of his vision admit of conflicting interpretations. His understanding of faith in particular—as that which grasps the highest reality and yet does so with the utmost inwardness— has engendered innumerable debates over the status of subjectivity. What is beyond debate is the impact of his reformulation and the fact that he stands as a pivotal figure between the classical and the modern periods.[8]

CHALLENGES AND CONTRIBUTIONS OF
MODERN CONSCIOUSNESS

Three Strata of Modernity

1. Reason as Critical: The Enlightenment

The thinkers of the Enlightenment sought to expunge from Christianity certain beliefs that were, in their opinion, the work of superstition. The basis for this doctrinal housecleaning was provided in large part by the notion of a universal rational and moral order accessible to any thinking person. The role of Christ was confined to that of a moral teacher, and it was in light of the moral order that even his teachings were interpreted and judged. But if one already has knowledge of truth, does one really need the particular figure of Jesus? And if on the other hand one does insist on Jesus as indispensable, is that not an arbitrary narrowing of what is rightfully universal? Here lie the roots of the "scandal of particularity," which is commonly associated with Gotthold Lessing's dictum, "Accidental truths of history can never become the proof of necessary truths of reason."[9] An "ugly ditch" had opened between the time of Christ and the present. It was equally a chasm between the accidental and the necessary—between the relativities of history, including the historical Jesus, and the matters most deserving of human trust and fidelity.

2. Reason as Self-Critical: Kant

The modern age is often identified with the Enlightenment and the rise of modern science. It is in this fashion that issues of religion and modernity are commonly portrayed. But to leave matters in these terms is to overlook the fact that the period of the Enlightenment, which so celebrated the achievements of science, culminated in a philosophy which strictly delimited the realm in which that science could claim authority. Quite arguably, the highest achievement of

8. My reading of Luther is particularly informed by Ian D. Kingston Siggins, *Martin Luther's Doctrine of Christ* (New Haven: Yale University Press, 1970).
9. Gotthold Lessing, "The Proof of the Spirit and of Power," in *Lessing's Theological Writings*, trans. Henry Chadwick (Stanford: Stanford University Press, 1956), p. 53.

the critical spirit was to criticize itself, and this was preeminently the work of Immanuel Kant.

Kant predicated his philosophy upon a radical distinction between two fundamental human capacities: that of theoretical reason, exemplified in the achievements of Newtonian physics, and that of practical reason, which governs the moral life. In this manner Kant appropriated an earlier metaphysical distinction, that between "nature" and "spirit," and translated it into the terms of his own "transcendental" philosophy, a philosophy centered upon the capacities and limitations of the human subject. So translated, the contrast was rendered the more acute, the more emphatic. Applied to theology, Kant's disjunction served as a basis for rejecting the various arguments for God's existence, whether adduced by Christian tradition or natural religion, as efforts to extend the operations of theoretical reason beyond their legitimate sphere. At the same time, Kant did find it possible to reintroduce the idea of God not as an object of knowledge but as a necessary postulate arising from the activities of practical reason. Similarly, the Christology Kant fashioned within these limits bears the mark of his fundamental disjunction. A strong distinction is drawn between Christ understood as the ideal of moral perfection and the empirical-historical figure of Jesus. To a large extent Kant's solution to the christological problem simply carried to its logical conclusion the problematic tendency encouraged by the Enlightenment and lamented by Lessing—the severance of ideality from history.

3. Reason as Self-Aware: Hegel

With Kant the spirit of the Enlightenment had become self-critical, but the effect of Kant's thought had been to absolutize certain dichotomies. The truths of religion, for example, were set apart from those of science. But there is something in the human mind which does not love a sharp dichotomy; that dichotomy creates a conceptual itch. For G. W. F. Hegel this spontaneous dissatisfaction was evidence that the inherited divisions were really the result of fragmentation, and Hegel was profoundly persuaded that fragmentation is finally error. For Hegel, the mind—or better, the spirit—is guided in its depths by a tacit awareness of the logic by which life itself evolves, a movement through diversity and conflict to convergence and reconciliation. Kant had been on the right track, Hegel believed, in the "Copernican revolution" whereby he had concentrated attention upon the fu damental capacities of the human subject. But he had failed to foll through on his crucial insight; he had not taken with full seriousness the character of human subjectivity as all-determinative and self-transcending. With Kant, reason had become self-critical, but it had not yet become self-aware.

Hegel held that in the course of the quest for self-awareness, finite spirit comes to recognize that by virtue of that very quest—by virtue of the unlimited, unconditional character of human questioning—it is already implicitly infinite. But the point at which this infinite character of the finite becomes most concrete and is thus most fully realized is in Jesus Christ, and there, as elsewhere, realization comes by way of conflict. Hegel's Christology focuses on the cross, where Christ suffers death, the fate of all finite beings. But in Christ it is God, the infinite, who is submitted to death. The crucifixion is the death of God. Yet in and through that extreme moment God remains God—and so it is death itself that dies. The bonds are broken, the finite is overcome; it is taken up into the infinite. This, in Hegel's view, is the true meaning of the resurrection and the ascension.[10]

One may with good reason dissent from Hegel's conclusions, but one cannot deny his achievement, which was nothing less than a reclaiming of history for theology. No longer the repository of merely "accidental" truths, history became the realm in which spirit attains its most profound self-recognition. Similarly, as regards particular doctrines, it would be wrong to dismiss Hegel as a simple rationalist, for he reclaimed the very doctrines that the rationalism of the Enlightenment despised: the incarnation, the atonement, the resurrection, and the Trinity. "Mystery" was no longer a term of opprobrium, but an invitation to deeper understanding.

An aspect of Hegel's influence, which is often unremarked, stems from the tendency in his system to identify salvation itself with the process of revelation. This Hegelian turn comported well with the modern emphasis upon experience. The result has been that it is often unclear in modern theology whether salvation is an event that one knows or the event of one's knowing. There is another aspect of Hegel, however, which has been less well received. Much of the

10. See Hegel, *Lectures on the Philosophy of Religion*, vol. 3, and *The Christian Religion*, pp. 169–229; and James Yerkes, *The Christology of Hegel* (Missoula: Scholars Press, 1978).

Hegelian achievement lay, to quote Claude Welch, in the insistence that "Christianity is neither mere feeling nor a kind of truth claim separate from the rest of man's knowing. In both respects Hegel stands in contrast to Schleiermacher." Certainly any responsible theology will hold that faith entails knowledge and truth in some important sense. But the modern penchant has been to regard religious knowledge as fundamentally distinctive and thus as set apart from the more ordinary forms. It is on just this point that "the disjunction between Schleiermacher and Hegel provided the shape of the issue for the nineteenth and twentieth centuries."[11] Perhaps because it is more congenial to the soteriology-Christology paradigm, Schleiermacher's stress upon religious experience has largely carried the day. Yet the very success of this procedure, with its penchant for a dividing of the conceptual terrain, may be in part responsible for the uneasy conviction, widespread in the present day, that modern Christology has yet to find a truly comprehensive and adequate context.[12]

Theological Reformulations

1. The Modern Turn: Schleiermacher

With Friedrich Schleiermacher the various strata of the modern period began to be assimilated into the mainstream of Christian theology. Schleiermacher fundamentally endorsed the Kantian turn to the subject: his own crucial contribution was to seek to found Christian doctrine in a thoroughgoing way upon the actualities of human experience. The effect of this innovation was quite clearly to place soteriology before Christology. In this sense his is a "functionalist" Christology: Christ is known as the indispensable "whence" of the common life of the Christian community; there is a kind of reading back from Christ's *effects* to his reality. Indeed, to speak of the divinity of Christ apart from his impact upon our experience is, in Schleiermacher's view, to surrender the living faith to metaphysics and mythology. For subsequent theology this conviction became in large part normative. The classical tradition had tended to reason that Christ is

11. Claude Welch, *Protestant Thought in the Nineteenth Century*, 1:106.
12. Those minority voices which have been most critical of the modern paradigm have taken their stand on a deepened appreciation of the noetic character of faith, that is, the character of faith as knowledge. See Karl Barth, *Church Dogmatics*, vol. 4/1, p. 758; and Wolfhart Pannenberg, *Basic Questions in Theology*, trans. George H. Kehm (Philadelphia: Fortress Press, 1970), 2:28–45.

divine and therefore able to save us. In Schleiermacher and much of modern teaching, Christ saves us; therefore we conclude he is divine.

But what of Lessing's problem? How is it that the experience of contemporary believers should be determined by this figure of past history, Jesus of Nazareth? For Schleiermacher the key was found in a developmental process occurring within history. In depicting this process, Schleiermacher offered a further variation upon the nature/spirit distinction; he suggested that we find within our awareness a lower and a higher consciousness. Our higher consciousness makes us aware that we depend upon God absolutely; the moment we gain this awareness, we know that it should be made to permeate our entire life, including the realm of our lower consciousness. But in fact this does not occur; we fall short of our own ideal, and this is the recognition of our sin.

At this point Jesus enters the picture, as the "archetype" of that which we cannot accomplish of ourselves, that is, the living out of the knowledge of God. But as archetype he is more than a mere example, as he was for the Enlightenment. While he does communicate the *form* of the authentic Christian life, he communicates a *power* as well. For Jesus' living out of the consciousness of God was itself a historical act which had a historical effect. It gave rise to the Christian community, which became in turn the further embodiment and communication of that act. In this manner Jesus' accomplishment is conveyed to us in the present time, as formative power and empowering form. Thus, Schleiermacher sought to overcome the estrangement of the truth of Christianity from the concreteness of history.[13]

It is not clear that Schleiermacher was ever entirely successful in uniting the two governing foci of his thought—the figure of Jesus and the character of Christian subjectivity. But then neither is it clear that the classical tradition ever realized its own twofold intent of affirming Christ's divinity and his humanity. In the tradition Christ's humanity tended to be regarded as itself miraculous in some way and thus as more than human; or contrariwise, it was regarded as peculiarly passive vis-à-vis the divinity and thus as not exercising a fully human freedom. Either way, a subtle Docetism seemed to be implied. In the

---

13. Friedrich Schleiermacher, *The Christian Faith*, secs. 88, 94; Richard R. Niebuhr, *Schleiermacher on Christ and Religion* (New York: Charles Scribner's Sons, 1964), p. 226.

face of these tendencies a profoundly enriching contribution of the modern period to Christian thought is the clear conviction that being human entails an unreserved participation in finitude and freedom. The notion that Jesus shared in the preconceptions of his times, that his self-understanding developed gradually and not without search and struggle, that he was in his very humanity one who freely chose and actively embraced the course he was to take—these are all distinctly modern propositions. And it was Schleiermacher who in large part began the vital task of appropriating such propositions into the fabric of Christology, not as mere concessions to modernity but as legitimate, deepened insights into the truth of the Christian gospel. In this and in many related features of his thought—the appeal to experience, the project of a Christology "from below," the priority accorded to soteriology, the effort to be entirely candid and self-critical—Schleiermacher fully merits his title as founder of modern Christian theology.

2. History and Apocalyptic

The persistence of Lessing's question was reflected in the course of the nineteenth century by the appearance of a great variety of efforts to recount the life of Jesus and thereby establish the historic core of the Christian faith. In 1906 this collective effort was brought up short by the publication of Albert Schweitzer's *Quest of the Historical Jesus*. Schweitzer argued that historians and popularists alike had failed to produce a coherent picture of Jesus' person and career. The problem, Schweitzer contended, lay with a congenital incapacity to take seriously that which Jesus himself had taken with ultimate seriousness: the expectation of an immanent ending of history. Ironically the historians had been blinded to this all-determining feature of Jesus' message by their own Enlightenment commitment to a vision of history as internally coherent and immune to disruption from without. Thus the world-affirming attitude which the modern age had won at such a price was called into question by the imperious, world-negating figure who emerged at the boundary of Schweitzer's research.

Chastened by Schweitzer's critique and informed by his insistence upon apocalyptic, the next generation of scholars proceeded more cautiously. Their approach is epitomized in the historical-critical work of Rudolf Bultmann, who took it as his fundamental premise that the New Testament is not history in the modern sense, not *reportage about* the historical Jesus, but the complex evidence of the early community's *response to* him. Attention thus shifted from the person of Jesus himself and centered instead upon the strands and elements of the community's faith. At the extreme point of skepticism the question arose whether one need posit the reality of the historical figure at all, or what difference it would make if one did not. More recently, however, such scholars as Ernst Käsemann have undertaken a "new quest," which has proceeded in full awareness of these strictures. After all, these scholars argue, if the Christian faith is not to be covertly Docetic, it must show that the figure of the historical Jesus can in *some* fashion bear the weight of the claims made on his behalf. Such, they believe, can indeed be shown if one attends to certain elements within the New Testament, notably in those parables and sayings of Jesus which do not bear the imprint of such subsequent events as the crucifixion. From these spare materials it is possible to derive a portrait of Jesus along the lines suggested at the beginning of the present essay.[14]

3. *Dialectical Theology*

The debate over the historical Jesus has carried us well into the present century. Now we must backtrack in order to pick up another thread, that of "dialectical theology." We may begin by recalling the distinction between spirit and nature which was so significant for the liberal theology of the nineteenth century. For many, the concept of spirit in particular served as a kind of conceptual link between divinity and the highest aspect, generally the religious aspect, of humankind. It is precisely this notion of some point of commonality between the divine and the human which Karl Barth attacked in his commentary on Romans. For Barth the quest for such a link, which is indeed the religious quest, is itself the work of presumption and sin.

14. See Ernst Käsemann, "The Problem of the Historical Jesus," in *Essays on New Testament Themes*, trans. W. J. Montague (London: SCM Press, 1964), pp. 15–47; and idem, "Blind Alleys in the 'Jesus of History' Controversy," in *New Testament Questions of Today*, trans. W. J. Montague (Philadelphia: Fortress Press, 1969), pp. 23–65; James M. Robinson, *A New Quest for the Historical Jesus*; and Norman Perrin, *Rediscovering the Teaching of Jesus* (New York: Harper & Row, 1976). For a popular presentation of the results of the new quest see Gunther Bornkamm, *Jesus of Nazareth*, trans. Irene and Fraser McLuskey with James M. Robinson (New York: Harper & Row, 1961).

So far from bringing us closer to God, it is the very mark of our separation. For Barth *both* spirit and nature, heaven and earth, in fact all creation, stood on one side of the ultimate chasm, while God, the infinite one, stood on the other. Thus a form of the eschatological vision uncovered by Schweitzer became the central tenet of theology.

To say that God is wholly other does not mean, however, that God must exist in isolation. It does mean that if the gulf between time and eternity is to be overcome the movement must derive entirely from the side of God. This is what has happened in Jesus Christ. But Barth insists that when we speak that name we must continue to recall the chasm—that Christ is really God and really human and that the two are infinitely different—even as we proclaim its overcoming. Only in this manner can we hope to be mindful of Jesus Christ as event and thus as gift.

The historical-critical fires that consumed the early quest for the historical Jesus were in considerable part the work of Rudolf Bultmann. In his capacity as theologian, Bultmann professed to celebrate the conflagration, for what was lost, in his estimation, was nothing more than the misguided effort to know Christ after the flesh, in the manner of this world—to establish facts which would secure a controlling knowledge of who and what Christ was. This hankering after objectivity was to Bultmann an evasion, a dodging of the personal risk inherent in Christian faith. The New Testament for Bultmann was not an idle compilation of historical data but a proclamation: the kerygma. Behind the writings lay the faith of the writers, and behind that faith lay the kerygma itself—the challenge to surrender the securities of the past, to be open to the inbreaking future, and above all to *decide* in the present moment, the absolute "now." Thus the task of demythologizing was not primarily a negative operation; it was an effort to recover the original challenge, to lay it bare, to let it speak anew. Dissolving the myth, we recover the word.

In attempting this recovery Bultmann drew heavily upon an existentialist philosophy inspired by Martin Heidegger. Heidegger interpreted human existence not as a being—not as some sort of thing—but as sheer possibility, recognizing and claiming itself in the moment of radical decision. Bultmann embraced this philosophical vision as profoundly consonant with the Christian kerygma, with the crucial proviso that the kerygma goes beyond mere philosophy in declaring such authentic existence as freely given in Jesus Christ. This is the key to Bultmann's rethinking, or demythologizing, of Chalcedonian Christology. Jesus is indeed the point of encounter between the human and divine, but that encounter must not be treated as a metaphysical datum located in the distant past. Rather, it is an event, a present event, centered in the act of proclamation.

Because Bultmann so denounced the historical quest and philosophical speculation of the previous century, one may miss the lines of continuity which nonetheless persist. It is apparent upon reflection that the result of much of existentialism has been to reinforce the Kantian disjunction between practical and theoretical reason. Bultmann is entirely within the premises of this tradition when he reduces the conceptual content of the kerygma to the barest minimum and places all the emphasis on the side of decision. In Bultmann's hands, Philipp Melanchthon's dictum that "to know Christ is to know his benefits" becomes a virtual definition of all one can know and should wish to know about the person of Christ. Thus Bultmann carries to a logical conclusion the modern tendency to accord primacy to soteriology. Christology is virtually absorbed into soteriology, and soteriology, shorn of its historical-conceptual content, is concentrated almost exclusively within the present moment.[15]

4. The Search for an Adequate Context

The thought of Bultmann, Tillich, and even the early Barth represents a profound appropriation of philosophical existentialism. It counters the earlier tendency, epitomized in Hegel, to sublate all distinctions, including that between the human and the divine, within a comprehensive notion of spirit. Insisting upon the frailty of reason, the risk of faith, and the transcendence of God, the existentialist movement exploded the liberal synthesis. In this sense it represented a chastened retreat from Hegelian expansiveness to a Kantian sense of limits. Moreover, in saying this one must avoid the all-too-common

---

15. Paul Tillich's existential ontology represents an important attempt to establish existentialism within a more adequate setting, but Tillich continues to adhere most emphatically to the modern paradigm and is accordingly distrustful of noetic claims on behalf of faith. See Tillich, *Systematic Theology*, 2:150; and David H. Kelsey, *The Fabric of Paul Tillich's Theology* (New Haven: Yale University Press, 1967), pp. 194–97. Thus it is not clear that Tillich marks a fundamental departure from the approach epitomized by Bultmann.

tendency to speak condescendingly of the existentialist heritage, as if it were nothing more than an overly pessimistic swing of the cultural pendulum. The eschatological demand is there to be reckoned with in the preaching of Jesus. The great merit of theological existentialism is that it strove to communicate that challenge undiminished, and any subsequent theology which neglects this task must be judged inadequate. Finally, among the appeals of this movement it must be noted that the existentialist disjunctions provided, or seemed to provide, a way of dealing with the abiding scandal of particularity. By distinguishing the historical Jesus from the kerygmatic Christ and concentrating salvific significance in the latter, it succeeded in diverting attention, at least temporarily, from the awkward questions of history.[16]

But this was its failing, for the existentialist tactic was an acute form of the penchant, noted earlier in Schleiermacher, for resolving problems of conflict by dividing the conceptual terrain. And thus it was inevitable that sooner or later the question Hegel addressed to Kant should reassert itself. Can a theology so fixed on a series of radical disjunctions—knowledge versus faith, history versus existence, immanence versus transcendence—be genuinely "concrete"? Can it, that is to say, provide an adequate conceptual context in which the divided, fragmentary facets of the truth may be seen to converge, if not yet fully to cohere? This question or some variant of it may underlie much of the recent exploration in Christology. Undoubtedly the various probings exhibit a great diversity, but many of the most significant may be understood as seeking some way in which Christian thought, while retaining the lessons of the first half of the century, might yet surmount the dichotomies of the once-dominant existentialism.[17]

Process theology is remarkably similar to existentialism in viewing human experience as profoundly oriented toward the future. But from the process perspective this openness is not unique to humankind, as in existentialism; rather, it is a clue by way of the human to

16. See Van Austin Harvey, The Historian and the Believer: The Morality of Historical Knowledge and Christian Belief (New York: Macmillan Co., 1966).

17. One of the finest discussions of theology and transcendental philosophy is still Dietrich Bonhoeffer's Act and Being (New York: Harper & Row, 1961). For further treatment of the issue of context, to somewhat different effect, see George Rupp, Christologies and Cultures: Toward a Typology of Religious Worldviews (The Hague: Mouton, 1974); and Eugene TeSelle, Christ in Context: Divine Purpose and Human Possibility (Philadelphia: Fortress Press, 1975).

all of reality. The entire cosmos is conceived as a complex of future-oriented events which are drawn into creative purpose by the lure of the divine Logos. Thus human activity, when properly understood, does not exclude divine initiative, and divine activity, properly understood, is persuasive and never coercive. This authentic relationship of the divine and the human, obscured by the substantialist metaphysic of the traditional creeds, finds its paradigmatic realization in the person of Jesus Christ. In the words of John Cobb, "Jesus, without in any way ceasing to be human, participated in that one structure of existence in which the self is coconstituted by the presence of God."[18] Here Christ is understood in the context of and at the head of what is quite arguably the most comprehensive setting possible—the entire process of cosmic creativity.

For the later Barth, as for the early Barth, there is no question of placing Christ within some allegedly more comprehensive context. Christ *is* the adequate context of Christian theology. But in the Romans commentary, Barth's understanding of that context was constrained by a dialectical method drawn from Kierkegaardian existentialism. In the course of the *Church Dogmatics*, by contrast, a number of developments become increasingly evident. First, Christology is conceived in conjunction with a fully developed doctrine of the Trinity. Second, a distinctive concept of analogy, an "analogy of faith," enables Barth to speak of the divine and the human conjointly rather than in opposition, giving greater coherence to his Christology and greater autonomy to creation. Third, the figure of Christ—previously depicted as a bare, enigmatic moment of crisis—is fleshed out with all the detail of the scriptural account of Jesus' earthly ministry. Finally, it is significant that in the soteriology which accompanies this replenished Christology, Barth's earlier language of destruction and re-creation is absorbed within an overarching framework of exchange.[19]

---

18. John B. Cobb, *Christ in a Pluralistic Age*, p. 171.
19. See Barth, *Church Dogmatics*, vol. 4/1, pp. 79–154; and Hans Urs von Balthasar, *The Theology of Karl Barth*, trans. John Drury (New York: Holt, Rinehart & Winston, 1971), pp. 100–150. See also Barth's essay "Rudolf Bultmann—An Attempt to Understand Him," in *Kerygma and Myth*, ed. Hans-Werner Bartsch, trans. Reginald H. Fuller (London: S.P.C.K., 1962), 2:83–132. Barth illustrates the fact that one does not have to regard Christ (or the Trinity) as an inadequate context in order to be concerned with context as an issue.

Karl Rahner may be seen as representing a middle course between the alternatives exemplified by Barth and process theology. He adopts a philosophical standpoint, but places strict limits on what philosophy can do. Rahner's approach resembles existentialism in taking the Kantian turn toward the subject, but it is amplified by a reverence for being and a respect for human nature which are drawn from classical Thomism. Rahner finds the crucial characteristic of humankind in a questing restlessness of spirit and in self-giving love. Accordingly he understands the incarnation of God as "the unique, *supreme*, case of the total actualization of human reality," which consists of the fact that we *are* insofar as we give up ourselves.[20] More recently Rahner has grounded his Christology in a view of world history interpreted in light of evolution and eschatology.

In many respects the work of Wolfhart Pannenberg marks a distinctive turn in contemporary theology, yet here too one finds an effort to appropriate and surmount the heritage of existentialism. History for Pannenberg is not simply human historicity; it is universal history. And faith is not just an absurd decision; it exhibits its own distinctive rationality. For those who are open to an understanding of history along the lines of Jewish apocalyptic, it becomes possible to affirm the resurrection of Jesus as a historical event. And the resurrection, so understood, enables us to see in Christ the proleptic embodiment of the meaning of world history. In Christ the conclusion of history— the end time when all will be made plain—is already, anticipatorily present.

Liberation theology, too, would ground Christology in a new vision of history. But whereas Pannenberg sees the historical problem largely as posed by the first stratum of modernity, the Enlightenment, the liberationists find more compelling the issues raised by a further stratum, namely, Karl Marx's searching critique of social-economic oppression. The real issues emerge not by an abstract consideration of freedom and reason, as occurs even in existentialism, but by concrete encounter with the negative realities of injustice and victimization. Salvation in this context is experienced as liberation, and Christology comes to center upon Jesus' ministry and crucifixion. By his active identification with the poor and outcast, Christ pronounces judgment

20. Karl Rahner, *Theological Investigations*, 4:110.

upon all the self-serving ideologies—including the complacent Christologies—which ignore and thus condone the hidden violence of the status quo. Thus the context the liberationists propose for Christology is not a generalized notion of history at all, but the concrete, self-critical practice of following in the way of Christ's own prophetic ministry.

ISSUES AND PROPOSALS

We have seen that from the earliest date Christology was informed by a certain soteriological interest, and we have noted how in the modern period that interest became a key to making Christology relevant. We have seen existentialism carry this modern strategy to a logical extreme, intensifying its strengths and weaknesses, and we have scanned a variety of recent explorations which, while yet influenced by existentialism, have found that position to be in some sense inadequate. But in what sense exactly? And do the shortcomings of existentialism, whatever they be, reflect upon the modern paradigm itself? If so, is the paradigm inherently defective, or does it simply require readjustment? The diagnoses offered on such questions are as various as the remedies prescribed.

The classical tradition is instructive in this regard. By roundly affirming that the one who saves must be the one who creates, the tradition made clear that the good news of salvation cannot be celebrated in splendid isolation. Salvation, if it be truly salvation, must be related in some fashion to all reality. In the course of its development, however, the classical tradition did create a de facto separation of Christology from soteriology by treating as discrete topics the "person" and "work" of Christ. Debating theories of salvation came to seem an enterprise unto itself, bearing only an external relationship to one's understanding of who Christ is.

The modern approach, which adopts soteriology as the inner meaning of Christology, may therefore be appreciated not only as an effort to render the figure of Christ more meaningful and credible, but also as an attempt to knit together two interdependent doctrines which had unfortunately grown apart. This modern reintegration has achieved much that any contemporary theology will wish to preserve. But it does seem clear that by beginning with soteriology the modern integration has tended to produce, in actual practice, a constricted Christology which has in turn entailed an inadequate soteriology.

In light of this situation, I should like briefly to submit three proposals for consideration: first, that Christology must not be divorced from the presence of Christ within the worshiping community; second, that the nature of this presence is in the strictest sense mysterious; and third, that Christology is profoundly related to the doctrine of the Trinity.

1. The Christ who is present is the one who reigns even now as Lord, known by the worshiping community but not confined within it. It is by virtue of this presence that the community is impelled, directed, and enlivened, that the story of Jesus' life is remembered and interpreted, and that the consummation of all things is awaited and hoped for. The earliest resurrection accounts were reports of Christ known as present. In this manner he was known as alive and thus as risen. As Dietrich Bonhoeffer has shown, a Christology pursued in this fashion need not become parochial. Yet it is for fear of being parochial, too narrow in its base, that modern Christology has generally neglected this crucial but elusive key.

2. At the same time, however, there is a sense in which modern Christology has been *too* oriented toward the present. The effort to begin with soteriology was an attempt to establish some experience or need in the present to which Christ might prove relevant. But inevitably this meant that the experience or need was defined to some extent independently of Christ; thus terms were established which would then constrain one's very notion of the presence of Christ. Hence the need for the second proposal. In the words of one commentator, the Christ who is present cannot be predefined; he "is not the representation of the self-consciousness of the believing community, the personification of the kerygma, or the like, but . . . he *owns* his own mode of presence."[21] We must be equally resolute in affirming *that* Christ is present and in denying that we have

---

21. Dietrich Ritschl, *Memory and Hope: An Inquiry Concerning the Presence of Christ*, p. 230. See also Dietrich Bonhoeffer, *Christ the Center*, pp. 27–34; and Hans W. Frei, *The Identity of Jesus Christ: The Hermeneutical Bases of Dogmatic Theology* (Philadelphia: Fortress Press, 1967), pp. 33–34. My proposals are indebted to the triumvirate of Bonhoeffer, Frei, and Ritschl. The next question, once the mysterious character of Christ's presence has been acknowledged, is how we can then have any clear knowledge of Christ; here Frei's work is especially suggestive. In a somewhat different vein, cf. Peter C. Hodgson, *Jesus—Word and Presence: An Essay in Christology* (Philadelphia: Fortress Press, 1971).

any independent knowledge of *how* he is present. Christ's presence is mysterious in the strictest sense: it is the presence of God—in God's own freedom.

In talking about salvation, we are drawn into some powerful terminology: life versus death, light versus darkness, heaven versus hell. It is crucial to remember that language of this sort, however legitimate, is open to immense abuse. If unaffected by the unifying power of an authentic Christology, such contrasts produce a theology which remains constitutionally divided, one might almost say schizophrenic, regardless of what it may say about reconciliation. Examples are found in many of the variants of the spirit/nature contrast and in the long-standing difficulty theology has experienced in its effort to affirm both the humanity and the divinity of Christ. It seems we continue to harbor the conviction that where God's freedom is active, human freedom is somehow diminished. The notion presents itself as common sense; it plays upon our deepest anxieties. But its effect is to deny the reality of reconciliation.[22]

3. To believe that God's freedom does not displace our freedom but rather creates and nourishes it is perhaps the inner meaning of saying that the one who saves is the one who creates. But these notions seem so difficult for us that it may be we are simply unable to appropriate them apart from the presence of Christ—which is to say, apart from the Holy Spirit. It is the Spirit who makes Christ present, as self-giving yet free. And it is this mysterious presence which in turn frees us—not simply from the world, but *into* it—to challenge and overcome the invidious and self-serving divisions which we ourselves have created in the vain attempt to effect our own salvation. By participating in this history of reconciliation, the people of God may share in the very life of that transcendent community which is the inner life of God. They become the body of Christ, and it is in this sense that Christology finds its adequate context within the life of the Trinity.

22. See D. M. Baillie, *God Was in Christ: An Essay on Incarnation and Atonement* (New York: Charles Scribner's Sons, 1948), pp. 106–18; and Karl Rahner, *Theological Investigations*, 1:162, 4:117.

SUGGESTIONS FOR FURTHER READING

Baillie, D. M. *God Was in Christ*. London: Faber & Faber, 1961.

Barth, Karl. *Church Dogmatics*. vols. 4/1, 4/2, 4/3.

Bonhoeffer, Dietrich. *Christ the Center*. Translated by John Bowden. New York: Harper & Row, 1966.

Brock, Rita Nakashima. *Journeys by Heart: A Christology of Erotic Power*. New York: Crossroad, 1988.

The Christological Controversy. Translated and edited by Richard A. Norris, Jr. Philadelphia: Fortress Press, 1980.

Christology of the Later Fathers. Edited by E. R. Hardy. *LCC* 3.

Coakley, Sarah. *Christ without Absolutes*. Oxford: Oxford University Press, 1988.

Cobb, John B. *Christ in a Pluralistic Age*. Philadelphia: Westminster Press, 1975.

Davis, Stephen T., editor. *Encountering Jesus: A Debate on Christology*. Atlanta: John Knox Press, 1988.

Franks, Robert S. *The Work of Christ: A Historical Study of Christian Doctrine*. London and New York: Nelson, 1962.

Fuller, Reginald H. *The Foundations of New Testament Christology*. New York: Charles Scribner's Sons, 1965.

Grillmeier, Alois. *Christ in Christian Tradition: From the Apostolic Age to Chalcedon*. 2d rev. ed. London: Mowbray, 1975.

Hendry, George S. *The Gospel of the Incarnation*. Philadelphia: Westminster Press, 1958.

Macquarrie, John. *Jesus Christ in Modern Thought*. Philadelphia: Trinity Press International, 1990.

Moltmann, Jürgen. *The Crucified God*. Translated by R. A. Wilson and John Bowden. Minneapolis: Fortress Press, 1993.

Pannenberg, Wolfhart. *Jesus: God and Man*. 2d ed. Translated by Lewis L. Wilkins and Duane A. Priebe. Philadelphia: Westminster Press, 1977.

Rahner, Karl. *Theological Investigations*. Vols. 1, 4, 5.

Ritschl, Dietrich. *Memory and Hope*. New York: Macmillan Co., 1967.

Robinson, James M. *A New Quest for the Historical Jesus*. London: SCM Press, 1959.

Schillebeeckx, Edward. *Jesus: An Experiment in Christology and Christ: The Experience of Jesus as Lord*.

Sellers, Robert Victor. *The Council of Chalcedon: A Historical and Doctrinal Survey*. London: S.P.C.K., 1961.

Sobrino, Jon. *Christology at the Crossroads: A Latin American Approach*. Maryknoll, N.Y.: Orbis Books, 1978.

Taylor, Mark Kline. *Remembering Esperanza*. Maryknoll, N.Y.: Orbis, 1990. Chapters 5 and 6.

9. THE CHURCH

WHERE WE ARE

Among the articles of Christian faith, "the church" has a peculiar status. Unlike the doctrines of God, Christ, Trinity, creation, fall, redemption, and so on, it was not specifically thematized in the patristic period, nor did it become the subject of controversy. Only when serious questions began to be raised about the church in the late Middle Ages did systematic treatises on this topic first appear. Yet obviously the reality of the church and commitment to it were present from the beginning of Christian faith and functioned as the largely unarticulated presupposition of all doctrines and beliefs.

In the strict sense, Christians do not believe *in* the church. Hans Küng and others have pointed out that, in general, the ancient creeds speak of believing *in* God and *in* the Holy Spirit, but of believing the church (*credo ecclesiam*).[1] To say that we believe the church means that the church is not God or Spirit or any sacred, divine, supernatural thing, despite the constant temptation to believe so. We do not believe *in* the church because we *are* the church—a sinful, fallible, pilgrim people who scarcely can be said to believe in themselves. Yet the creeds commit us to *believe* the church because it is an instrument of God's saving work and a locus of special divine presence.

The constant temptation has been to believe too much or too little about the church and thus to lose sight of what it essentially is. For example, we find today a new Catholic conservatism with its defense of a hierarchical and authoritarian institution; similarly, on the Protestant side, the charismatic and evangelical movements flourish with their extravagant claims for the Spirit, church authority, and credal orthodoxy. By contrast, there are many who, despairing of the church, deny the necessity of its existence or propose to dissolve its functions totally into the world. A subtler version of the tendency to

---

1. Hans Küng, *The Church*, pp. 53–59; Karl Barth, *Church Dogmatics*, vol. 4/1, p. 686.

believe too little about the church is found in its characteristically middle-class manifestation for which the church frequently is nothing other than a means of satisfying private, therapeutic needs through counseling, ideology, and clublike activities. Questions of truth and redemptive community are replaced by those having to do with the successful adjustment of individuals to the exigencies of life. Edward Farley suggests that, whereas the characteristically ancient form of the perversion of ecclesia was institutionalism (a form that certainly perpetuates itself), the characteristically modern form is individualism and privatism.[2] In either case the church confronts a loss of essence, a distortion into something other, something more or something less, than ecclesia.

THE DOCTRINE IN ITS CLASSIC FORMULATION

Images of Ecclesia

In secular Greek, *ekklēsia* simply means "assembly." Etymologically it suggests the act of assembling or "calling forth" (*ek* + *klēsis*, calling), but its more significant association is with the Hebraic term *qāhāl* or *qāhāl Yahweh*—"people (or congregation) of God"—of which *ekklēsia* is a frequent translation in the Septuagint (Greek Old Testament). This usage was well established when the early Greek-speaking Jewish-Christian community needed a term by which to designate itself. It expressed continuity with Israel, but also discontinuity, since another Septuagint rendering of *qāhāl*, namely, *synagōgē*, had come to be more commonly used of the Jewish religious community and place of worship. The Christian community came to think of itself as an ecclesia, not a synagogue. Moreover, the term selected, given its secular connotation, was decisively noncultic and nonsacral, a fact of enormous significance both historically and theologically. In a sense it was an empty, formal term, free of old cultic and religious associations, needing to be filled by a new content. This was accomplished by a rich profusion of metaphors, especially in Paul and in the deutero-Pauline and early Catholic epistles. Of the many New Testament images,[3] four in particular have dominated subsequent Chris-

---

2. Edward Farley, *Ecclesial Man: A Social Phenomenology of Faith and Reality*, pp. 182–85. On the distinction between "church" and "ecclesia," see above, p. 37.

3. Paul Minear lists nearly one hundred such images in his *Images of the Church in the New Testament*, although he focuses on the four we have designated.

tian understandings of the church. They are: people, body, communion, Spirit.

The earliest and most inclusive image, "people of God," marks Christianity's consciousness of being a new Israel related to, yet distinct from, the *qāhāl Yahweh*. The image carries with it national, ethnic, and political connotations that are never entirely lost but are profoundly modified. Paul broadens it to universal dimensions without losing sight of the fact that it specifies a temporal, historical reality. The ecclesia is a people without national boundaries or a common language and ethnic identity—a peculiar sort of people indeed.

The second image helps to specify the peculiarity: The *new* people of God is the "body of Christ." This second image is predominantly Pauline, but it has echoes elsewhere in the New Testament and has been commonly employed throughout church history, often with quite different meanings. "Body" is basically an ethical and social metaphor for Paul, not an organic one. The literal reference to the physical body of the crucified Jesus is already transfigured by the eucharistic words of institution into a symbol of self-sacrifice and self-divestment rather than of self-fulfillment, which is the customary association of the term. To this is added a second level of meaning when the community of faith itself is described by Paul as the "body of Christ." It is so not in the literal sense of being an organic extension of the incarnation, but rather in the sense that the self-giving love of Christ (his "body," given for us) now defines and constitutes its unique communal structure; he lives on in it and is corporately embodied by it to the extent that it actualizes the sacrificial quality of his life.

This interpretation is borne out by the third image: The body of Christ is in essence a new sort of "communion" or "fellowship" in which each individual finds identity and fulfillment through the other and in relation to Christ. In this fashion the distinctive love symbolized by Christ's own broken body is reenacted in the communal fabric of the church. Augustine in particular developed the theme of a fellowship of love, whereas among certain scholastic and Reformed theologians (notably Thomas Aquinas, William of Ockham, and Martin Luther) it was common to speak of the church as a fellowship of faith. Yet it is not faith that constitutes fellowship but the reverse, in the sense that community is the matrix in which faith occurs. Individual acts of faith do not together engender a communion; rather, the condition for the emergence of faith is the new possibility of existence represented by that very communion.

If we ask what constitutes true community in the Pauline sense, we are brought to the last and most elusive of the images, the creative work of the Spirit. As commonly used in the New Testament, "Spirit" refers to that modality of divine activity whereby God indwells and empowers not merely human subjectivity but also human *inter*subjectivity. True community embodies the distinctive love of Christ, and in that sense it belongs to the Son; yet it also derives from the creative work of the Spirit, and in that sense it is the "fellowship of the Holy Spirit." The themes of community and Spirit are woven tightly together by Paul and primitive Christianity, a connection reflected in the ancient creeds and elaborated throughout the tradition especially by Augustine and Aquinas, who described the Holy Spirit as the "soul" animating the body of the church.

Classic Marks of the Church

While the biblical images have stimulated theological reflection on the church throughout the history of tradition, they did not (perhaps regrettably) serve as a basis for a systematic doctrine of the church. In fact, there was no such systematic doctrine during the patristic and medieval periods, and since the Reformation the nature of the church has been a matter more of confessional conflict than of doctrinal consensus. The closest we come to a widely accepted creedal formulation is the famous statement introduced into the Constantinopolitan supplement to the Nicene Creed (381): "We believe . . . [in] the one, holy, catholic, and apostolic church." Subsequently the qualities of unity, holiness, catholicity, and apostolicity have been considered marks of the true church, although the actual meaning of these attributes is open to continual discussion. The simplest way to set forth the doctrine in its "classic formulation" is to look briefly at each of these marks. Later we shall consider how each has been relativized under the impact of modern consciousness.

Unity

Although Pauline theology located the principle of ecclesial unity in Christ (or the body of Christ), the third-century bishop Cyprian, who established the main lineaments of a Latin ecclesiology that prevailed for over a thousand years, relocated it in the episcopate. He argued that the unity in Christ was passed on to Peter and the apostles and that it now resides in the collective episcopate, not in a single representative. By contrast with this juridical approach, Augustine suggested, against the schismatics of his time (the Donatists), that it is love which demands unity and nonseparation—the love that is poured out by the Holy Spirit and is the very soul of the church. Love can be sundered and yet still unite; thus there is a reluctance on Augustine's part to conclude that the Donatists were in no sense in the church. But he agrees with Cyprian that "outside the [one, catholic] church there is no salvation."

Catholicity

Catholicity is a closely related attribute, as Cyprian's remarks indicate. Ignatius of Antioch was the first to speak of a "catholic church," meaning the whole or complete church in contrast to the local episcopal churches. This original and literal meaning of "universal" was gradually inflated, in response to various challenges and movements, to include the sense not only of "orthodox" (true, nonheretical, nonschismatic, i.e., doctrinal catholicity) but also of extension over the whole earth (geographical catholicity) and of a church larger in numbers than any other (numerical catholicity). Vincent of Lérins expressed these several senses in a famous formula, "That which is believed everywhere and always by all people," but it was Augustine who gave the notion of the *ecclesia catholica* (the only lawful religion of the Roman Empire after the edict of Theodosius in 380) full theological elaboration. The adjective was no longer a description but part of a proper name, the name of the universally accepted, official, consummate religion of the civilized world. He frequently described this church as "mother" ("You are safe who have God for your father and his church for your mother"), and he was so convinced of its inner vital power and the truthfulness of its message that he could say that he believed in the gospel only on the authority of the Catholic church.

Holiness

The tension between the church's essential being as the "body of Christ" or "community of the Spirit" and its actual historical exis-

253

tence as a sinful, fallible people was emphasized by a succession of rigorist, spiritualist sects. The first of these, the Montanists (mid-second century), claimed to be inspired by the Holy Spirit, allowed no forgiveness of postbaptismal sin, practiced an ascetic discipline, and welcomed martyrdom. Tertullian accepted certain of the Montanist practices, including the role of inspired prophets, and defined the church as a society of the Spirit whose true members are spiritual persons or "saints." Hippolytus went further, describing the church as "the holy society of those who live in righteousness," which must exclude sinners. A similar ecclesiology was championed by the Novatianists later on, in the third century, and by the Donatists in the fourth century.

In response to such pressures, a distinction gradually developed between the true, spiritual, or heavenly church and the empirical, historical church, which contained error and sin. Under Neoplatonic influence, Clement of Alexandria and Origen understood the heavenly church to be both preexistent and eschatological, the "ideal" toward which the earthly institution was oriented and for which it was to prepare its members. Neither would have accepted the later distinction between an "invisible" church containing only the elect and a "visible" church also including condemned sinners, since they were universalists who believed that all finally would be saved and that the empirical church would be subsumed in the spiritual. The "invisible-visible" distinction first appeared in Augustine under the impact of his predestinarian doctrine. In his view the invisible, true, or holy church is comprised of the fixed number of the saints predestined before the foundation of the world and known only to God. Although the distinction has proved useful in subsequent ecclesiology (notably that of the Reformers), Augustine's version of it was unnecessarily harsh, probably because of his long conflict with the Donatists and Pelagians.

A richer, more balanced theological elaboration of the "holiness" of the church is found in Aquinas's *Exposition on the Apostles' Creed*. "The church is holy," he writes, "by the indwelling of the blessed Trinity." In this *Exposition*, he describes the church, in the words of Yves Congar, as "a living body compacted out of a plurality of members, all quickened and governed by a single living principle . . . or soul," which is the Holy Spirit (more precisely, the Trinity indwelling as Spirit). Congar points out that the description of the Spirit as the soul quickening the body of humanity is not just a pious metaphor but a powerful technical factor in Aquinas's theology, since in his view "only a 'dynamic' principle genuinely divine can direct and move [humanity] toward the objects of the divine life." God as Spirit is "the dynamic power of the [ecclesial] life of humanity moving Godwards." Congar rightly adds: "Herein St. Thomas sees the first and deepest notion that can be had of the Church."[4]

Apostolicity

The term "apostolic" means "founded on or having a direct link with the apostles of Christ." According to tradition, the apostles possessed an original and unique authority by virtue of having been commissioned by Christ for missionary preaching and having witnessed the risen Lord. While the apostolic witness as such cannot be repeated, the apostolic *mission* remains, and in this sense there can be an "apostolic succession" (an idea first mentioned by Clement of Rome). Küng argues that the whole church, not just a few individuals, is the rightful successor of the apostles in obedience, and from this obedience derives its authority.[5] Nevertheless, a particular form of ecclesial polity emerged that used "apostolicity" as its legitimation, namely, one that was sacerdotal, episcopal, and hierarchical. By its very nature this polity vested authority in a group of specially sanctioned individuals, and its tendency was to become increasingly monarchical and absolutistic. Obviously it was necessary for the post-apostolic church to adopt some form of definite institutional structure, including an ordered and recognized ministry, and it was probably inevitable that this structure should reflect the patterns of religious and political authority characteristic of Hellenistic and Roman culture. What occurred was the loss of charismatic forms of ministry present in the apostolic church, and the adoption of a juridical model of reality with its accompanying system of rewards and punishments. While these developments are regrettable, it should be acknowledged that true Christian faith and practice survived in countless individuals, that the church helped to shape, for better or for worse, the values

4. Yves Congar, *The Mystery of the Church*, pp. 99–103; Thomas Aquinas, *Theological Texts*, ed. Thomas Gilby (London: Oxford University Press, 1955), p. 341.
5. Küng, *The Church*, p. 457; cf. pp. 443–61.

of Western civilization, and that, despite obvious abuses and corruption, the institution was for the most part effectively governed and led.

Details concerning the emergence of the episcopal system, its gradual transformation into a system of papal absolutism and Roman primacy, and the reaction of the conciliarists and late-medieval critics and reformers are available in other sources and will not be repeated here.

The Protestant Principle

"It is a defensible thesis," writes Geddes MacGregor, "that the Reformation was about the nature of the Church more than it was about justification or grace."[6] Those who oppose this thesis would argue that the Reformation introduced no new matters of doctrine and was directed primarily to the correction of abuses within a decadent Renaissance Catholicism. Those who favor it would contend that new and quite radical ecclesial principles did in fact emerge and that the various theological issues at stake were at root ecclesiological. One of the most forceful expositors of the latter view was the nineteenth-century historical theologian Ferdinand Christian Baur, who contended that, whereas in Catholicism the "idea" of the church had been completely identified with its concrete historical forms (notably the classic dogmas and the episcopal-hierarchical system), according to Protestantism the relation between idea and manifestation, or between the invisible and the visible church, is a dialectical-critical one: They are to be neither separated nor identified, but rather understood to exist in continuous tension with each other. There can be no ideal essence of ecclesia apart from its actual historical forms, but the latter can never be regarded as wholly adequate embodiments of the essential truth of the gospel. Thus all forms of ecclesiastical absolutism must give way to the freedom of the subject, the independence of the state vis-à-vis the church, and the principle of historical relativism. Baur suggested that the full implications of this "Protestant principle" were not worked out until the eighteenth-century Enlightenment[7]—a point to which we shall return shortly. The expression "Protestant principle," which Baur himself uses, is developed themati-

6. Geddes MacGregor, *Corpus Christi: The Nature of the Church according to the Reformed Tradition*, p. 5.
7. Ferdinand Christian Baur, *On the Writing of Church History*, pp. 242–43, 247–53.

cally by Paul Tillich, who defines it as the "protest against any absolute claim made for a relative reality, even if this claim is made by a Protestant church."[8]

It should be noted that the Reformers did not deny the classic marks of the church but added others which they thought were necessary to define the true church in the polemical situation of their time, namely, the pure teaching of the gospel and the right administration of the sacraments of baptism and the Lord's Supper.[9] Both Luther and Calvin embraced the Augustinian distinction between the invisible church and the visible church. By the former, Luther understood the "congregation of the faithful" or "communion of saints" wherever it may be found; as such it is hidden, an object of belief rather than perception, and its numbers are known to God alone. This true church or "spiritual internal Christendom" must find expression in a visible body or "physical external Christendom," the signs of which he enumerated; and it is said that Luther later came to realize more clearly the necessity of a historical institution and outward forms.[10] Still, as a critical theological principle which permitted quite radical criticism of the church's institutions, dogmas, and practices, Luther's distinction was revolutionary. Calvin's version of it was more traditionally Augustinian, since he understood the invisible church to be comprised of the total number of elect, living and dead, and he placed greater stress on the visible institution, "a living body which, being organized by Christ, its only head, exhibits structure. It is *corpus Christi*, the living instrument on earth of God's loving purpose and sovereign will."[11]

CHALLENGES AND CONTRIBUTIONS OF MODERN CONSCIOUSNESS

The Impact of the Enlightenment

The Enlightenment and post-Enlightenment period (from about the middle of the eighteenth century on) posed the second major crisis in the history of the Western church. The first was the Refor-

8. Paul Tillich, *The Protestant Era*, trans. James Luther Adams (Chicago: University of Chicago Press, 1948), p. 163.

9. Luther subsequently expanded the list to seven signs, including the power of the keys (to judge and forgive sin), ministry, public prayer, and Christian life.

10. MacGregor, *Corpus Christi*, pp. 8–10, 41–42.

11. Ibid., pp. 20–21, 45–47, 49–52, 55–56.

mation, which challenged the unity, holiness, and apostolicity of the Roman Catholic Church. The Enlightenment challenged the supernatural, suprahistorical character of the church left largely intact by the Reformers, thus radicalizing the critical principle of the Reformation itself. Post-Enlightenment theology articulated the relativity and historicity of the church, associating it with human quests for freedom and community while at the same time attempting to defend and transform the church-concept in the face of sectarianism, individualism, secularism, and thoroughgoing rationalism. In our own time we have entered upon what some have called a second wave of the Enlightenment, shattering the monolithic character and hegemony of the Western church as a whole, which has been predominantly Euro-American, white, bourgeois, and patriarchal. The ecumenical movement has played an important role here, as have the liberation movements, broadly conceived. Black religion in America, the liberation theologies of the Third World, and European political theology have set forth a new vision of ecclesia as pluralistic, emancipatory, prophetic, and eschatological, while feminist theology has unmasked and challenged the church's sexism and authoritarianism.

We turn first to the Enlightenment proper and its impact on transformations of the church concept. A new understanding of the church emerged in Enlightenment historiography, which viewed history in pragmatic, functionalist, nonsupernaturalist terms, distinguished between true religion ("spiritual, moral, free") and church doctrine, construed the church as an association on a par with other human societies such as the state, and stressed the principle of individuality and subjectivity. However, the first great post-Enlightenment ecclesiology was that of Friedrich Schleiermacher, who sought to avoid the reductionist tendencies of rationalism while incorporating its essential gains. Already in his *Speeches on Religion to Its Cultured Despisers*, (1799), under the influence of romanticism, he had stressed the essentially social and communal nature of true religion. But it was in *The Christian Faith* (1821, 1830)[12] that he systematically worked out a new concept of the church. Defining the church as the "fellowship of believers," which has a central place in "the constitution of the world in relation to redemption" (sec. 113), he locates the origin of the

---

12. References in the text are to the section numbers of the second edition.

church both in divine election (here he shares certain Augustinian-Calvinist themes) and in the "communication of the Holy Spirit." It is in developing the latter theme that Schleiermacher's own theological genius is most evident. He defines the Holy Spirit as "the common Spirit of the new corporate life founded by Christ" (sec. 121) or, more fully, as "the union of the divine essence and human nature in the form of the common Spirit animating the life in common of believers" (sec. 123). The Holy Spirit is "a specific divine efficaciousness working in believers"—a *common* Spirit, not a "person-forming union," as in the case of the two natures in Christ (secs. 123–25). What Schleiermacher is attempting here is to understand how the church is founded upon a divine reality working nonsupernaturalistically in the constitution of a human fellowship characterized by redemptive love. The union of the divine and the human in the church is analogous to that in Christ, yet with a difference, since in the one it occurs individually and in the other only communally (cf. sec. 122). Moreover, it is in and through the ecclesial community that "the redemption accomplished by Jesus of Nazareth" (sec. 11) is made efficacious for believers of all ages and communicated to the whole world.

Starting from quite different philosophical premises, G. W. F. Hegel arrived at a similar and equally seminal concept of the church in the final part of his lectures on the philosophy of religion (1821–31).[13] Hegel clearly recognizes the essential place of the cultus in religion: It gives expression to the "practical" form of the religious relationship, representing the moment of concrete communion with deity and of divine self-reconciliation. For the Christian religion, the church or "community of Spirit" originates with the transition from the sensible presence of God in Christ to God's spiritual presence in the community of faith. The essence of this community is a unique, transfigured intersubjectivity, distinguishable from all other forms of human love and friendship. Privatistic and exclusivistic modes of existence are set aside, as are distinctions based on mastery, power, position, sex, and wealth; in their place is actualized a truly universal justice and freedom. The name "Holy Spirit" signifies the unifying and liberating power of "divine love arising from infinite anguish"—

13. *Lectures on the Philosophy of Religion,* 3:133–62.

the same love that was objectively represented on the cross of Christ but that now works inwardly, subjectively, building up a new human community. "This is the Spirit of God, or God as present, actual Spirit, God dwelling in his community." Hegel goes on to examine how this community is institutionally embodied by the church and then "realized" in the cultural and political forms of the secular world, in the process of which the community as such may or may not "pass away" (the lectures end on an ambiguous, "discordant note").

Schleiermacher and Hegel have been of seminal importance to nineteenth- and twentieth-century theology (both Protestant and Catholic)[14] as it addressed two main systematic problems associated with the concept of the church, namely, the dialectic of spirituality and historicity and the problematic of the ecclesial community. Before turning to these issues, however, we shall examine the way in which the classic marks of the church have been relativized under the impact of modern critical consciousness.

Relativizing the Marks of the Church

It is evident today that the Christian church is not only united but also divided; not only catholic (in the double sense of universal and orthodox) but also partisan, particular, heterodox, and in continual need of renewal; not only holy but also profane and sinful; not only in possession of apostolic authority but also under constraint to serve the world and enhance human freedom. The question is how the church can be "both . . . and" without losing its identity, or how these polarities can be made productive rather than destructive. The fact that the attributes of the church are actualized only paradoxically and ambiguously[15] is a mark of its historicity, a sign that it too is subject to the contradictions and tensions of finite historical life.

The unity of the church is clearly an "essential" or "spiritual" reality based on the unity of God, for empirically the churches are

---

14. A group of early and mid-nineteenth-century Catholic theologians known as the Catholic Tübingen school (including J. S. Drey, J. A. Möhler, J. E. Kuhn, and F. A. Staudenmaier) sought to incorporate Schleiermacherian and Hegelian insights among other idealist and romantic sources into a vision of the church as the mystical body of Christ animated by the Holy Spirit. Despite opposition, they were forerunners of a new direction in Catholic ecclesiology (the *nouvelle théologie*) which understood the church as a sacrament, fellowship, or mystery, permeated by the divine life and issuing in worldly action. These developments reached a culmination in the encyclical *Mystici Corporis* and in the ecclesiology of Vatican II.

15. Cf. Paul Tillich, *Systematic Theology*, 3:165–72.

divided and disunited. On the one hand, true unity does not exclude diversity and plurality, which are facts of life and which may, as Karl Rahner suggests, help us to perceive the "radical and fundamental truths and realities of Christian faith and of Christian existence more clearly than perhaps would be the case if everyone were in the same social and ecclesial situation."[16] On the other hand, as Rahner, Küng, and others have pointed out, there really is no theological justification for the divisions in the church, which are the result of failure, guilt, sin.[17] The recognition of valid diversity, of productive plurality in belief, liturgy, and practice, should not be allowed to legitimate unproductive division, separation, and hostility.

Catholicity can no longer mean the intention of incorporating all peoples and religions into the church in a kind of grandiose Christian imperialism, nor can it permit the church to escape quite particular and often partisan commitments such as to the liberation of oppressed peoples and races. "Universality" must rather refer to an "inner wholeness" and to the future universal redemption of humanity.[18] Moreover, the doctrinal catholicity of the church must be subject to the Reformation dictum *ecclesia reformata et semper reformanda* ("the church reformed and always reforming"), for there is nothing in doctrine or practice that is static, nothing that does not require repentance, renewal, and reformulation. The church is at once catholic and reformed: catholic in substance, reformed in critical self-renewal.

The holiness of the church does not exclude its involvement in the ambiguities, imperfections, and sinfulness of the actual world. With Dietrich Bonhoeffer we must confess that it is not only the "communion of saints" but also the "communion of sinners";[19] that its sanctity derives not from its own merit or achievement but from the indwelling of God's Spirit. More specifically, the church is holy to the extent that it engages in acts of worship through which the redemptive relationship between God and humanity is concretely actualized. In worship the church is taken up into the life of God, but central to the same worship is the confession of sin and the recognition that everything is dependent upon divine grace and forgiveness.

16. Karl Rahner, *Foundations of Christian Faith*, p. 369.

17. Ibid., pp. 348–49; Küng, *The Church*, pp. 349–57.

18. Cf. Jürgen Moltmann, *The Church in the Power of the Spirit*, pp. 337–52.

19. Dietrich Bonhoeffer, *The Communion of Saints: A Dogmatic Inquiry into the Sociology of the Church*, pp. 86, 146–47.

Finally, the apostolicity of the church should not be used as a cover for authoritarianism, dogmatism, and hierarchalism. Küng points out that the New Testament term for ministry is *diakonia*, meaning service—service in the love of neighbor and of God—and that such service ought to characterize all ecclesial offices, including the highest, the petrine office, whose primacy should be one of service and ministry rather than dominion and authority.[20] True authority is exercised by means of service and issues in freedom—both within the church and on behalf of suffering, oppressed humanity.[21] Needless to say, such a ministry of service and liberation is all too rarely accomplished. Küng himself is unprepared to propose structural reforms by which the abuses of authority might be controlled, relying instead on the voluntary renunciation of power by those in high places.

The Dialectic of Spirituality and Historicity

The Enlightenment forced theology to thematize the historicity of the church as never before, recognizing it to be a finite, fallible, relative institution, sharing many of the characteristics of social groups in general. At the same time, no viable ecclesiology can surrender the conviction that the church is the continuous creative and redemptive work of God, who indwells and empowers it as Holy Spirit. The question is how the church can be both a divine gift and a human institution, both a spiritual and a historical reality, without confusing these dimensions of its being and without separating them. As we have seen, the tradition raised this question in terms of the distinction between the invisible and the visible church, but it has taken on new urgency since the emergence of critical-historical consciousness. It was addressed with consistency and rigor by German theology of the early nineteenth century, and it has been a central, perhaps irresolvable, question of twentieth-century ecclesiology. It is impossible to summarize this rich discussion in brief compass, and we have chosen to focus on one of its best representations, namely, the innovative ecclesiology of Paul Tillich.[22]

In accord with the tradition, Tillich states that the church is both a

---

20. Küng, *The Church*, pp. 495–611.
21. Moltmann, *The Church in the Power of the Spirit*, pp. 342–47, 352–61.
22. For the following see Paul Tillich, *Systematic Theology*, 3:107–10, 138–40, 149–61, 162–82.

spiritual reality ("the body of Christ," the "invisible" church) and a social group of individual Christians (the "visible" or empirical church).
To designate the first element or aspect, he has coined the term
"spiritual community." The spiritual community is constituted by the
"spiritual presence" (or the Spirit of God present, the presence of the
divine life within human life), which is the power that creates unambiguous yet fragmentary life both in individuals and in the sociohistorical process. The expression "unambiguous yet fragmentary"
means "appearing under the conditions of finitude but conquering
both estrangement and ambiguity." Tillich contends that the category
"spiritual community" is neither realistic (a supernatural, heavenly
realm of spiritual beings) nor idealistic (a construction of ideal attributes projected onto the screen of transcendence) but "essentialistic"
—a category pointing to the power of the essential behind and within
the existential. Its ontological status is that of "power"—not causal
power but creative and directive power. "The Spiritual Community
does not exist as an entity beside the churches, but it is their Spiritual
essence, effective in them through its power, its structure, and its
fight against their ambiguities." It is "the inner *telos* of the churches,"
the source of everything which makes them churches. The spiritual
community extends beyond the churches: It is latent as well as manifest; it is related dialectically to the other central symbols of unambiguous life, "kingdom of God" and "eternal life"; and by means of
it the three dimensions of human life—morality, culture, and religion—are united, no longer existing as separate realms. In other
words, for Tillich "spiritual community" is an ethical, cultural, and
eschatological symbol as well as an ecclesiological one.

The church is a "paradoxical" reality, participating both in the
unambiguous life of the spiritual community and in the ambiguities
of life in general and of religious life in particular. Its two aspects—
one theological, the other sociological—should be neither *identified*,
as in official pre-Vatican II Roman Catholic doctrine, "according to
which the Roman church is a sacred reality above the sociological
ambiguities of past and present," nor juxtaposed in unresolved *contradiction*, as in certain forms of Protestant ecclesiology. Rather, in
Tillich's view they are related *paradoxically*. As an indication of the
paradoxical character of the church, he argues that the "marks" of the
spiritual community—holiness, unity, universality, faith, love (note

that he drops apostolicity and adds two "Protestant" attributes, faith and love)—can be ascribed to the churches only by adding the qualifier "in spite of." The churches are holy in spite of their sinfulness, are essentially united in spite of their empirical divisions, are universal despite their particularity, are faithful despite their ambiguous religiosity, and are communities of love in spite of continuing estrangement.

Problematic of the Ecclesial Community

We suggested earlier that the characteristic perversion of ecclesia in our time is no longer institutionalism but individualism; that is, the notion that Christian faith consists essentially in private piety and morality and that the church exists for the sake of the salvation of individuals. Consequently, one of the major tasks of contemporary ecclesiology has been to obtain a fresh understanding of what constitutes *community* and to argue that ecclesia is intrinsically communal in structure. An important impetus in this direction was furnished by Schleiermacher and Hegel and carried further by the Ritschlian theologians. The American philosopher Josiah Royce, developing insights derived from Hegel, set forth an innovative theory of the "universal, divine, spiritual community," which he took to be intrinsic to the idea of Christianity.[23] Royce believed that community was a function of temporal process (memory and expectation), that it was constituted by acts of interpretation, that it issued in a community of loyalty and love, and that it was realized in, through, and for the church—yet beyond the church. Karl Barth's ecclesiology was elaborated in three extensive sections of the *Church Dogmatics* (vol. 4, secs. 62, 67, 72) devoted to the Holy Spirit and the "gathering," "upbuilding," and "sending" of the Christian community. While we have not attempted to summarize his position specifically, nuances of it are reflected throughout this chapter. Dietrich Bonhoeffer, under the influence of Hegel, the early Barth, and German sociology, attempted to work out a theological-sociological interpretation of the Christian community in his first book, *The Communion of Saints* (1927). He understood community to be a "collective person" mani-

---

23. See esp. Josiah Royce, *The Problem of Christianity.* Royce converted Hegel's "community of Spirit" (*Gemeinde des Geistes*) into "spiritual community," and he may be a source (though unacknowledged) of Tillich's use of this term.

festing an "objective spirit," and he established both a relation and a distinction between the Holy Spirit, the giver of faith and love, and the objective spirit of the empirical church. He believed that concrete I-Thou relations between persons, including relation to the divine Thou, could occur only within the framework of community.

Two contemporary American theologians have explored the problematic of the ecclesial community in especially helpful ways. In his book *Treasure in Earthen Vessels* (1961), James Gustafson intends to understand the church as a historical, human community possessing a unique center of meaning, the person-event Jesus Christ, which is rendered contemporary and efficacious through processes of communication, interpretation, understanding, reliving, and reenactment— all of which may be described in ordinary sociological categories. By contrast, Edward Farley in *Ecclesial Man* (1975) employs the tools of philosophical phenomenology to arrive at an understanding of the distinctive intersubjectivity of ecclesia as a community in which existence has been modified by the experience of redemption. This modification constitutes a community that is peculiarly "self-surpassing" and "nonprovincial" in character, knowing no ethnic, cultic, spatial, or temporal boundaries. Moreover, the realities of faith—God, Christ, creation, redemption—are apprehended only as socially mediated by the ecclesial community, not in terms of individual piety.

All these technical theological discussions of spirituality, historicity, and community need to be tested against the actual situation in which the church finds itself during the final decades of the twentieth century, namely, the quest for reunion of the churches in an increasingly pluralistic, non-Western world, and the impact of the liberation movements on the self-understanding of the community of faith. In the next section we shall confine our discussion to the latter.

Ecclesial Mission and Human Liberation

Liberation theologies of the Third World, and particularly of the black church in America, presuppose an idea of the church that is inclusive of political and secular realities, and an understanding of the church wherein social injustice and Christian mission affect each other dialectically. Accordingly, the ancient dogma "no salvation outside the church" must be called into question, since "salvation" occurs whenever and wherever human existence is moved toward liberation. In this situation, the issue shifts to one of discerning authentic liberation from ersatz liberation.

The conception of the church found in Latin American theologians such as Gustavo Gutiérrez and Juan Segundo is not ecclesiocentric. Neither sees the church as the only repository of salvific truth, since in their view the church, as custodian of the sacraments, is only one among the temporal structures God uses to bring salvation in history. Accordingly, its liturgical task and sacramental mission is to strive to orient itself toward "a new and radical service of people," "radically new social forms," and the "piloting of history."[24] For Segundo the church exists not so much as a vehicle of salvation and care for a privileged few, but rather to make a contribution to the world, to the "ecclesial way of living the love which is common to all men of good will." Gutiérrez observes that the work of Vatican II pointed a way for the church to exist "more in accord with the real challenges to the Christian faith of today." As a concrete social existence, the church should show that it can become a place of sociopolitical liberation.

Like all Christian theology, liberation theology is centered in God's saving activity, but the central claim of liberation theology is that divine saving action is directed more toward the plight of the poor, more toward the human than the exclusively Christian community. Hence, for Gutiérrez and Segundo the task of the church is to animate the secular order with the principles of social morality and a program of liberation representing a fearsome presence of Christ in today's human predicament. Where there are class differences, oppression, and poverty, the church as God's eucharistic fellowship is mandated to side with the oppressed and to work for the transformation of inhumane social relationships—even when this brings the ecclesial community into conflict with the power of the state.

Although its religious traditions and cultural resources are different, black theology in North America can affirm most of the major themes of Latin American liberation ecclesiology. Black theologians, utilizing the resources of Africa and the spiritual insights derived from the religious imagination of American slaves, understand the church to be the means whereby the liberating work of the Spirit is

24. Gustavo Gutiérrez, A Theology of Liberation, pp. 256, 56; Juan Luis Segundo, A Theology for Artisans of a New Humanity, 1:60.

actualized in the world. Yet these theologians also see the mission of the church as integrally linked to the humanizing of political forces and forms of social conditioning. These two poles reflect the experience of what W. E. B. DuBois once described as "double consciousness," the consciousness of being both black and American. If it is to be effective, the liberative work of the Spirit must be experienced at both poles of this bipolar reality: on the one hand, setting free the exploited by being present in their community in a special way; on the other hand, by destroying the oppressive power of the dominant culture.

Within the black community, the church has played an absolutely constitutive role. One of the ironies of history is that African slaves in America were indoctrinated in the religion of their masters, yet discovered the true, liberative meaning of the Christian gospel over against its cultural distortions. This happened in large part through the so-called invisible institution, the underground church that gathered secretly to sing, pray, shout, preach, and read. Here there occurred what might be described as a *clearing of freedom* within the harsh domain of oppression, a clearing in which slaves were transformed into human beings, seemingly silent and docile masses into a singing, resistant, hopeful people. Throughout much of black history, individuals found their true dignity and identity precisely and only in the black church—in that space of freedom cleared on Sunday morning and Wednesday evening, or whenever the community gathered. To "have church," as it was expressed, is to experience the presence of the Holy Spirit in the midst of the people, "empowering them with courage and strength to bear witness in their present existence to what they know is coming in God's own eschatological future."[25] The black church is a spiritual, eschatological, transformative event which has proven to be constitutive of the very survival of a people. As such it is a paradigm of what the church might be or become for all people, and it offers rich resources for ecclesial reflection.

For black theology, ecclesiology is grounded in both pneumatology

---

25. James H. Cone, "Sanctification, Liberation, and Black Worship," *Theology Today* 35 (July 1978): 139–52. See also his *Black Theology and Black Power*, esp. chaps. 3–4, and *The Spirituals and the Blues* (New York: Seabury Press, 1972); also E. Franklin Frazier, *The Negro Church in America* (New York: Schocken Books, 1963).

and Christology. The Spirit that is present in the church is the Spirit of Christ, and the work of the latter has been understood in both spiritual and political terms. While some black theologians such as Martin Luther King have stressed the spirituality of the church's power, others such as James Cone, orienting themselves to Jesus' ministry to the poor and oppressed, have seen it in more political terms, holding open the possibility even of participation in violent revolution. These two perspectives are not as totally irreconcilable as they may once have appeared during the heyday of black power, and recently some progress has been made in bringing them together. Recently, too, considerable interest has been expressed in connections between black church theology and the liberation struggles of peoples in the Third World.[26]

In contrast to the emphases of Latin American and black theologians on the mission of the church, feminist critics have directed attention primarily to issues internal to the church's constitution and tradition, namely, its dominant patriarchalism, sexism, and authoritarianism. Feminist theologians and historians such as Rosemary Ruether, Phyllis Trible, Elisabeth Fiorenza, Elaine Pagels, and Eleanor McLaughlin have shown how the role of women in the early Christian community and at other periods in church history has been systematically suppressed by the dominant tradition, as has feminine religious imagery.[27] While more radical feminist critics such as Mary Daly have called for the rejection of the Christian tradition entirely, others have seen that it is possible to reaffirm the central meaning of ecclesia by recovering lost elements of its tradition as well as fashioning new corporate and linguistic forms. As such, they are making an essential contribution to contemporary ecclesiology.

ISSUES AND PROPOSALS

Any attempt to reconstruct a doctrine of the church which takes into account its historical-spiritual, communal, ecumenical, and liberative dimensions must attend to at least four areas of concern: the

26. See the articles contained in Gayraud S. Wilmore and James H. Cone, eds., *Black Theology: A Documentary History, 1966–1979* (Maryknoll, N.Y.: Orbis Books, 1979), esp. parts 5, 6.

27. See esp. Rosemary Ruether and Eleanor McLaughlin, eds., *Women of Spirit: Female Leadership in the Jewish and Christian Traditions*, and Carol P. Christ and Judith Plaskow, eds., *Womanspirit Rising: A Feminist Reader in Religion* (New York: Harper & Row, 1979).

biblical-doctrinal, the cultural, the sociopolitical, and the theological. The first area pertains to the biblical images and classic marks of the church, while the second concerns the encounter between the Christian church and other religions. The third attends to the ecclesial vision of human freedom as it bears on the realities of oppression and victimization; and the fourth attempts to set forth a theological definition of the essence of the church that addresses these various issues.

1. From our review of "the doctrine in its classic formulation," it is not clear how the biblical images of the church (people, body, communion, Spirit) are to be correlated with the classic marks of the church (unity, catholicity, holiness, apostolicity), or how either the images or the marks can be constructively utilized today. To be sure, each of the classic marks has an obvious historical reference. The issue, however, is to determine in which form these marks, in their guise as a sort of ecclesiological "rule of faith," should or can be affirmed today. Should the biblical images be accorded a normative theological value above that of the marks? Or do the latter need to be modified or supplemented? For example, the liberation theologies of the 1970s tended to equate proper ecclesial witness with partisanship, charity, and suffering rather than to catholicity, holiness, and apostolicity. On the other hand, is it enough for contemporary ecclesiology simply to repeat the biblical images as though they are fixed and self-evident formulas for telling us what the church is? As such, they would be robbed of their imaginative, symbolic power. The question remains unanswered as to the proper usage and "mix" of biblical and creedal materials in contemporary theological reflection on the nature of the church.

2. The Christian faith is only one historically conditioned resource among humankind's rich reservoir of moral and spiritual symbol systems. This religious and cultural pluralism cannot be disregarded when assessing the future of the church or its constructive role in the world of today. Certainly apostolicity does not mean that the church has a corner on authority or truth; nor does catholicity mean that it has a manifest destiny to incorporate all peoples and religions into the *ecclesia catholica*. Perhaps if Christians can move toward resolving their internal theological feuds and their religious differences with non-Christians, it will be possible to conceive of an ecclesial community that espouses a view of humanity embracing the needs, wel-

fare, and aspirations of all peoples. Such a view of the church, as a community aware of its divine calling and committed to the nurture of others, could contribute to the actualization of world solidarity and a global religious consciousness.

3. Theologically, the church affirms a universal humanity as the basis of its identity in mission; yet its involvement in history too often included its identification with the dominant, oppressive, and patriarchal forces of Western society. Too often it has been a party to processes of mass victimization—of "pagans," Jews, women, blacks, native Americans, Third World peoples. This is a burdensome heritage not lightly to be escaped. It makes the church's commitment to human liberation, and an awareness of the political implications of its practice, all the more urgent in our time. What is required is that the logic of the oppressor-oppressed relationship be utterly broken and that in its place there should be built what Royce called the "universal community."[28] It will require transformations in Western theology that do what Walbert Bühlmann claims is necessary, namely, "the phasing-out of European hegemony and the spot-lighting of new groups of actors now taking the stage."[29]

It could be argued that the altered cultural and sociopolitical context in which the church finds itself today amounts to a second watershed in the modern history of the doctrine, comparable to the impact of the Enlightenment. The Enlightenment themes of historicity, relativity, freedom, and subjectivity are still valid, but the Western bourgeois cultural and political context in which they were developed is rapidly changing. New and more radical forms of religious consciousness, of communal existence, and of sociopolitical transformation must take shape, replacing the cultural imperialism, the privatism, and the laissez-faire capitalism that were negative heritages of the Enlightenment. The church should be in the vanguard of these changes rather than fighting rearguard actions, and these changes should have a profound impact on the church's self-understanding.

4. This brings us to the specifically theological task of working out a definition of the essential nature of the ecclesial community which takes into account the altered context to which we have referred and

28. *The Problem of Christianity*, pp. 75ff.
29. Walbert Bühlmann, *The Coming of the Third Church*, p. 3

which is also able to retrieve valid elements of the biblical and doc-trinal tradition. For purposes of discussion we offer the following definition: *Ecclesia is a transfigured mode of human community, comprised of a plurality of peoples and cultural traditions, founded upon the life, death, and resurrection of Christ, constituted by the redemptive presence of God as Spirit, in which privatistic, provincial, and hierarchical modes of existence are overcome, and in which is actualized a universal reconciling love that liberates from sin, aliena-tion, and oppression.* As such, the church is an anticipatory sign and sacrament of the coming kingdom of God, which is a "kingdom of freedom," a liberated communion of free subjects created and empowered by the indwelling Spirit of the God of freedom. This is the true "spirituality" of the church, its "invisible" essence, to which the empirical, historical church is always only ambiguously, paradox-ically related. Ecclesia is at once a historical and an eschatological reality, and the tension thus generated is the source of its true vitality.

Of course, no actual church adequately embodies the elements of our definition, but when an actual church asks itself what it ought to be, it cannot avoid reflecting upon itself in some such fashion as this unless it is willing to give up the question of its essential being. With-out the discipline of critical self-reflection, the church would succumb to its persistent tendency to lose its ecclesial essence—to drift into becoming a privatistic, alienated, merely human association serving certain social functions such as the disburdening of individuals and the maintenance of authority structures.

Our definition attempts to incorporate the biblical images: The church is the people of God comprised of a plurality of peoples; it is the body whose unique intersubjectivity is shaped by the life, death, and resurrection of Christ; it represents a transfigured mode of human community, a fellowship of faith, love, and freedom; and it is founded upon the creative, upbuilding work of the Spirit. The definition also attempts to reformulate the classic doctrinal marks: The church's unity is fashioned out of plurality and seeks the com-mon ground not only of Christian faith but also of religious expe-rience in general; its catholicity resides in overcoming privatistic, provincial, and hierarchical modes of existence and is oriented to the universal redemption of humanity; its holiness consists in its eschatological essence as a liberated communion fashioned by the

Spirit; and its apostolicity takes the form not only of witness to Christ, but also of service to the world—sharing in common struggles against dehumanization, alienation, and oppression. The definition reflects the ecumenical and liberative exigencies of our time and in that sense is a contingent, relative definition that is not perennially valid.

Obviously, definitions alone are not sufficient; the church must become in practice what it understands itself to be in essence, and often it only discovers in practice what it ought to be in essence. The task of critical self-reflection and practice is an unending one, and it lies at the heart of the doctrine of the church. The church's essence reveals itself both through its redemptive activity as a truly worldwide community and by means of theological reflection on its historical embodiments.

SUGGESTIONS FOR FURTHER READING

Barth, Karl. *Church Dogmatics*. Vols. 4/1 (sec. 62), 4/2 (sec. 67), 4/3 (sec. 72).

Baur, Ferdinand Christian. *On the Writing of Church History*. Edited and translated by P. C. Hodgson. *LPT* (1968).

Bonhoeffer, Dietrich. *The Communion of Saints: A Dogmatic Inquiry into the Sociology of the Church*. New York: Harper & Row, 1963.

Bühlmann, Walbert. *The Coming of the Third Church*. Maryknoll, N.Y.: Orbis Books, 1977.

Cooke, Bernard. *Ministry to Word and Sacraments*. Philadelphia: Fortress Press, 1976.

Cone, James H. *Black Theology and Black Power*. New York: Seabury Press, 1969.

Congar, Yves. *The Mystery of the Church*. Baltimore: Helicon Press, 1960.

Dulles, Avery, S. J. *Models of the Church*. New York: Doubleday, 1974.

Evans, Robert F. *One and Holy: The Church in Latin Patristic Thought*. London: S.P.C.K., 1972.

Farley, Edward. *Ecclesial Man: A Social Phenomenology of Faith and Reality*. Philadelphia: Fortress Press, 1975.

Gustafson, James M. *Treasure in Earthen Vessels: The Church as a Human Community*. New York: Harper & Bros., 1961.

Gutiérrez, Gustavo. *A New Way of Being Church*. Lima, Peru: Latin American Press, 1984.

———. *A Theology of Liberation*. Chap. 12.

Hegel, G. W. F. *Lectures on the Philosophy of Religion*, Vol. 3.

Hodgson, Peter C. *Revisioning the Church: Ecclesial Freedom in the New Paradigm*. Philadelphia: Fortress Press, 1988.

Jay, Eric G. *The Church: Its Changing Image through Twenty Centuries*. 2 vols. London: S.P.C.K., 1977–78.

Knox, John. *The Church and the Reality of Christ*. New York: Harper & Row, 1962.

Küng, Hans. *The Church*. New York: Image Books, 1976.

MacGregor, Geddes. *Corpus Christi: The Nature of the Church According to the Reformed Tradition*. Philadelphia: Westminster Press, 1958.

Minear, Paul S. *Images of the Church in the New Testament*. Philadelphia: Westminster Press, 1960.

Moltmann, Jürgen. *The Church in the Power of the Spirit*. Minneapolis: Fortress Press, 1993.

Niebuhr, H. Richard. *The Purpose of the Church and Its Ministry: Reflections on the Aims of Theological Education*. In collaboration with Daniel Day Williams and James M. Gustafson. New York: Harper & Row, 1956, 1977.

Pannenberg, Wolfhart. *The Church*. Philadelphia: Westminster Press, 1984.

———. *Theology and the Kingdom of God*. Philadelphia: Westminster Press, 1969.

Rahner, Karl. *The Church and the Sacraments*. Freiburg: Herder, 1965.

———. *Foundations of Christian Faith*. Chap. 7.

Royce, Josiah. *The Problem of Christianity*. Chicago: University of Chicago Press, 1968.

Ruether, Rosemary, and McLaughlin, Eleanor, eds. *Women of Spirit: Female Leadership in the Jewish and Christian Traditions*. New York: Simon & Schuster, 1979.

Schleiermacher, Friedrich. *The Christian Faith*. Pp. 525–722.

Schweizer, Eduard. *The Church as the Body of Christ*. Atlanta: John Knox Press, 1964.

Segundo, Juan Luis. *A Theology for Artisans of a New Humanity*, vol. 1.

Tillich, Paul. *Systematic Theology*. Vol. 3, esp. pp. 111–245.

Troeltsch, Ernst. *The Social Teaching of the Christian Churches*. 2 vols. New York: Macmillan Co., 1931.

Welch, Claude. *The Reality of the Church*. New York: Charles Scribner's Sons, 1958.

10. THE SACRAMENTS

WHERE WE ARE

Sacrament is the name given to certain specific rites of the Christian churches. Of the major denominations only the Quakers (Society of Friends) and the Salvation Army make no use of sacraments, but for all the others there are at least two, baptism and the Lord's Supper. According to both the contemporary Roman Catholic and Eastern Orthodox churches there are seven sacraments: baptism and the Lord's Supper (or Eucharist), but also confirmation, penance, extreme unction, ordination, and matrimony. Orthodoxy attaches less importance to the precise number than does the Roman tradition, which, under assault from the Protestant Reformers, fixed the number at seven at the seventh session of the Council of Trent in 1547.

Does the number of sacraments matter? Modern theology has come to think that the reasons that led Roman Catholics and Protestants to be so certain and vehement in their rival enumerations are far from cogent. On the other hand, the church developed in the course of its history a very large number of rituals, some local, some universal or nearly so; but of only some of these rituals is the claim made that they are sacraments. If sacraments are a special class of ritual, there must be something by which they are distinguished. Enumerating them is the consequence of knowing what sets these rituals apart.

In what follows it will not be presupposed that the number of the sacraments is known for certain. Indeed it will be shown that one cannot assume a definition of "sacrament," but must, rather, attend to the history of the arguments which have raged to and fro about what a sacrament might be. At the same time, if any Christian rites are correctly said to be sacraments, then baptism and the Lord's Supper are the least disputable examples. Therefore, in introducing here the theology of the sacraments, these two sacraments will be used as instances.

Scholastic theologians of the medieval period developed a distinction, which survives in Roman Catholic handbooks of theology to this day, between sacramental theology in general and the theology of the particular sacraments. The essence of a sacrament could be known, and each particular sacrament would then be presented as an example of the general nature of sacrament. The method to be pursued in this chapter is the exact reverse of this. If we are to speak of the sacraments at all, then it is of baptism and the Lord's Supper that we will speak with most assurance. We will proceed, in other words, from the particular sacraments to the possibility that there may be a generalized sacramental theology. It is not disputable that human beings communicate with each other by external means, rituals, signs, and symbols. The theological question is, however, what role is to be assigned to which ritual and why. If we can clarify the answers to these questions in respect of the two generally admitted sacraments, we will be in a better position to say how and why we can and should distinguish between the numerous incidental rituals which have grown up in the churches over the course of time and those privileged rites accorded the name of sacraments.

The contemporary discussion of sacramental theology has been shaped largely by movements within the Roman Catholic Church, culminating in the documents of the Second Vatican Council, as well as by studies prepared by the Faith and Order Commission of the World Council of Churches. At the same time, tendencies of a different kind have appeared in other parts of the church. There has grown up since the 1960s a rather unhealthy disjunction between the understandably somewhat traditional stance of an ecumenical sacramental theology and the concerns of a radical theology, focused on issues having to do with the meaning and relevance of religious language, with problems of epistemology and theological method, and most recently with liberation and society. The reason for this disjunction is, in large measure, attributable to the continuation in Protestant institutions of patterns of theological education which have either ignored the sacraments entirely or isolated them from the areas of debate about theological method. As we shall see, there is no good reason for the perpetuation of this gulf. The sacraments are not a specialized or rarified section of internal church life, to be held at arms length from issues concerning racial justice, poverty, sexism, or theological epistemology.

As we shall see, sacramental theology should be one of the liveliest areas of theological inquiry open to the contemporary student. One example will suffice, that of infant baptism. Here three types of questions arise. In the first place, what is the nature of the Christian revelation if it is said that human beings are saved by grace alone, to be received by faith alone, but that infants may fully participate in the fruits of baptism? Second, if there is a baptism for the forgiveness of sins, what view of the human person attributes sin to an infant? And third, what is the church's response to a society in which infants are presented for baptism by parents who have no discernible Christian practice? Fundamental questions concerning revelation, the human person, and the nature of the church are raised by the entirely practical question of whether the Christian churches are to continue the traditional activity of baptizing infants. They are merely complicated by the modern historical discussion about the integrity of the rite of Christian initiation, baptism, confirmation (or chrism), and first communication, and the possibility of its revival in the modern church. Furthermore, the realization that what is at issue is a *ritual* of deep human significance, on which social anthropologists have an important contribution to make, prevents one from the folly of supposing that the issues can simply be decided by the balance of pure theological argument or historical research. Sacramental theology is discernibly an area of profundity and complexity.

THE DOCTRINE IN ITS CLASSIC FORMULATION

Anthropologists affirm that, as a general rule, rituals precede any kind of developed clarification or explanation. Nonetheless the New Testament provides us with scanty evidence about how baptisms were performed, or the Lord's Supper celebrated, while containing some very striking interpretations, especially of baptism. We are entitled to assume that Christians assembled for worship and that the common life of the community included certain rituals. The development of distinctive patterns of Christian worship is the direct consequence of its separation from Judaism, which was by no means a uniform process. Where the evidence is so uncertain, historical reconstructions have frequently displayed denominational bias, with Protestants minimizing and Roman Catholics maximizing the importance and the uniformity of the church's liturgical life. But there can be no doubt, for example, that the Pauline churches observed the religious rituals of baptism and the Lord's Supper and that these rituals conform very closely to the ritual behavior of human beings as described by contemporary anthropology.

The history of sacramental theology has to be appreciated in close connection with the development of the rites in question. Three broad stages can be observed, first, growth in the elaborateness of the rituals; second, the imposition of order and uniformity upon them; and third, the criticism and reformulation of the rituals in the light of ancient models. Christian theology contains the seeds of each of these stages. It has a rich symbolical language in its literature, which invites dramatic representation (consider, for example, the symbolism of light). It promotes a sharp awareness of Christian identity and invites obedience to a single source of divine authority in its classic christology. And, by reason of its traditional teaching concerning "the heart," the hidden source of human willing, thinking, and feeling, Christianity is constantly capable of producing reform movements critical of mere conformity in externals. Sacramental theology constantly shows the repetition of a dialectic between external rite and interior intention.

Baptismal Regeneration

The apostle Paul's converts were encouraged to think of their baptism in extremely dramatic terms. Having been baptized, perhaps naked, by immersion in a river and then anointed, they were considered to have "put on Christ," and to have a new identity as "Abraham's offspring" and "sons of God" by adoption (Galatians 3 and 4). They have been "crucified with Christ," "buried with him," and "baptized into his death," so that they might participate in his resurrection (Rom. 6:3–8). Baptism would have been for them "a permanent threshold between the 'clean' group and the 'dirty' world."[1]

But hidden in this language is a problem concerning the precise relation between the ritual of baptism and the "rebirth" of the believer. Already an analogous issue had arisen over circumcision and had led to the remarkable idea of the need for a "circumcision of the heart" (Jer. 4:4 and Deut. 10:16), which Paul believed was the mark of a real Jew (Rom. 2:29). Classical theology closely followed Paul and other

---

1. Wayne A. Meeks, *The First Urban Christians: The Social World of the Apostle Paul* (New Haven: Yale University Press, 1983), p. 153.

New Testament writers in seeing the inner transformation of the believer in baptism as a miraculous act of God, the Holy Spirit. Its benefits were commonly summarized as remission of sins, deliverance from death, regeneration, and the bestowal of the Holy Spirit. In the New Testament all these are firmly linked to the last days, but with the waning of eschatological consciousness, the church increasingly placed emphasis on the literal possession in the present of supernatural qualities or gifts, especially the guarantee of passage through death to immortality.

The question arose, what then of baptism by heretics? In the middle of the third century, the Latin theologian Cyprian of Carthage argued with some consistency, on the premise of the unity of the church, that since the Holy Spirit indwells the church, there can be no bestowal of the Spirit by those separated from it. Those, moreover, in schism from the church are no better than heretics, since schismatics plainly do not believe in the church's indivisibility. Because they have become spiritually dead, they are in no position to bestow the Holy Spirit.

A century and a half later, Augustine was compelled to reexamine the basis of this theory and dissented from Cyprian. The church, he argued, is a mixed body. It is not the priest who conveys the Spirit, but the great high priest Christ acting through the priest. The priest may be a person of little spiritual capacity, or he may be in schism, or even a heretic. Nonetheless, if he administers Christian baptism, that person is validly baptized. But, and here is the rub, the *effects* of baptism will depend upon the state of the recipient. If the recipient persists in schism or heresy, that person receives no benefits; indeed he or she may be the more certainly damned.

The distinction between the validity and the efficacy of the sacrament is of great importance to the classical tradition, which followed Augustine in this matter. It enabled the church to assert the guaranteed and miraculous objectivity of the sacrament when administered in the authorized manner. For this the technical term, first appearing in the thirteenth century, was *ex opere operato* (by the deed done). But at the same time a reservation or caveat could be entered relating to the internal state of the recipient, who would receive no beneficial effect if he or she stubbornly persisted in offering an obstacle to the proffered salvation. In this case the effect of the sacrament would not be beneficial but disastrous.

One category of the baptized with whom the church was especially exercised was infants. Infant baptism, a practice at least as old as the third century, but by no means universal even in the fourth century, was in part motivated by the desire to ensure, in an age of high infant mortality, that the benefit of immortality might be theirs too. By the time of Augustine, the practice was sufficiently established for him to use it as an argument for the presence in infants of original sin. Augustine held that infants who died unbaptized were not saved, indeed they were punished, albeit lightly, for their sin. The view that baptism was literally necessary for salvation was the view held by the classical tradition, subject only to a few exceptions, such as those who died on their way to baptism. The enormity of the number of the damned led in later centuries to the theory of a "baptism of desire," among those persons of good will whose ignorance of the appointed way of salvation could not be held to be their fault.

A further problem for literalism existed in relation to postbaptismal sin. There are strands of the New Testament (for example, in Hebrews) which suggest that, after the baptismal forgiveness, no further opportunity for repentance existed. In the early church we hear that converts were occasionally in the habit of postponing baptism until their deathbed in order to ensure against the possibility of postbaptismal sin. But plainly such a practice was incompatible with the rapidly growing custom of infant baptism, and another method had to be found for the institutionalization of forgiveness. Here is the origin of sacramental penance—a term derived from the root *poena*, or punishment—the discipline imposed by a priest before or after absolution, as a satisfaction for sin. Since absolution could only be given by a priest in virtue of his endowment with the power of binding and loosing (the "power of the keys"), the integral character of the sacraments of baptism, penance, and ordination in the classic system comes into sight.

Eucharistic Miracle

The rite of initiation practiced in various ways in the fourth-century church included baptism, chrism (or confirmation), and the Eucharist. In the church at Jerusalem, for example, in the days of Cyril of Jerusalem, the full ritual was celebrated once a year at Easter. The rites took place in the night between Holy Saturday and Easter Day, with the impressive result that the newly baptized entered upon their mature Christian life with the celebration of the resurrection. The Eucharist signified participation in the risen body of Christ.

Two tendencies which we have already noted in relation to baptism are evident also in the history of eucharistic theology. The first is the impact of a declining eschatological consciousness. The ritual of the Lord's Supper, according to the account Paul gives in 1 Corinthians, expressed the sacred equality of each of the worshipers with each other in a world of unity and harmony, symbolized by the one bread of which each was partaker. The ritual involved a cultic commemoration of Jesus' last supper with his disciples, in which he designated the cup as "the new covenant in my blood" (1 Cor 11:24); it was to be cele-brated "until he comes." But just as baptism increasingly came to sig-nify the present possession of qualities and gifts, so eucharistic theology increasingly dwelt on the present miraculous transformation of the bread and wine effected by the priest. Thus the second parallel devel-opment can be observed, that of literalism in the interpretation of the rite. The difference, however, is that the eucharistic elements of bread and wine offered far greater opportunity than the water of baptism for identification with a miraculous transformation. Not merely is the bread and wine specifically blessed by Jesus, but the delivery of them to the worshipers is accompanied by a formula in each case, "This is my body. . . . This is my blood." The elements are not to be regarded as ordinary bread and wine but are transformed so as to be *saving* bread and wine. Because they are food in the natural order, the most popular image of interpretation becomes that of "nourishment" of the soul.

Throughout the early centuries there is abundant evidence both of great reverence accorded to the elements and of a freedom to interpret their spiritual meaning. By the time of Ambrose, a fourth-century bishop of Milan, the instruction of the newly baptized (contained in the influential *de Sacramentis*) included a clear statement that the word of Christ consecrates the sacrament, so that it becomes the re-deeming body and blood of Christ, powerful for the forgiveness of sins.

Controversy in the ninth and eleventh centuries about the degree of literalism with which the eucharistic miracle was to be interpreted eventually produced in the thirteenth century the word "transubstanti-ation." The bread and wine were held to be transubstantiated, that is to say, although they continue to have the appearance of bread and wine—with the properties, or "accidents," of color, taste, smell, and so forth—nonetheless at the level of "substance" they are wholly changed. In the form in which transubstantiation was expounded by

Thomas Aquinas, it was a highly sophisticated theory, based on an adaptation of Aristotelian metaphysics and designed to protect eucharistic theology from crude literalism. The term was adopted by the Council of Trent in 1551, without any precise theological definition, and has figured prominently in Roman Catholic apologetics ever since.

As with the theology of baptism, the history of eucharistic theology knows a continuous dialectic between insistence on the objectivity of the rite and the spiritual nourishment of the believer. The eucharistic miracle is performed, *ex opere operato,* by the consecrating priest. But the faithful are warned to approach the sacrament conscious of its holiness. Not to do so is to eat and drink judgment upon oneself. Thus the reception of the Eucharist is connected to the penitential system, which provides the appropriate means of preparation.

Precisely because the interior standards of preparation were set so high the classic tradition suffered from two unintended consequences. The first was the substitution of adoration of the eucharistic species for reception. To a very large extent congregations were spectators at the Eucharist, going about their own devotions, ignorant of the meaning of the Latin words being said by the priest. But once the miraculous transubstantiation had taken place, the congregation understood itself to be in the very presence of Christ himself, to whom devotion and adoration must be paid. Second, and as a corollary of the first consequence, frequency of participation in communion declined to the point where the majority of Christians came no more than once a year at the canonically prescribed attendance at Easter. Thus the Eucharist lost a considerable measure of its effectiveness as a sign of social solidarity in the body of Christ. Indeed, its social significance could plausibly be construed in quite another manner, as a means whereby a clerical caste exercised power in the context of chronic controversies with secular authority.

Sacramental Theory

The origin of a general theory of the nature of sacraments lies in the work of Augustine of Hippo. His theory of signs, developed in a work formative for the whole of medieval educational theory, *On Christian Doctrine* (396–427), embraces the sacraments as a means by which interior meanings are expressed by one agent to another. According to Augustine, a person who properly understands what is referred to by a sacrament is in a position to use and venerate it rightly. Christians have only a few, simple and sublime sacraments (here Augustine instances baptism and the Eucharist), which are contained in the teaching of Christ and the apostles.

There is, then, a distinction between the sacramental sign, the bread or wine, and the thing which is the sacrament, the act of being united with Christ in the fellowship of the church. A recipient may have one, but not the other, if that person fails to understand the spiritual sense or meaning of the sacrament or approaches it unworthily. This theory is coherent with Augustine's seminal understanding of sacrifice, according to which ritual acts of sacrifice signify the offering which God truly desires, namely, love of God and of the neighbor. When the Eucharist is offered by the church, it signifies the true sacrifice of Christians through the great High Priest. Augustine has no hesitation in following the traditional designation of the Eucharist as a sacrifice, because the whole theory of sacrifice is already embraced by a theory of signs. The "language" of signs is only dangerous to the spiritually obtuse. Accordingly there is no contradiction between this theory and the treatment of the sacramental elements with the utmost veneration.

Further developments built on Augustine's heritage. The standard textbook of Catholic theology during the Middle Ages, the *Sentences* of Peter Lombard, provided what Augustine had not offered, namely, a distinction between the sacraments proper—now enumerated as seven—and the other rites of the church. "Something is properly called a sacrament because it is a sign of God's grace, and is such an image of invisible grace that it bears its likeness and exists as its cause" (*Sentences* 4.1,2). In the light of this definition, of course, theologians could begin to explain how and why each of the seven rituals was a sacrament, and thus in the twelfth and thirteenth centuries sacramental theology achieved a high degree of technical precision. Every sacrament has a ritual (the *sacramentum tantum*, "the sign alone"); it has also the reality of the grace caused by the reception of the sacrament (the *res tantum*, "the reality alone"); and it has, further, that which is *both* reality *and* sign (*res et sacramentum*), the lasting effect of the sacrament, the change in the heart of the believer. The reality and permanence of this last was known as the sacramental character.

Augustine, as we have seen, had already used this concept in order to distinguish between the validity of the sacrament of baptism when administered by schismatics (its stamping of the soul of the baptized with an indelible mark) and the effect of the sacrament, namely, the grace conveyed. The medieval tradition was further to develop this theory in respect to each of the seven sacraments. Those that were unrepeatable, namely, confirmation and holy orders, were elucidated in the same way as baptism. The others were conceived of as conveying supernatural power by which the soul is continuously enabled to cooperate with God in its return to the divine. In the philosophical version of this theory advanced by Thomas Aquinas, the sacraments are referred to as "instrumental causes of grace," that is, means through which God acts in people's lives. They are signs because signs are necessary for communication with human beings; but they are *effective* signs, *ex opere operato*. The church is the institution that can guarantee the objective validity of sacramental ministrations; the sacraments are the God-appointed means by which human beings are raised out of the mire of sin to realize their God-given end.

Abuse and Criticism

Needless to say the sacramental system lent itself to abuse, not least by reason of its guaranteed objectivity. Three basic types of criticism have constantly reoccurred in the course of Christian history; first, concerning the lack of correlation between the administration or reception of the sacraments and personal morality or holiness; second, relating to the power or status bestowed on the priest by reason of his unique sacramental capacities; and third, criticism of the supernaturalism of sacramental theory as indistinguishable from magic. Each of these emerge with particular force at the Protestant Reformation, but their previous history indicates that the existence of sacramental rites in the Christian religion provokes chronic controversy.

1. Disputes about holiness—such as the Montanist, Novatianist, and Donatist movements in the early centuries of the church—led to the development by Augustine of a distinction between the true spiritual church and the empirical church, the latter being a mixed body containing both good and bad. Bad priests, he contended, do not invalidate the sacraments, and such has been the answer of the classic tradition to the rigorists of every age. The church, moreover, armed itself with the necessary powers to discipline those clergy whose lives

were an open scandal. The Christian protest against immorality was driven to schism when, with the centralization of church government under the papacy, the will to exercise discipline was undermined at the center.

Thus the ideal of apostolic Christian holiness was increasingly the aspiration of sectarian movements in and after the twelfth century. Their attacks focused on the use by the clergy of their monopoly of the sacramental means of grace for personal gain, on the abuse of the sacrament of penance, on infant baptism, and on the sacrificial interpretation of the Eucharist. But severe criticism of clerical ignorance and venality are to be found even in the writings of earlier orthodox thinkers, such as Bernard and Peter Abelard. In the early fourteenth century the poet Dante consigned several popes and leading churchmen to hell in his *Divine Comedy*.

2. Criticism of the power of the clergy likewise derived from an apostolic ideal of lowliness and humility. Power had accrued to the clergy on the conversion of Constantine by virtue of the mere fact that the advancement of the Christian faith could now become imperial policy. Christianity was launched on a long-standing and highly ambiguous participation and struggle with secular authority. The "Donation of Constantine," an eighth-century forgery purporting to confer on the pope of Rome huge powers of government, was regarded by Dante (who had no knowledge of its spuriousness) as an unmitigated disaster.

In the minds of the critics, such as the fourteenth-century Englishman John Wycliffe, the church—governed by men possessed with a lust for wealth and power—had become tyrannous. Only a reformation of the church would achieve the necessary changes, and Wycliffe called on the secular authorities to dispossess the church of its property and restore a true harmony of church and civil government. The philosophical undergirding for this appeal lay in a theory of double substances, divine and human, which he also applied to the Eucharist in his denial of transubstantiation. Wycliffe's theories were adopted by John Hus in Prague, and the eucharistic heresy thus became a symbol of the political revolution.

3. The criticism of superstition and magic also has deep roots in Christianity, since it was essential to the early church to differentiate its rights from those of the surrounding religions. The sacrificial char-

acter of the Eucharist was distinguished with care from pagan sacrifices, as not involving blood, as being spiritual, and as not implying the need to propitiate the deity. The Greek philosophical tradition of the true interior sacrifice was wholeheartedly appropriated by apologists and given Christian content and justification.

Magic and superstition have, however, deep roots in the human psyche, and one particular development in medieval sacramental theology facilitated the growth of a magical attitude to the sacraments. This was the influence, some would say the predominance, of legal over theological definitions after the breakdown of the scholastic synthesis in the later Middle Ages. The legal background to sacramental theology was of long standing. The very term *sacramentum* retained its legal connotation as an oath of allegiance and placed all the baptized under legal or quasi-legal obligation. The causal interpretation of the sacraments as means of grace encouraged a precise interpretation of the legal status, duties, and rights of both celebrants and participants. In the interests of precision a common terminology was devised to protect sacramental rites from illegalities. Each sacrament had particular "matter" (for example, materials and gestures) and particular "forms" (for example, prescribed words). Technical disputes resulted in the specification of what was correct in each case, which increasingly turned on the necessity of satisfying certain minimum criteria. Once these were fulfilled the beneficial results were guaranteed, and a host of unauthorized magical practices and attitudes were given an apparent basis.

Sacrifice and Memorial

Luther's rejection of the sacramental system included all of the traditional criticisms advanced above, together with some decisive considerations of his own that give his protest a theological force and coherence rivaled only by Wycliffe among his predecessors. This central consideration concerned unfruitful "works" and the identification of the sacrificing activity of the priesthood as a "work." Luther's protest began in relation to the theology accompanying the sale of indulgences, especially the idea that penitence was not required of a purchaser buying remission of purgatorial punishments for a member of his or her family. The dispute could have remained at a theological level but was quickly made a general matter of respect for papal authority. Luther responded with a generalized criticism of the sacramental system in his treatise on the *Babylonian Captivity of the Church* (1520).

Luther rejected the sacramental status of confirmation, marriage, orders, and extreme unction on the grounds that, by definition, sacraments are composed of two elements, sign and the word of promise found in scripture. Without condemning the use of rites of various kinds, he reserved the title of sacrament for the Eucharist and baptism, with penance as a salutary practice to remind one of baptismal faith. His attack on the Mass centered on the charge that, if it is said that we offer the Eucharist as a sacrifice, then it becomes a human work replacing dependence on Christ's sacrificial atonement on the cross. That it was in practice so regarded Luther took as proven from the schemes for clerical enrichment based on the purchase of requiem Masses for the departed. The whole system he regarded as a gross betrayal of the gospel of unmerited and gracious forgiveness, which we receive joyously as a promise. "The beginning of our salvation is a faith which clings to the word of a promising God."

Reliance on this promise was opposed by Luther to the various procedures devised in the classic tradition for dealing with the problem of sin after baptism, a system of control in the hands of a clerical elite. This, he believed, traded on human anxiety about ultimate salvation in the interests of the power and wealth of the hierarchy. Luther's aim was twofold, to return to ordinary Christians the power to determine their own eternal destiny and to provide them with assurance about the certainty of their salvation. The first he accomplished in his teaching about faith, and the second in his use of the idea of memory or recollection. To baptism is attached the promise that the one baptized will be saved (Mark 16:16), while the whole Christian life is to be conceived as a continuous recollection of the act of dying to sin and rising to newness of life, "that is, full and complete justification."

The same thought was applied by Luther to the Eucharist. The promise is the covenant with humanity, made in the incarnation and death of Christ, to forgive all human sin out of pure and free love. The sign or sacrament is his body and blood in the bread and wine, which serve as a reminder of the promise. The trouble with the medieval eucharistic tradition, he urged, was that it was so preoccupied with sacramental causality that it totally omitted to speak of faith in the promise.

Luther's concern was, in effect, to remind the church of the interior dimension of our grasp of the external ritual. He rightly and frequently appealed to Augustine and, like Augustine, saw no incompatibility between emphasis on the sign character of the sacrament and insistence on the fact that the body and blood of Christ are truly present in the bread and wine.

Calvin, who used the *Babylonian Captivity* extensively, was somewhat more reluctant to allow any union between the elements and divine grace. He strongly emphasized the role of the Holy Spirit in enabling the Christian believer to recognize Christ in the sacraments, which are "instruments through which God works as he pleases." At the same time he firmly opposed the solution of Zwingli who, he believed, held the sacraments to be simply testimonies of faith. They are, on the contrary, divinely appointed—even if subordinate—ways in which God nourishes the faith of his elect. Unbelievers, therefore, receive only the outward sign.

Denial or affirmation of the sacrificial character of the Mass passed into the confessional documents of the Reformation and of the Council of Trent. But in their theological elaboration they possessed a common assumption, that the offering of a sacrifice focused on the death of the victim. The highly influential seventeenth-century Spanish Jesuit John de Lugo defined sacrifice as "the immolation of a victim offered to God by a legitimate priest" and advanced a theory to account for the way in which the eucharistic sacrifice entailed the immolation of the divine victim. The artificiality of these and other similar theories persuaded Protestants that, despite their denials, Roman Catholics really intended to teach a repetition of Christ's sacrifice at the hands of the priest.

Three attempts have been made to transcend the impasse created by this opposition. The first, pursued by a number of seventeenth-century Anglicans, such as Lancelot Andrews, was to explore the figurative, or symbolic, representation of the sacrifice of the cross in what was spoken of as the "commemorative sacrifice" of the altar. This theory acquired in the twentieth century a deeper appreciation of the nature of symbol. The second attempt was based on a repudiation of de Lugo's emphasis on the immolation of the victim and spoke of the essence of sacrifice as the release of life or power made possible by the offering. The Eucharist thus conforms to the requirements of sacrifice, and a reappropriation of the patristic understanding is thereby said to be possible. The third route, much employed in modern ecumenical circles, is by means of reevaluation of the concept of *anamnesis*, or memorial. There is, it is said, a distinctively biblical understanding of memorial according to which what is ritually recalled is made present and active. Whether any of these precisely meet Luther's objection to the mass as a human work depends less on the theories themselves than on whether they are set in the context provided by an overarching doctrine of grace.

CHALLENGES AND CONTRIBUTIONS OF
MODERN CONSCIOUSNESS

Lutherans, Calvinists, and Zwinglians were unable to agree on eucharistic theology, and Protestant practice of the Lord's Supper became exceedingly diverse. There were, however, certain important common features. Considerable stress was placed, following Luther, on the subordination of the sign to the word. As a result, the celebration of the sacraments became an opportunity for considerable didactic display. Although both Luther and Calvin, and in England Archbishop Cranmer, had hoped for a weekly celebration of the Eucharist, this was not realized and the emphasis in Protestant worship fell heavily on the preaching of the word. Though a vigorous debate was maintained over the theology of the sacraments, especially concerning the eucharistic presence, in practice the rituals were devalued.

Anglicanism was a partial exception to this rule. The peculiar circumstances of the English Reformation led to the attempt to enforce unity of practice by means of the authorized *Book of Common Prayer*, a vernacular liturgy largely the work of Thomas Cranmer. Though strongly influenced by both Lutheran and Reformed theology, its intentions were comprehensive and comparatively conservative. Two revisions in 1549 and 1552, the latter more strongly reformed than the former, have continued to play a significant role in Anglican church life. The seventeenth and nineteenth centuries witnessed vigorous revivals of theologies of the real presence and eucharistic sacrifice and resulted in a general restoration of sacramental life in the Anglican Communion as a whole.

The Roman Catholic Church responded to the criticisms of the Protestant reformers with a general reform of the chaotic multiplicity of its liturgies, and the imposition of a universal standard. Latin was retained and the laity virtually excluded from active participation. The Council of Trent held that the sacrifice of the Mass required a sacrificing priesthood as a distinct order and rejected the Reformers' inferences from the New Testament doctrine of the priesthood of all believers. The missal (or Mass book) of Pope Pius V of 1570 fixed the rites of Roman Catholics for four centuries and confirmed the position of the private Mass as the norm. These and other developments in the Roman Catholic Church had the paradoxical effect of ensuring that there was a strongly developed apologetic doctrine of the sacraments in Roman Catholicism, while at the same time minimizing the participation of the whole church in the sacramental life. "It could almost be said that during the modern period the seven ecclesiastical sacraments became a central part of Catholic doctrine but a marginal part of Catholic religious life."[2]

Magic and Morality

As we have already seen, critics throughout the history of the church have been conscious of the need to differentiate the sacraments from magical performances. Sixteenth-century humanists—such as Erasmus, John Colet, and Thomas More—were openly contemptuous of contemporary superstition and credulity, and believed that the church could be purged of it by a reforming pope. That Protestantism was not itself free of superstition is proved by the persecution of "witches" throughout the seventh century. But as a whole the Reformation was characterized by critical alertness to the power of the clergy to exploit credulity, and rejection of Roman Catholic sacramental religion as "superstitious" was universal.

All of this made the application of the emerging scientific world view to the "miracles" of sacramental causality easier. Inasmuch as the "best defense of Christianity was to show its essential reasonableness and social utility,"[3] the sacraments could be reduced to the level of ritual reminders to the living of a good life. At a deeper level, however, the doctrine of the sacraments is inextricable from developments in the doctrines of creation and providence. If the material world was increasingly being conceived mechanistically, then any supposed change in

---

2. Joseph Martos, *Doors to the Sacred*, p. 127.
3. See above, p. 11.

the elements of bread and wine is, of necessity, an exceptional intervention. Again, the greater the emphasis placed on the separation between the laws governing bodies, and the freely functioning mind, the greater the attraction of subjective theories of the power of the sacraments, that is, views which relate to the intentions or dispositions of the recipients. This is a matter of degree. Both the Roman Catholic Descartes and the Lutheran Leibniz professed theories of sacramental change, the latter indeed believing that his doctrine of substance enabled him to reconcile Lutheran and Roman Catholic views of the Eucharist. Scandal could still be created by a book treating the theology of the Lord's Supper in a broadly rationalist and memorialist manner, which, when published in England in 1735, elicited more than twenty replies.[4]

One orthodox writer, conscious of Deist criticism of the miraculous, but whose arguments were widely deemed to have been victorious over them, was Bishop Joseph Butler. Convinced of the general ignorance of humanity, he argued that in construing the nature of the world in which we are set we must be content with probabilities, not certainties. With a wide range of arguments he set out the case for supposing there to be an analogy between God's moral government of the world and Christian revelation. Such arguments, moreover, must be practical in character since agents have to act in the world. The relevance of this philosophy to sacramental theology was correctly perceived by John Henry Newman a century later, when he spoke of Butler's *Analogy* as proposing a sacramental relation between nature and revelation.[5] The whole analogy of nature removes any presumption against the idea that there could be a principle of mediation at work between God and humanity. The existence of a visible, teaching church and the provision of means of grace are conceived as integral parts of a divine revelation.

A sharply contrasting response, strongly redolent of the rationalist inheritance of the Enlightenment, is contained in the brief but remarkable treatment of the sacraments at the close of Kant's *Religion within the Limits of Reason Alone* (1793). Here he is concerned with the illusions that religion promotes and that as a philosopher he feels

---

4. The author was an Anglican bishop, Benjamin Hoadley. One reply, that of William Law in 1737, is of more than passing interest in its conception of a eucharistic memorial which is of active force in the present.

5. John Henry Newman, *Apologia Pro Vita Sua* (London: Longmans, 1865), pp. 22–23, 29.

entitled to dispel. The principal illusion is that trust in the causal effi-cacy of what are called (misleadingly) the means of grace dispenses one from the effort of doing all that one can do to live a good life. Accord-ing to Kant's philosophical doctrines we cannot know anything at all about alleged supernatural aids. What we do know are the moral laws under which we must live a good life, and these provide us with the criteria for interpreting the major religious duties of private prayer, churchgoing, and the practice of the sacraments of baptism and the Eucharist. Pouring scorn on the "heathenish superstition" of suppos-ing that baptism washes away sin, Kant interprets initiation as a solemn beginning of a life of continuous moral education. Communal partici-pation in the Eucharist, he holds, promotes the idea of "a cosmopoli-tan moral community."

Here the impact of the substitution of a moral for a supernatural frame of reference is obvious. Kant is witheringly sarcastic of the way in which believers come to see themselves as divine favorites, but who fail by comparison with the naturally honest person. The importance of his critique is out of all proportion to its brevity. As the social perfor-mance of the church came increasingly under unfavorable scrutiny in the nineteenth century, the suspicion grew that its fundamental devo-tional life fostered dangerous illusions. The Marxist critique of reli-gion—resting on Feuerbach and, ultimately, Hegel—had its roots in Kant. And the encounter that modern theology has promoted between itself and liberation movements can be seen presaged in the Kantian thesis concerning the connection between the Eucharist and the uto-pian hope for a new world order.

Romanticism and Personalism

As we have argued, there has been in sacramental theology a contin-uous dialectic between the external rite and interior intention. The tendency of the classical tradition had been first to maximize, and then to defend, the guaranteed effectiveness of a validly performed sacra-mental ritual. But at every stage of the process a counterthesis can be observed which reemphasized the necessary dimension of interiority, the personal participation of the recipient in the meaning of the rite. In Augustine's heritage to Western theology, two elements played a vital role in preserving the dialectic. These have been, first, awareness of the sign character of all sacraments and, second, emphasis on the corporate nature of the church in its sacramental life. These two have constituted a permanent endowment merely awaiting favorable conditions for their rediscovery.

The Reformers, Luther and especially Calvin, strove to restore interiority to a tradition which they accused of having become mechanical. For Calvin the gifts we receive at the Lord's Supper are not the benefits of salvation, but Christ himself. We participate, above all, in his humanity. But the effect of the Reformation was to destroy the rite, so anxious had the Reformed churches become about orthodox doctrine and so insistent on freedom from ceremonial legislation.

It was the romantic movement that was again to alter the situation (permanently so far as one can judge at the present) in three respects. First, by reintroducing respect for antiquity the romantics greatly stimulated interest in the historical study of the past. Necessarily this movement had to pass through several stages. Patristic and liturgical scholarship, which underwent a dramatic renaissance in England in the early part of the nineteenth century, was initially governed by the needs of contemporary controversies. But in due course selective blindness and partiality were increasingly abandoned and the study of the past for its own sake began to yield impressive fruits. The churches that appealed to antiquity in justification of their sacramental theology discovered the need for a theory of development to account for its undoubted variations. At the same time, though somewhat later, the Protestant appeal to the norms of the apostolic period was itself discovered to entail internal variety.

The second impact of the romantic movement was a recovery of a sense of the mysterious depths of the natural world. John Henry Newman, one of the leaders of the Oxford movement in the Church of England until his reception into the Roman Church in 1845, correctly identified Coleridge, Southey, Wordsworth, and Scott as forerunners of the new sense of the symbolic character of nature. When combined with Butler's doctrine of mediation, Newman produced what he referred to as the doctrine of "the sacramental system," the idea that material phenomena are both the types and instruments of real things unseen. What is significant is that these considerations, which originate in a protest against eighteenth-century rationalism and constitute a general theory of signs, led Newman to become a Roman Catholic. The dialectic of the language of sign could only be applied fully in a church that had preserved its rituals.

Third, sacramental theology received a substantial impetus from the romantic concern for authentic personhood. Neither mechanistic concepts of grace nor moralizing reductions of the nature of religious fellowship are adequate to the nourishment of the mysterious communion of human personality with the divine life. Characteristic of this movement is a christological construction of what a human being really is. That is to say, the sacraments no longer are dominated by concern for remedies against human sin, in which the paradigm of humanity is provided by the story of Adam. Rather, there is concentration on the story of Jesus as the paradigm of true humanity, and the biblical images of participation and fellowship assume a position of prominence.

The impact of this development is most marked, of course, in modern Roman Catholic theology. While Catholic sacramental devotion had been strongly christocentric, sacramental theology was bound to remain confined within theories about modes of causality, so long as the scholastic inheritance predominated. The work of the Dominican Edward Schillebeeckx and of the Jesuit Karl Rahner has, however, opened up that tradition in a personalist direction. The basis of the new theory is consistent with Thomism, namely, that human being is predisposed toward revelation. For Schillebeeckx, the fact that God's personal gift of himself is as a human being addressing fellow human beings, is deployed, theologically as the justification for adopting and developing a philosophy of personal encounter. The sacraments are conceived as an encounter with God, and Christ is the primordial sacrament (*Ursakrament*). But human bodiliness is interiority made visible, a real presence of the being of a person in its forms of expression and patterns of behavior. The church, which is the earthly prolongation of Christ's glorified humanity, continues in its sacramental life the possibility of embodied encounter with Christ. At the same time, the church's celebration of the sacraments as worship is the communal act by which Christ's own worship is presented to the Father with that of his people. This is taken to explain the *ex opere operato* thesis, inasmuch as the prayer of Christ infallibly elicits the response of the Father.

Schillebeeckx's seminal work on the sacraments in the 1950s and 1960s has been modified by the conclusions of his more-recent christological writing. Karl Rahner, on the other hand, persisted with a traditional christology and continued to develop many of the themes he

shared earlier with Schillebeeckx. For Rahner, the church is the efficacious sign of salvation in which is expressed the eschatologically certain and victorious word of God to the human situation. There is,
therefore, a universal history of salvation (worked out in Rahner's theory of anonymous Christianity), an official history of salvation, and an
individual history of salvation. In the last of these Rahner strives to
show how, on the basis of his thesis of the genuine partnership between God and humanity, there is a necessary response to the efficacious word of the sacrament which preserves and enhances human
freedom.

Corporate Life

Augustine's doctrine of the Eucharist, as we have seen, laid particular stress on the fact that the eucharistic sacrifice is offered by the whole
church in the offering of its true head. Modern theology has considered the loss of this dimension of eucharistic theology to be one of the
major disasters of later medieval developments. Its recovery in recent
times is the fruit of a series of changes in which the Reformation, the
romantic movement, and developments in modern psychology have
all played a part.

The Reformation was important for the prominence it gave to the
congregation as the empirical realization of the "communion of
saints," devoted to each other in true fellowship. The romantic movement contributed a philosophical anthropology that stressed the im-
possibility of realizing personhood apart from the community. The
impact of this theory is plain in Schleiermacher's understanding of the
church. Against the individualism implicit in rationalist anthropologies, he insisted that it was of the nature of human piety that it should
express itself socially. The church is the essential medium by which
the impression of Christ's perfect consciousness of God is conveyed in
time, and the sacraments, especially the Lord's Supper, are the permanent means whereby the fellowship of believers with each other and
with Christ is nourished.

The impact of modern psychology, however, has been profound on
every aspect of the church's ritual life and understanding. The discovery of the unconscious has undermined excessive confidence in the
possibility of spiritual progress. The opportunity offered, by regular
participation in the sacramental means of grace, of escaping from the
consequences of sin has come to seem like an illusion. Human be-

ings have been exposed in psychological theory as chronically subject to subliminal motivations, whose power continues throughout life. Luther's thesis that sin does not completely die in us until the body dies has apparently been vindicated. To think otherwise is to court self-deception.

The consequence of this understanding of humanity has been to shift the emphasis in sacramental theology from concentration on sin and its removal, to emphasis on the new corporate life of reconciliation with God and with one's fellows. Since to a very large extent the sacraments had been seen as the means for dealing with postbaptismal sin, the revolution in attitude is of great importance. For it has undergirded the theological insight, central to the documents of the Second Vatican Council, that the sacraments are sacraments *of the church*, implying deeper participation in human fellowship and interpersonal exchange. It has also led to the interpretation of sin as communal rather than individual failure and to renewed interest in the patristic practice of public confession of faults and the assumption of corporate responsibility.

Communalism has also been strongly reinforced by the trend of the contemporary liturgical movement toward participatory liturgies. Roman Catholics, Anglicans, and Lutherans, not without controversy, have widely adopted the practice of celebration from behind the altar or table, with the priest facing the congregation, as a symbol of the corporateness of the eucharistic fellowship. But at the same time a particular and contrasting role has been played by the least "reformed" of all the churches, the Eastern Orthodox. Largely because of their relative isolation from the centers of the European Enlightenment, Orthodoxy was written off as moribund by Western theologians of the nineteenth and early twentieth centuries. After the Russian Revolution, however, a group of highly sophisticated theologians settled in Paris and the United States, and exposure to Orthodox theology and liturgy began to grow.

The attraction of Western Christians to Orthodox theology consists largely in its having avoided the inheritance of individualism by which classic Roman Catholic and Protestant understandings of the sacraments had become polarized. Where the Eucharist had centered for Roman Catholics on the representation of the sacrifice of Christ on the cross, and for Protestants on the memorial of the once-for-all redemption, Orthodoxy could claim that its liturgy focused on participation in the joy of the worship of heaven. Despite its length and complexity and the preeminence of the celebrating priest, the text of the liturgy powerfully evoked a communal sense of a church at one with the church in heaven, ascending to participate in a heavenly banquet. Orthodoxy also has greatly profited from its lack of technical and didactic concentration on formulae of consecration and philosophical theories of eucharistic change, or their didactic replacement by expositions of doctrines of the atonement. In a culture that has lost confidence in an instrumental understanding of sacramental causality, the expressive richness of Orthodox ritual has a strong appeal.

ISSUES AND PROPOSALS

Rites and Stories

The difficulty of an introduction to sacramental theology is its necessary reference to rituals that have varied widely in form and content over the course of church history. At the same time this fact serves to emphasize an important issue, namely, that sacraments have the nature of pretheological rites. The worship of the early church, of which we have little direct information in the New Testament, was presumably modeled upon that of the synagogue and transformed progressively in ways which matched the congregation's new experiences of the Spirit. We hear nothing of any deliberate attempts to mold worship anew according to agreed doctrinal norms. In this sense the heritage of the Reformation, in which theological assertion and denial played a leading role, is misleading as a paradigm for the formulation of sacramental theology. Anthropologists have insisted that rituals function in advance of elaborate explanation and that they are frequently related to the paradigmatic myths of a religion. Recent interest, therefore, in the role played by story in Christian theology offers the opportunity for some new developments.

But it should be noted that anthropological observation of the role of ritual in religion faces Protestants with something of a crisis. The accusation of the Reformers against the Roman Church was that it has reverted to the ritual slavery and legalism of Judaism. This necessarily entailed a sharp contrast between the pure religion of the apostles and their immediate followers, and the centuries of degeneration that had followed the primitive church. Even when critical scholars had exposed the internal disunity of the apostolic age, Protestant Old Testament scholarship consciously depicted cultic religion as inferior to the religion of the prophets, which, it was believed, Jesus had inherited. The attack on cultic religion was held to embody the authentic Christian heritage of freedom from law and bondage to human mediatorial priesthood.

Does Christianity have cultic rituals? The answer is not seriously in doubt. Contemporary study of Paul's references to baptism are unquestionably illuminated by modern anthropological theories of rites of passage. Rituals are ways in which frames are set around experience, and sacred boundries established. Where the symbolic transactions inspire confidence, the social and psychological effectiveness of a ritual is strongly documented. Criticism of the tendency of ritual forms to harden into substitutes for religious experience must stop short of the destruction of ritual as a mode of religious behavior.

The category of story, interpreted as the raw material of theology, has provided a valuable insight into the means by which Christian identity is sustained over time and in the midst of cultural changes. The sacraments of baptism and the Eucharist deploy the imagery of birth, death, and resurrection in their reorientation of the personhood of the convert. The new creation "in Christ" is a being whose personhood is now inseparately linked to the recollection of the story of Christ and to participation in the story of the people of God. Christian identity is structured alike by memory and by hope.

Sacraments as Worship

An issue that has come into the open in recent theology concerns the category of sacrament itself. There is little doubt that numerous artificial problems were created in the attempt to conform each of the seven sacraments to a formal definition of a sacrament. The identification of that precise number also rests on precarious assumptions, nor does there seem strong grounds for restricting them to two. Why then employ a general category at all? Schleiermacher, following Zwingli, looked forward to a time when the church would dispense with the word except insofar as it needed a collective term for reference to the continuing activity of Christ in baptism and the Lord's Supper.

A further reason for refusing to segregate the sacraments into a separate compartment of church witness lies in their character as worship. One way, indeed, in which the theology of the sacraments can be protected from becoming descriptions of the quasi-clinical operations of grace is their subsumption into a general theology of the praise of God in word and deed. That the Eucharist can be so incorporated needs no explanation, inasmuch as it constitutes a declaration of God's saving activity in Christ. But baptism is also worship, in three respects. It is, first, the acknowledgment of dependence upon the divine gift of life, which is received by the convert anew out of the waters of baptism. Second, baptism is itself a sacrificial offering, a putting to death of the old person and the joyous reception of new life in death. And, third, baptism in its aspect as the gift of the Holy Spirit is the precondition of the whole of the worshiping life, since all prayer is uttered with the assistance of the Spirit. The perception that the baptism of new members of the church is part of the normal life of a worshiping congregation has rightly transformed baptismal practice in the modern church.

The revival of awareness of the eschatological origins of Christian theology has also contributed to the grasp of the sacraments as worship. It was, as we have seen, the loss of eschatological consciousness that precipitated an undue emphasis on the literal and immediate possession here and now of the benefits of salvation. Although contemporary eschatology still shows the tension between other-worldly and this-worldly hopes, it has the potential for important contributions precisely to the question of the sacraments as worship and, in particular, to the relation of liturgy and political action.

In the first place, it serves to remind the church of the theme of judgment that belongs integrally to the sacraments of baptism and Eucharist. According to the apostle Paul, a baptized person has already passed through the death merited by sin and now walks in newness of life. Similarly, participation in the Eucharist requires a discriminatory perception about the nature of Christ's body of which the Christian is a member. Otherwise that person would eat and drink self-condemnation. In other words, these two rituals establish and reinforce a boundary between the world of sin and the holy community, which inescapably confronts the participant with a moral demand. This demand is nothing less than the presentation of the believer's self, body and soul, as a living sacrifice to God (Rom. 12:1). The whole of life is subsumed into the category of worship, of which specific acts of worship are but the focus and intensification.

The social and political significance of the eucharistic feast follows directly from this consideration. Inasmuch as the holy community is a sign of the whole human race and not an isolated entity pursuing its own ultimate salvation, the realization, or attempted realization, of holy equality inside the community constitutes a permanent judgment on the forms of segregation and inequality—racial, class, and sexual —practiced in society as a whole. Not that such equality has been invariably practiced. The history of the church shows the compromises that have found a ready home inside the church's own structures, let alone in the church's witness in society. Sociologically it seems that the cost of undermining the norms of a society is their partial adoption. The cost of the promotion of sacred equality in a rigidly structured society is the adoption of a hierarchy; the cost of the pursuit of universal brother- and sisterhood is the creation of a separated church conscious of its boundaries. A fenced Eucharist declaring the love of God for all humanity is the paradoxical consequence of the church's witness in the world. Thus internal revolution is the permanent state of the church as the costs are recurrently declared unacceptable.

Sacrifice and Commitment

Modern pluralistic societies create acute problems for religions in maintaining the strength of religious commitments. "Lack of commitment, lack of identity, meaninglessness, anomie and alienation are all very much related symptoms of societies in which definitions of reality are no longer taken for granted because competition has relativized each and all of them."[6] The problem is compounded by the fact that, as we have just indicated, the whole of Christian living is conceived as a sacrifice of self, a continuous identification with the death of Christ and participation in his resurrection. Although the classic tradition spoke principally of the Eucharist as a sacrifice in which the whole church and every member of it was offered to God, it is perfectly proper to refer also to baptism as a sacrifice, clarifying the priorities and strengthening the commitments of the convert.

Yet, as we know, the objections to sacrificial language in association with the sacraments are profound. It is said not merely that we have no cultural experience of the sacrifices performed in New Testament times, but the term has been abused beyond redemption by its use in relation to death in battle. Hitler, whose example has been imitated by

6. H. Mol, *Identity and the Sacred* (Oxford: Oxford University Press, 1976), p. 12.

every other totalitarian leader, required his followers to "sacrifice" personal liberties and human rights in the quest for national destiny. And insofar as sacrifice has specifically religious connotations in the modern mind, the notion of propitiation which early Christian theologians were so anxious to avoid has also persisted into the present time.

Nonetheless the category of sacrifice imposes itself as one of a complex of images used to explicate the death of Christ in the New Testament, and as an integral part of the traditional, pre-Reformation interpretation of the Eucharist. Moreover, its continued controversial deployment is guaranteed by the Tridentine defense of the thesis that there is a sacrifice in the Mass. Can anything be made of the idea in modern theology?

We return to the observation that the function of rituals is to structure experience. Specifically in the Christian religion, the rituals of baptism and Eucharist serve to demarcate the profane world from the people of God and to claim the latter as a sign of the ultimate triumph of the holy God over the worst that chaos, sin, and evil can achieve. So long as everyday experience lends support to the supposition that humanity is in progress from an age of superstition into new and hitherto unrealized freedoms, demarcation over against the threat of chaos, sin, and evil will seem a somewhat overdramatic structuring to adopt. On the contrary, forms of adaptation or assimilation to the norms of the culture will suggest themselves as appropriate to the onward progress of religion itself. But at the point reached in contemporary West European and North American societies, where the culture has largely accepted the thesis of an irreducible plurality of values, to the overt destruction of its will to realize the human good, the relevance of the early church's apocalyptic vision returns, and with it the synoptic structuring provided by its rituals. Self-sacrifice, for all its admitted dangers of masochism and ideological subversion, remains the criterion provided by the story of Jesus. The rites of baptism and the Eucharist will serve as a permanent reminder to the church of its sacrificial character.

SUGGESTIONS FOR FURTHER READING

Abbott, Walter, ed. *The Documents of Vatican II*. New York: Guild Press, 1966. Esp. The Constitution on the Sacred Liturgy.

Aquinas, Thomas. *Summa Theologica*. Part 3, questions 60–90.

Barth, Karl. *Church Dogmatics*. Vol. 4/4, Baptism as the Foundation of the Christian Life.

Brilioth, Yngve. *Eucharistic Faith and Practice, Evangelical and Catholic*. London: SPCK, 1930.

Cooke, Bernard. *Sacraments and Sacramentality*. Mystic, Conn.: Twenty-Third Publications, 1983.

Douglas, Mary. *Purity and Danger*. London: Routledge & Kegan Paul, 1966.

Eliade, Mircea. *The Sacred and the Profane*. New York: Harcourt, Brace & World, 1959.

Hatchett, Marion. *Sanctifying Life, Time and Space*. New York: Seabury Press, 1976.

Jones, Cheslyn; Wainwright, Geoffrey; and Yarnold, Edward. *The Study of Liturgy*. London: SPCK, 1978.

Kant, Immanuel. *Religion within the Limits of Reason Alone*. Translated by T. M. Greene & H. H. Hudson. New York: Harper & Row, 1960. Bk. 4.

Kavanagh, Aidan. *The Shape of Baptism: The Rite of Christian Initiation*. New York: Pueblo Publishing, 1978.

Luther, Martin. *The Babylonian Captivity of the Church* (= *The Pagan Servitude of the Church*). In *Martin Luther: Selections from His Writings*. Pp. 249–359.

Martos, Joseph. *Doors to the Sacred: A Historical Introduction to Sacraments in the Catholic Church*. New York: Doubleday & Co., 1982.

Moule, Charles F. D. *Worship in the New Testament*. London: Lutterworth Press, 1961.

Quick, Oliver. *The Christian Sacraments*. London: Nisbet, 1927.

Rahner, Karl. *The Church and the Sacraments*. New York: Herder & Herder, 1963.

———. *Foundations of Christian Faith*. Chap. 8.

Schlink, Edmund. *The Doctrine of Baptism*. St. Louis: Concordia Publishing House, 1972.

Schillebeeckx, Edward. *Christ the Sacrament of the Encounter with God*. New York: Sheed & Ward, 1963.

———. *The Eucharist*. New York: Sheed & Ward, 1968.

Schleiermacher, Friedrich. *The Christian Faith*. Pp. 582–695.

Schmemann, Alexander. *Sacraments and Orthodoxy*. New York: Herder & Herder, 1965.

———. *The World as Sacrament*. London: Darton, Longman & Todd, 1966.

Thurian, Max, ed. *Ecumenical Perspectives on Baptism, Eucharist and Ministry*. Geneva: World Council of Churches, 1983.

Wainwright, Geoffrey. *Eucharist and Eschatology*. London: Epworth Press, 1971.

DAVID B. BURRELL

11. THE SPIRIT AND THE CHRISTIAN LIFE

WHERE WE ARE

The Christian life has been regarded from the beginning as a following of Jesus. Erstwhile Christians have ever been invited to step into the shoes of that first band of followers, twelve of whom he explicitly chose to be carriers of the word—apostles. Indeed, we may surmise that the role they play in the Gospels was shaped with an eye to later followers: their humble origins; their persistent inability to get the point; their impetuous desire to share in his lot, followed by their disappearance at the critical moment. And the Gospel of John reminds us how, in being called to follow him, we are not merely being conscripted into his service, but are rather invited to become his friends.

An invitation to friendship with divinity taxes our credulity, so much so that to accept it *is* to believe Christianly. That seemingly impossible barrier being breached, it is a relatively small step to speak of intimacy with God—both as individuals and as a people, for this God has already acknowledged delight in being with us. The capacity of divinity to delight in us creates in its turn an entirely new dimension of receptivity in us. This new person, this self transformed, is itself a sign of the promise as he or she displays a newfound familiarity with God as well as a correlative capacity for receiving and forgiving one's fellows. The promise of a relation between God and ourselves, which has the qualities of and potentialities for friendship, opens up similarly new possibilities among ourselves.

That, I take it, is the character of the promise offered to humankind in Jesus. That promise might best be called *faith*, if we were to understand faith as naming a new mode of life which is a new way of relating—to God.[1] Since, however, that term so easily slides into *belief*, which focuses primarily and often exclusively on the human

1. Wilfred Cantwell Smith, *Faith and Belief*.

302

dispositions involved, it seems preferable to speak of the Spirit. It is the Spirit who shapes that new mode of life, and to refer this life to its primary agent reminds us that we are always speaking of an active relating—dispositional in character, it is true, but ever accessible to those who share in the life of faith.

The expression "spirit" conveys a sense of relating, because its now accustomed use (since medieval times) has been to render our capacity to relate and to be related intentionally to all things.[2] The two characteristic modes of intentional relating—knowing and loving—complement one another in accounting for what we find distinctively human. To speak of a spiritual dimension to human beings is not, in the first instance, to make an odd metaphysical claim so much as it is to remark our capacity to respond intelligently and affectively to the world about us, to other intentional beings, and to our own selves—to respond potentially, at least, to all things and to their source and goal as well.

That we possess such a capacity to respond is clearly presupposed to anyone's being called forth, for it is that capacity which must be addressed. So the term "spirit" will stand for both: the character of the one called and the call itself (or the caller). Moreover, since intentional relationships contain the capacity for making us over, if anything does, the very notion of a continuing friendship with God must be understood to be a transforming relationship. As Aristotle put it, "A friend is in on that relationship whereby one relates to one's own self."[3] And if Søren Kierkegaard is accurate in characterizing the self *as* a relating, the friend then becomes quite truly "another self."[4]

Christianity, then, names a doctrine only secondarily, for the set of beliefs that term connotes forms the skeleton of a flesh-and-blood relating that can only be described as a new mode of life.[5] This relating is a spiritual one, not in the disincarnate sense of that term, but because any intentional relating must be spiritual. As we have seen, the primary sense of "spiritual" derives precisely from our capacity to enter into relationships of this kind. In its inward shape,

2. John S. Dunne, *Time and Myth.*
3. Aristotle, *Nicomachean Ethics*, Book 9.
4. Søren Kierkegaard, *Sickness Unto Death.*
5. Kenneth Kirk, *The Vision of God.*

then, the new life offered us in Christ is at once a gift and a call, and so elicits from us a response of gratitude. It is the character of that response which gives the Christian life its distinctive shape; it is a eucharistic life.

Hence the doctrine of the Spirit intersects with at least three established sectors of Christian theology: (1) that of grace and sacramental life, (2) that of church and ministry, and (3) the distinctively Christian treatment of God as Father, Son, and Holy Spirit. By reminding ourselves at the outset how the Christian life must be conceived as a response to divine initiative, we have underscored the primary element in the doctrine of the Spirit. Since we can hope to understand that initiative, however, only by scrutinizing how Christians have deemed it appropriate to respond, this chapter will concern itself with outlining and analyzing the characteristic forms which that response has taken since the momentous celebration of Pentecost in Jerusalem. By grouping the various responses into characteristic types, we will be able to identify the elements in each which will call forth critical scrutiny and demand some theological assessment. All this is offered, moreover, in an attempt to understand that new relationship offered to us—communally and personally—"in Christ Jesus."

THE DOCTRINE IN ITS CLASSIC FORMULATION

Toward a Definition of the Christian Life

Throughout most of the church's history there has been a fairly well articulated doctrine of the Spirit in relation to the Trinity, but no real doctrine of the Spirit in relation to the Christian life. There have, however, been many influential attempts to give expression to the new relationship to God constituted by Christ and his Spirit, so that it is possible to infer at least the beginnings of such a doctrine. The simplest way to typify these attempts would be to show one set concentrating on the personal implications of this new relationship and another developing its communal dimensions. It would then be convenient to locate a third group attempting to find a middle way to incorporate both perspectives. Such a typology presents two obvious dangers: It reinforces a peculiarly modern contrast between individual and social dimensions, and it may lead us to exaggerate the extremes in order to occupy the more desirable middle ground. Yet in so synoptic a presentation, the best we can do is forewarn ourselves against such inbuilt distortions and proceed with the typology as our best approach to a classic formulation of the doctrine.

I shall work consistently to correct the tendency to oppose individual to community, notably by preferring the word "personal" to "individual." If what distinguishes persons, classically, is their spiritual capacities, and if "spiritual" describes in the first instance one's capacity to relate—to others, to the environment, to oneself, and potentially to all there is—then *person* implies *community*. To be unrelated is to be that much less a person.

One of the ironies of cultural history is that the folkways of more traditional societies could presume this sense of inclusion, since it was effectively communicated by the mores; think of the Greek *polis* for a quite sophisticated example. As individuals were taught to focus more on their own development, however, *relating* turned into an issue. Without the supporting structures, people began to ponder the difficulties involved in relating to others, the environment, and oneself—to say nothing of all that remains. That is a curious self-conception, to be sure, since we all grew up in microcosmic communities; yet it is a clear testimony to the way in which pervasive philosophical perspectives can have a hand in estranging us from our own roots, our very selves.

The doctrine of the Spirit grew as any doctrine grows—now reacting to, now incorporating these shifting cultural horizons. More than most, however, this doctrine first evidenced itself in the hearts of people and those movements which sprang from charismatic initiatives. Invariably, we shall see, these movements expressed a self-understanding of Christian faith as offering an alternative to the current ethos: a sign of God's intention to renew creation, accompanied by an appropriate response on the part of those who would allow themselves to be so transformed. In this way, the initial biblical themes of the Spirit have continued to shape the history of those who have wished to become God's own people and the vanguard of the kingdom of God.

Friendship with God

I suggested at the outset how arresting it is to offer any hope of friendship with God, yet that is precisely what Christianity claims to

305

bestow as well as to promise. The First Letter of John casts this dynamic in terms of familial intimacy:

> My dear people, we are already the children of God
> But what we are to be in the future has not yet been revealed;
> all we know is, that when it is revealed we shall be like him
> because we shall see him as he really is (3:2, JB).

Paul speaks continually of Jesus actually reconciling us to the Father as well as Jews to Gentiles, "destroying in his own person the hostility" so that we are now "part of God's household" or "are being built into a house where God lives, in the Spirit" (Eph. 2:14, 19, 22, JB). While the referent is always a community, what happens can be verified by the individuals themselves in their new relations to one another and to all things—"in the Spirit" or "in Christ."

Hence a central metaphor for articulating the new life bestowed by and in the Spirit becomes friendship with God. The initiative, as we have seen, always lies with the Lord, so that one can also liken this new life to the original disciples' response to Jesus' call to leave everything and follow him. The early monks, epitomized in Anthony (ca. 270), offered dramatic examples of such self-renunciation and quickly became an implicit norm for most Christians. In their desire to conquer their "lower natures," their personal austerities could easily obscure the graciousness of the original call; yet in their counseling capacity they were remembered to be people of exquisite "sweetness," quite clearly on intimate terms with God.[6] The explicit condition of celibacy clearly shows both sides of this response, for it could be understood and lived as a reproach to the rest, who could not help "gratifying their lower natures," or it could be embraced as a way of dramatizing one's wish to respond wholeheartedly to that original invitation.

Augustine is a useful fourth-century witness in this regard, for his attitudes in the *Confessions* display a bit of both. In fact, he never clarifies why he considers his own espousal of Christian faith to be so intimately linked with a celibate way of life—which he clearly does. Perhaps that is because he was still not clear about it ten years after the fact. Yet his account has proved to be as useful as it has because he took so much care to delineate the labyrinthine ways of his own

---

6. In his *Making of Late Antiquity* (Cambridge, Mass.: Harvard University Press, 1978), Peter Brown shows how hermits came to play the role of counselor to many as well as to offer a symbolic focus to specific communities.

eventual response to God—that he was not thereby compelled to "leave the world" to become a monk and engage in singular austerities. So the *Confessions* of Augustine not only manage to translate into a poignantly personal idiom the psalmist's injunction to Israel to proclaim the great deeds God has done for his people, but also offer some initial help in living with that pervasive environment called "the world."

Fledgling Christians have never lacked for advisers in negotiating "the world," but most of these advisers have preferred to formulate rules for others rather than offer an account of the vicissitudes of their own journey. If the distortion attendant on the early monastic response was *rigorism*, the distortion accompanying more domesticated forms of Christianity has always been *formalism*: Our normal penchant for codification, giving way to the "tendency to exaggerate the idea of Christianity as a new law, to substitute obedience for faith, to exalt the precepts above the grace of God."[7] Despite the incisive warning against formalism incorporated into the New Testament personae of "scribes and Pharisees," the penchant to codify always threatens to nullify the root metaphor of friendship with God. Thomas Aquinas, writing in the thirteenth century, crafted the reconciling formula: "The new law is principally the grace of the Holy Spirit . . . written in the hearts of those who believe in Christ." But the power of the legal metaphor usually prevailed to elevate to principal status what he considered secondary, namely, "instruction to the faithful concerning what they should believe and do."[8]

The Psychology of Interiority

The rise of entrepreneurial initiatives, spurred on by the discoveries of untapped regions across the ocean, made the search for God a more and more individual venture. Those who came forward to guide this quest were able to delineate the pathways of personal experience with God to a degree of accuracy and refinement which remains a classic achievement. Four figures—three Spanish and one French—stand out as directors of prayer and the inner life: Ignatius of Loyola, Francis de Sales, John of the Cross, and Teresa of Avila. Each of these was also involved in forming or re-forming a religious congregation as well. Aquinas's creativity should in part be attributed to the new form

7. Kirk, *Vision*, p. 137.
8. *Summa Theologica*, Part 1a2ae, question 106, art. 1.

of religious life for which he explicitly opted over strong familial objections. The friars—inspired by Francis and Dominic—reflected the newfound mobility of the thirteenth century, effecting a presence in town and university centers. Their emergence as an alternative to the more settled monastic order reflects something of the religious pluralism of the medieval period.

By the sixteenth century, however, the sheer number of religious, the diversity of their professions, and the varying degrees of observance displayed would project a decidedly negative impression on the North European Reformers. Furthermore, the fact that these religious continued to embody, however differently, the separation from ordinary life wrought by a threefold commitment to poverty, celibacy, and obedience would give Luther sufficient warrant to consider theirs to be a contrary witness, for so evident an institutionalization of the "two ways" could not but impede lay folk from taking the whole gospel to heart. The very presence of "religious" would itself encourage the vast majority of the faithful to settle for a reduced program, even a minimal one—in short, for a set of "works" proposed by monks for those who would be content with a lesser road.

Indeed, the desire to open the gospel revelation to everyone seemed to permeate this postmedieval age. John of the Cross's insistence that he was writing only for those explicitly called to a life of prayer must be interpreted in the light of the Spanish Inquisition's concern about the number of lay people drawn to prayer. Ignatius developed his "Spiritual Exercises" precisely for seekers of this sort, and Francis de Sales's *Introduction to the Devout Life* was explicitly addressed to "persons living in the world." Whatever form the spirit of reform would take, it clearly reflected a widespread yearning on the part of people in all walks of life to learn how they might respond wholeheartedly to the promises tendered to all people in the gospel. Luther's way of contrasting gospel with law offered a glimpse of the spirit abroad: to recapture what is *new* in the New Testament.

Ignatius of Loyola proposed a way of laying hold of this gospel invitation in a simple yet revolutionary scheme for meditation which released individual readers (or hearers) to put themselves into the particular scene and actively and imaginatively participate in the action. The method advised a close adherence to the gospel narrative itself, and the presence of a director would help to prune luxuriant interpretations by focusing the application onto the course of one's own life. It should be clear, however, how powerful a proposal this was. (It was too powerful even for Ignatius's own religious family, which before a century had elapsed would take unto itself the responsibility for *preaching* the Exercises—a practice only recently reversed in favor of the original emphasis on individual direction.) Yet the medieval legacy of order would prevail—even if in a restrained and somewhat formalistic way—in presenting meditation as a series of steps.

Francis de Sales offered a less rigorous road, and spoke even more freely than Ignatius of the "affections of the heart." Together they helped undermine the presumed prerogatives of the cloister, thereby opening a way of prayer to all people. Moreover, their innate respect for order also tempered the inevitable enthusiasm that can carry the untutored off in bizarre directions. The anxieties of the Inquisition were met not by its repressive tendencies but by opening to all people what had previously been presented as available only to a few. The essential work of the reform was to be carried on in the hearts of believers.

Of Teresa and John of the Cross less need be said. Their influence was not as pervasive as that of Ignatius and Francis de Sales, yet their writings stand as a recurring reference point for students of prayer in each successive age. Christians who find their confessional practice barren may turn to other religious traditions for spiritual nurture. When they do, they will invariably find themselves discovering classics hidden in their own tradition. As this process has occurred in those who have become attuned to meditation, they have found in the writings of John of the Cross and Teresa an especially acute psychology of interiority. It is uncanny how these two writers can articulate features of contemplative practice cognate to Eastern or Islamic traditions, yet do so in a way that is unmistakably a development of the Gospels. Put in a more clinical mode, their success lies in their ability to delineate the psychological contours of a loving human response to divine initiative, and to do so with an accuracy that carries a near guarantee of authenticity.

When we view the polemics of the Reformation in retrospect, it cannot help but appear that the reactions of both sides left a broad sane center unoccupied, and for some time unoccupiable—a virtual no man's land. Luther's violent aversion to monasticism led in two directions at once: to a healthy tolerance of natural joys and recreations and an encouragement of domestic piety, and to a concern that believers themselves put the lie to the traditional doctrine of "two ways" by living the gospel as fully as possible. This latter demand led quite naturally to a renewal of rigorism and legalism, albeit in somewhat different guises, especially among the followers of Calvin and of the Anabaptist movement. These latter showed particular consternation at an antinomian interpretation of the *sola fide* doctrine.

In any case, whatever the promise, Kirk is surely right in saying that "in so far . . . as Christian liberty was the child of the Reformation, it died in infancy."[9] Nor were the issues simply ecclesiastical or political. It is true that except for Anabaptists the Reformers were all too ready to appeal to civil magistrates to enforce church discipline. Yet the difficulty cut even deeper than an unreflective reliance on a traditional alliance between church and state; it emerged in the conflict between a doctrinal avowal which tended to weigh personal assurance of God's forgiveness above everything else, and a growing concern to see the reformed communities clearly distinguish themselves as Christian. Interior communion would clash with external conformity—for a clear distinction demands codification, and is all the clearer for being rigorously so.

God's Own People: A New Israel

We contemporary Americans can easily criticize the Puritan enthusiasm to make a new beginning in a new land, finding it both politically and theologically naive, until we realize how many of our ordinary presumptions embody just such a theology. Why else do we spontaneously consider any situation we meet as a "problem to be solved"? How can we explain the depth of *dis*illusionment accompanying Vietnam unless Americans had been even more deeply "illusioned" about the character of the wars *we* fight? It is important, therefore, to set alongside the more personal modes of embodying the Christian life the communal expectations that have also shaped our thinking and feeling from early times—foremost among them the millenarian expectations that have swept portions of Europe and America since the time of the Crusades.

The principal theologian of this millennialism was Joachim of Fiore, a twelfth-century Calabrian monk. Wars of righteousness had always

9. Kirk, *Vision*, p. 424.

claimed the inspiration of the Spirit, but after his typology of history it was possible to articulate that claim in a distinctive ideology. What he did was propound "an interpretation of history as an ascent through three successive ages, each of them presided over by one of the persons of the Trinity. The first age was the age of the Father or of the law; the second age was the age of the Son or of the gospel; the third age would be the age of the Spirit and . . . would be one of love, joy and freedom, when the knowledge of God would be revealed directly in the hearts of all men."[10] Never was a doctrine (the Trinity) so effectively converted into a social and political ideology. Without so intending it, Joachim had overturned the view accepted since Augustine that the kingdom of God had been realized in principle in the reconciling action of God in Christ, with the actual task of accomplishment turned over to his followers as a leaven in history. It is to these very followers that the Spirit of Jesus has been promised. By detaching the Spirit from the Son and by leaving the age of the Spirit to be determined, Joachim's typology gave to each charismatic leader who would emerge the opportunity of inaugurating this third age by giving a specific interpretation to the apocalyptic pronouncements in the New Testament.

For the next four hundred years, portions of Europe would again and again have to reckon with the stirring proclamation that the new age was upon them. Always appealing to the Spirit, these movements would usually begin with a powerful preacher recalling the people to the purity of their faith in Jesus. The presumed vehicle of that faith— the church and notably the clergy—would be the evident target for the preacher's polemic, who would then be quite naturally drawn to proclaim the age of the Spirit in opposition to the now corrupted age of the Son. The antiestablishment character of such preaching tended to appeal to the dispossessed elements of society, so that Norman Cohn has been able to correlate their rise (and fall) with economic cycles or with large-scale epidemics.

When Luther began to galvanize the religious energies in Saxony to reform Christendom, he was soon confronted in the person of Thomas Müntzer with a yet more radical reformer. A reading of the Augsburg Confession (1530) will show how ardently the lay followers of Luther wished to reform the *ecclesia catholica*, for whatever objec-

10. Norman Cohn, *The Pursuit of the Millennium*, p. 108.

tions they had to Roman practices paled before the opposition they felt it necessary to direct toward "the Anabaptists." They readily perceived how explosive it was to claim the sanction of the Spirit to use the apocalyptic portions of the scriptures to fuel one's own cause. Spiritual illumination would replace learning as the Spirit overcame a worldly church and a corrupt world. The oppositions embodied in the early desert monastic challenge took on a new impetus, given the directing force of Joachim's ideology and the power of a mass movement. Nor was the sword to be laid aside, for the apocalyptic battle had clearly begun.

The most celebrated example of this power at work was certainly the proclamation of the city of Münster as the "New Jerusalem" in 1534. It was to be "purified of all uncleanness," first by expelling any remaining Catholics or Lutherans and then by requiring everyone to be baptized, so that the town would be "inhabited solely by the children of God."[11] As these events presaged, more and more power became concentrated in the theocratic rulers, one of whom soon had himself crowned king. The ecclesiastical and civil powers they had dethroned took their inordinate measure of revenge within the year, reestablishing Münster to its original order. Yet the power of an apocalyptic spiritual movement had been broken only to have been demonstrated.

Secular counterparts have devastated the landscape of the twentieth century, showing how Joachim's typology can be carried to the point where a "third Reich" could be proclaimed, devoid of any connection at all to the age of the Son and yet able to galvanize immense human energies that can only be called "spiritual," even in their utter perversion. If the doctrine of the Spirit—cut loose from its doctrinal moorings as the Spirit of Jesus and devoid of the ecclesial disciplines of worship and service—can wreak such havoc, some indirect testimony is rendered to its power for transformation as well and to the correlative inadequacy of a "merely rational" account of human life. As our century has displayed in grotesque ways, replacing a religious idiom by a secular one only hinders the necessary task of discerning what spirit is indeed at work.

11. Ibid., pp. 261–80.

CHALLENGES AND CONTRIBUTIONS OF
MODERN CONSCIOUSNESS

The Pattern of Christendom

Once we grasp *spirit* as the capacity for relating, we will more easily understand the peculiar ways in which modern consciousness has challenged this doctrine. Indeed, one might even say that it was only in the modern period that the doctrine of the Spirit came into its own, for under the pressures of modernity the church was led to broaden the doctrine as never before and to give it a "secular" and not merely ecclesiastical meaning. What was previously developed to articulate the individual's relation to God, or what erupted as a novel .way of organizing humankind's response to God's invitation, had now to be made explicit for everyone. In its struggle to free itself from social and political patterns shaped by ecclesiastical and hierarchical presumptions, the Enlightenment was to force the church to relate to the world and, in doing so, to show more actively just how we are called to relate to one another and to the Creator of all.

The dynamic is subtle but obvious once it is recognized. As long as the church had been accepted as the place where one relates to God (as in "going to church") and was also presumed to offer legitimacy to the social order, there was no need actively to relate either to the Lord or to the surrounding world. As long as one belonged to a worshiping community and played out a proper social role, things were in order. It is plausible to trace this state of affairs to Constantine's incorporation of the Christian religion as the official cult of the empire, though it took many centuries for the pattern to coalesce. Once it did, however, in the set of structures known as Christendom, that movement which originated as a call to friendship with divinity came rather to serve as the central "plausibility structure" for an entire society.[12] Monastic and religious communities offered alternatives within the structure, where the call to discipleship and service was explicitly taken up; yet those very efforts, while displaying the transforming power of the Spirit, also legitimated the overall pattern as it made room for them as well.

---

12. For the notion of "plausibility structure," see Peter L. Berger and Thomas Luckmann, *Social Construction of Reality* (New York: Doubleday, 1967).

This grand conception inspired much of Western art and architecture as well as the flourishing philosophical and theological activity of the Middle Ages. Many classical thinkers incorporated this vision of a Christian society into their syntheses, offering it as an elegant justification. Yet the pattern proved vulnerable to economic and social factors which emerged, along with intellectual rumblings, to challenge its validity. At the same time, doubtless influenced by these seams appearing in the robe, some perceived a spiritual lacuna as well. What we now call the Reformation began as a series of reform movements which the larger ecclesial unity proved unable to assimilate. The authors of the Augsburg Confession placed themselves firmly within the Catholic church, proposing to alter its policies and structures precisely with a view to mission—to the more adequate relating of revelation to the world in which they lived. As we have noted, the pattern of Christendom often prevailed so that reformed bodies were incorporated into the body politic in the established fashion. Yet the challenge had been issued: The church must measure itself against its gospel mandate and articulate its mission to the world.

The call to a mission demands an explicit activity of relating; the Spirit is called forth when Christendom wanes. The history of missions as we know them, of course, often represented valiant efforts to transplant the structures of an established church to other lands and cultures. A pattern as pervasive as Christendom will inevitably persist, and in fairness it should be said that its noble vision continued to inspire generous workers. Still there were efforts both in Europe and abroad to establish a new social and political synthesis. Where it did not jell, the reaction of taking refuge in one's individual relationship to God betrayed the mission in another way, "saving" the individual soul but leaving the world as an organized fabric of human relations to shift for itself. What was needed was a new set of images and metaphors that would do justice to the Spirit by developing explicit patterns of relating to God's world as well as to God's own self.

Secular Challenges to the Christian Life

Images latent in a tradition as rich as Christianity have a way of arising in response to needs and challenges such as this, and the nineteenth and twentieth centuries were certainly no exception. But before we consider the new ways of conceiving the Christian life which developed from within the tradition, we need to acknowledge the challenge to Christianity that came from outside, in particular from the great secular movements of the day, for if there has been one major impetus for the church to engage the world in the modern period, it has been the emergence of secular movements which challenged its claim to be a transforming power for the good in human affairs and offered in its place alternative schemes of salvation. I shall call attention to three such schemes, each of which has its roots in the nineteenth century and has nearly run its course in the twentieth: Marxism, Freudian psychotherapy, and the cult of progress.

Marxism

Tawney called Marx the "last of the scholastics" because he presumed to have forged a theory comprehensive enough to offer a thoroughgoing analysis of the workings of human society. Machiavelli had challenged the Aristotelian model of explaining social organization from a goal related to human good. Liberal political thought had come to replace the common good with competing interest groups. The marketplace became a pervasive image for the play of social and political ideas as well as of economic forces. So there was considerable precedent for employing economic metaphors to illuminate social and political process, yet no one had been so bold as Marx to offer a straightforward explanation squarely on the basis of economic behavior, making everything else in society turn specifically on the mode of ownership of the means of production.

Alter that fundamental economic feature of a society, and everything else will follow, Marx argued, including the transformation of human relations within a family; for economic organization governs everything else. Marx had much more to say, of course, and especially about the quality of relationship that should characterize human life, but what singles him out is his confident assertion that he had found the key to human transformation and social interaction in an economic theory. In that respect, Marx was typically a child of the Enlightenment and specifically of Hegel; scholastic explanatory schemes, while far-reaching, tended to be more holistic in conception. Marx's disdain for politics, which he consistently regarded as foolishness, follows directly from his single-strand explanatory model.

On the other hand, his idealized patterns for human interaction, involving maximal participation of each worker in all phases of production, never quite squared with the simple economic advantage associated with division of labor. So a reader of Marx will always feel the discrepancy between his descriptions and the procedures we have come to associate with Marxist-Leninist strategies.

Contemporary European Marxists continue to debate whether his animosity to religion as the "opiate of the people" follows directly from his materialistic metaphysics, which would of course find no room for worship; or whether his perspective was unalterably clouded by the alliance between the churches in Europe and the *ancien régime*, reestablished so insistently at the Congress of Vienna. Much of the discussion turns on the actual relevance of materialism—largely that of Friedrich Engels—to Marx's social theory. What has certainly proven to be the case, however, is that Marxist societies have no way of justifying anything so useless as worship. Harnessing the spirit to work for human betterment raises, before long, severe questions regarding one's goals for humankind. Whether the pinch is felt in worship or in the creative arts, it does not take long before some will ask: Does this improvement represent our real good? or Is it worth the human cost entailed?

Such questions are seldom raised from a situation of manifest oppression, so Marxism remains a powerful lure as an alternative to economic servitude. Yet one cannot help but be struck by the vagueness of Marx's own vision for human society. It is as though he simply *believed* that so basic an economic alteration could only lead the people somewhere better. Notwithstanding this telling lacuna, however, his program of economic analysis initiated a powerful consciousness-raising instrument. To be able to trace the lines of power affecting one's current destiny represents an obvious advantage, even if that knowledge will not of itself spell out a constructive alternative.

It is, of course, the character of that alternative, as actually displayed in societies which have adopted the analysis as a program, which gives one reflective pause before Marx's promise of a viable salvation scheme for human society. Yet carrying out the analysis to a point of self-reflection promises far greater self-awareness than pursuing an anticommunist crusade, for however one is brought to assess Marx's theory, it offers the intellectual leverage we have come to find in any powerful conceptual scheme. And its premises can awaken a Christian believer to dimensions of the gospel often left unexamined in a nominally Christian society.

Freud

The name "Freud" stands not only for an individual, Sigmund Freud, but also for an entire movement, including branches at variance with Freud's explicit teachings—notably followers of Carl Jung. Yet the fact of doctrinal differences has proven less significant in the long run than the introduction of a distinctive and definite "psychological point of view." Not unlike Marx, Freud had aspired to an explanation of the workings of the individual psyche which was thoroughly scientific, materialist in its essential elements, and related to a single dynamic feature: repression of libidinal (sexual) energy. Much about his Victorian clientele reinforced such a single-minded explanatory scheme, although some of his more independent coworkers (notably Alfred Adler and Jung) challenged it relatively early on therapeutic as well as logical grounds. Moreover, Freud's own therapeutic experience led him to postulate a second drive—the "death-instinct"—to account for pathological phenomena which he could not relate to the basic dynamics of repression. Yet his demand for a single explanatory scheme remained for him a scientific ideal.

Religion stood squarely in the way of Freud's program, as it did for Marx, and for roughly the same reasons: It distracted from the concentrated effort it would take to put the program into practice. For Freud, religion offered an irrational escape from the business at hand of clearly identifying the sources of repression, and it conveniently served as a massive projection device whereby familial dynamics might be displaced to a cosmic theater. Moreover, his experience was that religious practice contributed far more to psychic pathology than it offered by way of healing.

Intellectually, again like Marxism, the movement inspired by Freud conspired with a skeptical temper and with the ethical reduction of Christianity to render religion superfluous, or at least to ask that it defend itself in therapeutic terms. That such a ploy could even succeed for a while, however, testifies to the collusion of the elements noted, for Freud, like Marx, is notoriously vague in his conception of a healthy individual. In fact, his own descriptions of a psychological cure usually amount to some form of social adjustment. Yet if society is itself enmeshed in oppressive practices, adjusting oneself to them can hardly be adjudged a success. Here the interaction of Marx's analyses with Freud's proposals has led to particularly fruitful discussions of the human good—personal and social —yet more to the detriment than the enhancement of their particular theories. If Marx's scheme tends to overlook the individual, Freud's program for individuals remains quite blind to systemic disorder.

More recent writers in a Freudian vein—notably Norman O. Brown and Ernest Becker—have sought to combine these two perspectives. Brown tends to resolve the difficulties by recourse to a utopian social order ruled by a freedom from repression. Writing later and in appreciation of Brown, Becker nevertheless criticizes his solution as naive.[13] He traces the roots of human malaise to a repression yet more basic than the sexual: a repressed fear of death. This strategy allows him to incorporate both the drives which Freud contended were at work into a yet more basic dynamism stemming from our unconscious handling of our impending demise. By focusing on so existential a theme, Becker finds himself turning to such theological writers as Søren Kierkegaard and Paul Tillich, discovering their analyses to be more serviceable to his project of understanding and more congenial to therapeutic practice, rather than pretending to a more rigidly scientific scheme.

Cult of Progress

I have identified each of these schemes as offering alternatives to the human transformation promised in Christ and have associated each with the nineteenth century (for Freud's scientific attitudes more clearly square with the century past than with our own). I also suggested that each has nearly run its course in the twentieth century. That may sound strange, given the actual hold and potential attraction of Marxism for so many millions of people, and the virtual intellectual hegemony of some psychological viewpoints over the West. Yet I would contend that few regard these ideologies any longer as salvation schemes, because their record at human improvement is incredibly mixed and their resources to articulate a good for

13. The key works are Norman O. Brown's *Life Against Death* and Ernest Becker's *The Denial of Death*.

humankind have proven to be peculiarly weak. The same can be said for the Western counterpart to Marxism: economic growth and progress. In fact, Anthony Burgess's stringent satire A *Clockwork Orange*, projecting a generation into the future, dramatizes how similarly bankrupt in value structure are the capitalist and Marxist worlds.

Progress takes on cultic trappings when it resists analysis and becomes identified with annual percentage growth in gross national product. No one may ask whether such an increment actually contributes to human betterment, even though ironies abound. The squeeze on developing nations is especially telling when one appreciates what fraction of their total resources needs to be expended on status symbols like jet aircraft for a national airline, not to mention showy armaments. Yet so-called developed nations have come to realize as well the remote and proximate ceilings on their resources (or access to resources). The near proximity between decolonization and the publishing of *Limits to Growth* was hardly coincidental. The Club of Rome was bound to be more sensitive than American entrepreneurs to limitations on access to resources, yet the United States' programmed dependence on oil brought the same message home a decade later.

E. F. Schumacher's likening of resources to capital investment put the matter dramatically: We have been digging into the principal for some time now.[14] This homely analogy would fail to make its point, of course, were the natural endowment unlimited, for any fraction of infinity is itself infinite. So the peculiar heedlessness which has fueled the myth of indefinite progress involved a simple presumption of boundless resources. At just this point the myth supported a salvation scheme called "unlimited development."

Renewal of the Spirit

The foregoing critical appraisal of these three schemes for human development offers an object lesson in forging a doctrine of the Spirit and the Christian life. It is that special perspective on the human which derives from a worshiping community that allows one to see these three as salvation schemes. The same perspective allows us to profit from their way of understanding humankind without needing

14. E. F. Schumacher, *Small Is Beautiful* (New York: Harper & Row, 1973), chap. 1.

to adopt their pretense to save. Nor need we trouble to refute them, for that would hinder our learning from them. If they cannot succeed in saving humankind, they can nevertheless help us discover new ways of understanding and expressing the saving power of God. So have Christians learned to appreciate various proposals for a secular social order; in denying religion its conventional role, they have left room for the Spirit to call forth new ways of relating the power of the gospel to human institutions.

What has resulted is a church renewed in ways of which the early Reformers could never have dreamed, and in an ecumenical spirit of unity which seeks to overcome the divisions that the Reformation handed on to us. We can see this especially in those parts of the world where the church has been constrained to find new ways of being an evangelical community to societies in change or especially resistant to change: in South America, Africa, and Asia especially, yet with resonances in North America and Europe as well.[15] In a neat reversal the Christian peoples who sent missionaries in recent centuries are now receiving a fresh witness from those very people whom once they taught. It remains to be seen whether we will prove as receptive as they were.

Yet this witness did not emerge overnight. It has been in preparation for more than a century in theological inquiries into fruitful ways for believers to relate to a world in the making and to influence the shape it takes. Individual piety is never enough, for individuals presuppose a social order. Yet Christianity in the post-Christendom era often settled for a program of piety, lacking the imagination to formulate a new relation to society. It is to the credit of nineteenth-century German theologians like Johann Adam Möhler and early twentieth-century French thinkers like Yves Congar and Henri de Lubac that a fresh understanding of church-to-the-world was developed to the point where it could break out in the deliberations and actions of Vatican II (1962–65).[16]

Working closely with lay movements, and so embodying a new fashion of thinking and acting, theologians learned to reflect on

15. For a useful survey see Walbert Buhlmann, *The Coming of the Third Church*.
16. The standard source is *The Documents of Vatican II*, ed. Walter M. Abbott (New York: Guild Press, 1966). The key work of Henri de Lubac is *Catholicism: A Study of Dogma in Relation to the Corporate Destiny of Mankind* (London: Burns, Oates & Washbourne, 1950). The work of Möhler and others has been summarized in Leonard Swidler, *Aufklärung Catholicism 1780–1850* (Missoula: Scholars Press, 1978).

social and political processes in the terms of those fashioning them. They also took heart and vision from church leaders who called for Christians to take up the traditional cause of the poor and oppressed in a more organized fashion, notably the social encyclicals of Popes Leo XIII (1891), Pius XI (1931), and John XXIII (1962). By demanding that believers assume a social and political position somewhere between Marxism and liberal capitalism, these messages reached a world wider than the Catholic faithful and wider even than the Christian churches, showing all people how the Spirit of Jesus might give direction to new societies in the making.

Anyone who reads *Rerum Novarum* (1891) with even a passing acquaintance with Marx will immediately note how Pope Leo XIII was able to learn from Marx's analysis of society, yet avoid his messianic pretenses by connecting that analysis with a rich tradition of social teaching. It was their earlier collaboration in the Resistance with all manner of unbelievers which inspired French theologians in the 1950s to develop views on the relation of Christ's kingdom to the world—views which underlay Vatican II's "Declaration on the Church in the Modern World" and which have been a formative influence for Latin American theologies of liberation.[17] Needless to say, individuals and governments who preferred the Christendom model, however vestigial, or who were more comfortable with a "privatized" religion, have been quick to brand these efforts as "communist." Yet they can be distinguished from Marxist ideology precisely in their clear affirmation of a transcendent human destiny, and unlike their critics, they challenge Christians to relate to the world in which we live. In this passionate concern for *relating* the promise of God to the facts of human existence, and humankind to the yet undiscovered reaches of that promise, we can most clearly see the doctrine of the Spirit developing, and at work, in our time.

ISSUES AND PROPOSALS

The transformations Christianity has undergone in recent decades testify to a smoldering vitality in the churches whose patterns seemed to have continued in the mold of Christendom. In many corners of the world and in different strata of society can be found the leavening

---

17. A glance at the documentation in Gustavo Gutiérrez's A *Theology of Liberation* will verify this lineage.

presence of men and women ministering to human need. Witnessing to that secret vitality are ministries which have emerged to conform themselves to the shape of specific needs. In each case, people have found in the gospel a way of better understanding how to see what others have overlooked and how to respond to what they see.

Among the various images for this renewed sense of ministry to the world, that which offers greatest promise is the image of a "pilgrim people." It was appealing to the dissenters who wished to begin again in the New World and, under quite different circumstances, to the bishops assembled three centuries later in Rome for the Second Vatican Council. Each group intended to renew its church with a view to renewing the world. The sense of being a *people* picks up the communitarian dimension emphasized in the millenarian movements, while the quality of *pilgrim* connotes the journey of faith underscored by those intent on friendship with God. In other words, the ministry of those who follow Jesus intends to be a force powerful enough to revolutionize the social order, yet from within as a leaven.

The problem is that the polarities so often experienced in our lives as opposites—individual/society, mystical/revolutionary, contemplative/active—incline us all too easily to adapt the gospel to one pole or another. This very fact, however, may suggest a redefinition of the Spirit as that power which permits us to hope for what history has shown humankind so incapable of realizing: the reconciliation of these very opposites. Such a formulation would contain the principal elements of the classic doctrine of the Spirit: a divine initiative eliciting the sort of response which calls forth a community. It would also remind us that we can never claim a clear vision of that divine initiative, but can only discern its character as it reveals itself in the contours of the community shaped by our response to it.

With this understanding in mind, let us conclude by considering three practical issues confronting Christians who would be responsive to the Spirit in the present day.

1. *Ecological Alternatives.* The point of view singled out as "ecological" is nothing but an attempt to *think* the world in which we live as systemically as that world is itself organized. Like the decision to begin calculating costs we have cavalierly called "externalities," it can only be regarded as good sense to use advances in systems analysis and cybernetics to attempt to understand the complex information

system we know nature to be. Yet keeping our consciousness so alert calls for a sense of responsibility we would prefer to evade. Whether we will allow ourselves to continue to do so will in part depend on the larger story into which we insert ourselves and the natural world.

The Genesis accounts of creation form the setting in which Christians and Jews can allow their attitudes toward the world to be shaped. The rabbinic commentaries converge on a central theme: Everything which the Lord God made and saw to be good is in some measure entrusted to those whom he created in his own image, created male and female. The rest of creation is given over to this one part of creation which images the Creator. But to what end? The text itself is unclear; the terse command "Be fruitful, multiply, fill the earth and conquer it" (Gen. 1:28, JB) hardly describes a task. The commentaries flesh it out: to continue the creation God himself began. Then the necessity for the *shabbat* appears. Without so insistent a reminder we would soon presume the work to be completely our own; we would forget how it had been given us, and that we were to think of ourselves as continuing the work of the Lord.

"Steward" is the New Testament image for our status: Luke 16–18 spells out discipleship in terms appropriate to stewardship. To be entrusted with something for which we are to care—such is the invitation extended to those called to act according to that divine image within them. Yet to image ourselves in so subordinate a status will inevitably appear demeaning. Some day some among us are bound to ask why they are not boss. Several answers may be given to such a question, yet there is one only that will be able to be heard— some tangible reminder that in this domain my glory lies not in initiating but in responding. Something analogous to the *shabbat* must provide Christians with an ear to hear the rest of creation convey the message Augustine ascribes to all things: "We did not make ourselves, but he who abides forever made us" (*Confessions* 9.10). It seems that nothing short of a periodic encounter with the contemplative dimension within ourselves, where our spirit meets the Spirit, can hope to reorient us to be stewards—continuing God's creation by caring for it.

2. *Aspirations to Justice.* The social and political analogue to an environmental consciousness demands more sane measures of economic well-being than gross increments in production and consump-

tion. Goals for development are being scrutinized, whether the arena be the first, second, or third world, as thinking about growth encounters concern with equity. And *equity* can be identified with that proportionality which Aristotle introduces into any discussion of justice, not with "equal distribution." The tendency for those preoccupied with justice to favor a planning model elicits understandable fears from more classical economists and most average citizens, yet it need not follow that we must oppose a desire for freedom to a concern for justice. In fact, the time-honored principle of subsidiarity, which pushes decision-making to the viable social or political unit closest to the issue, can often help mediate standard conservative/liberal discussions on these issues.

What is becoming increasingly clear, in fact, is that no society can survive, much less pursue, goals that offer some viable future for humankind, without the constant catalyst of "mediating structures."[18] A review of the social encyclicals delivered over the past century by each successive pope, together with the literature forming the social gospel movement from Walter Rauschenbusch to Reinhold Niebuhr to the most recent statements of the World Council of Churches, reveals a concerted attempt to wrest the discussion of justice from Marxist hands by scrutinizing standard Marxist presuppositions and claiming yet more consistent grounds for pursuit of justice in the Christian tradition. I say more consistent because that tradition recognizes richer dimensions to the human person than Marxist theory will allow, and more *politically* consistent because it is predicated on the free action of subgroups within a society, notably ecclesial and prophetic associations.

3. *Action as Response.* The human ideal presumed by liberal political theory and spelled out in current Western literature on human development is exemplified by the autonomous individual. The worth of such individuals will be measured by their achievements: Their association with one another is considered to be secondary (if not peripheral) to those achievements, and any lasting or systemic bonds would have to be regarded as incidental, however much one might desire them. The self so conceived is initiator par exellence. Indeed, that is what *autonomy* amounts to: being a self-starter.

18. Peter L. Berger and Richard John Neuhaus, *To Empower People: The Role of Mediating Structures in Public Policy.*

But what if such a one were to succeed in these terms, only to find success tasting more like defeat? What if the touted capacity to move oneself were to feel more and more like being driven? What if, after living by and into such a conception of ourselves, we were to yearn for the unaffected relatedness of friendship, only to find ourselves ill-equipped for it? These themes are familiar in contemporary literature, and they can only reveal a growing disillusionment with the prevailing story of an autonomous self. More positively expressed as a quest for community, this desire too can easily give way before the taxing demands of communal endeavors, for the tasks involved, both personal and public, are strictly incompatible with a self-image that aspires to an ideal of autonomy.

The New Testament contains an even more trenchant critique yet offers a promise as well, utilizing images that have the power to recast our individual and communal stories. The transforming images are contained in the passion narratives of Jesus. They are framed to bring us to the point where we recognize how the pursuit of autonomy necessarily involves crucifying that self in each of us who would otherwise recognize Jesus to be the "Son of man"—that is, the one whom our heart desires. That recognition is essential to understanding how the death of Jesus can be an atonement for our sins and the resurrection of Jesus our new life.[19] The response is itself ingredient in the action of atonement, just as the recognition releases us to a new self-conception: that in one situation (the most self-shaping and significant of all) it is better to be second than first, better to respond than to initiate. In that constituting relation, whereby the self is "grounded in the power that constitutes it" (Kierkegaard), the most exalted agency is response.

The effect of such a realization should alter one's entire attitude, one's characteristic way of relating to everything else! Yet that capacity—the capacity to be related to all that is—is what we call "spirit." Hence the power to alter our actual relationship to *everything* rightly deserves the name "Spirit": the Holy Spirit or, as the New Testament tends to prefer, the Spirit of Jesus. To become in the roots of one's being a *responder* is, in the words of John, to "receive the Holy Spirit" (20:22). The consequence of that reception is a new

19. Sebastian Moore, *The Crucified Jesus Is No Stranger.*

325

receptivity spelled out in various new capacities which were hitherto impossibilities: Forgiven, we might forgive others (John 20:23); healed, we might now heal, unafraid even of deadly poison (Mark 16:18). The initiator may be vulnerable, but the responder can no longer be harmed.

The promise of the Spirit, then, is the promise of a new sort of life—at once a participation in the inner life of God and an activation of that divine image which each of us was created to display. That activation must be a liberation, however, from the posturing to which we are all so prone, the pretense of autonomy. The specific contribution of the doctrine of the Spirit is to show us how that liberation takes place: by altering our very self-conception above all to become responders to the initiative of God in our behalf. By articulating that initiative as Father, Son, and Holy Spirit, the Christian tradition provides us with abundant reminders of the inner life of God. The doctrine of the Spirit indicates how we may participate therein, becoming new selves and "friends of God."

SUGGESTIONS FOR FURTHER READING

Barrett, C. K. *The Holy Spirit and the Gospel Tradition.* London: S.P.C.K. 1966.

Barth, Karl. *Church Dogmatics.* Vol. 4/4, pp. 3–40.

Becker, Ernest. *The Denial of Death.* New York: Free Press, 1973.

Berger, Peter, and Neuhaus, Richard. *To Empower People: The Role of Mediating Structures in Public Policy.* Washington: American Enterprise Institute for Public Policy Research, 1977.

Bonhoeffer, Dietrich. *The Cost of Discipleship.* New York: Macmillan Co., 1963.

Brown, Norman O. *Life against Death.* New York: Vintage Books, 1959.

Bühlmann, Walbert. *The Coming of the Third Church.* Maryknoll, N.Y.: Orbis Books, 1977.

Cohn, Norman. *Pursuit of the Millennium.* New York: Oxford University Press, 1970.

Congar, Yves. *I Believe in the Spirit.* 3 Volumes, translated by David Smith. New York: Seabury Press, 1983.

Dunne, John S. *Time and Myth.* New York: Doubleday, 1973.

Francis de Sales. *Introduction to the Devout Life.* New York: Doubleday, 1972.

Ignatius of Loyola. *Spiritual Exercises.* New York: Doubleday, 1973.

Joachim of Fiore. *Apocalyptic Spirituality.* Edited and translated by Bernard McGinn. New York: Paulist Press, 1979.

John of the Cross. *Collected Works.* Edited by K. Kavanaugh and O. Rodriguez. Washington: Institute of Carmelite Studies, 1970.

Kierkegaard, Søren. *The Sickness unto Death.* Translated by Howard V. Hong and Edna H. Hong. Princeton: Princeton University Press, 1980.

Kirk, Kenneth. *The Vision of God.* New ed. Edinburgh: J. Clarke, 1977.

Kovel, Joel. *History and Spirit: An Inquiry into the Philosophy of Liberation.* Boston: Beacon Press, 1991.

Lampe, George. *God as Spirit.* London: SCM Press, 1977.

Law, William. *A Serious Call to a Devout and Holy Life.* Edited by Paul Stanwood. New York: Paulist Press, 1978.

Lubac, Henri de. *The Church: Paradox and Mystery.* New York: Alba House, 1969.

Moore, Sebastian. *The Crucified Jesus Is No Stranger.* New York: Seabury Press, 1977.

———. *The Fire and the Rose Are One.* New York: Seabury Press, 1980.

Phillips, D. Z. *The Concept of Prayer.* London: Routledge & Kegal Paul, 1965.

Prenter, Regin. *Spiritus Creator.* Philadelphia: Muhlenberg, 1953.

Rahner, Karl. *On Prayer.* New York: Paulist Press, 1968.

———. *Theological Investigations,* vol. 3.

Robinson, H. W. *The Christian Experience of the Holy Spirit.* London: Nisbet, 1928.

Smith, Steven G. *The Concept of the Spiritual: An Essay in First Philosophy.* Philadelphia: Temple University Press, 1988.

Smith, Wilfred Cantwell. *Faith and Belief.* Princeton: Princeton University Press, 1979.

Teresa of Avila. *Collected Works:* Washington: Institute of Carmelite Studies, 1977–.

Williams, Robert. *Recognition: Fichte and Hegel on the Other.* Albany: State University of New York Press, 1992.

12. THE KINGDOM OF GOD AND LIFE EVERLASTING

WHERE WE ARE

Eschatology has traditionally been defined as the doctrine of "the last things." It appeared as the final chapter in the classic systems of dogmatics under the heading *de novissimis* in Latin and *ta eschata* in Greek texts. This dogmatic locus dealt with events that still belong to the future, such as death and resurrection, the last judgment and the end of the world, eternal damnation (hell) and eternal life (heaven). It covered the future destiny of each individual after death as well as the final consummation of the world.

In the period of Protestant scholasticism (seventeenth century), the treatment of eschatological topics became petrified in the last chapter of dogmatics. Karl Barth spoke ironically of this approach as "lulling us to sleep by adding at the conclusion of Christian Dogmatics a short and perfectly harmless chapter entitled—'Eschatology.'"[1] To a large extent the mainline churches, both Protestant and Roman Catholic, permitted the sects to claim the subject of eschatology as their specialty. Their literalistic preaching from the Bible about the end of the world has tended to inoculate the mainline bodies of Christianity against this virus of eschatology.[2] Despite this fact there has occurred a renaissance of eschatological thinking in twentieth-century theology unparalleled in the history of Christian thought.

Eschatology is no longer confined to the concluding chapter of dogmatics as teaching about the last things. The whole of Christian theology is penetrated by eschatology. Every theological statement is at the same time an eschatological statement in the sense that eschatology deals with what is ultimate, and to speak of God is to speak of our "ultimate concern" (Tillich). There is a consensus among the various schools of theology that the eschatological perspective is basic

---

1. Karl Barth, *The Epistle to the Romans*, p. 500.
2. The most popular example of this type of literalism is Hal Lindsey's *The Late Great Planet Earth* (Grand Rapids: Zondervan, 1973).

to the understanding of the Christian faith. At the beginning of his long theological career, Barth inaugurated the eschatological renaissance in Christian theology with this striking claim: "Christianity that is not entirely and altogether eschatology has entirely and altogether nothing to do with Christ."[3] Echoing this mandate a half century later, Jürgen Moltmann insisted: "The eschatological is not one element *of* Christianity, but it is the medium of Christian faith as such. . . . Hence eschatology cannot really be only a part of Christian doctrine. Rather, the eschatological outlook is characteristic of all Christian proclamation, of every Christian existence and of the whole church."[4]

There are several reasons for the emphasis on eschatology in today's theology. The first reason is the general philosophical discovery of the phenomenon of hope in human existence that generates questions pointing in the direction of eschatology.[5] The second reason is the historical rediscovery of the eschatological core of the message of Jesus and of biblical faith as a whole.[6] Leading philosophers and psychologists—Bloch, Marcel, Marcuse, Fromm, Polak, Ricoeur, Maslow, Menninger, and numerous others—have made noteworthy contributions to the phenomenology of hope in human existence. The meaningfulness of Christian eschatology depends on its structural correspondence to the factor of hope in human life. Eschatology promises fulfillment; hope presupposes something lacking. Human beings hope for what they lack. If we are in bondage, we hope for deliverance; if we sit in darkness, we hope for light. The lack may be described by such metaphors as illness, darkness, slavery, alienation, lostness, exile, even death. It is the mission of hope to respond to a situation of distress by sending out a signal for help.

Correlated with this existential phenomenology of hope is the renewal of biblical eschatology that began around the turn of the century with the studies of Johannes Weiss and Albert Schweitzer. The renaissance of eschatology was brought about as a result of the application of the historical-scientific method to the study of the New Testament. The historical knowledge that the eschatological theme

3. Barth, *Epistle to the Romans*, p. 314.
4. Jürgen Moltmann, *Theology of Hope*, p. 16.
5. See, e.g., Ernst Bloch, *Das Prinzip Hoffnung* (Frankfurt: Suhrkamp Verlag, 1959).
6. See Johannes Weiss's seminal work of 1892, *Jesus' Proclamation of the Kingdom of God*.

lies at the heart of the Bible and determined the message of Jesus and early Christianity became all the more influential in theology by the fact that scholars like Weiss and Schweitzer had no theological interest in their own findings. They were not pro-eschatological; they looked upon the eschatological outlook of the Bible as antiquated. Their purely historical findings were not integrated into their own modern religious interpretation of faith and life.

The eschatological hypothesis in biblical interpretation produced a serious crisis in theology. If eschatology belongs to the essence of primitive Christianity but appears unintelligible to the modern mind, how is it possible to interpret what is essentially Christian in terms that make sense today? It could be that eschatological thought is a dead issue for modern people, including Christians among them. The relevance of eschatology cannot be established simply by showing how "biblical" it is. It took the crisis of modern culture to open the imagination to new ways of interpreting biblical eschatology. Since then theology has been productive of many types of eschatology, differentiated both by how they interpret the meaning of eschatology in the New Testament and how they understand its relevance for modern times.

THE DOCTRINE IN ITS CLASSIC FORMULATION

The Biblical Roots of Eschatology

One of the chief problems of biblical interpretation has been that of finding the thread of continuity that ties the two testaments of the Bible together. Since the awakening of the eschatological perspective in theology, it has become evident that the people of God, from the days of Israel in the Old Testament to the period of the church in the New, have moved forward in history in expectation of future salvation, however much this expectation was always founded on historical events in which God had intervened in the past.

In the Old Testament the coming of eschatological salvation was announced in different terms, for example, the day of Yahweh, the day of judgment, the coming of the Messiah, the kingdom of God, and the new Jerusalem. The eschatology of Israel underwent a continual process of change and development. Originally Israel held a predominantly this-worldly eschatology; its vision of the promised future belonged to this world of space and time. This is the case with early prophetic eschatology. The prophets expected a coming paradise *on earth*. The coming kingdom, which Yahweh was to establish for his people, enjoyed the same material reality as the promised land. It would be a land flowing with milk and honey. The faithful remnant of Israel would be drawn to the holy mountain as their dwelling place. There is no specific hope for heaven or life after death. Salvation will be something to see; the earth will be extremely fruitful, people will be inwardly renewed, society will become righteous, and the nations will be at peace. Israel, the least of the nations, will be exalted above all the others, provided the people remain faithful to the ancient covenant.

The Israelites began to have doubts that the prophetic vision of a future paradise would ever be translated into the world of here and now, or even that they would ever be delivered from exile and return to the homeland. Gradually, otherworldly eschatological traits were mingled with future hope as they came into contact with Iranian and Hellenistic influences. A process of transcending took place which shifted the focus of attention from this world to the next, a transition that would be mediated by an apocalyptic transformation of the present age into a spiritual realm beyond space and time.

Apocalyptic eschatology flourished especially during the period between the two testaments, although it had already made its breakthrough in the postexilic books of the Old Testament, particularly Daniel, Ezekiel, and Second Isaiah. Apocalypticism, however, was not wholly discontinuous with earlier prophetic eschatology. Both kept the fires of hope burning for salvation and liberation during times of wretchedness and oppression. Both pictured the God of Israel as the God of history who will come to change the world, to put down what is evil and recreate what is good both for Israel and for the nations. Nevertheless, Jewish apocalypticism brought new dimensions into eschatological thought, preparing the stage for Jesus' message of the kingdom of God.

Apocalypticism sharpened the contrast between this age and the age to come. It depicted a complete break in time, prophesying calamity and chaos of cosmic proportions before the new age could dawn. The contrast between good and evil was drawn in black and white terms, painted against the backdrop of a dualism of opposing forces,

God and the devil. Demonology and angelology also entered in. The powers of God and the devil were mediated in human history and the world by good and evil spirits. Writings that claimed to hold the secret to the revealed mysteries concerning the end-time were published under pseudonyms borrowed from such famous Old Testament figures as Adam, Noah, Enoch, Abraham, and Daniel. These writings are called apocalyptic because "apocalypse" means "revelation." They contain esoteric revelations, expressed in numbers and symbols, of the whole course of world history and the plan of salvation from beginning to end. The apocalyptic trend thus moved away from earthly to heavenly expectations, from seeking a better future in history for Israel and the nations to a totally other destiny of humanity and the world above and beyond history.

The Christian revision of Jewish apocalyptic eschatology was determined by the modifications which Jesus of Nazareth himself effected through his preaching of the kingdom of God and the double ending of his life: his *death* on the cross and his *resurrection* to a new form of being. The central motif of Jesus' message was the coming kingdom of God. The eschatological rule of God which Jesus preached was the power determining both the content of his message and the activities of his ministry. However, there is no consensus among contemporary theologians on how to interpret Jesus' expectation of the kingdom of God. Did Jesus think of the kingdom of God as something otherworldly and future (traditional orthodoxy)? Or as something otherworldly and present (Karl Barth and dialectical theology)? Or as something this-worldly and present (Rudolf Bultmann and existentialist theology)? Or as something this-worldly and future (Christian Marxism and liberation theology)? Perhaps there is an element of truth in all these viewpoints, each forming one facet of a multidimensional vision of the kingdom of God.

A major debate among New Testament scholars is whether Jesus built on the foundations of apocalyptic eschatology current in his time or reached back to the earlier forms of prophetic eschatology. There has been a tendency among scholars to exempt Jesus from the apocalyptic world view. Ernst Käsemann has written, "His own preaching was not constitutively stamped by apocalyptic."[7] More plausible is the view of Ulrich Wilkens that although Jesus was not a

7. Ernst Käsemann, "The Beginnings of Christian Theology," in *Apocalypticism, Journal for Theology and the Church*, vol. 7 (New York: Herder & Herder, 1969), p. 40.

typical apocalyptist, his message was delivered in the medium of apocalyptic thought forms.[8]

Jesus expected the coming of the kingdom in the immediate future. He made an urgent appeal to his hearers to repent and believe, for there was barely enough time to get ready for the advent of God's approaching rule. One of the most hotly debated issues among scholars has been whether Jesus expected the arrival of the kingdom in the very near future, or whether it was already being fulfilled at that moment. Do we have in Jesus' message the basis for a future-oriented eschatology or a present-oriented eschatology? The alternative is a false one. There are passages that point in both directions. The future reign of God is pictured as drawing so near as already to have a present impact through the person of Jesus. The kingdom is not yet fulfilled, but its initial force is already being felt in the words and works of Jesus' ministry.

After Easter and Pentecost the early church became convinced that Jesus was the Messiah, the bringer of eschatological salvation. Features of eschatological fulfillment due to Easter were etched into the apostolic picture of Jesus' earthly ministry. Coupled with its memory of the historical Jesus, the early church also looked forward in hope of future fulfillment coinciding with the return of Christ. In this way the eschatology of primitive Christianity became three-dimensional. The Revelation of John refers to the Christ "who is and who was and who is to come" (Rev. 1:4,8). It is significant that the present tense comes first. The early Christians believed that the risen Christ was really present among them according to the Spirit. This present dimension of experience is the basis of what scholars have called Christ-mysticism, most vividly represented in the writings of Paul and John. However, their witness to the eschatological Christ was never reduced to the single time-dimension of the present. The present Christ is identical with the one who was—the Jesus of history. The risen Lord is continuous with the crucified Jesus. And this Christ who is and who was will come again. The primitive Christian community looked forward to the glory of the coming of the Lord in the end-time. In this respect the New Testament continued the trend inaugurated by the Old Testament to portray the people of God as an

8. Ulrich Wilkens, "The Understanding of Revelation within the History of Primitive Christianity," in *Revelation as History*, ed. Wolfhart Pannenberg, et al. (New York: Macmillan Co., 1968), pp. 57–121.

exodus community that lives by faith toward a fulfilling future embodied in the word of promise. All three dimensions of time—present, past and future—determine the structure of eschatological thought in the early church.

The Transformation of Eschatology in the Patristic Era

The earliest Christians were convinced that the parousia was imminent, that Christ was coming soon, and that history was about to come to a smashing end. Gradually, however, the eschatological consciousness began to wane among second- and third-century Christians. They had to adjust to an indefinite postponement of the parousia and begin to cope with the exigencies of ongoing history. Eschatological intensity gave way to ecclesiastical developments. The original eschatological tension in Christianity was relaxed by this growing trend toward institutionalization which some New Testament scholars have called "early Catholicism." Occasionally a high-pitched eschatological hope would return, as in the case of Montanism, taking the form of a protest against the secularization of the church and a call to purity of moral and spiritual life.

In the patristic age the list of "last things" was divided between those that concern the individual person and those that relate to the world in general. Death became the focus of each individual's eschaton. The nearness of the parousia in early Christian eschatology was transformed into the idea of the suddenness of death. The offices and sacraments of the church were legitimized as means to prepare the individual to face death. Personal death was imminent, not so much the parousia. The "last things" of the world in general were postponed to a remote future. The last day, the resurrection of the body, the final judgment, and the end of the world—events that were expected in the *near* future in the New Testament—were still affirmed but now removed to the *distant* future. These were no longer objects of passionate expectation. Instead, fear of one's personal eschaton in death provided the occasion for the church to take control of the eternal destiny of each individual. In this atmosphere it was possible for the organized church to require obedience to its authority as the absolute condition of salvation.

The positive significance of eschatology in the age of the church fathers must be seen in terms of the church's intellectual encounter with Hellenistic philosophy. The eschatological perspective equipped these early church thinkers to transform the categories of Greek philosophy in their theological interpretation of the cosmos and of human nature. It would be erroneous to fault them for having completely lost the eschatological horizon of early Christianity. What happened instead was that eschatology paid off in other terms, bearing on broader cultural and philosophical issues.

Eschatology opened history to the experience of novelty. The coming of God's kingdom in history radically changed the human situation. The historical events on which the salvation of humanity is based are unique, unrepeatable, and decisive. These events happened once for all and contribute something to the final meaning of all things. According to Greek philosophy, the cosmos was eternal. Everything that *is* coincides with what is necessary, and if necessary then eternal; so everything that exists had to exist from eternity. In this view there can be no real novelty, no future that is really innovative. The cosmos is revolutionary; it revolves, goes round and round. Everything is inextricably trapped in a cycle of endless repetition. At bottom everything remains always the same, the cosmos itself being caught in a system of eternal bondage to immutable and invariable laws, without beginning or end. At this point patristic thought broke away from the Hellenistic scheme and framed its picture of the world with the doctrines of creation and eschatology. The world was created from nothing (*ex nihilo*), and in the end there will be a consummation that represents advance, achievement, maturity, and novelty far surpassing in glory the beginning of things. The Hellenistic axiom "The end is always like the beginning" gave way to the dominical saying "Behold, I make all things new."

The church fathers also drew upon biblical eschatology to formulate a new doctrine of the nature and destiny of humankind. Belief in the bodily resurrection of the dead was a part of the Christian hope. Christians were ridiculed by Celsus, the pagan philosopher, for being philosomatic (a body-loving people). Porphyry reported of Plotinus, another important philosopher, that he was ashamed of having a body. "The true philosopher is entirely concerned with the soul and not the body. He would like, as far as he can, to get away from the body."[9] Contrary to such a viewpoint the apostle Paul said, "Your

9. Quoted by D. R. G. Owen, *Body and Soul* (Philadelphia: Westminster Press, 1956), p. 39.

body is a temple of the Holy Spirit within you" (1 Cor. 6:19). The philosopher hoped to escape the dungeon of the body by means of the immortal life of the soul. The apostle looked for the glorification of life in the body by the resurrection of the dead. The difference is clear: salvation *from* the body or *with* the body.

Christian eschatology offered a way out of a dilemma posed by Greek philosophy. If there is hope for life after death, it is based on a separation of body and soul. The body is mortal, the soul immortal. This was the teaching of Plato. If, on the other hand, body and soul form an inseparable unity, as Aristotle taught, then nothing human —not even the soul—survives the grave. With Plato the church fathers affirmed life after death, and with Aristotle they held that an individual is a living unit composed of body and soul. The resurrection of the body was the key to effect a synthesis of the Platonic hope for life after death and the Aristotelian idea of the psychosomatic unity of human being. The idea of bodily resurrection overcame the spiritualism of Plato as well as the naturalism of Aristotle. These are examples of how elements of Christian eschatology contributed to a transformation of Greek thought-forms in the theology of the church fathers.

The Place of Eschatology in the Scholastic Synthesis

The tendency to view the Middle Ages as a static period of a thousand years is easily exploded by considering the various streams of eschatological thinking that developed during this period. Augustine identified the kingdom of God with the visible form of the hierarchical church. The millennium was equated with the period of the church running between the first and second coming of Christ. The millennial rule of Christ was now taking place in the offices and sacraments of the church. This conservative institutional interpretation of the kingdom governed the imperial church throughout the Middle Ages.

However, old millennial hopes surfaced time and again in popular piety and reform movements. Strange mixtures of apocalyptic and revolutionary eschatological ideas flourished in such heretical and sectarian movements as the Albigensians, the Waldensians, and the Joachimites. Vivid portrayals of heaven, hell, purgatory, the second coming of Christ, the end of the world, and the final judgment were the major themes of popular eschatology. The work of Joachim of Fiore (d. 1202) merits special notice. Joachim's eschatology was not church-centered, as in Augustine. In fact, his eschatological scheme took a critical turn *against* the church. History was divided into three ages: the age of the Father, the age of the Son, and the age of the Spirit. The third and final age of the Spirit was still to come. The center of gravity belonged to the future, when the Spirit would create a truly spiritual community utterly opposed to the imperial church. Joachim planted seeds of thought that were later to be secularized in the form of socialism.[10]

In the Middle Ages the topics of eschatology were also treated by the great scholastic thinkers. Peter Lombard incorporated eschatology into the total system of scholastic theology, and there it became frozen for centuries in a highly atomistic and conceptual schematization. By the end of the seventeenth century the doctrine of "the last things" reached its highest point of development in the voluminous systems of Lutheran, Reformed, and Roman Catholic scholasticism. The issues were academically treated by the use of Aristotelian methodology. The last things were literally discussed as events that will happen when the present world comes to an end. They are: death, the resurrection of the dead, the final judgment, the end of the world, eternal damnation, and eternal life.[11] Controversial questions that divided Protestants and Catholics were subject to lengthy polemical treatment. The overall picture, however, is fairly simple.

Death in the scholastic systems was not viewed as a total annihilation of the person. Rather, death is merely the end of natural life, causing a separation of soul and body. The body ceases to exist, but the soul lives on with all its power. The immortality of the soul can be proved by reason and scripture. As soon as death occurs, the soul faces either a happy lot or an unhappy lot, either heaven or hell immediately. The Protestants rejected the idea of an intermediate state where souls linger as in a state of sleep. They also rejected the Roman Catholic idea of purgatory and the notion of limbo, a special place for the souls of unbaptized children and another for the souls of the patriarchs who died before the coming of Christ.

10. Norman Cohn, *The Pursuit of the Millennium* (New York: Harper & Row, 1961), pp. 99ff.

11. See, e.g., Heinrich Schmid, *The Doctrinal Theology of the Evangelical Lutheran Church*, pp. 624–63.

The scholastics taught, further, that the time will come when the body will be resurrected and reunited with the soul. This will be the very same body as before, only now endowed with attributes appropriate to spiritual life beyond this earthly realm. The resurrected body will last forever, look glorious, enjoy perfection, and feel no need for food or sex.[12] This is a belief that reason cannot discover; it is revealed solely by scripture.

The final judgment immediately follows the resurrection of the dead. Some people will still be living when the world comes to an end. Their bodies will not need to be resurrected, only transformed according to the specifications of spiritual life. No one knows when the final judgment will take place, but there will be signs from which the approach of that day can be inferred. In general, these signs have to do with times getting worse, Satan becoming stronger, an increase of wickedness among people, and more suffering for the righteous. Then Christ will visibly appear in glory to judge all people, bringing consolation to the faithful and terror to the wicked, executing judgment upon the godly and the ungodly according to the standards revealed by the word of God.

Millennialism, otherwise known as chiliasm, was rejected by the theologians of Protestant orthodoxy. There will be no rule of Christ and his elect on earth for a thousand years, between his second advent and the final judgment. The rejection of chiliasm in orthodoxy is the root of its later antagonism to all utopian systems of thought. This means, in effect, that no future occurrence can displace the importance of the organized church between Pentecost and the parousia.

When the final judgment takes place, the world will come to an end. It will burn up in a ball of fire and come to naught. At the base of this scholastic eschatology there is a pessimism about this present world order. It is not evolving toward a glorious consummation; it is not being transformed by gradual progress in the direction of a new heaven and earth. Rather, what is to be expected is an absolute annihilation of the substance of the present world.

In the end there will be a complete separation of the righteous and the unrighteous, the former going to heaven and the latter to hell.

12. Ibid., p. 641.

Hell means eternal damnation and death, a state of torment and misery of endless duration meted out according to what each person deserves to pay for earthly sins. Heaven means eternal life, perfect joy in the face of God forever, an everlasting reward for the saints.

This scholastic system of eschatological thought was placed in the last chapter of dogmatics. There it languished in a pitiable state and finally succumbed to the onslaughts of rationalistic criticism in the Enlightenment and new formulations with the rise of modern Protestant theology.

CHALLENGES AND CONTRIBUTIONS OF MODERN CONSCIOUSNESS

The Transformation of Eschatology in the Post-Enlightenment Period

Beginning with the last part of the seventeenth century, traditional Christian eschatology took a plunge into a confusion of modern movements, generally labeled rationalism, naturalism, romanticism, idealism, and positivism. This is the age of the Enlightenment, born with the discovery of a new world view, derived in large part from the work of Isaac Newton. Here we can characterize the fate of the Christian idea of the kingdom of God in the period of the Enlightenment in a few broad strokes.

The Newtonian world view pictured God as a rational divine being who shaped the universe according to eternal laws. The system in nature is essentially rational, including both human nature and society with all its institutions. Everything is conceived to exist according to laws of nature that can be known by the operation of reason. The rational harmony that Newton discovered in the order of nature was transferred to the social order so that, as Adam Smith believed, there is an "invisible hand" at work in all social structures guided by a wonderful natural law of harmony. The thinkers of the Enlightenment believed that underlying the apparent disharmony, chaos, and misery there is a basically good natural order founded on eternal laws that God himself built into the world. If something is wrong, it is because human beings have not heeded the original laws written into the nature of things. Thus, Jean Jacques Rousseau, the father of romanticism, looked at the mess which history calls civilization and pleaded for a return to the original state of humanity. This is a paradise in which people were naturally good and lived together like "noble savages" in a condition unspoiled by civilization—in liberty, equality, and fraternity. The cry here was to get back to the rational order, back to nature, back to the lost paradise. Eschatology thus suffers a reversal at the hands of the backward-looking myth of a golden age in the past. The earthly task of humankind is to retrieve the primitive state of nature, which lacks nothing in perfection.

The world view of the Enlightenment, whether along the lines of Newton, Adam Smith, or Rousseau, collapsed the biblical God of history into the laws of nature and the eschatological vision of Christianity into a harmonious social order. The old image of the kingdom of God became a workable social model to be realized by the ability of human reason to conform itself to the order of nature. Throughout the Enlightenment the eschatological kingdom of God was brought down to the size of *this world*, as something to be realized by human beings in history. Its focus was on the *human*: human society, human welfare, human happiness. Religion was reduced to what is natural and reasonable, striving for the highest possible elevation of humanity and society.

The setting for eschatology in the mind of the Enlightenment is very much in this world. However, the effect of translating eschatology into this-worldly expectations produced a revolutionary mentality. The end of the eighteenth century was a period of revolution. People were beginning to take fate into their own hands and to convert the eschatological kingdom of peace and righteousness into a society of equality and justice here on earth. The eschatological kingdom was becoming utopian socialism.[13]

Utopian socialists, followers of Saint-Simon, appeared in France at the beginning of the nineteenth century. The most famous disciple of this socialist movement was Auguste Comte, who was imbued with the sense that something new was happening in his time. Comte attempted to translate the chiliastic expectations of earlier times, such as we find in Thomas Müntzer in the sixteenth century, into a system of universal principles based on philosophy and science. Comte enthusiastically proclaimed his new positivistic science as a new religion, even a new church with its appropriate dogmatics.

13. *Utopias and Utopian Thought*, ed. Frank E. Manuel (Boston: Beacon Press, 1966).

Comte saw history unfolding in three stages: the mythological stage of theology, where orthodox Christianity remains bogged down; the metaphysical stage of Western philosophy; and a final positivist scientific stage, which is the wave of the future. Comte's theory became enormously influential in the process of absorbing the contents of eschatology into the dialectics of progress in history, still perhaps the dominant myth of modern times.

Eschatology undergoes a further transformation in the dialectics of the historical process in the thought of Karl Marx. Marx transformed utopian socialism into a system of "scientific" revolutionary thought. In this system the eschatological factor becomes the negative principle of a dialectical process to bring about a new order in this world, leading from capitalism to communism. All that remains of eschatology within the historical process is the breach in time, the old time before the revolution and the new time after, as well as the dramatic reversal in the order of things, capitalism coming to an end and the miserable working class, the proletariat, taking control. The upper class is pushed down, the underclass enthroned, resulting in a workers' paradise on earth.

Although Marx rejected utopian socialism, there is no doubt that he transformed eschatological hopes into utopian ideals that appeal to the masses. The masses, deeply entrenched in misery, are given promises of a new order bound to materialize. There will be no more unemployment, slave labor, poverty, and oppression by the exploiting class of capitalists. Power will fall into the hands of the people, and the state will finally wither away. No more false authority, abuse of power, or misuse of law. There will emerge a new humanity in a new society, totally liberated and free for the reign of peace and justice here on earth. Like the paradisiacal state of Adam and Eve before the fall, Marx's vision of the end-state is of a classless society rising from the ashes of an apocalyptic-type struggle of good and evil forces. Here religious eschatology, mediated in its heretical chiliastic forms, becomes radically secularized.[14] The transcendent becomes immanent, the theological becomes teleological, the hereafter nothing but the postrevolutionary future.

14. Paul Tillich, "The Christian and the Marxist View of Man," unpublished (Tillich Archives, Harvard Divinity School, Cambridge, Mass). This document was prepared as a study document for the "Universal Christian Council for Life and Work," December 1935.

Contemporary with the Marxist revolutionary transformation of eschatology was the nineteenth-century evolutionary myth of progress. The optimistic spirit prevailed in all branches of knowledge, including theology. Original sin could no longer be maintained, because it put the brakes on the indefinite march of progress. The wheels of progress appeared to be irresistible and unceasing. An inevitably better future was coming because of new science and technology. Before Marx spelled out his revolutionary vision of the future, Immanuel Kant had proposed an ethical interpretation of the kingdom of God on earth, the realization of which depended on the sum total of morally responsible actions performed by human beings. The kingdom of God which Jesus announced became very much something of and for this world, dependent not on the will of God but solely on human achievement. The establishment of the kingdom on earth was tied to the forward motion of progress.

Nineteenth-century Protestant theology incorporated the myth of progress into its own ethical concept of the kingdom of God. In liberal Protestantism the kingdom of God represented a new social order that will come about as a result of human activity and through moral progress in history. In this scheme, eschatology functions as a kind of teleological process in which the future goal of the kingdom is gradually being realized by the present ethical achievements of humanity. The "kingdom of God" thus became the watchword of the Social Gospel movement in America, under the leadership of Walter Rauschenbusch. It was expected that a better social order would be established through enlightened social policy and moral progress. Confidence in the potential of humanity to better its lot on earth weakened the eschatological images of traditional Christianity. The question was whether the realization of a blessed human future would come about through revolution or through evolution.

The Renewal of Eschatological Thought in the Twentieth Century

In the nineteenth century, Christianity became increasingly a pale religious reflection of a progressively secularized culture. Jacob Taubes concluded his brilliant study of Western eschatology with a section on G. W. F. Hegel, Søren Kierkegaard, and Marx, and for him that was apparently the end of the subject.[15] This judgment parallels the verdict of Ernst Troeltsch, who said just before World War I, "The eschatological bureau is closed these days."[16] The original eschatology of Christianity could still be heard in the churches as a doctrine abut personal salvation and life after death.

Albert Schweitzer's monumental book, *The Quest of the Historical Jesus* (1906), represented the rediscovery in the twentieth century of eschatology in the message of Jesus and of primitive Christianity. This came as a shock to Protestant theology, which was intent on conforming Christianity to modern trends and ideas. Eschatology had been dismissed as part of the primitive world view of New Testament times and thus bound up with the husk of the Christian faith, not the kernel. Schweitzer's study shows conclusively that for Jesus eschatology was at the core of his message and that apart from his belief in a speedy coming of the kingdom of God not even his ethical teachings make any sense. Jesus lived, preached, healed, suffered, and died in the power of his commitment to the coming of God's rule on earth, bringing life and salvation to all humanity and the world. Schweitzer's view is commonly called "consistent" or "thoroughgoing" eschatology because of his proposal to understand everything the Gospels say about Jesus in light of his eschatological hypothesis.

Building on Schweitzer's eschatological reading of the New Testament, Karl Barth announced that the message of the Bible stands in stark contrast to the cultured views of modern times. In Barth's "theology of crisis," eschatology became a doctrine revealing the unbridgeable gap between human history here and now and the totally other world of God in heaven and eternity. The eschatological event as the eternal now can only touch history at a tangent, but cannot itself have a history. Jesus Christ is the bare mathematical point where time and eternity meet. The resurrection of Christ is called an "eschatological" event and therefore not a "historical" event in the sense in which critical historiography uses the term. Traditional eschatological symbols—the parousia, the end of the world, the final judgment, the second coming of Christ, the resurrection of the dead, and everlasting life—have nothing to do with real events which

15. Jacob Taubes, *Abendländische Eschatologie* (Bern: A. Francke, 1947).
16. Quoted by F. L. Polak, *The Image of the Future* (New York: Oceana Publications, 1961), 2:43.

Christian hope expects will happen in the future. They are dimensions of a transcendental eschatological Word that descends vertically from the alpine heights of eternity, never taking shape incarnationally in the horizontal categories of history, past, present, and future.

Barth revised his interpretation of eschatology with each shift of emphasis in his theological development. He became aware of the inadequacy of an eschatology that relocates the future of hope from "ahead" to "above." He broke out of a starkly abstract dialectic of eternity and time to give expression to the Christian hope for a real future fulfillment. In the end, however, Barth never wrote the volume on eschatology, the "last things," for his *Church Dogmatics*. There was perhaps nothing new to say, for everything that could be said *Christianly* was already contained in the incarnational revelation. The future could only have noetic significance, bringing forth a fuller *knowledge* of the revelation in Christ. Barth's eschatology did not call for any new things still to happen, only for a final unveiling of the accomplished revelation of God in the incarnate Word.

Rudolf Bultmann, like Barth, agreed that New Testament Christianity is essentially eschatological. The word "eschatological" became fixed in the vocabulary of Bultmann's existentialist theology. He appropriated the existentialist categories of Martin Heidegger, author of the philosophical work *Being and Time*, to make the kerygma of primitive Christianity understandable to modern people. Thus the individual exists in radical openness to the future; bondage to sin is enslavement to the law of one's past; authentic existence is the openness of trust toward the future; faith is freedom from the past; salvation is an ever-coming occurrence out of the future, to be grasped through faith alone. The grace of God is the power to assure the meaning of each existential moment, in spite of the anticipation of death as one's own most certain destiny.

Bultmann's dependence on existentialist philosophy meant that the biblical symbol of God's coming kingdom was reduced to the element of bare futurity in the temporal structure of human existence. Eschatology became scarcely more than the factor of meaning in each existential moment. In the Bible the symbol of the kingdom of God and eternal life embraces not only hope for the individual person in the struggles of existence, but also hope for the future of all things, for the wider human community of nations, and even for the whole cosmos of nature and history. In Bultmann's eschatology, limited as it was by existentialist hermeneutics, there was no way to prevent the future from being reduced to the ever-receding horizon of existential openness, without shape or content, without power or reality grounded in the nature and activity of God.

Paul Tillich made the greatest contribution to the interpretation of the kingdom of God among the theological leaders of the last generation. He defined the problem of eschatology as the question of the meaning and goal of history or as the quest for the kingdom of God. The symbol of the kingdom of God has two sides—an inner-historical side and a trans-historical side. The prophetic revolutionary aspect of Tillich's social thought drew its power from the dynamics of the kingdom of God in history. He saw history as a movement in which the new is created, in which unique and unrepeatable events occur, yet which runs toward a future goal. This means that the Christian faith looks ahead for the future transformation of all reality; it interprets the past and acts in the present in light of the future goal toward which history runs. The "new being" is expected predominantly in a horizontal direction rather than a vertical one. Christianity hopes for the realization of the kingdom of God, the divine rule of peace, love, and righteousness in a new heaven and a new earth.

The Role of Eschatology in Contemporary Theology

The quest for an adequate eschatology has been continued beyond Barth, Bultmann, and Tillich by the present generation of systematic theologians. Wolfhart Pannenberg and Jürgen Moltmann in particular have criticized an eschatology in which the horizon of the future is swallowed up by the eternal blitzing in from above. Dialectical theology did not think of eschatological hope as having anything to do with the concrete future. Future tenses were as often as possible converted into talk about the presence of the kingdom of God here and now.

According to Pannenberg, theology must accept Jesus' message of the kingdom of God as the basic starting point for any Christology or doctrine of salvation. "This resounding motif of Jesus' message—the imminent Kingdom of God—must be recovered as a key to the whole of Christian theology."[17] The kingdom of God is the eschatological future which God himself brings about. This is to be thought of as the power of the future determining the destiny of everything that exists. It is possible to call God eternal, not in the timeless sense of Plato and Parmenides, but in the sense that he is the future both of our present and of every age that is past.

Moltmann also speaks of the future as a "new paradigm of transcendence."[18] This future is not to be thought of as the progress of the world developing out of the present. There is no transcendence in that. Rather, the future can be a paradigm of transcendence only by bringing into the present something qualitatively new. If we blow up the present into the future, without radical change in the foundations of personal and social reality, the power of evil is magnified along with the good. Then our last state is no better than our first. The transcendent future is a power to attack the conditions of evil in the foundations of reality and to lead it forward through a process of revolutionary transformation. From within history and suffering the pain of its conflicts, it is possible to project a transcendent future of history, which is qualitatively other than just future history. A better future in history can be hoped for on the basis of the power emanating from the transcendent future of history, opening up new prospects and possibilities.

Liberation theology is also trying to come to terms with the contemporary eschatological reading of the biblical message. Liberation theologians, whether black, feminist, or Third World, have been influenced by the European discussions on the "theology of hope" and "political theology." Liberation theology starts with an analysis of the concrete situation rather than with a summary of biblical truths which only need to be applied as a second step. Gustavo Gutiérrez's definition of theology has become classic: Theology is critical reflection on historical praxis. Truth emerges in language that reflects a community's engagement in the liberating transformation of the world. In such liberating praxis we can find clues to what God is doing in the world.

17. Wolfhart Pannenberg, *Theology and the Kingdom of God*, p. 53.
18. Jürgen Moltmann, *Religion, Revolution and the Future* (New York: Charles Scribner's Sons, 1969), pp. 177ff.

Some liberation theologians, particularly in Latin America, have consciously adopted the Marxist analysis of society. They have committed themselves to a revolutionary praxis that aims to socialize the means of production, overcome the classist society, and awaken the masses to share in the political process that decides the circumstances of their daily lives. A favorite text of scripture is frequently quoted from the Magnificat:

> He has put down the mighty from their thrones,
>   and exalted those of low degree;
> he has filled the hungry with good things,
>   and the rich he has sent empty away. (Luke 1:52–54)

Liberation theology resists any attempt to neutralize the concrete political meaning of this passage in the interest of an abstract spiritualization that leaves the real world the way it is. This means that the eschatological symbols of the Bible are turned away from an otherworldly future to the historical transformation of the material conditions of life. To some extent the eschatology operative in today's liberation theology resembles the nineteenth-century interpretation of the kingdom of God that began with Kant, developed in Ritschlianism, and ended with the Social Gospel movement.

ISSUES AND PROPOSALS

Christianity today stands at the crossroads between two diametrically opposed interpretations of eschatology. On one side are the "conservative evangelicals" in all Christian denominations who think of eschatology in the traditional sense of "last things" to occur in some near or distant future. On the other side there are "post-Enlightenment" Christians who think of eschatology more concretely in relation to social-ethical objectives. In its traditional meaning, eschatology refers to the final consummation of this world and the eternal destiny of all people. But what does the biblical promise of eschatological salvation have to do with the real world in which human beings struggle for a meaningful life? In the current situation there are many issues that keep the debate on eschatology still fluid.

1. The renewal of biblical eschatology in contemporary theology is trying to overcome a false dichotomizing of eschatology into other-

worldly and this-worldly hopes. The symbolic elements in the eschatological traditions of the Bible cover the entire spectrum of human hope. Hope may be described as an expectant looking toward the future for what is *new*. But how can one express new things that lie in the future if they have not already happened, if they are not simply already there? This can happen only through language that functions in terms of a dialectical reversal. The principle which seems to have guided hope in its formation of language is what Paul Tillich has called "the negation of the negative." The negativities in human experience are negated. The symbols we use to express our hope depend on our reading of the human condition.

2. In the Bible there is a progressive escalation of hope from prophetic to apocalyptic eschatology. Prophetic eschatology centers on the history of Israel amid the nations of the world and points to a future *in* history with promises of a better life. Apocalyptic eschatology looks beyond Israel to the cosmos, beyond the salvation of Israel to the final future *of* history itself, when the whole of creation will be ushered into the redemption in the last days. There was always the danger that apocalypticism would zoom off into a never-never land of fantasy and speculation, losing touch with the real life of people and nations in concrete history. Because much of traditional eschatology appears to have left the ground of real history and taken off into the clouds of another world of time and space, it is necessary to retrace the steps of Israel, as it were, and to start our eschatology like the prophets with the struggles of people in this life. Then it will be possible to escalate human hope, as the apocalyptists did, to enfold the totality of reality in a cosmic eschatology.

3. A real historical grounding of eschatology is needed today as a corrective to the church's tendency to relate gospel hopes to purely private concerns, thus ignoring the public issues of human life. The gospel is the good news of the advent of God's kingdom. The purely personal and interpersonal sphere cannot contain the full meaning of the kingdom, minus all social, political, economic, and cultural realities which determine the contexts and possibilities of human existence. The recovery of the full concept of the kingdom of God can help us overcome what Johannes B. Metz calls the "trend toward the private" and to sound the political and social notes of the Christian message.

The Christian hope drives us to seek ever more adequate actualization of God's kingdom in the open fields of public life, so that the vision of freedom, peace, and justice may achieve provisional embodiment in institutional structures that determine the conditions under which individuals exist in society. Without this political grounding, the Christian hope runs the risk of becoming a palliative, an opiate, an ideological servant of the status quo. The image of the kingdom of God represents hope for both personal and social fulfillment. The promised kingdom points to a situation in which bodily and spiritual ills are healed, in which shalom will reign among all creatures, and in which love will create harmony for the good of all.

4. Two strands have been woven together in the Christian tradition concerning life after death; one stems from the Greek myth of the immortality of the soul and the other from the New Testament message of the resurrection of the body. Immortality and resurrection both express hope for life beyond the eternal clutch of death. If the soul is understood as the innermost core of personal identity, the "true self," then the doctrine of the immortality of the soul expresses the hope that what is essentially human will survive death. If, however, the body is an integral part of the human personality, so that without my body I would be no-body at all, then it too must be integrated into the hope of eternal life. So the ancient Christian creeds affirm the resurrection of the body. Still, they do not literally mean the physical body. The apostle Paul made it clear that through resurrection the physical body is transformed into a spiritual body. This means that salvation, as distinct from the Hellenistic *soteria*, is not a matter of salvaging the soul from its dungeon in the body.

The Christian hope for eternal life ultimately accepts an integration of body and soul. The happiness of the soul is bound up with its somatic form of life and does not occur by loosening its links with the body, as in some metaphysical and mystical forms of spirituality. The incarnational thrust of the Christian gospel is too powerful to be lost in the end. What is at stake is the present ethical implications of an eschatological image of the psychosomatic unity of human being. What people hope for in the end legitimates what they practice in the present. If the body is good for nothing in the end, it cannot hold a high value in the present. But if the body is the temple of the Holy Spirit, as Paul said, if each individual is a member of the body of

Christ, and if we share a foretaste of eternal life now by partaking of this eucharistic body, then we will hear an ethical imperative in Paul's saying: "You glorify God in your bodies!" This means that the power of eternal life is not something stored up elsewhere, to become real at some other time and place. Rather, impulses of life eternal are being released into the personal, social, and political body of this very life. This grants us the possibility of attempting new things, of engaging in a resurrection politics and a liberation practice ahead of the times. We do not have to wait until we are dead before we live at least in a partial way the new life which occurred in the history of Jesus Christ.

5. The question is still being debated among contemporary Christians whether the Christian hope is ultimately universal or particular in scope. A minority of theologians have taught a doctrine of universal salvation, the "return of all things." The majority of churches and theologians have resisted the teaching of universal salvation. Why? It seems that Christians have done what comes naturally—to hope chiefly for themselves, their own family and friends, and let the rest go to hell. This is most natural, but is it Christian? The question is whether our human solidarity with the whole cosmos will not expand the base of our hope beyond individual personal fulfillment in the end. Guided by the universal scope of divine love, Christian hope will rebel against every doctrinal restriction which sets limits to the vision of hope.

What will the final future of life in the kingdom of God look like? We can only speak about God and God's kingdom in language limited by the conditions of human finitude. But we do know that there is a drive toward infinite freedom within human beings which seeks a total unburdening from every limitation. Humans possess an unquenchable thirst for the infinite. Augustine said that our hearts are restless until they find their rest in God, and this God may be defined as the term of pure and unlimited freedom. Human being is not satisfied to stand still within the confines of the finite. It belongs to human nature to go forward to new being and live from the unfettered source of freedom in God.

Is the final goal of the kingdom to be thought of as a static finale to the dynamic struggle for freedom? Is the world of nature and history now in motion only to stand still in the end? Is there a final resting place—a mansion—to which everyone will retire from the struggles of life? Then the kingdom of God would resemble Nirvana, an eschaton of nothingness. It would be better to envision the kingdom of God as the power of the future which ceaselessly opens up new possibilities. The essence of God is the pure freedom which humanity is seeking when in search of the truth and reality of its own identity. God is pure freedom—the only being free to be on its own. The reality God enjoys is underived freedom as such. The freedom humanity seeks is derived from beyond itself, from the source of freedom in the being of God. The salvation humanity seeks—paradise, heaven, eternal life—is not the peace and quiet of a retirement center. It is the final ecstasy of life, a vital movement beyond every stasis. The symbol of the resurrection teaches us to hope for an ecstasy of life beyond the stasis of death. The final Christian hope, on the ground of the resurrection of Jesus Christ, is to be finally reconciled to God with all things and thus to share in life everlasting.

SUGGESTIONS FOR FURTHER READING

Altizer, Thomas J. J. *Genesis and Apocalypse: A Theological Voyage toward Authentic Christianity.* Louisville: Westminster, 1990.

Alves, Rubem. A *Theology of Human Hope.* Washington, D.C.: Corpus Books, 1969.

Baillie, John. *And the Life Everlasting.* New York: Charles Scribner's Sons, 1933.

Barth, Karl. *The Epistle to the Romans.* London: Oxford University Press, 1933.

Benz, Ernst. *Evolution and Christian Hope: Man's Concept of the Future from the Early Fathers to Teilhard de Chardin.* New York: Doubleday, 1966.

Braaten, Carl E. *Eschatology and Ethics.* Minneapolis: Augsburg Publishing House, 1974.

Brunner, Emil. *Eternal Hope.* Philadelphia: Westminster Press, 1954.

Bultmann, Rudolf. *History and Eschatology.* Edinburgh: University Press, 1957.

Chilton, Bruce, editor. *The Kingdom of God in the Teaching of Jesus.* Philadelphia: Fortress Press, 1984.

Eliade, Mircea. *Cosmos and History. The Myth of Eternal Return.* New York: Harper & Bros., 1959.

Gutiérrez, Gustavo. *The God of Life.* Translated by Matthew J. O'Connell. Maryknoll, N.Y.: Orbis Books, 1991.

Hayes, Zachary. *Visions of a Future: A Study of Christian Eschatology*. Wilmington: M. Glazier, 1989.

Heim, Karl. *The World: Its Creation and Consummation*. Edinburgh: Oliver & Boyd, 1952.

Hick, John H. *Death and Eternal Life*. New York: Harper & Row, 1976.

Küng, Hans. *Eternal Life? Life after Death as a Medical, Philosophical, and Theological Problem*. New York: Doubleday, 1984.

Martin, James. *The Last Judgment in Protestant Theology from Orthodoxy to Ritschl*. Edinburgh: Oliver & Boyd, 1963.

Minear, Paul. *Christian Hope and the Second Coming*. Philadelphia Fortress Press, 1974.

Moltmann, Jürgen. *Theology of Hope*. Translated by James W. Leitsch. Minneapolis: Fortress Press, 1993.

———. *The Trinity and the Kingdom*.

Niebuhr, H. Richard. *The Kingdom of God in America*. New York: Harper & Bros., 1937.

Pannenberg, Wolfhart. *Theology and the Kingdom of God*. Philadelphia Westminster Press, 1969.

Robinson, J. A. T. *In the End God*. London: Collins, 1968.

Rosenstock-Huessy, Eugen. *The Christian Future*. New York: Harper & Row, 1966.

Rowley, H. H. *The Relevance of Apocalyptic*. London: Lutterworth Press, 1944.

Schweitzer, Albert. *The Quest of the Historical Jesus*. 3d edition. London: A. & C. Black, 1954.

Suchocki, Marjorie. *End of Evil: Process Eschatology in Historical Context*. Albany: State University of New York Press, 1988.

Tillich, Paul. *Systematic Theology*. Vol. 3.

Weiss, Johannes. *Jesus' Proclamation of the Kingdom of God*. Translated by Richard H. Hiers and D. Larrimore Holland. Philadelphia: Fortress Press, 1971.

13. THE RELIGIONS

WHERE WE ARE

To be a Christian seems to entail the judgment that being a Christian is superior to being anything else. To display this superiority has often been seen as the task of Christian apologetics. This has not necessarily meant a claim that Christians are morally or humanly superior to others, but it has normally meant the conviction that the God from whom alone salvation can be received is known or present to Christians as nowhere else.

Today this habit of thought is severely challenged by increasing awareness of the many impressive ways in which human beings are organizing their lives and seeking and finding truth, wholeness, or salvation. To more and more Christians, approaching others with the assumption of the superiority of their own religion seems false to Christian love. Is it not better to listen appreciatively to what others have learned and experienced than to assume that we already know better?

But this gives rise to problems too. Does it mean that we abandon the conviction that Jesus Christ is the savior or liberator of all? Do we become relativistic, accepting private decisions of others as beyond criticism? Does this charitable tolerance extend to everyone—to racists, for example? Or does our faith provide grounds to decide in advance what the limits of respect should be? If so, are we being truly open to those others whom we are called to love and who judge by other norms?

Prior to World War I, the problem was often formulated as that of the finality or absoluteness of Christianity. Can we appreciate the achievements of other religious traditions and still evaluate them from the Christian point of view? Has Christianity in principle already grasped the final truth, or must we recognize that Christianity is just one way of believing and living alongside others which have equal justification for their exclusive claims?

In the nineteenth century the problem was formulated in terms of Christianity and other religions. Philosophers of religion sought the essence of the universal human phenomenon of religion, and theologians undertook to show that this essence attained its purest and most perfect form in Christianity. The category "religion" thus became the basic context within which such matters were discussed. Theologians understood their task as explaining the beliefs of the Christian religion. Following this understanding, colleges and universities have developed departments of religion. And this chapter is entitled "The Religions."

Nevertheless, this approach has become problematic in the period since World War I. Karl Barth, the most important theologian of this period, pointed out that faith has to do with what God has done in Jesus Christ and is not merely a particular expression of a universal human religiousness. Such religiousness is real enough, even among Christians. But to study Christianity as one form of religion among others is to miss its character as response to the unique act of God.

Since Barth, the category "religion" has become more and more problematic. Barth understood religion as the human effort to attain salvation, and he supposed that apart from Jesus Christ all people are engaged in some such effort. Hence he did not challenge the use of the category in relation to the great traditions of Asia. But representatives of these traditions have noted that religion is a Western category imposed upon them, often quite uncongenial from their point of view and grouping together quite disparate phenomena. If we continue to speak of "the religions," it is partly because of custom and partly because of the lack of consensus about a better way to communicate.

As a result of theological developments typified by Karl Barth, theology separated itself from the context of the academic study of religion and the religions. This discipline was pursued in colleges and universities as comparative religion or the history of religions, while theology was largely studied in seminaries. But theologians have recognized in recent years that they cannot continue to ignore the other religious traditions, and some historians of religion, notably Wilfred Cantwell Smith, have recognized that their discipline is impoverished when it turns away from the normative question of religious truth and value. As a result, the relation of theology to the history of religions is now in a healthy flux.

Christian reflection on "the religions" may come last in a book such as this, but it informs thought on all Christian doctrines. Awareness of living Judaism, for example, must influence the way we speak of Jesus Christ. Awareness of Buddhist saints who do not believe in God must affect the way we think of the relation of God and holiness.

In some respects these problems are new. The encounter with the great traditions of India and China alters the context in which Christians think, and this was not important before the sixteenth century. The nineteenth century introduced a new awareness of the sociohistorical conditioning of all thought. In the twentieth century, Westerners are finally abandoning the deep-seated assumption of the superiority of Christian culture.

But from the beginning, Christians have been aware of religious people who were not Christian. At least some of the available options for viewing these people were forged already in the early centuries of the church. The next section will deal with these classic formulations, while the following section will consider how the broadening of horizons and the rise of historical consciousness deepened the problem and called forth new solutions. Finally, we shall return to the present situation and suggest the character of faithful response today.

THE DOCTRINE
IN ITS CLASSIC FORMULATION

There is no orthodox doctrine about the religions. Indeed, there is no classic position on the subject thus posed. This is partly because the category "religions" was not employed until modern times. It is also because reflection about most of the living movements we call religions was not central to Christian theology. The primary focus has usually been on people as individuals who believe, or do not believe, in Jesus Christ. Nevertheless, attitudes toward and beliefs about Judaism, pagan religions, and Islam are expressed in classical Christian literature. Moreover, in the early modern period the traditions of China, especially Confucianism, assumed some importance. The fact that these reflections were not subsumed under the common heading "religions" before the modern period may have been an advantage.

Determinants of Christian Attitudes Toward Others

One element in shaping the attitudes of Christians toward others is a virtually universal tendency to divide the world into "us" and "them." Just as Jews opposed themselves to Gentiles and Greeks to barbarians, so also Christians have opposed themselves to the heathen or infidels. This fact and its expression in Christian history and contemporary society is of great historical and sociological importance. But theologically our interest is more in the ways in which Christian thought has given a distinct cast to this universal tendency.

Three themes are important here. First, Christianity has been an intensely missionary movement. Since the "us-them" distinction for Christians was not based on given characteristics such as ancestry, it could be overcome. "They" could and should join "us." Their ignorance of the salvation to which we witness can only be overcome as we carry the gospel to them. Hence Christians have at times engaged in heroic efforts to evangelize others. The ideal and goal has been one of the union of all people in acknowledgment of Jesus Christ as Lord and Savior.

Second, the same understanding that leads toward overcoming all natural barriers "in Christ" leads to disappointment and even anger when others who hear the word of what God has done for them in Christ are indifferent or reject it. When the distinction of "we" and "they" is established by race or even culture, "we" may feel contempt for "them," but we do not regard them as individually to blame for their condition. But when, as with Christians, "we" are convinced that once "they" have heard and only stubbornness and willful viciousness prevent their believing, then the attitude toward them can become much more harsh. Christians have at times exercised great cruelty toward others in the endeavor to convert them or to make them suffer for their refusal.

Third, most Christians have recognized that there is much of value in the lives, thought, and culture of those who are not Christian. The earliest believers understood themselves to be the heirs of Abraham and the prophets, the true inheritors and continuers of Israel. As participants in Greek culture, most believers in the Mediterranean world affirmed much of that inheritance as well. Many Christians were convinced that their Savior, Jesus Christ, was one with the universal divine principle, the Word or Logos, that informed all people and all cultures. The prologue of the Gospel of John is the *locus classicus* for this immensely important aspect of Christian teaching. When this is emphasized, the person who is not a Christian is approached not merely as unbeliever but also as one in whom and through whom the everlasting Word acts and speaks.

These three motifs—readiness to extend Christian fellowship, enmity toward those who refuse the offer, and respect for the work of the Word even where Jesus Christ is not acknowledged—have produced varied and inconsistent doctrines through the centuries of Christian history. They serve primarily to relate Christians to other individuals who are not Christians, but they also affect Christian understanding of the religions.

Interpretations of Judaism, Paganism, Islam, and Confucianism

Theologically, the most developed understanding has been in relation to Judaism. At first the synagogue and the church shared a common scripture. Even when Christians canonized additional writings, they retained the Jewish scriptures as well. Christians and Jews viewed one another more as heretics than as adherents of different religions. That is, each saw the claims of the other as a false reading of the scriptures.

Central to Christian self-understanding was the view that the Jews were in error. Christians claimed to be the heirs of the promises of the shared scriptures, and that meant that the Jews could not be the elect people. The Jewish rejection of Jesus had to be shown as based on error and even sin. Christian theologians and preachers did not differ substantially in their denunciation of Judaism. They differed only in that some were more vitriolic than others. In relation to Jews, although the door to Christian conversion was always open, it was the second of the three motifs listed above that dominated. Christian theology encouraged the persecution of Judaism.

Theologians did not, however, support the extermination of Judaism. Whereas they often encouraged the annihilation of heresy and other competitors with orthodox Christianity, they supported a narrowly circumscribed legal status for Judaism. Jews were to exist in a condition of misery until the end as a negative witness to the truth of Christianity. At the end they would finally be forced to acknowledge the perverseness of their error. Of course such subtle limits to the approved persecution of the Jews did not prevent popular riots, Crusader massacres, and pogroms. And it was often Christian theologians and saints who then prevented the government from making reparations to the Jews.

Greco-Roman paganism required a more differentiated response. On the one hand, Christians joined Jews in refusing to participate in what they deemed superstition and idolatry. They would not, for example, acknowledge the deity of the Caesar. They opposed magical and occult practices, and when they came to power, they outlawed these practices.

They were more tolerant toward cultic acts of political religion. These were not outlawed at once, and there were even instances of Christian emperors participating in public ceremonies at pagan temples. Nevertheless, once in power, Christianity moved to displace these observances.

The great challenge lay in the philosophical schools, especially Neoplatonism. It was in relation to these movements that the doctrine of the universal work of the divine Word was employed most positively. Where Neoplatonism flourished in separation from magical and occult practices, as in Alexandria, Christian theologians recognized it as an admirable adversary, and it was allowed to continue under the Christian empire.

Today we might make the mistake of supposing that since Neoplatonism was "only" a philosophy it would not constitute a competitor to Christianity. This is to read back into the Roman world the fragmentation of our own. Philosophy is now one academic discipline alongside others, and Christian theology has largely accepted a role as another such discipline. But then philosophy and theology both claimed to offer the encompassing truth and to point the way to salvation. Among thoughtful people, Neoplatonism was Christianity's greatest competitor for total allegiance.

Christian theologians respected Neoplatonism and learned from it. Indeed, they incorporated much of it into their own theology. The Christianity that won the struggle for the mind of the later Roman world was a Neoplatonized Christianity. In the competition between Christianity and Neoplatonism, Christianity won because it was able to assimilate the wisdom of Neoplatonism, whereas Neoplatonism was unable or unwilling to assimilate the wisdom of Christianity.

The rise of Islam raised a different question for Christians. Whereas Judaism and paganism were internal challenges within Christendom, Islam was a powerful military threat which conquered half the Christian world. The chief Christian response was at first defense, and later the offensive reactions of the Crusades and the reconquest of Spain. In both defense and offense, Muslims were viewed chiefly as infidels.

Nevertheless, there was some theological response. The cultural and intellectual superiority of Islam over Western Christianity made it a conduit of scholarship to the West. Especially important for medieval theology was the new understanding of the philosophy of Aristotle. This philosophy seemed to embody a knowledge which could be common to Jews, Muslims, and Christians. For example, Christianity, Judaism, Islam, and much of Greek philosophy were seen as sharing a belief in the unity of God. This gave encouragement to the idea of natural theology, the view that human reason alone can establish many of the truths of faith. This idea was worked out most fully and influentially by Thomas Aquinas. For him, natural theology required completion by truths which could be known only by supernatural revelation. But in the seventeenth and eighteenth centuries the truths that are known by reason came to be regarded as all sufficient and as the norm by which to judge the several positive religions. This normative natural religion is basically an ethical monotheism free from historical particularity and nonethical regulations.

The gradually increasing knowledge of China, beginning with Marco Polo, introduced Confucianism to the Christian consciousness. On the whole, the image of China in Christendom was quite positive. Hence the Christian attitude toward Confucianism was affirmative. Nevertheless, it was clear that Confucianism was not Christianity, and Christian faith was understood to call for the conversion of the Chinese.

In the sixteenth and seventeenth centuries, Jesuit missionaries achieved positions of influence in the Chinese court, and Catholic Christianity won a considerable following in many parts of the country. The success of the Christian mission posed problems analogous to those of the church in the Roman Empire. To what extent must Chinese culture and religious practice be rejected by converts to

Christianity, and to what extent could they be assimilated? For example, could Christians participate in Confucian rites honoring the ancestors and especially Confucius himself?

Most of the Jesuit missionaries wanted to develop a Confucian Christianity analogous to the Neoplatonic Christianity that won the Roman world. In this effort they at times had support from the papacy. But during a century of struggle, beginning in the middle of the seventeenth century and continuing into the eighteenth (the so-called "rites controversy"), the papal position became more rigid. Confucian practices were proscribed, and tolerant missionaries were punished. Christianity in China was thereby limited to the status of a foreign religion.

It is interesting to see that in this struggle "religion" became a crucial issue. If Confucianism, with its pervasive influence on Chinese culture, was a religion, then Christians must refuse participation. If, however, the Confucian rites and practices so integral to Chinese life could be viewed as "political," then the church need not oppose them. The friendly Manchu emperor K'ang-hsi officially supported the Jesuit argument that they were political, and it was the refusal of the pope to accept this position that led to the loss of imperial support for the Christian mission.

These brief comments about the Christian relation to Judaism, paganism, Islam, and Confucianism should make clear that there was no one Christian view of "the religions." Each religious tradition posed its own problems for the church, and there was little effort to generalize. By the nineteenth century, however, the situation had changed. Christians understood themselves in a global context in which there were other religions. The understanding of these other religions became for many the central issue in the understanding of Christianity itself.

CHALLENGES AND CONTRIBUTIONS OF MODERN CONSCIOUSNESS

Post-Enlightenment Views of the Religions

Immanuel Kant, who climaxed the rationalism of the Enlightenment, also effected a "Copernican revolution" in philosophy which paved the way for radical historical thinking. Whereas the other rationalists had thought of reason as a means of learning objective truth about an objective world, Kant argued that the mind has the more basic function of constituting a rationally ordered world. Although he generally thought of this constituting activity as that of human mind as such at all times and places, increasing knowledge of the diversity of cultures led his followers to see that in many respects human beings have constituted their worlds quite differently. The study of the ways the human mind has developed thus assumed primacy. The discussion of religion shifted from an effort to discover the universal rational religion to an evaluation of the actual diversity of religions.

G. W. F. Hegel undertook to read the entire history of religion as one linear movement. This did not mean that he failed to recognize the contemporaneous existence of a variety of religions, but he distinguished the creative moment of each from its sheer continuation. He saw in these creative moments a continuous development of spirit itself, which is at once divine and human. He discerned this creative movement as beginning in China, moving to India, Persia, Israel, Greece, and Rome, and finally coming to its fulfillment in Germanic Protestantism and Western European culture. One of the questions with which Hegel wrestled philosophically was whether religion itself, including Christianity, had like art now become "for us a thing of the past."

Although Hegel opened up whole new vistas for thinking about the religions and continues to be an immensely influential figure, few have followed him in his linear view of the relation of Eastern and Western religions. Others have also discerned patterns of progress in religion, but they have acknowledged the continuing and competitive validity of several forms more or less at the same level. Usually this is done by seeing all religions as expressive of a common essence. For example, Schleiermacher saw the essence of all religion in the feeling of absolute dependence. He could then distinguish primitive from developed expressions of religion in a linear fashion, but he could also recognize that there exists today a multiplicity of high religions, specifically Judaism, Islam, and Christianity. All these are marked by monotheism. Schleiermacher distinguishes them first according to their aesthetic and ethical orientations, classifying Islam as aesthetic and Judaism and Christianity as ethical. He describes the two religious forms in such a way as to imply the superiority of the ethical over the aesthetic, and then proceeds to display the superiority of

Christianity over Judaism on the basis of idolatrous remnants in the latter.

By the end of the nineteenth century it was no longer possible so easily to relegate the religions of India and China to inferior status as having failed to achieve monotheism. If Christianity was to be shown to be the supreme form of religion, a much fuller wrestling with the self-understanding of other religious traditions would be required.

Ernst Troeltsch devoted extensive attention to the problem of what he termed "the absoluteness of Christianity." In his book by that title, he argues that religion, which he regarded as the manifestation of the divine life in human history, achieves its purest and most universal form in Christianity. He supports his argument by showing how expressions other than Christian are closely bound to particular nations or cultures, or are primarily philosophical in character. The Christian understanding of God's self-manifestation in persons breaks these boundaries.

However, Troeltsch himself could not rest with this formulation. His further studies of Christianity forced him to recognize the great diversity of Christian forms and the extent to which all of them are culture-bound. His studies also forced him to acknowledge the capacity of other traditions, especially Buddhism and Hinduism, to transcend national and cultural limits. Hence there was no longer any basis for persisting in the claim to Christian absoluteness. Although religion exists as a distinct element in each tradition, in its actual forms it cannot be abstracted from the culture as a whole. If we are to compare religions, we must compare the civilizations in which they are embodied and expressed. We have no criteria independent of the diversity of cultural values by which to make an objective judgment. We must accept Christianity as absolute for us, while recognizing that other religions may be absolute for other cultures.

Other scholars attempted to arrive at an understanding of religion on more objective grounds. Nathan Söderblom maintained that the idea of God or a supreme being is far more limited than the experience of the holy. Rudolf Otto came to a similar conclusion and declared the holy to be a universal category of human experience. Otto argued that Christianity expresses the holy in a distinctive and thoroughly ethicized way, thus making an argument for its superiority. Yet the effect of his work was primarily to turn attention from theological to phenomenological formulations. He illumined Christian beliefs by setting them in the context of the experience and beliefs of other religious communities. He also showed that religion is a necessary and universal feature of human experience, so that the question is not the justification of religion in a secular world but how it is best expressed.

It was the role of Karl Barth vigorously to reintroduce into this situation the perspective of the Reformers. More consistently even than they, he insisted upon a wholly christocentric mode of reflection. It is the task of the Christian to witness to what God has made known to us in Jesus Christ. This is both a "no" to all our human efforts to find saving truth apart from Christ and a "yes" to us as persons redeemed by Christ. Insofar as religion is to be understood as the human effort to attain salvation, it must be condemned. This goes as much for Christian religion as any other. Only as religion is understood as a human effort to respond to the divine self-revelation can a qualified affirmation be admitted.

In any case, Barth calls for a separation of theology from the study of religion. That study is completely justified just as any science is. Christians are free to study all human phenomena, including religion. Because in studying religion they have no need to show that one religion is better than another, the study of religion can attain a fuller objectivity and openness. But all this throws no light on Christian doctrine. The theologian looks only to Christ.

For two generations most Christian theology followed the direction pointed by Barth even when theologians have not agreed with him in detail. That is, for half a century the work of Christian theology was carried on outside the context of history-of-religions. Those theologians who against Barth's advice continued to attend to other religions usually did so only to display the contrast between the religions and Christian faith as response to divine revelation. Emil Brunner argued that either the Christian must deny that Christian faith is a religion at all, or else assert that it is true religion in sharp contrast to all others as false. Of those holding this position, Hendrik Kraemer engaged in the most detailed and responsible study of other religions in order to support this fundamental contrast.

The opposition of revelation to human religion could also function to ally Christianity with secularization. If religion as a human phenomenon expresses a lack of faith in Christ, then the de-religionizing of the world is, from the Christian point of view, a gain. Dietrich Bonhoeffer called for a "religionless" Christianity and a nonreligious hermeneutic of scripture. A tradition of secular Christianity emerged. More recently there have been powerful calls for a political interpretation of the gospel which will make clear the concrete meaning of liberation from the actual oppressions operative in our world. Meanwhile, Arend Th. van Leeuwen has attempted to show what the association of Christianity with secularization has meant in relation to other religions. In his view, Christianity supports the movements for secularization against all the traditional religions of Asia, and it sees these movements as implementing its own message. For this strand of Christian thinking, it is typically Marxism rather than other religions with which dialogue is important and alliance appropriate.

Continuing Efforts to Locate Christianity in the Horizon of Religion

Until recently most contemporary professional theologians have been caught up in this nonreligious interpretation of Christianity. However, on the fringes of theology the tradition of viewing Christianity within the horizon of religion has continued, and the work done there has had a great influence on the habits of mind and modes of thought of Christians, especially in the English-speaking world. An important expression of this approach was that of William Ernest Hocking, a philosopher and lay Christian. He called for Christians to adopt "the way of reconception." He defined religion as "a passion for righteousness, and for the spread of righteousness, conceived as a cosmic demand." He then argued that all religions, while sharing this common essence, develop different apprehensions of the truth. As they meet each other, each has much to learn from the others and in the process needs to reconceive its own truth. Thus each can grow toward an inclusive form. He believed that Christianity has a peculiar capacity to develop into such an inclusive religion. Later he came to understand religion in a more mystical way.

The understanding of the essence of religion as mystical experience has probably been the most influential in recent times, at least in the United States, despite its lack of acceptance among theologians. Aldous Huxley and Arnold Toynbee did much to popularize the view that all religions express in diverse ways the unitive experience of mysticism. More recently, this esoteric core of religions has been distinguished from their exoteric manifestations by Frithjof Schuon, seconded and supported by Huston Smith. Meanwhile it has had an important practical effect on the way Eastern religions have been approached, especially by such Roman Catholics as Thomas Merton.

Beginning with Vatican II, Roman Catholics have taken the lead in relating Christianity to other religions both in theory and in practice. For the first time the church has taken an official stand toward other religions. It did so with specific reference to Buddhism, Hinduism, Islam, and Judaism. In all cases it expressed a positive and friendly attitude. It has been the responsibility of its theologians to clarify the relation between this positive stance and the continuing insistence on the supernatural centrality of Christ and the importance of the church.

Karl Rahner has been the most important thinker to take up this task. He has developed the doctrine that implicit faith can be found outside the church and has introduced the category of the "anonymous Christian" to refer to those who have received this faith apart from the church. Faith is no less the work of God among anonymous Christians than among the people of the church. Further, the religions of the world are channels for expression of this faith and for its encouragement. They are thus instruments of salvation.

This does not lead to a relativistic attitude on the part of Christians. What is anonymous, inchoate, and fragmentary has been fully manifest in Jesus Christ. When the opportunity presents itself to enter the church in which this full truth is celebrated, it is the duty of the anonymous Christian to do so. When the church arrives, the other religions are no longer needed. But the approach to these other religions should be dialogical rather than polemical. Christianity can learn from them as well as teach them. All can gain from their mutual encounter with the possibility of moving toward convergence.

Of particular importance are the specific statements of Vatican II on Judaism. Although the Catholic Church never officially taught the responsibility of all Jews for the crucifixion of Jesus, much Christian theology and preaching had stated that the Jewish people as a whole are guilty. The Council repudiated this teaching and rejected anti-Semitism. This paved the way for an important and badly needed dialogue between Catholics and Jews.

The shift from polemic to dialogue in the Catholic church, and

the corresponding shift which has occurred in much of Protestantism, could be supported from a variety of theological points of view.
In some cases dialogue has been a means of better understanding the
community from which converts were sought. In others it has been
conceived as a subtle approach to the conversion of the dialogue
partner. In still others it has expressed the conviction that all comparative judgments as to the respective merits of different religions are
objectionable. But whatever its motivation, it has had a pervasive
effect upon the Christian view of other religions and the self-understanding of Christians. To view representatives of other religions as
partners in dialogue is, provisionally at least, to see Christianity as
one religious movement among others.

Paul Tillich is an interesting embodiment of this development. In
principle his theology was always open to viewing Christianity in the
context of the history of religions, since he recognized a universal
revelation of God in all cultures and all religions. Following in the
tradition of Schleiermacher, Troeltsch, and Otto, he viewed Christianity as a concrete realization of a universal dimension of human
existence. He described this universal dimension as ultimate concern. In principle he was interested in how ultimate concern is expressed in all religions, but in fact he gave more attention to the
movements that were most important in Europe during his formative
years: humanism, communism, and fascism. These he called quasi-
religions. He also struggled to formulate his distinctive theological
position in relation to the dominant Barthian rejection of religion as
the context of theological study. In his later years, however, he developed this interest, made personal contacts with Asian religions
(especially Buddhism), and expressed regret that he had not developed his theology more fully in the context of the study of the
religions. He saw that as the task for the future.

Wolfhart Pannenberg also represents a movement toward reestablishing the religions as the context for the understanding of Christianity. For him the universal characteristic of human beings which
expresses itself everywhere is the anticipation of an end which will
retrospectively give meaning to all that has been. The confirmation
of this anticipation and the revelation of what it entails are to be
found in the resurrection of Jesus, so that the history within which
that event occurred is of central importance. But because it is of

central importance for the whole world, it needs to be displayed as such in the context of universal history. Such a history is primarily the history of religions, and the Christian affirmation can only be vindicated as the resurrection of Jesus Christ can be shown to be the proleptic fulfillment of what is anticipated in all religions. This, in turn, can be done only as objective rational inquiry into all religions supports this interpretation. Hence Christian theology in the context of the history of religions becomes the theology of religion.

Both Tillich and Pannenberg claim a certain superiority or absoluteness for Christianity, but they avoid the types of claims made during the nineteenth century. For Tillich the criterion of absoluteness of a religion is the success of its central symbol in pointing beyond itself to the absolute. It is the particular merit of the cross that it does so. Hence there is no argument for the superiority of the actual institutions and beliefs or moral practices of Christianity, only the claim that the central symbol of Christian faith is transparent to the absolute precisely insofar as it refuses its own absolutization.

For Pannenberg, in a similar way, all religions are incomplete and unfulfilled; this is as true of Christianity as of any other. What is important is that this incompleteness be recognized and that a religion point beyond itself to the ultimate fulfillment of all. Christian eschatology, in its doctrine of the universal resurrection, meets this requirement.

The Critique of "Religion"

The pursuit of dialogue with other traditions has raised critically the question mentioned at the outset as to the usefulness of the category "religion." Attention to "religion" has led either to viewing Christianity as one among many embodiments of a common essence or a priori, or else to the contrasting of Christianity with all the others as a revelation or a movement of secularization. In either case the traditions other than Christianity are grouped together under a common rubric on the assumption that they are all engaged in essentially the same task. Generalizations about this common task are sought through phenomenology or anthropology or metaphysics. These generalizations then provide the categories with which the several movements are approached.

Wilfred Cantwell Smith has been the most vigorous critic of the category "religion." He too has noticed that it is a Western category that imposes meanings on other traditions which are alien to them. He has seen how often these meanings are pejorative. Also, if we begin with Western ideas about religion, the relationship of religions seems inevitably competitive. The use of this concept compartmentalizes us into adherents of a given number of movements, ignoring the actuality of personal faith as faith develops in diverse contexts and cultures. He recommends that we encounter people in terms of their faith, talking with them person-to-person instead of as adherents of different religions.

George Rupp develops one feature of this direction of thought. He points out that the divisions within what have been called religions are often greater than the differences among the religions. Liberal Christians may find more in common with liberal Buddhists than with fundamentalist Christians. Although Rupp does not issue a polemic against the category of religion, he does call for a typology that cuts across the lines that have been established when we think of the religions.

The actual practice of dialogue raises another issue of equal importance. This is the problem of understanding. Our normal way of understanding is to fit what we encounter into the established categories of our thought. If, for example, we have a theory of the nature and function of religion and then categorize some movement as a religion, we can study it, or enter into dialogue with its representatives, in order to learn the particular way in which that movement expresses what are already assumed to be universal characteristics of religion. The problem arises if our dialogue partners find our questions inappropriate and try to explain something that falls outside our established categories. We must then decide that our dialogue partners have not understood us, that they are ignorant of their own movements, or that our questions are not appropriate. If we make the latter decision, we will either try again to work out the appropriate questions from our own resources or try to learn how to question by listening to the unanticipated answers.

The actual situation always involves some of both, if the dialogue proceeds effectively. We cannot break altogether from established habits of mind, but our ways of questioning and thinking will be gradually altered as we listen attentively to those who have different habits. Nevertheless, some who have participated long and seriously in dialogue despair of achieving any real understanding of the deeply different modes of thought and experience with which they are confronted merely through dialogue.

Two alternatives are then possible. First, people may participate in the spiritual disciplines of the other tradition and come through them to experiences more analogous to those that are being described. This is an approach in which Roman Catholics have taken the lead. There is a Catholic Zen center near Tokyo where many Catholics have participated in Zen-type experiences. In the United States both Zen and yoga have been practiced in Catholic convents and monasteries. Certainly the result is an improved understanding of what Hindus and Buddhists are saying.

The second possibility is the employment of speculative philosophy. Although the dominant Western tradition has organized the world of thought and experience in ways quite alien to those of India and China, there are some thinkers who have protested against the dominant mode and have pointed to radical alternatives. Schopenhauer is an outstanding example in the early nineteenth century. He interpreted the normal Western consciousness as one in which reality is organized by the will, and he saw the consequences as eminently destructive. Hence in his own quest for truth and salvation he developed the idea of the annihilation of the will as the route to serenity and truth. He believed that this was what happened in some forms of mysticism. When he encountered fragments of Buddhist literature, he saw in nirvana the realization of that extinction of the will to which his own speculations had led him. Although he never became a scholar of Buddhism, his grasp of Buddhist soteriology was far deeper than that of the leading scholars of the nineteenth century.

In the twentieth century, Martin Heidegger performed a similar service for the West. After he turned away from the typically Western understanding of existence developed in *Being and Time,* his thought moved more and more into an actual immersion in being. The rational conceptual approach of Western thought gave way to an openness to being which allowed him to experience himself as one through whom being is. The tendencies toward substantialism and dualism in his early thought give way to a mode of realization of what one is as an instance of being. This is remarkably similar to a

Mahayana Buddhist realization of what one is as an instance of Buddha-nature. The approximation of Heidegger to Buddhism was recognized by Heidegger himself and has been frequently appreciated by Oriental Buddhists.

Although Arthur Schopenhauer and Heidegger have contributed greatly to the possibility of Westerners understanding Eastern thought, a price is exacted for accepting their assistance. One can understand Buddhism only at the cost of rejecting the whole structure of Western thought and experience. If one would continue to be a Christian believer, it must be in terms of a very different form of Christianity than any that has yet appeared, a form so different that one must question its continuity with our biblical roots.

For this reason another type of philosophical project appears more promising for dialogue, although it is not yet as influential. A philosopher may attempt not so much to shift from one thought form to another as to show how a multiplicity of thought forms are equally valid. Ludwig Wittgenstein's language games lend themselves to this type of use. Also in other ways Wittgenstein's thought is suggestive of still largely unexplored approaches through which Westerners may be able to understand an Eastern mode of thought without being removed from their own.

The first major book which systematically developed a complementary view of East and West was F. S. C. Northrop's *Philosophy East and West*. Northrop argues that human experience begins with a differentiated aesthetic continuum, that is, an experience of such things as colors, shapes, and sounds spatially arranged. From this starting point the Greeks and the West as a whole shifted attention to differentiating forms within the continuum. They abstracted these and reflected about them. This made possible the development of mathematics, science, technology, and a whole style of rational, conceptual organization. On the other hand, the East regarded these differentiating forms as superficial and sought the deeper reality in the undifferentiated aesthetic continuum. While acceptance of Northrop's position does not make it immediately easy to grasp the experience of the undifferentiated aesthetic continuum, or to understand the language in which it is expressed, it does make intelligible to Westerners what is being discussed. We can see why a different language is needed. In principle it enables Westerners to cross over to a strange world of thought and life without repudiating their own.

Meanwhile it enables Westerners to view the two worlds as complementary rather than mutually exclusive. Those who participate in dialogue on this basis will understand why they have much to learn and will also be freed from the assumption that dialogue is possible only on the basis of a common essence or shared experience.

Although Northrop's book is important as providing a way in which different traditions can be understood as complementary, it is inadequate and even misleading in its accounts both of Christianity and of the several Eastern traditions. Hence the task of clarifying the complementary contributions of East and West largely remains to be done. Northrop's own teacher, Alfred North Whitehead, offers possibilities for this task which were neglected by Northrop and which are now being explored.

Theological Reconceptualization and Mission

As Hocking saw, the encounter of traditions leads to reconceptualization in all. He thought this was grounded in a common essence, which he described first in terms of moral passion and subsequently more mystically. Many have continued to suppose that dialogue and mutual influence can occur only between movements that are grounded in the same experience or have the same end. However, we have now seen that dialogue can also occur among movements which have complementary modes of experience. Indeed, the significance of the reconceptualization that follows an encounter with expressions of a radically complementary mode of experience may be even greater.

Today the encounter of Christians with Eastern traditions has already led to extensive experimentation with new meditational disciplines, as noted earlier. It has led to the incorporation of Oriental insights into Western psychology and therapy and has made its mark in Western literature.

In the early centuries of Christianity a vital faith was able to reconceptualize itself in and through its engagement with the wisdom of Greece. In the process it so assimilated the achievements of Greek thought that philosophers could become Christian without abandoning the truths to which their thought had led them. Today it seems that the dialogical relation with the religions of Asia offers a similar opportunity for reconceptualization in and through engagement with Eastern wisdom.

Thus far most Christian theological reflection has been stimulated by encounter with the other "higher" religions, but within American culture there is a new interest in "primitive" religions as well. American Indian religions have been reappraised as having much to teach us. Both African theologians and black theologians in the United States have opened to us the achievement and power of traditional African religion. In their quest to understand the religious experience of women, some feminists have forced a reappraisal of what has long been dismissed and berated as witchcraft. It seems that Christianity must not only learn from the great religious traditions of Asia but also come to terms with aspects of religious experience which it has repressed and suppressed in its rise to ascendancy. The task of understanding these manifold phenomena and reinterpreting theology in light of them has scarcely begun.

The process of such reconceptualization need not be viewed as antithetical to the concern for evangelization. Just as it was a reconceived Christianity which could win classical philosophers to the faith, so it may be a reconceived Christianity alone which can win those who have deeply tasted of the wisdom of the East or gained new appreciation for what was once dismissed as primitive.

There remains a still deeper question. Is there alongside the mission of evangelization of individuals another and different mission to "the religions"? This is suggested in Roman Catholic theology. Hans Küng, for example, has spoken of the church's task to be of service to the other "religions." The extensive missiological literature on "Christian presence" in non-Christian cultures suggests a similar stance. Perhaps through presence, service, dialogue, and Christianity's own rigorous reconceptualization, the process of reconceptualization in other traditions can proceed in a way that involves their progressive incorporation of that truth to which Christians have uniquely witnessed.

ISSUES AND PROPOSALS

Ours is a time of fresh opportunity. We can pick up the struggles of the nineteenth-century theologians to understand their faith in the global context, and we can do so with many advantages. Today we are much more ready to learn from other cultures since the assumption of the superiority of European culture over others no longer grips us. Both through scholarship and through personal contacts we have access to other traditions which our theological ancestors lacked.

Our advantages can also be our dangers. We may be so ready to learn from others, so ashamed of the imperialistic attitudes of our past, and so unsure of our inherited beliefs that encounter with new wisdom causes us to abandon our own inheritance. Often the issue is formulated as that of narrow faithfulness to our tradition or broad openness to the whole of human experience. Those who opt for the latter may feel themselves to be separating from the heart of Christian faith. Christianity comes to be viewed even by such Christians as most fully represented in its narrowest and most doctrinaire members, those who would continue the most negative aspects of our tradition. Conservatives see the vagueness and loss of rootedness that often follow from an open and receptive attitude, and build their defenses higher. Thus the encounter with other religious traditions, while it offers fresh opportunity for growth and vigor, can lead to the sterile choice of narrow-minded bigotry or lukewarm compromising liberalism.

The theological challenge is to make clear another option, specifically the option of faith. That requires once again clarifying what Christian faith really is as faith in Jesus Christ. We must show that faith in Jesus Christ is neither an attitude of rigid defense of inherited doctrines and attitudes, nor the pretense of standing on some neutral ground and supposing that from that perspective we can judge the merits of all the world's great religious traditions.

Insofar as we lack faith, we will try to establish our own security. We may do so either by absolutizing our relative heritage or by claiming neutrality and objectivity. If we do have faith, we will abandon the effort to establish our own security, and will trust Christ instead. That means we can listen nondefensively to what others believe and learn from them even when they deny Christ. The more deeply we trust Christ, the more openly receptive we will be to wisdom from any source, and the more responsibly critical we will be both of our own received habits of mind and of the limitations and distortions of others.

In the early church, faith led to the assimilation and transformation of Hellenic wisdom. In the process, the biblical heritage was itself transformed. Like all historical occurrences this one was ambiguous. Much of what has handicapped Christian thought in the twentieth century came from this incorporation of Hellenic modes of thought in the early church. But much of what was learned was of permanent value, and a church that failed to learn from the best thought of that day might long since have perished in its rigid isolation.

Similarly, we today confront the wisdom of ancient traditions, especially those of India and China but also of traditions that go back before the rise of civilization. These show their power of attraction through their penetration of Western culture. Faith calls us to assimilate and transform this wisdom. In the process we will again be transformed. Such transformation will not be the consummatory end of Christian history. It too will be ambiguous. There is danger that we will lose sight of important elements of our own tradition and uncritically ingest what should be radically transformed. But to fail to open ourselves to this process will be to declare our lack of faith, our insistence on establishing our own security on the basis of what has happened in the past, our refusal of Christ's future. It will have the practical result of making Christian faith merely one among many options confronted by the next generation, and one that looks peculiarly parochial and closed. Better to live by faith and take the risk of making many mistakes than to make the unquestionable mistake of trusting our ideas instead of the living Christ.

Of all the encounters with other religious movements, the most disturbing for Christians is the encounter with Judaism. It is most disturbing because for so long we have falsely supposed that we have already adequately assimilated and transformed the wisdom of Judaism, and we have treated the ongoing Jewish community more as a fossil than as a living movement. It is disturbing also because of the growing awareness of the enormous suffering we have inflicted upon the Jews in the name of Jesus Christ. The one who for us is the symbol and bearer of liberation, transformation, and reconciliation is for the Jew the symbol of oppression, abuse, and persecution. The Jew knows the underside of our history, the half that we have repressed.

We have much yet to learn from Jewish wisdom. But what we have especially to gain from our encounter with living Judaism is a realization of our own collective evil. We cannot be healed until our active memory integrates the vicious anti-Semitism of our saints, our repeated pogroms against Jewish communities, and the Holocaust itself. And unless we are healed, the Jews will have reason to fear the repetition of our depraved behavior.

Still we will do no favor to the Jews by abandoning all talk of Christ because it is offensive to them, for it is only in Christ that our healing can occur, and it is only as we are healed that Christ can cease to be their enemy. Indeed, Christians who seek understanding across the lines of religious traditions do themselves a disservice if they minimize the distinctive character of their own faith. Of course, there must be openness to change, and in the course of time we may find aspects of our traditional teaching which can only be repented and rejected. But if we are to learn from others and be transformed through them, we must bring into the encounter the full richness of our heritage. Christianity can grow broader and more inclusive only as it revitalizes its relations with its own deepest roots.

SUGGESTIONS FOR FURTHER READING

Augustine. "In Answer to the Jews. Adversus Judaeos." Translated by Marie Liguori. *FC* 27:387–416.

Barth, Karl. *Church Dogmatics*. Vol. 1/2.

———. *The Epistle to the Romans*. London: Oxford University Press, 1933.

Cobb, John B., and Ives, Christopher, eds. *The Emptying God: A Buddhist-Jewish-Christian Conversation*. Maryknoll, N.Y.: Orbis Books, 1990.

D'Costa, Gavin, ed. *Christian Uniqueness Reconsidered: The Myth of a Pluralistic Theology of Religions*. Maryknoll, N.Y.: Orbis Books, 1990.

Griffiths, Paul J., ed. *Christianity through Non-Christian Eyes*. Maryknoll, N.Y.: Orbis Books, 1990.

———. *An Apology for Apologetics: A Study in the Logic of Interreligious Dialogue*. Maryknoll, N.Y.: Orbis Books, 1991.

Hegel, G. W. F. *Lectures on the Philosophy of Religion*. Part 2.

Heidegger, Martin. *On the Way to Language*. New York: Harper & Row, 1971. Esp. chap. 1.

Hick, John, and Knitter, Paul, eds. *The Myth of Christian Uniqueness: Toward a Pluralistic Theology of Religions*. Maryknoll, N.Y.: Orbis Books, 1987.

———. *Problems of Religious Pluralism*. New York: St. Martin's Press, 1985.

Hocking, William Ernest. *Living Religions and a World Faith*. New York: Macmillan Co., 1940.

Knitter, Paul. *No Other Name? A Critical Survey of Christian Attitudes toward the World Religions.* Maryknoll, N.Y.: Orbis Books, 1985.

Kraemer, Hendrik. *The Christian Message in a Non-Christian World.* London: Harper & Bros., 1938.

Nicholas de Cusa. "De Pace Fidei," in *Unity and Reform: Selected Writings of Nicholas de Cusa.* Edited by John P. Dolan. Notre Dame: University of Notre Dame Press, 1962.

Northrop, Filmer Stuart Cuckow. *The Meeting of East and West: An Inquiry Concerning World Understanding.* New York: Macmillan Co. 1946.

Origen. "Against Celsus." ANF 4.

Panikkar, Raimundo. *The Silence of God: The Answer of Buddha.* Maryknoll, N.Y.: Orbis Books, 1988.

Pannenberg, Wolfhart. *Theology and the Philosophy of Science.* Philadelphia: Westminster Press, 1976.

Pieris, Aloysius. *Love Meets Wisdom: A Christian Experience of Buddhism.* Maryknoll, N.Y.: Orbis Books, 1989.

Ruether, Rosemary Radford. *Faith and Fratricide: The Theological Roots of Anti-Semitism.* New York: Seabury Press, 1974.

Rupp, George. *Beyond Existentialism and Zen: Religion in a Pluralistic World.* New York: Oxford University Press, 1979.

Schleiermacher, Friedrich. *The Christian Faith.* Esp. pp. 31–52.

———. *On Religion: Speeches to Its Cultured Despisers.* Translated by John Oman. New York: Harper & Bros., 1958.

Smith, Huston. *Forgotten Truth: The Primordial Tradition.* New York: Harper & Row, 1976.

Smith, Wilfred Cantwell. *The Meaning and End of Religion.* New York: Mentor, 1963.

———. *Towards a World Theology: Faith and the Comparative History of Religion.* Philadelphia: Westminster Press, 1980.

Swidler, Leonard, ed. *Toward a Universal Theology of Religions.* Maryknoll, N.Y.: Orbis Books, 1987.

Tertullian. "An Answer to the Jews" and "The Prescription Against Heretics." ANF 3.

Tillich, Paul. *Christianity and the Encounter of the World Religions.* Minneapolis: Fortress Press, 1994.

———. *The Future of Religions.* New York: Harper & Row, 1966.

Troeltsch, Ernst. *The Absoluteness of Christianity and the History of Religions.* Richmond: John Knox Press, 1971.

Toynbee, Arnold Joseph. *Christianity among the Religions of the World.* New York: Charles Scribner's Sons, 1957.

Van Leeuwen, Arend Th. *Christianity in World History: The Meeting of East and West.* London: Edinburg House, 1964.

Whitehead, Alfred North. *Religion in the Making.* New York: New American Library, 1960.

AN EPILOGUE: THE CHRISTIAN PARADIGM

If there can be said to be a single overriding task for theology at the present time, it is to recover a sense of the *wholeness*, the *unity* and *integrity*, of the Christian witness.

This statement by Robert King in the opening chapter of this book identifies the perennial task of Christian theology. It used to be called "the essence of Christianity," but regardless of the words used it is or should be always the central task of theological reflection to point to what is essential in Christian faith. This has never been easy, and it is even more difficult today when we are aware in ways our foremothers and forefathers were not that theology is a constructive enterprise and that Christianity is but one religion among many.

As almost every contributor to this volume has stressed, the Enlightenment posed a major challenge to identification of the essence of Christianity, for it brought to the foreground awareness that the human "world," whether religious, political, sociological, or personal, is a constructed world and hence a relative one. Since the Enlightenment and especially since Immanuel Kant, it has not been possible to turn to a deposit of the faith in scripture or tradition and find there an absolute or certain basis for religious truth. We have come to realize that there is no naked eye, no innocent eye, that all our ways of being in the world are *our* ways, and that the ways in which we construct our world are determined by our time and place. Moreover, the liberation theologies of recent years have driven the knife of relativity deeper into our settled worlds, for they insist that the self which constructs the world is not isolated or neutral as it does its work, but profoundly influenced by its economic, political, and cultural setting. We are selves-in-relationship from the very beginning to the end of our days and hence deeply influenced in ways beyond our knowing or our control.

Given this situation of radical relativity, it might appear that identification of the essence of Christianity is hopeless. It might appear that the pluralism which characterizes much of contemporary theological reflection is an acknowledgment of despair over being able to say what Christianity is and is not. Yet the essays in this book do not witness to such despair. On the contrary, they see the present situation, in which Christianity is not to be identified with an absolute deposit of sacred writings or with an infallible tradition of interpretation or with one particular set of models for the divine-human relationship, as freeing the essential core of Christianity to live once again in people's lives. This essential core is not any book or doctrine or interpretation, but the transformative *event* of new life, a new way of being in the world that is grounded in the life and death of Jesus of Nazareth. Scripture is testimony to this event; doctrines are consensus attempts to formulate its significance; theologies are interpretations of it; but *as event* it stands behind, beneath, and before all our constructions of it. It cannot be captured by any of our interpretations.

The contemporary awareness of the relativity of all our constructions has freed the event from idolatrous human control while at the same time sharpening our wills and our intellects to interpret it more appropriately and more universally. In this sense all theologians today embrace "the Protestant principle" that no human construct can embody the relationship of God with humanity. We are, then, on the brink of another "reformation," not the sort of reformation which would reduce Christianity to what the modern consciousness will accept, or absorb Christianity into other religions, but one which would enable us to appreciate its truth as well as its relativity. As John Cobb says in his essay, "the more deeply we trust Christ, the more openly receptive we will be to wisdom from any source, and the more responsibly critical we will be both of our own received habits of mind and of the limitations and distortions of others." It is not easy to maintain this stance—a stance which believes in the Christian way as a true way, but not the only way—for it involves commitment to relative truths. But it is, as the essays in this book uniformly insist, a necessary stance for informed, contemporary persons. It is also implied in Christianity, which at its core does not dictate a set of beliefs but proclaims a saving event. Relativism is not just a modern burden; it is an implication of Christianity's witness to the universal saving activity of the one and only God.

Hence the reformation of Christianity coming out of the Enlightenment and the more recent liberation theologies is a genuine one in that it makes a conscious attempt to return to the roots of the faith. Those who insist that a canonical view of scripture is not possible; that a dynamic rather than a static view of God is appropriate; that stress on the work rather than on the person of Jesus Christ is right; that hierarchical, patriarchal models of God's relationship to the world are oppressive and destructive; that other religions, which emphasize impersonal and natural models of God in contrast to the personalistic Western models, offer a needed corrective to Christianity—all who emphasize these points do not do so merely to accommodate the relativism of the modern consciousness, but because they believe that the essence of Christianity demands such emphasis. The authors of this volume believe that Christianity is proclaimed more appropriately and fully *by* such insistence, that the event which is at the core of Christianity demands such relativity, dynamism, openness, correction, and transformation of oppressive structures.

Much of what has been said in these closing comments can be summed up by the frequent use in this book of the term "paradigm" in relation to Christianity. A "paradigm" is an exemplary formulation; in theology, it can refer to such formulations as those of Augustine, Thomas Aquinas, John Calvin, Friedrich Schleiermacher, and the liberation theologies. Such theologies are "exemplars," standard models which include basic assumptions and accepted forms of articulation. These paradigms all refer to *the* exemplar which is their base, what one of our essays calls "the originative event, . . . the paradigmatic figure Jesus of Nazareth." This Jesus of Nazareth is "the model of models" behind all the tentative, exemplary formulations which attempt to interpret the transformation of existence embodied in his story. While it might be said that the theologies of the Reformers or of Schleiermacher or of the liberationists involve "paradigm shifts," in that distinctive emphases emerged with each of these interpretations of Christianity, the *intent* of each of these theologies was not to change the basic assumptions of Christianity, but to recover what was truly essential in what had somehow become distorted or obscured. In science a paradigm shift such as the change from New-tonian to quantum physics involves a revolution in basic assumptions; the old is left behind and everything is seen from a new perspective. Such is not the case in theology. Old interpretations are cast aside, but the basic assumptions of the religion remain, since they are not after all settled theories. Rather, what is paradigmatic in Christianity is the *event* of transformed existence associated with Jesus of Nazareth, and all reformers claim merely to be interpreting this event more truly and more relevantly.

Hence it could be said that Christianity itself constitutes a "para-digm," a comprehensive interpretation of God's ways with the world which has characteristic assumptions and emphases. As one of our essays remarks, "the Christian faith is only one historically condi-tioned resource among humankind's rich reservoir of moral and spiri-tual symbol systems." This is the broadest understanding of paradigm in relation to Christianity; it emphasizes the relativity of Christian faith in relationship to other world religions as well as underscoring the continuity, in spite of distinctive emphases, of interpretations within the tradition. It would be helpful in attempting to assess the direction implied for theological reflection in this book to understand Christianity as one paradigm alongside other paradigms of the divine-human relationship and to see within that paradigm shifts in empha-sis which, while distinctive and significant, do not constitute the creation of a new religion. This perspective will allow us to appreci-ate other religions in ways not characteristic of the Christian tradition and to see how Christian reformers, including contemporary reform-ers, can offer new interpretations of the faith which do not constitute a new religion but which open up the core meaning of this faith for contemporary women and men.

I would like to illustrate this thesis by analyzing four characteristic notes emerging in this book: (1) the open relationship of Christianity to other religions; (2) the relative authority of scripture; (3) the oppres-sive nature of the hierarchical, imperialistic, patriarchal model for the divine-human relationship; and (4) the emphasis on openness to the future rather than on the absolutism of the past. Each is preemi-nently contemporary as well as part of an overall conviction that the emerging identification of the essence of Christianity evident in these motifs is more appropriate to the transformation of existence asso-ciated with the paradigmatic figure of Jesus of Nazareth than previous interpretations of these issues.

The Relativity of Religion

If one views Christianity as one paradigm of the divine-human relationship among many others, then Christianity becomes relative. Arguments for the absoluteness, superiority, or uniqueness of Chris-tianity become difficult if not impossible. To many people this situa-tion appears intolerable. How can one believe in a religion which is not *the* religion? What sort of truth does such a religion proclaim? To see Christianity as a paradigm or one way of modeling the divine-human relationship among others relativizes Christianity, but not the God whose work it proclaims. The problem with believing *in* Chris-tianity or in any other religion is that the religion, not God, becomes absolute. The relativizing of Christianity is an implicit recognition that the God worshiped in Christianity is not a tribal God, not "the God of Christians," but the one and only universal God. To see Christianity as a paradigm acknowledges that all our ways of imagin-ing and talking about God are inadequate and partial, but by that very admission we are saved from worshiping the creations of our own minds. Moreover, we can appreciate the limitations of even our best—the classic—attempts to model the divine-human relation-ship.

Many recent thinkers, both within the Christian community and outside it, have noted the catastrophic results on the natural environ-ment of the Judaic-Christian transcendent, personalistic model for God. One of the strengths of the Western tradition has been this model; but unbalanced by Eastern models of immanence, which stress the interconnection of all life, it has given human beings li-cense to dominate and desecrate the nonhuman world. If the God whom we worship is the one and only true and universal God, then a model of God which not only permits but encourages the laying waste of the natural world is severely distorted. If the essence of Christianity is the event of the transformation of existence, then any formulation of that event should seek to be universal in its under-standing of that transformation, which surely includes a harmonious and fulfilling relationship between the human and natural orders. It is not our formulations that are sacred; hence we can acknowledge where they have been amiss. To see Christianity as one paradigm among many frees Christians to make this acknowledgment. To be a contemporary Christian fully conscious of the relativism of the Christian model frees the mind from idolatry and opens it to needed corrections from other religions.

But then what sort of truth is being proclaimed by Christianity? How does one know that *this* paradigm contains any truth at all? Are all religions equally valid? These questions have plagued Christians for centuries because of the assumption that a universal religion must be the absolute and only one. Relativity and universality, however, are not opposites: a poem which is particular and relative in its expression of a profound human reality, such as the experiences of love or death, is no less universal for being partial. In fact, a poem can be universal only by being radically concrete and particular and hence necessarily partial and relative. No human expression, poetic or religious, can be complete or absolute; nevertheless, in its relativism it can be "true."

What is the nature of such truth? The truth of any model of reality—and Christianity as a paradigm of God's ways with the world provides such a model—can be judged by a number of factors: its internal consistency, its capacity to comprehend the various dimensions of existence, its "fit" with life as lived, its ability to deal with personal and public evil, and its fruitfulness for understanding the depths and heights of existence. Such factors are relative ones, but all together they work to support the judgment (or not to support it) that the paradigm in question *is* a true, though partial, model of reality. Commitment to a paradigm is a judgment of relative adequacy; this is but another way of saying we live by faith, not by knowledge. We *believe*—not without evidence or in spite of evidence, but on the basis of partial evidence—that a particular paradigm is *one* appropriate way to express what can never be fully or adequately expressed: the event of God's transforming love. If we worship God and not our own paradigms, then as Cobb says, "the more deeply we trust Christ, the more openly receptive we will be to wisdom from any source." Relativism does not diminish faith in God, only faith in our own formulations of God's redeeming love.

382

The Authority of Scripture

For Christians the issues we have been reflecting on come into sharp focus when we turn to the authority of scripture. Christianity has in many ways been a "book" religion. The character of contemporary relativism is nowhere seen more acutely than in the changes that have occurred over the last two hundred years regarding the question of scriptural authority. Historical criticism has insisted that scripture is a text like other human texts: it was written from various points of view; it was influenced by the cultural, economic, political, and personal circumstances of its authors; it is a poetic text composed of stories and images which permit many different interpretations. The constructive, relativistic character of modernity is evident in the shift from seeing scripture as a divinely inspired, closed deposit of truth to seeing it as a vehicle proclaiming the transforming event of God's love associated with Jesus of Nazareth. Scripture is now understood to be a human expression of that event as it occurred in the lives of various people and communities. The forms of expression vary as different authors attempt to say what that transformation entails: images of God as healer, father, savior, word, reconciler, king, redeemer are but partial and inadequate (as well as culturally conditioned) attempts to express the change in their existence experienced in relationship to the life and death of Jesus of Nazareth.

The relativization of scripture means that this text can no longer be seen as absolute or closed; it is not these particular writings that are sacred, but the event to which they point. Hence other modes of expression, images not central in scripture, might be authoritative or appropriate if they point to dimensions of the transformation of existence in ways that fit with the quality of the new life introduced by Jesus of Nazareth. The criterion is not whether it is "in the Bible" but whether it is an appropriate (though partial) expression of that transformed way of life. For instance, while the images of God as "liberator" or "mother" are not central to the New Testament (they are much more evident in the Old Testament), each expresses a profound dimension of God's transforming love. "Liberator" points to freedom from oppression, especially at the social and political levels, while "mother" captures as no other image can the awareness of rebirth, nurture, acceptance, and compassion common to Christian experiences of God's love. The end of a closed canon and of the absolutism of scripture means a greater possibility of *relevancy* in language expressing the divine-human relationship, especially for peoples who have traditionally felt excluded by the particular images of scripture.

If scriptural language models the divine-human relationship, it does not capture or hold it; other models are needed to correct the biases and partiality of its models. But what is the status of the biblical models? What is the authority of scripture? There are many ways to express the special place which the Bible has for Christians who accept its relative status. One such way is to see it as a "classic," analogous to other classics which have gained authority because of their intrinsic power to express certain truths about reality. A classic is *given* authority because it is judged to merit it. Likewise the writings which comprise the Bible are in this perspective given authority by people who experience the transforming love of God associated with the paradigmatic figure of Jesus of Nazareth, because these writings are judged to express dimensions of that experience more adequately than other rejected writings. The criterion is adequacy in expressing that event; as such, they become "classics," foundational but not exclusive texts, models which provide guidance but which are admittedly partial and biased. A text which is understood as absolute and divinely inspired *imposes* its authority regardless of its relevance; a text which is understood as a classic must *win* its authority by its ability to speak to all kinds of people in varying circumstances. The former kind of text is not more "true" than the latter; in fact, it pretends to a kind of truth—absolute truth—which is never available to human beings and which is at base idolatrous. Many Christians have worshiped and still do worship a book, not God; the Bible as classic text permits foundational but partial authority to scripture, the only kind of authority which any human text can legitimately claim.

Models of the Divine-Human Relationship

The issues of the relevance as well as the relativity of the Christian paradigm also emerge when we turn to contemporary awareness of the oppressive nature of the hierarchical, imperialistic, patriarchal model for the divine-human relationship. This model is so ingrained in the Christian tradition that to many people it is identical with the Christian paradigm. However, one of the major shifts within this paradigm, as noted by several of the contributors to the present volume, has been severe contemporary criticism of this way of modeling the divine-human relationship. Many Third World and feminist theologians insist that if Christianity is inexorably wedded to the imperialistic, patriarchal model, then there is little possibility that it can address the oppressive structures of racism, poverty, and sexism under which they suffer. They point out that this model of the divine-human relationship has contributed substantially *to* these oppressive structures, not simply because of the choice of such models as "king," "lord," and "father" for God, but also because of the legitimization of these models as divinely inspired and absolute to the exclusion of other complementary or alternative models. With the relativization of scripture and the tradition, however, the imperialistic, patriarchal model is recognized not only as being but *one* way to imagine the relationship between God and humanity, but also as a way which has served the political and personal privilege of white, affluent males to the detriment of many other kinds of people.

Since this model has certainly been a central one in the Christian paradigm, two questions arise in relation to its status: How does it compare with models of the divine-human relationship in other religious paradigms? And is it central to the essence of Christianity? If one compares it to models in other religions, one is immediately struck by its oddity, for while there are certainly imperialistic, patriarchal notes in many religions, one aspect of the Judaic-Christian model is unique: its lack of female or feminine imagery for God. One does find, to be sure, especially in the Old Testament, maternal imagery for God's relationship to humanity, as well as tendencies to interpret the wisdom of God in female terms; moreover, the medieval mystics often spoke of God's love in maternal language. However, these sources do not constitute a sufficient counter to the main tradition, which is profoundly patriarchal. Most other world religions, more influenced than Christianity by the goddess religions and fertility cults, balance male imagery for God with female imagery either through complementary deities or dual aspects of the one deity. This fact alone relativizes the Christian pattern, but it does not necessarily mean that the classic Christian model is wrong because it is unique. The more basic question is the second one: Is the imperialistic, patriarchal pattern central to the essence of Christianity? We have noted that what is essential in Christianity is not any theory or set of images about the divine-human relationship, but a transforming event associated with Jesus of Nazareth which introduces a new way of being in the world.

While interpreters will differ in their understanding of the nature of this event, some characteristic notes emerge, at least among the contributors to this volume. One summary of these motifs appears in the definition of the church: "Ecclesia is a transfigured mode of human community, comprised of a plurality of peoples and cultural traditions, founded upon the life, death, and resurrection of Christ, constituted by the redemptive presence of God as Spirit, in which privatistic, provincial, and hierarchical modes of existence are over-come, and in which is actualized a universal reconciling love that liberates from sin, alienation, and oppression." The notes empha-sized in this definition are the universal, liberating, nonhierarchical, communal, and transfiguring mode of existence as characteristic of genuine Christian life. Such a definition can be seen as an attempt to interpret Jesus' preaching on "the kingdom of God" as setting forth a kind of "rule" radically at odds with conventional hierarchies of all sorts, as advocating a disorientation to worldly standards and a reori-entation to God's way of relating to us not according to what we deserve but according to the measure of freely given love.

While the radically unsettling and transforming character of this event has been deeply compromised by the hierarchical, patriarchal model—a model which is intrinsically supportive of the conven-tional, imperialistic status quo—every major reformation within the church has been sparked by the insight that the essence of Christian-ity does not support conventional standards. The monastic move-ments, at least in their early stages, are obvious examples of this insight, as are also Martin Luther's "justification by grace through faith," Friedrich Schleiermacher's universal feeling of absolute de-pendence, Karl Barth's doctrine of the election of all peoples to salvation, the many reforms of Vatican II stressing reciprocity be-tween church and world, and the liberation theologians' insistence that God is the liberator of the oppressed. A case can be made, then, that not only to the contributors of this volume but also to the major reformers of the church, the hierarchical, patriarchal pattern is *not* a central constituent of Christianity—in fact, it is a perversion of it.

If this is true, then one might ask, How should the divine-human relationship be modeled? If the traditional pattern is no longer acceptable, what are the alternatives? Two points appear relevant in the attempt to suggest a preliminary answer. First, no *single* model is desirable or possible. One of the basic difficulties with the traditional model is its hegemony, which has led both to idolatry and to irrelevance. In addition to its oppressive and destructive character, this model, as the only major one, has become an idol in the sense that the distance between the image and the reality it represents has collapsed. As a result, God's "name" to many people *is* "Father," which not only absolutizes the "fatherhood" of God, but also prohibits other complementary or alternative ways of speaking about our relationship to God which are more relevant to many people. Second, another *kind* of model or models is actually more appropriate than the traditional one, given what we have identified as central in Christianity. What is central is the transforming event associated with the life and death of Jesus of Nazareth, a transformation that brings about a new way of relating both to God and to other human beings. The stress is on the new quality of relationship which is seen not as a settled state of affairs between a static, substantial, imperialistic God and comparably static, substantial, dependent human beings, but as a dynamic process between a responsive, loving deity redeeming the suffering and supporting the growth of humanity. The imperialistic, patriarchal model has no place in such an understanding of the basic relationship between God and humanity. While the "father" model, if interpreted nonpatriarchally, is certainly an appropriate one, other models are also necessary to express dimensions of the new, transforming relationship with God which lies at the base of Christianity —models which stress aspects which the father model cannot, such as friend, lover, mother, liberator, healer, comrade, helper.

If models are seen primarily not as describing God's nature—as picture models—but as suggesting various dimensions of the transforming relationship with God, then it will be clear that many models are needed to express the richness of this relationship, and they will be more readily accepted. To be sure, theologians rightly abstract from the relationship to talk about divine and human "natures," yet the focus in Christianity is not on natures as such but on the transforming event which creates a new kind of relationship between God and humanity. As phenomenologists, process philosophers, sociologists, psychologists, and many others point out, we exist only as selves-in-relationship to others and to our environment. Relationship appears to be the law of the universe, not only for human beings and all other forms of life but also for the most basic constituents of matter—for example, the components of the atom—which can be best understood not as separate entities but as parts of structural relationships.

Openness to the Future

These comments lead us naturally to our final point: the contemporary emphasis on openness to the future rather than on the absolutizing of the past. Traditional Christianity's peculiar and distinctive relationship to history—the fact that it is grounded in the story of a particular human being who lived almost two thousand years ago—has tended to absolutize the past, especially its early history, and to suppose that its reformation depends on a return to the purity of primitive Christianity. Patterns of ecclesiastical polity, models of God, relations with culture and politics, personal life styles for believers—all these issues and more have frequently been seen within the framework of first-century Christianity. The relativization of scripture and tradition, as well as the critique of classical Christianity by the liberation theologies, have raised the question of Christianity's orientation to the past in a serious way. Of equal importance, the future is now seen by many theologians to be more viable than the past as a source for transforming the present. The envisioning of an alternative future—epitomized for some by Jesus' preaching of the coming kingdom as a way of being in the world at odds with conventional, present ways—creates a critical perspective from which the oppressive structures of the present can be changed. The transforming event of God's love is seen not in private or static terms, but in communal, dynamic terms. People become Christians not by personally accepting certain dogmas derived from the work of a bygone savior, but by living now in the presence of God's love to bring about universal transformation and fulfillment.

One distinctive note of the essays in this book is the insistence on pluralism and openness regarding what Christianity is and will be. The hesitancy this perspective engenders is seen in our reluctance or inability to engage in monumental systematic theologies as in the past. Theologians today are less certain than in the past about how to present a metaphysical systematization of Christian faith. However, the other side of this pluralism and openness is the willingness to entertain models of the divine-human relationship from both non-Christian religions and the traditionally dispossessed within Christianity. If one understands the divine-human relationship not as a matter settled in the past but as an event whose fulfillment is before us, then one necessarily lives with less certainty and more openness. The authors of this volume do not, however, appear to find this situation demoralizing. On the contrary, a settled, static, absolutistic interpretation of Christianity avoids the cutting edge of the faith, which can never be any theory or dogma or theology, but which entails participation in the redemptive love of God as it moves toward the transformation of the world.

As we bring these comments to a close, we recall that we opened them with the statement that the two principal contemporary shifts within the Christian paradigm have been brought about by the Enlightenment and the liberation theologies. Both have involved the relativization of Christianity. The first stressed the interpretive capacities of the self in the construction of its world; the second stresses the cultural conditioning of all such constructions. These "shifts" have seriously brought into question the classic Christian paradigm, and it may be that this paradigm will not be able to survive the critique. However, it is my contention (and I believe also the contention of most of the contributors to this book) that Christian faith can never be identified with any particular paradigm. Its "essence" is not any set of assumptions or theories, but a transforming event of existence which no paradigm can capture. Interpreters will continue to agonize and differ over the nature and meaning of this event. However, if we believe that this event is genuinely definitive of God's way with the world and universal in its scope, then we will neither absolutize our own ways of understanding it nor fail to appreciate ways which, while different from our own, nonetheless embody dimensions that our limitations have overlooked and to which our sin has blinded us.

SUGGESTIONS FOR FURTHER READING

Barbour, Ian G. *Myths, Models, and Paradigms: A Comparative Study in Science and Religion.* New York: Harper & Row, 1974.

———. *Religion in an Age of Science.* San Francisco: Harper & Row, 1990.

Barr, James. *The Bible in the Modern World.* London: SCM Press, 1973.

Berger, Peter L. *The Social Reality of Religion.* London: Faber & Faber, 1969.

Black, Max. *Models and Metaphors.* New York: Cornell University Press, 1962.

Chopp, Rebecca S. *The Power to Speak: Feminism, Language and God.* New York: Crossroad, 1989.

Christ, Carol P., and Plaskow, Judith, editors. *Weaving the Visions: New Patterns in Feminist Spirituality.* San Francisco: Harper & Row, 1990.

Goodman, Nelson. *Languages of Art: An Approach to the Theory of Symbols.* 2d ed. Indianapolis: Hackett, 1976.

Krieger, David J. *The New Universalism: Foundations for a Global Theology.* Maryknoll, N.Y.: Orbis Books, 1991.

Kuhn, Thomas. *The Structure of Scientific Revolutions.* Chicago: University of Chicago Press, 1962.

McFague, Sallie, *Models of God: Theology for an Ecological, Nuclear Age.* Philadelphia: Fortress Press, 1987.

———. *The Body of God: An Ecological Theology.* Minneapolis: Fortress Press, 1993.

Niebuhr, H. Richard. *Christ and Culture.* New York: Harper & Row, 1951.

———. *Radical Monotheism in Western Culture.* New York: Harper & Row, 1960.

Ricoeur, Paul. *Biblical Hermeneutics.* Semeia 4. Edited by. J. D. Crossan. Missoula: Scholars Press, 1975.

Ruether, Rosemary Radford. *Gaia and God: An Ecofeminist Theology of Earth Healing.* San Francisco: Harper & Row, 1992.

Tracy, David. *The Analogical Imagination: Christian Theology and the Culture of Pluralism.*

Trible, Phyllis. *God and the Rhetoric of Sexuality.* Philadelphia: Fortress Press. 1978.

CONTRIBUTORS

CARL E. BRAATEN

Professor of Systematic Theology, Lutheran School of Theology at Chicago, and Director of the Center for Catholic and Evangelical Theology. His major works include *Principles of Lutheran Theology, The Apostolic Imperative*, and *Justification: The Article by Which the Church Stands or Falls.*

DAVID B. BURRELL, C.S.C.

Theodore M. Hesburgh Professor of Philosophy and Theology, University of Notre Dame. His recent work, notably *Knowing the Unknowable God* and *Freedom and Creation in Three Traditions*, focuses on Islamic and Jewish influences on the formation of the classic Christian doctrine of God.

JOHN B. COBB, JR.

Ingraham Professor of Theology, Emeritus, School of Theology at Claremont. Among his recent publications are *Christ in a Pluralistic Age, Beyond Dialogue: Toward a Mutual Transformation of Christianity and Buddhism*, and *Sustainability: Economics, Ecology and Justice.*

EDWARD FARLEY

Professor of Theology, Divinity School, Vanderbilt University. He is author of *Ecclesial Reflection: An Anatomy of Theological Method, Theologia: The Fragmentation and Unity of Theological Education*, and *Good and Evil: Interpreting a Human Condition.*

LANGDON GILKEY

Shailer Mathews Professor of Theology, Emeritus, Divinity School, University of Chicago. Former President, American Academy of Religion. His books include *Message and Existence: An Introduction to Christian Theology, Society and the Sacred: Towards a Theology of Culture in Decline*, and *Nature, Reality, and the Sacred: The Nexus of Science and Religion.*

JULIAN N. HARTT

William Kenan, Jr., Professor of Religious Studies, Emeritus, University of Virginia. Formerly Noah Porter Professor of Philosophical Theology, Yale University. His most recent publications are *Theological Method and the Imagination* and *The Critique of Modernity*.

PETER C. HODGSON

Professor of Theology, Divinity School, Vanderbilt University. His recent publications include a new edition and translation of Hegel's *Lectures on the Philosophy of Religion, Revisioning the Church, God in History*, and *Winds of the Spirit: A Constructive Christian Theology*.

DAVID H. KELSEY

Luther A. Weigle Professor of Theology, Divinity School, Yale University. His books include *The Uses of Scripture in Recent Theology, To Understand God Truly: What's Theological about a Theological School*, and *Between Athens and Berlin*.

ROBERT H. KING

Vice-President and Dean, Millsaps College. Formerly Professor of Philosophy and Religion, DePauw University. Author of *The Meaning of God*, he is a regular contributor to *The Christian Century* and other journals.

WALTER LOWE

Professor of Systematic Theology, Candler School of Theology, Emory University. He is author of *Mystery and the Unconscious, Evil and the Unconscious*, and most recently *Theology and Difference: The Wound of Reason*.

SALLIE MCFAGUE

Carpenter Professor of Theology, Divinity School, Vanderbilt University. Formerly Dean, Vanderbilt Divinity School. Her recent writings include *Models of God: Theology for an Ecological, Nuclear Age* and *The Body of God: An Ecological Theology*.

GEORGE W. STROUP

Professor of Theology, Columbia Theological Seminary. He is author of *The Promise of Narrative Theology: Recovering the Gospel in the Church* and *Jesus Christ for Today*.

STEPHEN W. SYKES

Bishop of Ely, England. Formerly Regius Professor of Divinity, Cambridge University, England. Author of *Christian Theology Today, The Integrity of Anglicanism,* and *The Identity of Christianity,* he also coedited *The Study of Anglicanism.*

DAVID TRACY

Distinguished Service Professor of Roman Catholic Studies, Divinity School, University of Chicago. He is author of *Plurality and Ambiguity: Hermeneutics, Religion and Hope, Religion and the Public Realm,* and *Dialogue with the Other.*

ROBERT C. WILLIAMS

Taught philosophy and religion at Vanderbilt University prior to his death in 1987. His interests focused on African, African-American, and American philosophy along with philosophy of religion and religious studies.

ROBERT R. WILLIAMS

Professor of Philosophy, Hiram College. Author of *Recognition: Fichte and Hegel on the Other* and *Schleiermacher the Theologian,* he is editor and translator of I. A. Dorner's *Divine Immutability.*

INDEX

Abelard, Peter, 231, 284
Adam, story of (Adamic myth), 168, 170,
171–72, 173, 174, 175, 177–78, 182,
194–95, 196–98, 200–204, 207–8, 211
African religion, 372
Ambrose, 280
American Indian religion, 372
Anabaptists, 310, 312
Analytic philosophy, 23
Andrews, Lancelot, 287
Anselm, 7, 149 n.4, 230–31
Anthony the Hermit, 306
Anthropology, theological, 167. *See also*
Human being
Apocalyptic, 238, 240, 331–33, 348. *See
also* Eschatology
Apologists, 226–27
Aquinas, Thomas, 146–47, 148, 149 n.4,
232, 251, 307, 359; on the holiness of the
church, 254–55; on the human intellect,
118–19; on implicit knowledge of God,
171; on the sacraments, 280–81, 283; on
sin, 203–4; on subordination of women,
174; *Summa Theologica*, 7–8
Arians, 94
Aristotle, 303, 324, 336, 359
Arius, 227
Athanasius, 94, 227
Atonement, 230–31. *See also* Salvation;
Soteriology
Augsburg Confession, 311–12, 314
Augustine, 70, 146, 172, 194, 251, 253,
254, 306–7, 323, 336; and the Augustinian synthesis, 5–7; on baptism, 279; on
distortion of the image of God, 177–78;
on illumination, 118; on intuition of
God, 171; on sacramental signs, 281–82;
on the sacraments, 291–92; on sin,
198–203, 205–7; on subordination of
women to men, body to soul, 173–74

Baptism, sacrament of, 274, 275, 276–77;
of and by heretics and schismatics, 278;
infant, 276, 278–79; as regeneration,
277–79
Barr, James, 80, 135
Barth, Karl, 101–2, 105, 136, 264, 328,
329, 354; challenge of, to the liberal consensus, 19–20, 239–40; on Christ as the
context of theology, 243; on creation and
providence, 160–61, 162; on eschatology,
343–44; on the grounding of the human
being in God's decision, 188–90; on religion, 363; on revelation as the Word of

God, 130–31; on Scripture as authorita-
tive, 78, 80–81
Bartsch, Hans-Werner, 77–78
Baur, Ferdinand Christian, 74, 256–57
Becker, Ernest, 318
Berkouwer, G. C., 80
Bernard of Clairvaux, 284
Bible. *See* Scripture
Biblical exegesis, use in church and theol-
ogy, 82
Bibliographic aids, 28–34
Black church, 265, 266–67
Black theology, 83, 107–8, 191, 258,
266–68, 372
Bonhoeffer, Dietrich, 242 n.17, 246, 261,
264–65, 364
Bornkamm, Gunther, 239 n.14
Brown, Norman O., 318
Brown, Peter, 306 n.6
Brunner, Emil, 130, 363
Buddhism, 112, 362, 369–70; Zen, 53, 369
Bühlmann, Walbert, 270
Bultmann, Rudolf, 51, 74, 79, 80–81, 106,
161–62, 238–39; on eschatology,
344–45; program of demythologizing,
240–41; on revelation as event, 121–22;
on self-understanding, 184–85
Butler, Joseph, 290

Calvin, John, 70, 96, 148, 204, 257; *Institutes of the Christian Religion*, 9; on revelation, 119–21; on the sacraments,
274–75, 287, 288
Canon, 68–69, 80, 81, 383–84
Catholic theology: *nouvelle theologie* movement in, 260 n.14, 320, 321; and the sacraments, 274–75; and social encyclicals,
321, 324; transcendental method in, 21,
132–33; Trent, Council of, and, 121,
274, 281; Tübingen School of, 260 n.14,
320; Vatican I and, 71–72; Vatican II
and, 260 n.14, 266, 275, 320, 321, 322,
365
Chalcedon, Council of, 226, 228–30
Christendom, 313–14, 321
Christianity: claims to superiority, 353–54;
and Confucianism, 359–60; essence or
identity of, 60–61, 67–68, 83–84, 111,
135–36, 222, 377–80, 381, 386–88,
389; finality or absoluteness, 353, 362,
367, 380–82, 389; and Greco-Roman paganism, 358; and Islam, 359; and Judaism, 357–58, 365, 374–75; and other religions, 353–75; reconceptualization of,

394

Printed in the United States
138841LV00001B/90/A